ABSTRACT

Ref.: Sales No. E.84.II.B.6,
F.84.II.B.6 and S.84.II.B.6
(ID/325)

June 1985
New York

INPUT-OUTPUT TABLES FOR DEVELOPING COUNTRIES
Volume I

TABLEAUX ENTREES-SORTIES DES PAYS EN DEVELOPPEMENT
Volume I

CUADROS DE INSUMO-PRODUCTO PARA PAISES EN DESARROLLO
Volumen I

ABSTRACT / SOMMAIRE / EXTRACTO

Printed in Austria
V.85-28579—August 1985—4,600

ID/325/Abstract
English/French/Spanish

ABSTRACT

A methodological introduction in volume I of *Input-Output Tables for Developing Countries* helps to familiarize the reader with the basic problems of compilation and to establish a sound conceptual basis for the interpretation of the input-output technique.

First the relationships between national accounts and input-output systems are presented and the consistencies and divergencies between the two systems are explained.

A theoretical overview of the inter-industry system prepares the reader to enter into more detailed problems of compilation. Possible versions of the set-up, the different valuation concepts, the use of different prices and the concepts and methods involved in handling imports have been treated extensively.

Twenty country tables with, in some cases, very detailed technical descriptions have also been included.

This conceptual introduction will also help the reader in the interpretation of the tables contained in volume II of *Input-Output Tables for Developing Countries.*

SOMMAIRE

L'introduction méthodologique du volume I des *Tableaux entrées-sorties des pays en développement* aide le lecteur à se familiariser avec les principaux problèmes liés à la compilation des données et lui permet de disposer d'une base théorique pour l'interprétation de la technique des entrées-sorties.

D'abord, les rapports entre le système de comptabilité nationale et le système d'entrées-sorties sont présentés et les concordances et les divergences entre les deux systèmes sont expliquées.

Un aperçu théorique du système des échanges interindustriels prépare le lecteur aux problèmes plus détaillés que pose la compilation des données. Les différentes présentations et méthodes d'évaluation possibles, l'utilisation de prix différents et les notions et méthodes liées au traitement des importations sont examinées en détail.

Ce volume comporte également 20 tableaux par pays, accompagnés de descriptions techniques très détaillées.

L'introduction théorique aidera également le lecteur à interpréter les tableaux figurant dans le volume II des *Tableaux entrées-sorties des pays en développement.*

EXTRACTO

En el volumen I de *Cuadros de insumo-producto para países en desarrollo* figura una introducción metodológica que tiene como objetivo familiarizar al lector con los problemas fundamentales de la compilación y establecer una base conceptual sólida para la interpretación de la técnica de insumo-producto.

En primer lugar, se hace una exposición de las relaciones existentes entre los sistemas de cuentas nacionales y de insumo-producto y se explican las coincidencias y divergencias entre ambos sistemas.

Una consideración teórica general del sistema basado en la relación entre industrias prepara al lector para introducirse en un estudio más detallado de los problemas de la compilación. Se han tratado con amplitud las diferentes versiones de la proyección, los diferentes conceptos de valoración, el uso de diferentes precios y los conceptos y métodos relacionados con el tratamiento de las importaciones.

En el mismo volumen se han incluido también 20 cuadros de países, en algunos casos con descripciones técnicas muy detalladas.

Esta introducción teórica ayudará también al lector en la interpretación de los cuadros que figuran en el volumen II de *Cuadros de insumo-producto para países en desarrollo.*

INPUT-OUTPUT TABLES
FOR DEVELOPING COUNTRIES

Volume I

UNITED NATIONS INDUSTRIAL DEVELOPMENT ORGANIZATION
Vienna

INPUT-OUTPUT TABLES
FOR DEVELOPING COUNTRIES

Volume I

UNITED NATIONS
New York, 1985

The designations employed and the presentation of material in this publication do not imply the expression of any opinion whatsoever on the part of the Secretariat of the United Nations concerning the legal status of any country, territory, city or area or of its authorities, or concerning the delimitation of its frontiers or boundaries.

Where the designation country or area appears in the heading of tables, it covers countries, territories, cities or areas.

Material in this publication may be freely quoted or reprinted, but acknowledgement is requested, together with a copy of the publication containing the quotation or reprint.

ID/325

UNITED NATIONS PUBLICATION

Sales No.: E.84.II.B.6

ISBN 92-1-106198-9

03000P

Preface

Input-output tables have been compiled for many countries but, especially for developing countries, they tend to be dispersed over a wide number of publications. It can therefore be difficult for researchers interested in comparative studies to assemble a collection of tables for this purpose. The present volume therefore contains a selection of input-output tables which is hoped may be useful for the analysis of developing economies. The tables vary very much in size, statistical treatment and age, but may be drawn upon for information as to the internal structure of economies at different stages of development.

The concentration has been upon developing countries because input-output tables in standardized form are already published by the United Nations Economic Commission for Europe.[1] It should be noted however that the tables in the present work have been standardized only with respect to presentation, in that a common format has been adopted to summarize the characteristics of the tables and to present the data. The tables cannot be used for comparative purposes without consideration of the different sectoral classifications, treatments of imports, pricing methods etc., that have been adopted by the original compilers of the tables. The points are discussed in more detail in the methodological introduction that follows this preface.

The preparation of the volume has been carried out jointly by the United Nations Industrial Development Organization (UNIDO) in Vienna and the German Institute of Economic Research (DIW) in Berlin. While DIW was mainly engaged in processing and storing the data, UNIDO provided the institutional and technical framework of the data bank.[2]

In addition, the United Nations Statistical Office has prepared country chapters accompanying some of the input-output tables in this volume. They contain detailed information on various aspects of the analytical framework of the tables and on the statistical sources and compilation methods used. Aspects examined include the available forms of the table, the valuation standards, the classification and units, and the treatment of selected transactions, such as in secondary or non-marked products, etc. It is hoped that, by making explicit the incompatibilities between the input-output data of different countries, the volume can thus be a contribution to further standardization of input-output tables.

---

[1]See, for instance *Input-Output Tables for Years Around 1975* (United Nations publication, Sales No. E.82.II.E.24). As far as developing countries are concerned, the United Nations Economic Commission for Latin America has recently published a collection of tables for countries of that region—*Tablas de insumo-producto en América Latina* (United Nations publication, Sales No. S.83.II.G.11).

[2]See "The UNIDO input-output data bank" (UNIDO/IS.328, 9 July 1982).

In this connection it should be noted that the only international standards for input-output statistics are those of the system of national accounts (SNA), as defined in two United Nations publications.[3] The methodological introduction to input-output tables, which follows, is not intended either to define these or to replace them, but only to give a brief overview of some of the issues encountered with tables as actually compiled.

A second volume of existing input-output tables is under preparation and, beginning in 1985, publications will be continued by the United Nations Statistical Office in its National Accounts Series every five years. Each successive publication will present input-output tables compiled by individual countries in the intervening period.

    [3]*A System of National Accounts,* Studies in Methods, Series F, No. 2, Rev. 3 (United Nations publication, Sales No. E.81.XVII.15); *Input-Output Tables and Analysis,* Studies in Methods, Series F, No. 14, Rev. 1 (United Nations publication, Sales No. E.73.XVII.11).

EXPLANATORY NOTES

For technical reasons, the method of presentation of statistical data in tables may not follow normal practice.

Abbreviations

c.i.f.   cost, insurance, freight

f.o.b.   free on board

GDP   gross domestic product

ILO   International Labour Organisation

ISIC   International Standard Classification of All Economic Activities

n.e.s.   not elsewhere specified

SNA   United Nations system of national accounts

UNDP   United Nations Development Programme

CONTENTS

CONTENTS

Part one

METHODOLOGY

The relationship between national accounts and input-output tables

Theoretical approach

National accounts and input-output tables have been developed separately, despite their strong theoretical links. In some countries, they are compiled by different institutions and the information they provide is not necessarily consistent. The reason for the distinct development of the two schemes is the different types of uses to which each of them have been applied. Input-output tables were created and developed mainly for use in a special type of economic analysis. National accounts were developed as a consistent bookkeeping scheme, containing data which could be used for any type of economic analysis or planning. National accounts may be defined as a system for registration of transactions, or flows, in goods and services, financial claims and assets and transfers, which are generated by distinct transformation processes, as in the system of national accounts in its revised version as of 1968. Each transformation process is represented by a separate account in which incoming and outgoing flows are registered. In the United Nations system of national accounts (SNA), the technical transformation process is represented by the production accounts and the non-technical ones by the consumption and the accumulation accounts. A fourth account for transactions with the rest of the world deals with the relations of these three accounts for the country under consideration with all other countries.

Each flow is only registered once, that is at the intersection of the column which represents the account from which the flow leaves, and the row which stands for the account into which it enters. For instance, the flow of consumption expenditures is registered at the intersection of the production row (incoming money flow) and the consumption column (outgoing money flow). Similarly, value added is an incoming flow into the consumption account and an outgoing flow in the production account, and is consequently registered at the intersection of the production column and the consumption row. The rows and columns of the matrix correspond to the debit and credit sides, respectively, of the corresponding accounts. The row and column totals for any particular account must be equal.

Elements on the main diagonal of the matrix, however, register flows between transformation processes in the same group. These flows could be netted out. Whichever procedure is followed, row and column totals remain equal because any amount registered in a diagonal element increases the row and column totals by the same amount. In the production account, representing the deliveries from one production process to another, the diagonal element is of special interest for input-output analysis. To focus attention on this element, the rows and columns of the consumption, accumulation and rest of the world accounts are restricted to the production of industries, i.e. of commodities, and the supply of commodities from imports and the uses to which the supply of these commodities are put. The distinction is in recognition of the fact that there is not a one-to-one correspondence between the output of a commodity and the output of an industry producing that commodity as principal product. It is unusual for the output of an industry to fall completely within one commodity group, while conversely the total output of a commodity group may be drawn from several different industries.

By subdividing the production process by industries, the total amount of intermediate flows—completely internal before—is split into a series of intermediate deliveries and receipts. As a consequence of subdividing the production activity, the other elements of the rows and columns which concern industries also have to be split. The commodities entering into intermediate and final uses are classified according to the industry where the commodities are characteristically produced.

For the purpose of input-output analysis in the SNA the approach is taken to include data on the cost structures of industries and on the supply and disposition of commodities that are practical to gather and compile and that may be converted into commodity-by-commodity or industry-by-industry input-output tables without undue difficulties. For this purpose, establishments are defined as units that engage in the production of the most homogeneous group of goods and services for which the necessary input data can be gathered, and the classification of commodities is bound to the classification by kind of economic activity. The categories of the commodity classification are defined as the characteristic products of each kind of economic activity.

Difficulties in practice

In principle, the aggregate value of total final expenditure which, in an input-output table, is equal to the sum of the column totals of final demand minus imports should be equal to the equivalent gross domestic expenditure concept established in the systems of national accounts. The sum of the row totals of the primary inputs (excluding imports) in the typical table should likewise be equal in value to the corresponding income flow aggregate. Similarly, in countries with market economies the aggregate value of the final demand columns minus imports constitutes the gross domestic product at market prices. The same aggregate can be shown in the following account derived from the SNA accounts:

Compensation of employees	Private consumption expenditure
+ Operating surplus	+ Government purchases of goods and services

+ Depreciation	+ Gross domestic fixed capital formation
+ Net indirect taxes	+ Net additions to stocks
	+ Exports of goods and services
	− Imports of goods and services
= Gross domestic product at market prices	= Expenditure on the gross domestic product

In practice, a difference may exist between the estimates of the two systems, which may be due either to differences in the methods of valuation or differences in methods of accounting, or both. The nature and extent of the differences naturally vary between the countries.

Given an aggregate income and production concept, such as gross domestic product at market prices, the following two conditions for consistency with the corresponding input-output aggregate may be stated:

(a)   All transactions must be valued on the same basis;

(b)   The same transactions must be included in the aggregate.

These conditions would require, for example, that the system of national accounts or balances adopt the same conventions for valuing foreign trade, income-in-kind, the services of owner-occupied dwellings, the services of financial institutions etc., as the input-output table. It would also require that the two systems draw the same line between transactions considered to be intermediate, and those regarded as final.

If a more detailed reconciliation is required, for example, if the various components of domestic expenditure are to be reconciled with the final demand column totals of the input-output table, and the primary input row totals with the distributive shares of the income aggregate, still more detailed adjustments might be required to ensure that condition (b) held for each component separately. If the production account were disaggregated by sector of production some major adjustments would be required so that the totals of the production sectors in the resulting table would be consistent with those of a typical input-output table of transactions. In particular, it would be necessary to have an auxiliary table of marketing costs in order to cope with the problem of purchasers' and producers' prices (see below). These are some of the principal reasons why input-output tables cannot easily be linked with other industrial statistics.

Framework and main features of input-output analysis

The input-output method is an adaptation of the theory of general equilibrium to the empirical study of the quantitative interdependence between economic activities. It was originally developed to analyse and to measure the connections between the various producing and consuming sectors within a national economy. But it has also been successfully applied to the analysis of smaller units like regional or metropolitan areas or even of a large integrated individual enterprise, as well as to the analysis of international economic relationships.

In all instances, the method of approach is basically the same. The interdependence between the individual sectors of the given system is described by a set of linear equations, its specific structural characteristics are thus reflected in the numerical magnitude of the coefficients of these equations. These coefficients must be determined empirically; in the analysis of the structural characteristics of an entire national economy they usually are derived from a so-called statistical input-output table.

It is helpful to distinguish at the outset the input-output table from the analytical system to which it is related. The table is a statistical description of the inputs and outputs of the different branches of an economic system during a particular period of time. The input-output system is a theoretical scheme, a set of simultaneous linear equations in which the unknowns are the levels of output of the various branches, and in which the parameters are to be empirically estimated from the information contained in the input-output table. Accordingly, the assumptions of the theoretical scheme strongly influence the accounting conventions used in the table.

Basic assumptions

The use of input-output tables in analysis depends on some basic assumptions. Failure to meet these requirements can lead to inaccurate results. The most important assumptions with regard to the structure of the input-output matrix are as follows:

(a) The homogeneity assumption requires that each sector only produces one type of product, called the characteristic product of this industry, which has a single input structure. There is no substitution possible among the inputs in the production of any good or service;

(b) The proportionality assumption states that there exists a fixed ratio between the gross output of each industry and its inputs, i.e., that the input-output coefficients are constant. In other words, the amount of each kind of input absorbed by any particular sector varies in direct proportion to that sector's total output. Although not absolutely necessary in input-output analysis, this assumption is sometimes extended to value added, i.e., value added coefficients are assumed to be constant as well. The assumption of constant returns to scale is contested on the ground that functions more complex than simple proportions are necessary to describe production processes realistically, particularly in industries such as railways and utilities, where at least one large installation (for example, a railway track, a dam, or a telephone line) must be provided before any output appears. It is defended chiefly on grounds of simplicity;

(c) The additivity assumption refers to the condition that the total effect of carrying on several types of production is the sum of the separate effects. Thus, external economies and diseconomies are ruled out.

The validity of each of these assumptions depends both on the nature of production in single plants and on the way in which these units are aggregated into sectors. Some assumptions may be more valid for aggregates than for individual units, as for example the exclusion of joint products and external

4

economies. Others may hold for single productive processes but not necessarily for sectors.

In the pure theory of input-output the coefficients are regarded as relating to the physical quantities of commodities used in producing a given physical quantity of another commodity. In practice, however, almost all tables are prepared in money values. This is necessary because commodities are usually too heterogeneous to permit a purely physical measure, and some, such as services, are simply not measurable in physical terms. It is important, however, that the coefficients in value terms should be interpreted as if they were technical coefficients. As a consequence, whenever input-output tables are being compared intertemporally they must be valued at constant prices.

The interindustry accounting system

Since interindustry analysis is concerned with interrelations arising from production, the main function of interindustry accounts is to trace the flow of goods and services from one productive sector to another.

The basic design of the transaction matrix is derived from the division of uses into two categories, intermediate and final, and the corresponding division of inputs into produced and primary. The first distinction is logically similar to that which is made in Keynesian income analysis between induced and autonomous elements. In both models, there is some choice as to the uses which will be considered autonomous (or final, in input-output terminology), which must be determined from both theoretical and empirical considerations. The distinction between intermediate and final use of output, on the one hand, and produced and primary inputs, on the other, leads to four types of transactions, which are customarily grouped as follows:

(a) Quadrant 1 shows the intermediate transactions, that is the flows of goods and services which are both produced and consumed in the process of current production. Since it is precisely upon these relations between the sectors of production that input-output analysis focuses attention, they are shown in greater detail, so that quadrant 1 usually occupies the largest part of any table. Unfortunately, there is no close correspondence between the detailed schemes of sector classification used in different countries. The composition of each sector is in practice governed by the industrial classification system in each country, since the information presented in input-output tables is largely derived from industrial censuses. However, the theoretical input-output system imposes certain requirements upon the table which may be formulated as classification criteria.

(b) Quadrant 2 contains the final use of produced commodities and services, broken down by major types of use. Consumption by households makes up the largest part, but four other components of final demand are commonly distinguished: consumption by Government (that is all the purchases of goods and services by the Government and its agencies, excluding production activities); gross domestic fixed capital formation; net additions to stock; and exports. Each of these sectors is highly aggregated in comparison to the sectors of production, yet each is conceptually quite distinct and corresponds closely to the related national accounting category. In some tables imports may be treated as a deduction from final use, as in national income accounting, or may be added to primary inputs (see below for the treatment of imports).

5

(c) Quadrant 3 contains, corresponding to the final demand columns, rows showing the primary inputs. These inputs are usually described as primary because they are not part of the output of current production. In a static model, the use of existing capital stock is a primary input, as is the use of the customary primary factors, labour and land. Primary inputs into current production represent the value added in each sector of production as well as imports. They can be divided into the following categories: imports; depreciation; net indirect taxes; income of employees; and profits of enterprises and income of the self-employed (or operating surplus). Not all actual tables present primary inputs in such detail, but occasionally they are shown in an even finer breakdown. The total payment for primary inputs by each sector corresponds to the value added in production, being the difference between the value of output and the cost of input.

(d) Quadrant 4 contains the direct input of primary factors to final use, of which an example is household service. The fourth quadrant is sometimes omitted from published input-output tables, but for the sake of completeness it deserves to be mentioned.

It is important to note that there is no necessary correspondence between totals of the individual columns of final demand and the total use of any single primary imput. From the accounting point of view, the significant difference between the two types of sector is that the productive sectors must have balanced budgets (total input equal to total output). But no such equality is imposed upon the individual final and primary input sector; the values of primary input and final uses must only balance in the aggregate. In cases where the entire table, or some of its rows, are described in the appropriate physical rather than monetary units, the balancing of row and column totals is of course impossible.

Concepts of compilation

Matrix variants

Some establishments produce only one commodity or group of commodities which is the characteristic product of the industry under which they are classified. However, as noted before, a number of establishments also produce other commodities which are not among the characteristic products of the industry under which they are classified. The existence of such secondary production and the lack of complete correspondence between industries and commodities present problems in deriving pure input-output tables. These may be either commodity × commodity tables (recording the inputs of commodities into the production of commodities) or industry × industry tables.

For practical purposes, it emerges that the commodity × commodity table will be found to be more suitable in most applications. Demand is for a particular commodity or group of commodities and not for the mixed range of output of an industry, and there is no need to transform the demand vectors from one unit to another. One should note, however, that such a transformation is also necessary if commodity × commodity tables are used in an application which includes primary inputs, although because of the degree of similarity between primary input structures this may present less difficulty than the transformation of final demand in the case of industry × industry models.

Even with the most sophisticated statistical methods, it is not possible to define the establishment in such a way that the homogeneity assumption of input-output analysis will be completely satisfied. The result is a table of a mixed character. The columns represent industries which produce more than one product. The data on intermediate consumption are usually in product terms and are matched with the industries which produce them as their main product. In this context, it has become customary for analytical purposes to distinguish between the make matrix and the absorption matrix. In the make matrix the information on the commodity outputs of each industry is registered by industry rows and commodity columns. As a consequence, each row shows the commodity compositions of the output of a particular industry. In the absorption version, the matrix is formed by commodity rows and industry columns.

In the make matrix, the diagonal elements are the characteristic products produced by the industry itself. The size and number of off-diagonal elements show the degree to which the establishments of a given industry are in practice inhomogeneous production units. These elements represent two types of commodities: subsidiary products and by-products.

The subsidiary products of an industry are made through different production processes than that of the characteristic products of the industry (examples are electricity produced by a mining company or the construction activity of a manufacturing firm). The production of by-products and secondary products is, however, inseparably linked with the production of the characteristic product of an industry. Examples of such joint products are milk and cream, coke and gas and many products of the chemical industry. Also, certain scraps and waste products, which can be produced separately in another type of production process appear in the non-diagonal elements of the matrix.

The construction of commodity × commodity or industry × industry tables from the basic data available involves transfers of inputs and outputs between sectors. The transfer of outputs is a comparatively simple matter since the production of non-characteristic products is being recorded. The transfer of inputs, however, is not nearly so simple, as much of the basic data on inputs relates to inputs into industries and not to the particular commodities produced in those industries. It may be possible to obtain some data at a level below that of the establishment, and in some cases engineering data may be available on inputs into certain commodities. But, as a rule, supplementary information of this kind is incomplete. Hence, the transfer of inputs has to be carried out on the basis of specific technology assumptions.

Valuation

As in national accounting, it is important that all transactions should be valued in the same way. There are two main problems in ensuring uniform valuation. First, where taxes are levied on outputs, purchases may be valued either including or excluding the tax, that is, either at producers' values or at basic values. Secondly, there is the effect of trade and transport margins and the choice between producers' values and purchasers' values.

Basic values

The elimination of one of the causes of inequalities in the pricing of gross output, i.e. net commodity taxes, is facilitated once the distinction between industries and commodities has been made. Net commodity taxes consist of indirect taxes less subsidies, which vary with the quantities or values of commodities produced or sold. They include the taxes levied on domestic production as well as import duties. If these taxes are deducted from the value of the flows on which they are levied, the remaining value will have a more homogeneous price structure than before.

Each commodity flow value, which is presented in the commodity rows and columns, may contain commodity taxes levied on its output and on the direct and indirect requirements of inputs in the successive stages of its production. Ideally, therefore, the net commodity taxes levied not only on the output of a commodity, but also those levied on its inputs and the inputs into its inputs and so on, should be deducted from the value of each commodity flow in order completely to eliminate the disturbing effect of the net commodity taxes on the input or output coefficients. The resulting value is called the true basic value.

In practice, however, no information is usually available on commodity taxes levied on the indirect input requirements of each commodity flow. Because of this the SNA instead recommends the use of approximate basic values. These are, for output, the producers' value minus the net commodity taxes paid by the producer, and for intermediate inputs and final demand, the producers' value minus the net commodity taxes paid by the last producer of the flows concerned. In fact, approximate basic values are always larger than or equal to true basic values.

Producers' prices and purchasers' prices

Any transaction, if described in monetary rather than physical units, may be valued at either the price received by the producer or the price paid by the purchaser. The difference is composed of marketing costs, which include such items as transport costs, wholesale and retail distributive mark-ups, insurance and warehouse costs. Input-output tables (and the associated vectors of final demand) may, therefore, be valued at either producers' or purchasers' values, depending on how trade and transport margins are treated.

It is often felt desirable to show distribution and transport margins as two separate entries because their input structures are different and many official industrial classifications place the activities in different groups. It may be found that the necessary data are not readily available to permit this disaggregation of the margins across all purchasers, although the total margins paid by each purchaser may be estimated. In this case an alternative treatment is possible. Here all margins are treated as distribution margins and the distribution industry is shown as purchasing units of transport and its output and sales are increased by the same amount. It should be noted here that the gross output of the distribution and transport industries should not include the value of the goods handled. Gross output is defined as the value of the mark-up, that is, the difference between the selling and buying values in the case of distribution or the

8

charge made for transportation. The reason for this is clear. If the goods handled were included in the outputs and inputs of these industries, the homogeneity of the sectors, and thus some of the usefulness of the table, would be lost.

Since most statistics record transactions at the price paid by the purchaser, tables using that system of valuation are more easily prepared. And for certain purposes, the table in purchasers' prices may even be more useful. But such a table suffers from three disadvantages, which in general are sufficient to make producers' prices the preferred system of valuation in an input-output table:

(a) First, under the purchasers' price system, the row total of each sector, which forms the output control total for computing input coefficients, includes the marketing costs incurred in each delivery of the output of that sector. Marketing costs will probably vary as the pattern of output changes, and thus lead to variations in the recorded value of total output even if actual production of that sector remains unchanged. This means that coefficients estimated in the base year are unlikely to be stable. However, under the system of producers' prices, marketing costs will vary with the input structure of an industry, which is generally more stable than the output structure, so that coefficients computed in the base year from a table valued under this system are likely to be more stable than those valued under the purchasers' price system;

(b) Secondly, under this system, all marketing costs are counted twice, in the value of output of the producing industry and as inputs to that industry from the distribution and transport sectors. Under the producers' price system, on the other hand, all outputs including the control totals, are valued f.o.b. plant, and marketing costs are therefore counted only once; in other words, duplication does not occur. Thus a system of producers' values will give the important uniformity of valuation which is unlikely to occur with purchasers' values;

(c) Finally, the system of purchasers' prices explicitly separates each element which makes up the final purchasers' value, so that the value of each transaction corresponds more closely to the flow in physical units.

From the point of view of the treatment of indirect taxes (not considering problems raised by distributive margins), it may be concluded that basic values are preferable to producers' values. The treatment of margins, assuming no indirect taxation, was also discussed. In practice, however, these two problems cannot be considered—nor can decisions on methods of valuation be made—in isolation. Purchasers' values differ from basic values by the amount of tax and by the amount of margins. Producers' values differ from purchasers' values by the amount of margins and from basic values by the amount of tax.

The added stability of the coefficient matrix usually justifies the extra statistical information necessary to compile the table in producers' prices. Ideally, all the important marketing cost elements should be identified in order to reconcile completely the accounts of each sector. Supporting tables should be prepared, showing the marketing costs entering into each transaction, in the row of the producing industry and the column of the purchasers' industry. If this can be done, it is possible to translate a given table of transactions into whichever price system is most appropriate for the purpose at hand.

Foreign trade sector

General characteristics

A foreign trade sector is a necessary part of all input-output tables. It is necessary in order to obtain an accounting balance of inputs and outputs in current domestic production, since some of the inputs absorbed are imported from abroad, while part of the output is exported abroad. For those economies in which foreign trade is particularly important, one of the most likely applications of input-output analysis will be to the problems of exports and imports. The method of recording exports is perfectly straightforward: that part of the output of a given sector which is exported is entered in a final demand column. Whereas this treatment of exports is universal, several methods are used for recording imports. The difference between them rests upon the meaning of the input coefficients which result in each case.

The treatment of imports in input-output tables varies considerably between countries. The treatment varies in the amount of statistical data it requires and accordingly some treatments have their appeal from this standpoint but, as is often the case, the simplest treatment is not always the most useful in application of the tables. When an input-output table is being used to assess the output of commodities required to meet a given level of final demand, it is useful to be able to extend the analysis to determine the proportions in which the required supplies of the various commodities will be produced domestically or imported. This assessment of import requirements enables one to assess the implications for the balance of trade of a postulated set of final demands. In many economies imports represent a significant share of total supplies and balance of payments problems often restrict economic growth. It is therefore important to be able to analyse import requirements accurately in input-output models.

In discussing imports in the context of input-output analysis it is helpful to begin by making a distinction between competitive and non-competitive imports. Even if this distinction is not always made in practice, it throws light on the merits and demerits of the alternative conventions used to record imports. A competitive import can be defined as a commodity which is a good substitute for some domestically produced commodity. Clearly, the interpretation of the phrase a good substitute is a matter of judgement. A non-competitive import, on the other hand, is one for which there is no domestic counterpart.

If the supply of a competitive import is distributed along any row other than that of the corresponding domestic product, then substitution which may easily occur between these two sources as inputs to some third sector will cause variance in the two input coefficients—from the competing import and from the domestic product—to the third sector. Constancy, or stability, of the input coefficients is of critical importance, yet substitution between a domestic product and a competitive import may take place in a short period of time. If, however, the competitive import and the domestic product are distributed along the same row, substitution between them will not affect their joint input to a third sector, which is technically determined. Thus the technical coefficient is likely to be much more stable than either of its two components, the domestic input coefficient and the competing import coefficient.

If, on the other hand, a non-competitive import is distributed along a row with a broadly similar (but non-substitutable) domestic product, the coefficients formed from their joint flow create an indirect demand for domestic output which in fact is a demand for imports. But if the non-competitive import is distributed along an entirely separate row, then the input coefficients formed by its flow will be quite stable in the sense that they are not substitutable for the outputs of other sectors.

Valuation of imports

The importance of the uniformity of valuation of transactions has been emphasized. This applies both when considering supplies of commodities and when considering purchases of commodities. Domestically produced commodities may be valued at basic values, that is, excluding any commodity taxes and distribution and transport margins. The valuation for imports which corresponds most closely conceptually to that used for domestic products is the value of import goods at the border of the importing country, which may be termed the domestic border or port value. This will be the c.i.f. value of imports plus protective import duties. The c.i.f. value of imports consists of three items: the value of goods when leaving the exporting country; freight charges to the domestic port of entry; and insurance charges.

It is appropriate to add to the c.i.f. value only those import duties which can be regarded as protective duties, or duties levied in order to raise the cost of the import in relation to the corresponding domestic cost with the aim of putting the domestic and foreign producers in an equally competitive position. Other import duties aim mainly at raising revenue or discouraging consumption and are often matched by a corresponding excise duty on the domestically produced commodity. This treatment of imports will ensure that they are valued in a manner comparable to the ex-factory pre-tax valuation used for domestic goods. Any distributive or transport margins involved in transferring imported goods from their port of entry to purchasers should be treated in the same way as similar margins on the transfer of domestic goods from the producer to the purchaser.

Alternative treatment of imports

The following observations should be borne in mind when considering the alternative treatments of imports.

Method A. All imports are allocated in a single row to the consuming sectors. This treatment is perfectly acceptable to the extent that imports are non-competing. To the extent that they are competing, substitution will tend to occur, restricting the usefulness of the input coefficient matrix as time passes. In this case, all intermediate flows are of domestic products only, and the construction of the import row requires an identification of the destination of imports.

Method B. All imports are distributed along the row of a similar domestic sector. Unlike the previous convention, this means that flows contain imported and domestically produced elements without distinction. In this case there is no problem of instability, but the presence of non-competing imports in the rows may give rise to inaccurate estimates of output requirements when the inverse matrix computed from this version of the table is post-multiplied by a bill of goods comprising final domestic demand and exports.

Two slightly different coefficient matrices may be computed from a flow table of this type: in the first case the row total, that is, the sum of all imports and domestic output, may be taken as the denominator in forming the coefficients. In this case, a further instability is introduced since there is no necessary relation between changes in total supply, which may be confined to imports, and changes in domestic inputs. Furthermore, this instability will affect the value of every coefficient in any column where significant substitution between imports and domestic production takes place. The second possibility is that if the total imports in each row are known, they may be entered with a negative sign in the final demand quadrant, so that the value of the row total equals domestic output: coefficients computed on this base should be well-behaved. One advantage of this method is statistical simplicity. No information is needed on the destination of imports, only on their origin and this can usually be easily obtained from customs sources.

Method C. The third method tries to combine the virtues of the previous two while avoiding their faults, by distributing only those imports which are judged to be competing along the rows of the corresponding domestic sector (thus obtaining stable input coefficients) and distributing the non-competing imports as a separate row (thus preserving the homogeneity of the output structure). All intermediate flows thus consist of domestic product plus competing imports, and the total of the latter are entered as a negative column in the final bill of goods. In this case, as in Method B, it is necessary to specify the actual import requirements in any computation. However, it seems likely that this can be done more accurately with competing imports. If not, an adjustment to the diagonal elements in the coefficient matrix makes it possible to compute a solution on the assumption that the supply of competing imports will be in some proportion (which may be varied for each sector) to the corresponding domestic output. It should be mentioned that the data requirements for this method are not too demanding and it is more accurate than the previous method.

Method D. A final possibility is that all imported goods can be distinguished both by origin and by destination. This is equivalent to the preparation of two tables—one for domestic flows and one for imported products. Naturally, the statistical requirements are demanding, but the results make possible a considerable flexibility in the treatment of imports. It is certainly worthwhile making the effort to distinguish between competing and non-competing imports, and relegate the latter to a row at the foot of the table. An immediate advantage of this method is that information about import substitution in particular elements can be accurately incorporated in the table. Thus a domestic flow matrix can be constantly revised, so that the problem of substitutability can be minimized. Imports can either be aggregated by column, and treated as in Method A, or aggregated by row, and treated as in Method B.

The statistical requirements of this approach are demanding but the results make possible a considerable flexibility in the treatment of imports and permit a very clear analysis to be made of the impact of demand on home and foreign supplies. The records of firms and other purchasers generally do not contain information as to the origin (domestic or foreign) of a purchased commodity. Indeed, a firm may not even know the origin if the commodity has been purchased from a wholesale dealer.

Bibliography

Aidenoff, A. Input-output data in the United Nations system of national accounts. *In* Applications of input-output analysis. Carter *and* Brody, *eds.* Proceedings of the 4th International Conference on Input-Output Techniques.

Bulmer-Thomas, V. Input-output analysis in developing countries. New York, John Wiley, 1982.

Chenery, H. B. *and* P. G. Clark. Interindustry economics. New York, 1959.

Leontief, W. Input-output economics. New York, 1966.

United Nations. Department of Economic and Social Affairs. Problems of input-output tables and analysis. Studies in methods. Series F, No. 14.
   Sales No.: 66.XVII.8.

_____ Input-output tables and analysis. Studies in methods. Series F, No. 14, Revision 1.
   Sales No.: 73.XVII.11.

_____ Economic Commission for Africa. The objectives, concepts and methods of input-output analysis. (E/CN.14/NAC/46/Rev.1)

_____ Economic Commission for Asia and the Far East. Input-output: some problems of compilation. (ASTAT/NA.6/PA/6)

Part two

INPUT-OUTPUT TABLES

Presentation of the tables

The tables are presented in a consistent format and usually in their original breakdown by industries. In the case of Mexico, Papua New Guinea and Sri Lanka an aggregation was performed. Any inconsistencies arising, *inter alia*, due to imperfect accounting practices in the original table or misprints in the source have been deleted, in some cases by inserting a row or column for adjustments. This step proved to be very time-consuming in individual cases, depending on the quality of the original table and the legibility of the printed version.

The first quadrant is usually square, that is, as to rows and columns the number of industries or commodities is identical, but not always. If the transactions are valued at purchasers' prices and the trade margins are given as a column (with negative sign) in the second quadrant, a row for industry trade has been introduced showing only zero entries in the first quadrant and the trade margin totals in the trade margin columns. Thus, the total deliveries of industry trade are equal to its total purchases.

The nomenclature for gross output used in the original tables varies considerably, but has been carried over. For each industry the input and output are equal. This equality is given from the beginning in most tables under consideration, as they were formally balanced by one procedure or another. In preparing the present tables it has often been difficult to identify the statistical unit as being either industries or commodities. In tables that explicitly show deviations between the output values by industries and by commodity groups, an appropriate vector of differences has been inserted.

With regard to the presentation of imports, when they are contained in the first quadrant, the practice of the original tables is followed. Thus they may appear as a column to be subtracted from total (intermediate + final) demand to yield total output, or, alternatively as a row in the third quadrant to be added to total domestic production to yield total resources.

Each table is introduced by a brief characterization as to: country; reference year; source; currency units; pricing system (purchasers' prices, producers' prices, basic values); treatment of trade margins in purchasers' price tables (column or row); treatment of imports (separated from domestic products or not); total number of rows; total number of columns; availability of import matrices or more detailed transaction matrices; statistical unit of quadrant 1; and status of quadrant 4.

More details on the contents of the individual rows and columns can be seen from their designations given with the data. The text was taken from the source and, if possible, supplemented by information on whether employers' contributions to social security are included in wages and salaries or not as well as on the price basis of imports and exports.

Each input-output table is individual and, strictly speaking, not completely comparable with the other tables. Moreover, the information given in the source is very often limited. In particular, this holds for the consideration of social security contributions and the treatment of secondary products and taxes. However, the aim is not to reproduce every documented peculiarity of individual tables. For such information the reader is referred to the original version. The aim is rather to present features of individual tables in a common framework in order to determine those that are by and large comparable.

ALGERIA

Reference year: 1974

Entries in table: Total flows

Source: Algérie, Secrétariat d'Etat au plan, direction des statistiques, *Annuaire statistique de l'Algérie, 1976*

Computerized: UNIDO

Currency units: Dinars of Y 1974
Scale factor: 1,000,000

Pricing system: Purchasers' current prices
Intermediate sectors: 20 × 21
Treatment of trade margins: Trade margins disaggregated by intermediate and final demands

Treatment of imports: Import columns for imports c.i.f. and import duties
Availability of import matrix: Not available

Total number of rows: 28
Statistical unit of quadrant 1: Industry

Total number of columns: 44
Statistical unit of quadrant 1: Industry

Fourth quadrant: Not occupied
Note: Quadrant 1 is not symmetric

Input-Output Table of Algeria for the Year 1974

ALGERIA 1974 | FLOWS In millions of Dinars of Y 1974 | PURCHASERS CURRENT MARKET PRICES

INDUSTRY:	1 Agriculture Forestry.Fisher	2 Energy Water Supply	3 Petroleum Natural Gas	4 Mining and Quarrying	5 Metal Industry Equipments	6 Non-Metallic Mineral Prods
* TOTAL INDUSTRY TRANSACTIONS *						
1 Agriculture Forestry.Fishery	489.8	0.5	0.0	0.5	0.0	20.0
2 Energy and Water Suply	37.4	21.0	2.0	1.3	15.1	22.7
3 Petroleum Natural Gas	61.4	29.7	2306.8	1.4	3.0	35.0
4 Mining and Quarrying		47.9	18.0	23.0	11.7	1.1
5 Metal Industry Equipment	133.0	45.0	182.5	23.3	1212.6	33.3
6 Non-Metallic Mineral Prods		23.0	5.3	0.0	23.0	
7 Construction & Public Works	0.0	2.3	3.4	0.0	0.0	14.0
8 Petroleum Ind.&Servs(Govmt)	0.0	0.0	1573.4	1.0	9.0	0.0
9 Chemical & Plastic Products	246.5	2.3	29.4	7.0	90.2	1.0
10 Manufacture of Food Products	112.3	0.0	0.0	0.0	0.0	0.0
11 Textiles		0.0	0.0	0.0	6.0	
12 Leather					2.0	
13 Wood, Paper and Printing	8.0	3.2	7.6	3.0	12.3	1.0
14 Other Industries	0.7	4.8	0.0	0.9	0.0	0.4
15 Transport	19.7	5.0	61.7	52.9	86.1	7.7
16 Communications		0.2	1.9	0.9	17.4	2.6
17 Hotels, Restaurants, Bars	0.0	0.5	0.0	4.3	0.0	0.0
18 Real Estate	0.9	0.0		0.0	8.0	13.0
19 Services Giv. to Enterprises	73.9	0.0	245.0	2.0	86.0	
20 Services Given to Households	0.0	0.0		0.0	0.0	
21 Total Intermediate Inputs	1186.5	166.9	4460.3	154.2	1702.8	171.9
22 Value Added	3576.9	603.8	18418.2	372.8	1083.4	338.5
23 Compensation of Employees	784.3	199.8	284.1	123.9	542.7	159.4
24 Social Security	151.9	57.3	58.2	56.8	143.9	46.0
25 Indirect Taxes less Subsid.	87.9	50.7	3996.3	23.5	417.0	86.0
26 Consumption of Fixed Capital	268.8	141.2	737.9	55.0	163.3	64.7
27 Net Operating Surplus	2284.5	154.7	13341.9	113.6	-183.3	-17.8
28 Gross Output	4763.4	770.7	22878.5	527.0	2786.2	510.4

Input-Output Table of Algeria for the Year 1974

ALGERIA 1974 FLOWS in millions of Dinars of Y 1974 PURCHASERS CURRENT MARKET PRICES

INDUSTRY:	7 Construction & Public Works	8 Petroleum Ind. & Servs(Govmtl)	9 Chemical and Plastic Product	10 Food-processing	11 Textiles	12 Leather
* TOTAL TRANSACTIONS *						
INDUSTRY						
1 Agriculture,Forestry,Fishery	24.2	0.0	13.6	1402.1	20.3	62.1
2 Energy and Water Supply	12.2	7.0	11.2	26.1	15.4	3.0
3 Petroleum, Natural Gas	126.5	32.2	20.4	31.9	8.6	2.0
4 Mining and Quarrying	237.2	7.2	74.6	76.0	19.8	6.5
5 Metal Industry Equipment	1298.4	384.1	50.6	77.9	9.3	14.0
6 Non-Metallic Mineral Prods	730.7	5.6	23.5	14.3	3.0	0.0
7 Construction & Public Works	7.6	7.6	4.1	0.0	3.0	0.6
8 Petroleum Ind.&Servs(Govmtl)	0.0	920.9	548.4	0.0		
9 Chemical & Plastic Products	168.2	600.0		92.8	726.8	171.0
10 Manufacture of Food	0.0	0.0	6.3	1530.6		6.6
11 Textiles	8.0	2.0	14.0	2.0	1073.00	65.4
12 Leather	0.0	0.0				147.4
13 Wood, Paper and Printing	317.3	14.3	23.90	108.8	24.3	10.2
14 Other Industries	31.7	98.9	1.2	4.1	26.5	8.1
15 Transport	17.6		23.2	2.9	3.1	2.4
16 Communications	14.6	22.9				
17 Hotels, Restaurants, Bars	15.5	166.5	2.0	60.8	62.8	13.0
18 Real Estate	14.2		23.0			
19 Services Giv. to Enterprises	341.0			40.0		
20 Services Given to Households	0.0	0.0	0.0		0.0	
21 Total Intermediate Inputs	3522.0	1754.6	864.3	3398.0	2006.2	504.3
22 Value Added	3972.2	1434.5	531.3	1567.0	901.7	288.0
23 Compensation of Employees	1728.4	421.5	151.5	142.4	363.2	105.5
24 Social Security less Subsid.	487.9	90.7	44.7	147.5	104.2	29.5
25 Indirect Taxes less Subsid.	491.8	45.3	108.8	193.5	250.0	76.8
26 Consumption of Fixed Capital	213.1	426.0	138.8	103.0	96.1	32.5
27 Net Operating Surplus	1051.0	450.9	94.8	82.0	87.4	43.7
28 Gross Output	7494.2	3189.1	1395.6	4965.0	2907.9	792.3

19

Input-Output Table of Algeria for the Year 1974

ALGERIA 1974 FLOWS in millions of Dinars of Y 1974 PURCHASERS CURRENT MARKET PRICES

INDUSTRY:	13 Wood, Paper and Printing	14 Other Industries	15 Transport	16 Communications	17 Wholesale and Retail Trade	18 Hotels, Bars Restaurants
* TOTAL TRANSACTIONS						
* TOTAL INDUSTRY						
1 Agriculture,Forestry,Fishery	26.3	0.3	0.0	0.2	0.0	48.0
2 Energy and Water Supply	4.7	0.2	12.8	2.7	44.0	6.5
3 Petroleum, Natural Gas	0.4	0.4	205.8	2.0	135.0	3.0
4 Metal and Quarrying	0.3	0.0	0.5	8.0	0.3	0.2
5 Metal Industry Equipment	62.8	25.8	165.2	9.0	85.3	11.6
6 Non-Metalic Mineral Prods	3.2	0.0	2.8	0.5	50.2	9.6
7 Construction Ind.&Public Works	0.0	0.0	0.7	0.0	69.2	10.0
8 Petroleum Ind.&Servs(Govml)	60.0	9.0	28.0	3.0	63.0	157.9
9 Chemicals & plastic Products	0.6	7.0	0.7	0.8	5.6	1.0
10 Manufacture of Food Products	60.0	0.0	0.9	0.1	0.0	0.4
11 Textiles	23.0	2.0	3.0	2.5	57.2	0.5
12 Leather						
13 Wood, Paper and Printing	405.7	1.6	1.4	7.3	86.1	8.0
14 Other Industries	19.6	8.0	41.2	0.0	19.2	9.0
15 Transport	5.3	0.2	9.0	4.6	105.4	0.0
16 Communications	4.2	0.3	1.0	2.3	3.0	0.5
17 Hotels, Restaurants, Bars						
18 Real Estate	36.0	0.2	115.0	0.0	303.6	7.5
19 Services Giv. to Enterprises						
20 Services Given to Households						
21 Total Intermediate Inputs	665.0	60.3	1006.7	56.1	1814.9	290.3
22 Value Added	512.4	40.2	2276.5	238.1	4838.3	453.4
23 Compensation of Employees	241.3	9.8	712.0	187.2	937.9	166.1
24 Social Security less Subsid.	69.2	2.8	213.0	47.2	238.9	38.6
25 Indirect Taxes less Subsid.	16.9	14.6	87.0	4.5	242.4	152.0
26 Consumption of Fixed Capital	37.7	1.9	391.3	70.9	323.0	131.2
27 Net Operating Surplus	57.3	11.9	832.3	-71.7	3096.9	75.5
28 Gross Output	1177.4	100.5	3283.2	295.4	6653.2	743.7

Input-Output Table of Algeria for the Year 1974

ALGERIA 1974   FLOWS in millions of Dinars of Y 1974   PURCHASERS CURRENT MARKET PRICES

INDUSTRY:	19 Real Estate	20 Services Given to Enterprises	21 Services Given to Households	22 Total Intermed Consumption	23 Government Consumption	24 Private Consumption
* TOTAL TRANSACTIONS *						
INDUSTRY						
1 Agriculture,Forestry,Fishery	0.0	0.2	0.0	2086.7	162.7	5977.9
2 Energy and Water Supply	0.0	10.2	8.0	292.4	88.7	247.5
3 Petroleum, Natural Gas	5.0	5.0	4.0	3013.7	88.7	667.4
4 Mining and Quarrying	0.0	0.0	0.0	476.5	37.0	14.3
5 Metal Industry Equipment	50.0	95.0	113.6	4045.9	31.6	880.2
6 Non-Metallic Mineral Prods	0.0	0.0	5.0	925.6	3.0	95.4
7 Construction & Public Works	50.0	10.0	0.0	224.4	5.0	0.0
8 Petroleum Ind.&Servs(Govmtl)	0.0	0.0	50.2	2535.4	182.2	1395.7
9 Chemical & Plastic Products	-1.0	0.0	0.0	2401.4	231.2	5029.3
10 Manufacture of Food	0.0	0.0	55.0	1807.2	30.6	2545.2
11 Textiles	0.0	0.0	0.0	1202.2	106.6	826.8
12 Leather	0.0	15.0	6.1	151.8	33.7	598.8
13 Wood, Paper and Printing	0.8	3.0	2.4	1049.2	77.6	529.0
14 Other Industries	0.0	10.3	8.0	1920.9	47.5	845.9
15 Transport	0.0	0.0	8.0	108.5	73.5	117.8
16 Communications	0.0	2.5	33.9	243.0	148.9	796.5
17 Hotels, Restaurants, Bars	5.0	60.0	30.5	1661.2	7.9	1257.0
18 Real Estate	2.0					961.4
19 Services Giv. to Enterprises						
20 Services Given to Households						
21 Total Intermediate Inputs	71.8	216.0	276.4	24350.1	1453.2	22380.3
22 Value Added	144.2	399.6	767.9	4059.5	0.0	0.0
23 Compensation of Employees	54.6	14.0	201.9	2098.5	0.0	0.0
24 Social Security	9.2	2.8	15.4	209.3	0.0	0.0
25 Indirect Taxes less Subsid.	49.6	80.3	88.3	7200.0	0.0	0.0
26 Consumption of Fixed Capital	124.7	101.9	80.3	3508.7	0.0	0.0
27 Net Operating Surplus	1208.7	183.8	360.4	2325.9	0.0	0.0
28 Gross Output	1516.0	615.6	1044.3	68409.6	0.0	0.0

21

Input-Output Table of Algeria for the Year 1974

ALGERIA 1974   FLOWS in millions of Dinars of Y 1974   PURCHASERS CURRENT MARKET PRICES

TOTAL TRANSACTIONS * INDUSTRY	25 Total Consumption	26 Gr. Enterprises Fxd Cap Form	27 Government Gr Fxd Cap Form	28 Households Gr Fxd Cap Form	29 Total Gross Fix Capital Format	30 Changes in Stocks
1 Agriculture,Forestry,Fishery	6140.6	134.3	12.1		146.4	192.6
2 Energy and Water Supply	336.2	0.0	0.0		0.0	0.0
3 Petroleum, Natural Gas	756.1	0.0			0.0	244.6
4 Mining and Quarrying	917.4					84.7
5 Metal Industry,Equipment	126.4	6634.3	817.0		7451.3	2546.7
6 Non-Metallic Mineral Prods	5.6					113.2
7 Construction & Public Works	0.0	1781.5	4695.5	700.0	7177.0	0.0
8 Petroleum Ind.&Servs(Govmtl)		1778.0			1778.0	
9 Chemical & Plastic Products	1577.9	0.0	0.0		0.0	649.0
10 Manufacture of Food	5260.5					420.4
11 Textiles	2575.8					235.2
12 Leather	849.8					532.4
13 Wood, Paper and Printing	706.5	180.0	120.0		300.0	586.5
14 Other Industries	158.7	0.0	0.0		0.0	
15 Transport	918.5	0.0	0.0		0.0	
16 Communications	164.7	0.0	0.0		0.0	
17 Hotels, Restaurants, Bars	869.7	0.0	0.0		0.0	
18 Real Estate	1273.0	0.0	0.0		0.0	
19 Services Giv. to Enterprises	148.5	881.9	0.0		881.9	
20 Services Given to Households	1033.3	0.0	0.0		0.0	
21 Total Intermediate Inputs	23833.5	11390.1	5644.6	700.0	17734.7	5110.8
22 Value Added	0.0	0.0	0.0	0.0	0.0	0.0
23 Compensation of Employees	0.0	0.0	0.0	0.0	0.0	0.0
24 Social Security	0.0	0.0	0.0	0.0	0.0	0.0
25 Indirect Taxes less Subsid	0.0	0.0	0.0	0.0	0.0	0.0
26 Consumption of Fixed Capital	0.0	0.0	0.0	0.0	0.0	0.0
27 Net Operating Surplus	0.0	0.0	0.0	0.0	0.0	0.0
28 Gross Output	0.0	0.0	0.0	0.0	0.0	0.0

Input-Output Table of Algeria for the Year 1974

ALGERIA 1974   FLOWS in millions of Dinars for Y 1974   PURCHASERS CURRENT MARKET PRICES

	31 Exports	32 Total Use	33 Imports	34 Duties & Taxes on Imports	35 Gross Output Producers Price	36 Transfers of Products
* TOTAL TRANSACTIONS *						
INDUSTRY						
1 Agriculture,Forestry,Fishery	577.1	9143.4	2441.9	95.4	4763.4	0.0
2 Energy and Water Supply	0.0	628.6	0.0	0.0	770.7	-142.1
3 Petroleum, Natural Gas	18621.3	22635.7	395.2	43.1	22878.5	-1269.7
4 Mining and Quarrying	229.3	804.7	116.6	20.9	527.0	-79.7
5 Metal Industry, Equipment	191.2	15152.1	8979.8	2112.4	2786.2	-233.2
6 Non-Metallic Mineral Prods	0.0	1165.9	527.0	88.4	510.4	-22.2
7 Construction & Public Works	0.0	7407.2	0.0	0.0	7494.2	-87.0
8 Petroleum Ind.&Servs(Govmt)	0.0	4313.8	0.0	0.0	3189.1	1124.7
9 Chemical & Plastic Products	85.5	4713.9	2109.8	698.1	1395.6	47.7
10 Manufacture of Food	97.1	7585.2	1767.4	270.1	4965.0	-176.2
11 Textiles	28.1	4041.6	206.2	123.9	2907.9	-73.5
12 Leather	24.6	1054.5	22.1	14.8	1792.3	-31.3
13 Wood, Paper and Printing	24.8	2667.0	929.8	246.4	1177.2	-72.8
14 Other Industries	20.5	2242.6	65.7	36.3	100.5	-11.3
15 Transport	213.8	3053.0	114.9	0.0	3283.2	-345.1
16 Communications	3.9	277.5	0.0	0.0	295.7	-23.7
17 Hotels, Restaurants, Bars	92.7	1074.5	35.4	0.0	743.7	0.0
18 Real Estate	0.0	1516.8	330.8	0.0	1516.6	1035.9
19 Services Giv. to Enterprises	146.6	2843.2	119.7	0.0	1615.6	0.0
20 Services Given to Households	0.0	1044.3	0.0	0.0	1044.3	0.0
21 Total Intermediate Inputs	20335.2	91364.3	19205.1	3749.6	61756.4	-202.1
22 Value Added	0.0	0.0	0.0	0.0	0.0	0.0
23 Compensation of Employees	0.0	0.0	0.0	0.0	0.0	0.0
24 Social Security	0.0	0.0	0.0	0.0	0.0	0.0
25 Indirect Taxes less Subsid	0.0	0.0	0.0	0.0	0.0	0.0
26 Consumption of Fixed Capital	0.0	0.0	0.0	0.0	0.0	0.0
27 Net Operating Surplus	0.0	0.0	0.0	0.0	0.0	0.0
28 Gross Output	0.0	0.0	0.0	0.0	0.0	0.0

Input-Output Table of Algeria for the Year 1974

ALGERIA 1974   FLOWS in millions of Dinars of Y 1974   PURCHASERS CURRENT MARKET PRICES

	Trade Margin on 37 Intermed Demand	Trade Margin on 38 Houshld Consump	Trade Margin on 39 Gov't Consumpt	Trade Margin on 40 Gr Fxd Cap Form	Trade Margin on 41 Stocks	Trade Margin on 42 Exports
* TOTAL TRANSACTIONS *						
INDUSTRY						
1 Agriculture,Forestry,Fishery	-486.6	2141.3	2.1	0.0	-37.3	223.2
2 Energy and Water Supply	99.0	0.0	0.0	0.0	0.0	0.0
3 Petroleum, Natural Gas	56.4	151.7	20.4	0.0	0.0	317.5
4 Mining and Quarrying	256.0	0.0	0.0	0.0	0.0	0.0
5 Metal Industry Equipment	39.8	154.2	5.9	977.0	99.6	13.9
6 Non-Metallic Mineral Prods	0.0	2.0	-0.3	0.0	0.0	0.0
7 Construction & Public Works	6.7	0.0	0.0	0.0	0.0	0.0
8 Petroleum Ind.&Servs(Govmtl)	0.0	0.0	0.0	0.0	0.0	0.0
9 Chemical & Plastic Products	-132.4	376.2	23.8	0.0	53.4	2.8
10 Manufacture of Food	141.4	874.9	8.6	0.0	-8.7	18.0
11 Textiles	18.5	721.7	3.6	0.0	7.0	3.4
12 Leather	139.5	235.6	19.9	0.0	0.0	2.7
13 Wood, Paper and Printing	14.8	148.1	7.0	0.0	0.0	3.7
14 Other Industries	0.0	28.9	0.0	75.0	0.0	0.0
15 Transport	0.0	0.0	0.0	0.0	0.0	0.0
16 Communications	0.0	0.0	0.0	0.0	0.0	0.0
17 Hotels,Restaurants, Bars	0.0	0.0	0.0	0.0	0.0	0.0
18 Real Estate	0.0	0.0	0.0	0.0	0.0	0.0
19 Services Giv. to Enterprises	0.0	0.0	0.0	0.0	0.0	0.0
20 Services Given to Households	0.0	0.0	0.0	0.0	0.0	0.0
21 Total Intermediate Inputs	153.4	4858.7	91.7	1052.3	114.0	585.2
22 Value Added	0.0	0.0	0.0	0.0	0.0	0.0
23 Compensation of Employees	0.0	0.0	0.0	0.0	0.0	0.0
24 Social Security	0.0	0.0	0.0	0.0	0.0	0.0
25 Indirect Taxes less Subsid.	0.0	0.0	0.0	0.0	0.0	0.0
26 Consumption of Fixed Capital	0.0	0.0	0.0	0.0	0.0	0.0
27 Net Operating Surplus	0.0	0.0	0.0	0.0	0.0	0.0
28 Gross Output	0.0	0.0	0.0	0.0	0.0	0.0

Input-Output Table of Algeria for the Year 1974

ALGERIA 1974   FLOWS in millions of Dinars of Y 1974

PURCHASERS CURRENT MARKET PRICES

	43 Total Trade Margins	44 Total Resources
* TOTAL TRANSACTIONS *		
INDUSTRY		
1 Agriculture,Forestry,Fishery	1842.7	9143.4
2 Energy and Water Supply	0.0	628.6
3 Petroleum, Natural Gas	588.6	22635.7
4 Mining and Quarrying	80.5	804.7
5 Metal Industry,Equipment	1506.9	15152.1
6 Non-Metallic Mineral Prods	61.5	1185.9
7 Construction & Public Works	0.0	7407.2
8 Petroleum Ind.&Servs(Govmtl)	0.0	4313.8
9 Chemical & Plastic Products	482.7	4713.9
10 Manufacture of Food	760.9	7585.2
11 Textiles	877.1	4041.6
12 Leather	256.8	1054.5
13 Wood, Paper and Printing	386.4	2667.0
14 Other Industries	51.4	242.6
15 Transport	0.0	3053.0
16 Communications	0.0	277.1
17 Hotels,Restaurants, Bars	0.0	1074.5
18 Real Estate	0.0	1516.0
19 Services Giv. to Enterprises	0.0	2843.2
20 Services Given to Households	0.0	1044.3
21 Total Intermediate Inputs	6855.3	91364.3
22 Value Added	0.0	0.0
23 Compensation of Employees	0.0	0.0
24 Social Security less Subsid.	0.0	0.0
25 Indirect Taxes less Subsid.	0.0	0.0
26 Consumption of Fixed Capital	0.0	0.0
27 Net Operating Surplus	0.0	0.0
28 Gross Output	0.0	0.0

BANGLADESH

Reference year: 1962/63

Entries in table: Total flows

Source: A. R. Khan and A. MacEwan, *Regional current input-output tables for East and West Pakistan* (Karachi, Pakistan Institute of Development Economics, 1967)

Computerized: Sozialökonomisches Seminar, Hamburg

Currency units: Rupees of Y 1962/63
Scale factor: 100,000

Pricing system: Purchasers' current prices
Intermediate sectors: 35 × 35
Treatment of trade margins: Inputs, row 32

Treatment of imports: Columns 41-45 in final demand
Availability of import matrix: Not available

Total number of rows: 39
Statistical unit of quadrant 1: Industry

Total number of columns: 46
Statistical unit of quadrant 1: Industry

Fourth quadrant: Not occupied

Input-Output Table of BANGLADESH (East Pakistan) for Year 1962/63

BANGLADESH (PAKISTAN EAST) 1962 — FLOWS In hundred thousand Rupees of Y 1962/63 — PURCHASERS CURRENT MARKET PRICES

INDUSTRY:	1 Rice Growing and Processing	2 Wheat Growing and Processing	3 Jute Growing and Baling	4 Cotton Growing and Ginning	5 Tea Growing and Processing	6 All Oth Agric. Forstry, Fishing
* TOTAL TRANSACTIONS * INDUSTRY						
1 Rice Growing and Processing	3273	0	0	0	0	6587
2 Wheat Growing and Processing	0	16	137	0	0	13
3 Jute Growing and Baling	0	0	0	0	0	10
4 Cotton Growing and Ginning	0	0	0	7	0	0
5 Tea Growing and Processing	0	0	0	0	45	45
6 Oth. Agric. Forestry. Fishing	10723	110	676	15	44	1426
7 Sugar Refining & Gur Making	0	0	0	0	0	0
8 Edible Oils	0	0	0	0	0	0
9 Cigarettes, Bidi& Oth Tobacco	0	0	0	0	0	0
10 Other Food and Drink	0	0	0	0	0	0
11 Cotton Textiles	172	0	0	0	0	0
12 Jute Textiles	0	0	0	0	0	0
13 Other Textiles	22	0	0	0	0	0
14 Paper and Printing	0	0	0	0	0	0
15 Leather and Leather Products	0	0	0	0	0	0
16 Rubber and Rubber Products	0	4	2	0	9	41
17 Fertilizer	392	0	9	2	1	1
18 Other Chemicals	114	0	0	0	8	8
19 Cement, Concrete and Bricks	0	0	0	0	0	0
20 Basic Metals	0	0	0	0	0	0
21 Metal Products	0	0	0	0	0	0
22 Machinery	297	3	24	0	1	57
23 Transport Equipment	0	0	0	0	0	0
24 Wood, Cork and Furniture	0	0	0	0	0	0
25 Const. of Residential Bldg.	0	0	0	0	0	0
26 Const. of Non-Resden. Bldg	0	0	0	0	0	0
27 All Other Construction	0	0	0	0	0	0
28 Miscellaneous Manufactures	0	0	0	0	0	0
29 Coal & Petroleum Products	68	0	0	0	0	0
30 Electricity and Gas	0	0	0	0	0	0
31 Transport	1895	1	393	2	46	2104
32 Trade	2461	1	1176	5	185	4390
33 Ownership of Dwellings	0	0	0	0	0	0
34 Government (Admin & Defence)	30	0	0	0	1	0
35 Services, n.e.s.	0	0	19	0	21	9
36 Intermediate Inputs	19464	138	2455	31	357	14645
37 Indirect Taxation	-310	-3	782	-1	342	186
38 Gross Value Added	56041	98	7148	41	1893	46977
39 Total Output	75195	231	10385	71	2592	61808

27

Input-Output Table of BANGLADESH (East Pakistan) for Year 1962/63

BANGLADESH (PAKISTAN EAST) 1962   FLOWS in hundred thousand Rupees of Y 1962/63   PURCHASERS CURRENT MARKET PRICES

INDUSTRY:	7 Sugar Refining & Gur Making	8 Edible Oils	9 Cigarettes,Bidi & Oth.Tobacco	10 Other Food and Drink	11 Cotton Textiles	12 Jute Textiles
TOTAL INDUSTRY TRANSACTIONS						
1 Rice Growing and Processing	0	0	0	0	0	0
2 Wheat Growing and Processing	0	0	0	235	0	0
3 Jute Growing and Baling	0	0	0	0	0	1667
4 Cotton Growing and Ginning	0	0	0	0	1248	0
5 Tea Growing and Processing	0	0	0	237	0	0
6 Oth.Growing,forestry,fishing	2250	1595	516	311	8	0
7 Sugar Refining & Gur Making	0	0	0	104	0	0
8 Edible Oils	0	150	0	0	0	0
9 Cigarettes,Bidi& Oth.Tobacco	0	0	0	0	0	0
10 Other Food and Drink	0	0	0	5	0	0
11 Cotton Textiles	0	0	0	0	4310	0
12 Jute Textiles	0	0	0	0	0	0
13 Other Textiles	0	0	0	16	4	0
14 Paper and Printing	0	0	8	0	381	13
15 Leather and Leather Products	2	17	19	35	0	0
16 Rubber and Rubber Products	0	0	0	0	10	0
17 Fertilizer	4	2	0	0	0	0
18 Other Chemicals	0	0	9	12	554	57
19 Cement, Concrete and Bricks	0	0	0	0	0	0
20 Basic Metals	0	4	1	24	0	0
21 Metal Products	0	0	0	0	13	53
22 Machinery	0	0	0	0	9	0
23 Transport Equipment	0	0	0	0	0	3
24 Wood, Cork and Furniture	0	0	0	0	0	0
25 Constr.of Residential Bldg.	0	0	0	0	0	0
26 Constr.of Non-Residen.Bldg.	0	0	0	0	0	0
27 All Other Construction	0	0	1	0	0	0
28 Miscellaneous Manufactures	0	8	6	4	220	46
29 Coal & Petroleum Products	0	8	2	2	43	116
30 Electricity and Gas	15	8	31	31	84	125
31 Transport	183	52	31	186	237	431
32 Trade	358	227	194		839	
33 Ownership of Dwellings	0	0	0	0	0	0
34 Government (Admin.& Defence)	1	1	0	0	6	3
35 Services, n.e.s.	18	6	2	3	36	54
36 Intermediate Inputs	2831	2115	798	1208	8002	2568
37 Indirect Tax on Output	112	21	205	9	300	92
38 Gross Value Added	1160	506	574	1075	3307	3177
39 Total Output	4103	2642	1577	2292	11609	5837

28

Input-Output Table of BANGLADESH (East Pakistan) for Year 1962/63

BANGLADESH (PAKISTAN EAST) 1962   FLOWS in hundred thousand Rupees of Y 1962/63   PURCHASERS CURRENT MARKET PRICES

#	INDUSTRY:	13 Other Textiles	14 Paper and Printing	15 Leather and Leather Prods	16 Rubber and Rubber Products	17 Fertilizer	18 Other Chemicals
	TOTAL TRANSACTIONS *						
1	Rice Growing and Processing	0	0	0	0	0	0
2	Wheat Growing and Processing	0	0	0	0	0	0
3	Jute Growing and Baling	0	0	0	0	0	0
4	Cotton Growing and Ginning	0	0	0	0	0	0
5	Tea Growing and Processing	6	157	276	0	6	61
6	Oth.Agric.Forestry.Fishing	0	0	0	0	0	1
7	Sugar Refining & Gur Making	0	0	0	0	0	43
8	Edible Oils.Bidi& Oth.Tobacco	0	0	0	0	0	0
9	Cigarettes.Bidi& Oth.Tobacco	0	0	19	0	0	0
10	Other Food	1080	0	6	2	0	0
11	Cotton Textiles	789	0	5	0	27	0
12	Jute Textiles	0	350	105	0	0	40
13	Other Textiles	2	0	0	23	0	0
14	Paper and Printing	55	154	89	7	9	317
15	Leather and Leather Products	0	0	0	0	0	0
16	Rubber and Rubber Products	13	9	3	4	0	6
17	Fertilizer	0	2	0	0	0	5
18	Other Chemicals	0	0	0	0	0	53
19	Cement.Concrete and Bricks	0	0	0	0	0	0
20	Basic Metals	0	41	7	15	14	35
21	Metal Products	55	79	3	3	23	30
22	Machinery	2	193	5	5	54	6
23	Transport Equipment	342	73	18	13	25	39
24	Wood.Cork and Furniture	1	168	173	0	58	247
25	Constr.of Residential Bldg.						
26	Constr.of Non-Resden.Bldg						
27	All Other Construction						
28	Miscellaneous Manufactures						
29	Coal & Petroleum Products						
30	Electricity and Gas						
31	Transport						
32	Trade						
33	Ownership of Dwellings	1	13	0	0	0	4
34	Government (Admin.& Defence)						
35	Services,n.e.s.	3	18	2	2	16	16
36	Intermediate Inputs	2359	1257	716	78	232	913
37	Indirect Tax on Output	3	64	30	2		263
38	Gross Value Added	938	365	304	26	213	808
39	Total Output	3300	1686	1050	104	445	1984

Input-Output Table of BANGLADESH (East Pakistan) for Year 1962/63

BANGLADESH (PAKISTAN EAST) 1962   FLOWS in hundred thousand Rupees of Y 1962/63   PURCHASERS CURRENT MARKET PRICES

INDUSTRY:	19 Cement,Concrete and Bricks	20 Basic Metals	21 Metal Products	22 Machinery	23 Transport Equipment	24 Wood, Cork and Furniture
* TOTAL INDUSTRY TRANSACTIONS						
1 Rice Growing and Processing	0	0	0	0	0	0
2 Wheat Growing and Processing	0	0	0	0	0	0
3 Jute Growing and Bating	0	0	0	0	0	0
4 Cotton Growing and Ginning	0	0	0	0	0	0
5 Tea Growing and Processing	52	0	0	0	0	0
6 Oth. Agric. Forestry.Fishing	0	0	0	9	102	657
7 Sugar Refining & Gur Making	0	0	0	0	0	0
8 Edible Oils	0	0	0	0	0	0
9 Cigarettes.Bidi& Oth.Tobacco	0	0	8	0	0	0
10 Other Food and Drink	0	0	0	0	0	0
11 Cotton Textiles	0	0	0	0	0	0
12 Jute Textiles	19	0	0	0	0	0
13 Other Textiles	0	0	1	0	2	0
14 Paper and Printing Products	0	2	0	0	0	0
15 Leather and Leather Products	0	0	2	0	0	0
16 Rubber and Rubber Products	0	2	4	34	18	2
17 Fertilizer	0	0	0	1	5	0
18 Other Chemicals	93	362	38	341	15	13
19 Cement,Concrete and Bricks	2	13	710	50	37	57
20 Basic Metals	2	2	738	21	83	3
21 Metal Products	0	0	7	0	0	30
22 Machinery	0	0	0	0	0	0
23 Transport Equipment	0	0	0	0	0	0
24 Wood, Cork and Furniture	16	0	21	7	3	4
25 Const. of Res-Nedtal Bldg.	0	0	31	40	0	0
26 Const. of Non-Resdel. Bldg.	17	15	35	2	7	13
27 All Other Construction	178	40	110	15	59	47
28 Misc.Other Manufactures	150	70	6	50	2	49
29 Coal & Petroleum Products	3	12	2	5	2	1
30 Electricity and Gas						
31 Transport						
32 Trade						
33 Ownership of Dwellings						
34 Government (Admin.& Defence)						
35 Services n.e.s						
36 Intermediate Inputs	558	534	1043	627	360	895
37 Indirect Tax on Output	17	30	6	7		
38 Gross Value Added	1206	284	1058	490	229	382
39 Total Output	1781	848	2107	1124	589	1298

Input-Output Table of BANGLADESH (East Pakistan) for Year 1962/63

BANGLADESH (PAKISTAN EAST) 1962   FLOWS in hundred thousand Rupees of Y 1962/63   PURCHASERS CURRENT MARKET PRICES

INDUSTRY:	25 Construction Resident. Bldg	26 Construction of Non-Resden.Bldg	27 All Other Construction	28 Miscellaneous Manufacture	29 Coal&Petroleum Products	30 Electricity and Gas
* TOTAL TRANSACTIONS *						
INDUSTRY						
1 Rice Growing and Processing	845	0	0	0	0	0
2 Wheat Growing and Processing	1	0	0	0	0	0
3 Jute Growing and Baling	0	0	0	0	0	0
4 Cotton Growing and Ginning	0	0	0	0	0	0
5 Tea Growing and Processing	0	0	0	0	0	0
6 Oth.Agric.Forestry.Fishing	751	269	204	440	0	0
7 Sugar Refining & Gur Making	0	0	0	0	0	0
8 Edible Oils	0	0	0	0	0	0
9 Cigarettes.Bidi& Oth.Tobacco	0	0	0	3	0	0
10 Other Food and Drink	0	0	0	36	0	0
11 Cotton Textiles	0	0	0	67	0	0
12 Jute Textiles	0	0	0	3	0	5
13 Other Textiles	0	0	0	0	0	0
14 Paper and Printing	0	0	0	0	0	0
15 Leather and Leather Products	0	0	0	0	0	0
16 Rubber and Rubber Products	0	0	0	0	0	0
17 Fertilizer	0	0	136	51	0	0
18 Other Chemicals	130	377	1469	20	0	0
19 Cement.Concrete and Bricks	206	376	613	59	0	0
20 Basic Metals	99	170	40	50	0	20
21 Metal Products	454	179	0	0	0	0
22 Machinery	35	0	0	0	0	0
23 Transport Equipment	0	0	0	5	0	0
24 Wood.Cork and Furniture	0	0	0	0	0	0
25 Constr.of Residential Bldg	0	0	0	0	0	0
26 Constr.of Non-Resden.Bldg	0	0	0	0	0	0
27 All Other Construction	0	0	0	0	0	0
28 Miscellaneous Manufactures	6	36	68	76	0	190
29 Coal&Petroleum Products	0	0	42	12	0	66
30 Electricity and Gas	0	0	0	39	0	0
31 Transport	0	0	0	173	0	0
32 Trade	0	0	0	3	0	4
33 Ownership of Dwellings	0	0	0	0	0	0
34 Government (Admin.& Defence)	0	0	29	3	0	0
35 Services.n.e.s.	28	15	6	3	0	0
36 Intermediate Inputs	2356	1499	2607	1073	0	285
37 Indirect Tax on Output	4115	0	0	33	0	17
38 Gross Value Added	0	2082	4209	691	0	879
39 Total Output	6471	3581	6816	1797	0	1181

31

Input-Output Table of BANGLADESH (East Pakistan) for Year 1962/63

BANGLADESH (PAKISTAN EAST) 1962

FLOWS in hundred thousand Rupees of Y 1962/63

PURCHASERS CURRENT MARKET PRICES

INDUSTRY:	31 Transport	32 Trade	33 Ownership of Dwellings	34 Govt. (Admin & Defence)	35 Services n.e.s.	36 Intermediate Consumption
* TOTAL INDUSTRY TRANSACTIONS *						
1 Rice Growing and Processing	0	0	0	0	0	10505
2 Wheat Growing and Processing	0	0	0	0	0	265
3 Jute Growing and Processing	0	0	0	0	0	1804
4 Cotton Growing and Baling	0	0	0	0	0	1255
5 Tea Growing and Gining	0	0	0	0	0	
6 Oth. Agric. Forestry Fishing	62	0	0	0	0	20759
7 Sugar Refining & Gur Making	0	0	0	7	0	322
8 Edible Oils	0	0	0	0	0	305
9 Cigarettes,Bidi& Oth Tobacco	0	0	0	0	0	
10 Other Food and Drink	0	0	0	0	0	27
11 Cotton Textiles	4	0	0	0	0	5425
12 Jute Textiles	3	0	0	0	0	1292
13 Other Textiles	0	0	0	0	0	637
14 Paper and Printing	22	9	0	1	42	105
15 Leather and Leather Products	0	0	0	0	0	121
16 Rubber and Rubber Products	59	0	0	43	0	469
17 Fertilizer	0	0	0	0	0	1897
18 Other Chemicals	0	0	0	0	0	2145
19 Cement Concrete and Bricks	0	0	0	0	0	2559
20 Basic Metals	0	0	0	0	0	1086
21 Metal Products	58	45	0	15	7	835
22 Machinery	74	0	0	6	0	157
23 Transport Equipment	0	0	0	2	1	106
24 Wood Cork and Furniture	0	0	0	0	9	301
25 Constr. of Residential Bldg.	0	0	0	0	0	0
26 Constr. of Non-Resden. Bldg.	0	0	0	0	2	0
27 All Other Construction	0	0	0	0	0	0
28 Miscellaneous Manufactures	336	2	0	0	0	647
29 Coal & Petroleum Products	336	3	0	0	15	1123
30 Electricity and Gas	21	0	0	0	2	867
31 Transport	0	0	0	10	20	6197
32 Trade	0	0	0	63	0	12134
33 Ownership of Dwellings	0	0	3013	149	0	0
34 Government (Admin.& Defence)	43	2	0	545	53	586
35 Services, n.e.s.	19	91	71	363	12	642
36 Intermediate Inputs	770	200	3084	1366	161	77581
37 Indirect Tax on Output	31	30	0	0	0	2291
38 Gross Value Added	9226	18005	6674	5056	9043	188278
39 Total Output	10027	18235	9758	6422	9204	268150

Input-Output Table of BANGLADESH (East Pakistan) for Year 1962/63

BANGLADESH (PAKISTAN EAST) 1962

FLOWS in hundred thousand Rupees of Y 1962/63

PURCHASERS CURRENT MARKET PRICES

* TOTAL TRANSACTIONS * * INDUSTRY	37 Consumption	38 Fixed Investment	39 Increase In Working Capital	40 Exports Abroad	41 Exports to West Pakistan	42 Imports from Abroad
1 Rice Growing and Processing	67870	0	0	0	0	-972
2 Wheat Growing and Processing	3047	0	0	0	0	-3005
3 Jute Growing and Baling	229	0	-423	7929	0	0
4 Cotton Growing and Ginning	0	0	-114	46	1528	-146
5 Tea Growing and Processing	980	0	0	64	599	-25
6 Oth.Agric.Forestry.Fishing	42126	0	0	1097	0	-612
7 Sugar Refining & Gur Making	4090	0	0	48	0	-291
8 Edible Oils	3908	0	0	0	0	-1468
9 Cigarettes,Bidi& Oth.Tobacco	1683	0	0	0	13	0
10 Other Food and Drink	2325	0	0	0	883	-14
11 Cotton Textiles	9302	0	1610	29	81	-190
12 Jute Textiles	0	0	0	3052	595	0
13 Other Textiles	2027	0	0	47	124	-47
14 Paper and Printing	874	0	0	75	0	-407
15 Leather and Leather Products	880	0	0	56	296	-11
16 Rubber and Rubber Products	274	0	0	0	0	-217
17 Fertilizer	0	0	0	0	1	-24
18 Other Chemicals	1399	0	0	1	0	-1236
19 Cement,Concrete and Bricks	0	0	217	2	0	-97
20 Basic Metals	0	94	0	0	10	-1728
21 Metal Products	1502	2971	0	34	31	-466
22 Transport Equipment	86	1287	0	4	0	-3438
23 Machinery	0	90	0	0	0	-945
24 Wood,Cork and Furniture	1247	3458	0	0	0	-146
25 Const.of Residential Bldg.	0	3581	0	0	0	0
26 Const.of Non-Residen.Bldg.	0	6816	0	0	0	0
27 All Other Construction	0	0	0	0	0	0
28 Miscellaneous Manufactures	2294	0	0	5	657	-172
29 Coal & Petroleum Products	931	0	0	0	0	-1989
30 Electricity and Gas	314	0	0	0	0	0
31 Transport	2669	0	0	215	0	-294
32 Trade	9758	0	0	0	0	0
33 Ownership of Dwellings	5836	0	0	0	0	0
34 Government (Admin.& Defence)	8571	0	0	0	0	0
35 Services,n.e.s.		0	0	24	0	-33
36 Intermediate Inputs	175296	18297	2136	12739	4818	-17971
37 Indirect Tax on Output	0	0	0	0	0	0
38 Gross Value Added	0	0	0	0	0	0
39 Total Output	175296	18297	2136	12739	4818	-17971

Input-Output Table of BANGLADESH (East Pakistan) for Year 1962/63

BANGLADESH (PAKISTAN EAST) 1962   FLOWS in hundred thousand Rupees of Y 1962/63   PURCHASERS CURRENT MARKET PRICES

	TOTAL TRANSACTIONS *	43 Imports from West Pakistan Inputs to West Pakistan	44 Trade&Transport Inputs to Imprt	45 Imported Wheat Processing	46 Total Output
1	Rice Growing and Processing	-2208			75195
2	Wheat Growing and Processing	-76			231
3	Jute Growing and Baling				10385
4	Tob Growing and Ginning	-970			2592
5	Oth Growing and Processing	-2161			61808
6	Sugar Refining & Gur Making	-18			4103
7	Oth Agric,Forestry,Fishing	-151			2642
8	Edible Oils	-306			1577
9	Cigarettes,Bidi& Oth.Tobacco	-48			2292
10	Other Food and Drink	-2910			11609
11	Cotton Textiles	-59			5837
12	Jute Textiles	-88			3300
13	Other Textiles	-104			1686
14	Paper and Printing	-74			1050
15	Leather and Leather Products	-397			104
16	Rubber and Rubber Products	-267			445
17	Fertilizer	-201			1984
18	Other Chemicals	-224		13	1781
19	Cement,Concrete and Bricks				848
20	Basic Metals				2107
21	Metal Products				1124
22	Machinery			39	589
23	Transport Equipment				1298
24	Wood,Cork and Furniture				6471
25	Constr.of Residential Bldg				3581
26	Constr.of Non-Resden.Bldg				6816
27	All Other Construction				1797
28	Miscellaneous Manufactures	-1634			0
29	Coal & Petroleum Products	-65			1181
30	Electricity and Gas				10027
31	Transport		1240		18235
32	Trade		6101		9758
33	Ownership of Dwellings				6422
34	Government(Admin.& Defence)				9204
35	Services.n.e.s.				
36	Intermediate Inputs	-12139	7341	52	268150
37	Indirect Tax on Output	0	0		2291
38	Gross Value Added	0	0	270	180554
39	Total Output	-12139	7341	328	450995

34

BURUNDI

Reference year: 1970

Entries in table: Domestic flows

Source: Burundi, Bureau du Plan, Ministère des affaires étrangères et de la coopération, *Comptes économiques du Burundi, 1970*

Computerized: Deutsches Institut für Wirtschaftsforschung, Berlin

Currency units: Burundi francs of Y 1970
Scale factor: 1,000,000

Pricing system: Producers' current prices
Intermediate sectors: 36 × 36
Treatment of trade margins: —

Treatment of imports: Imports c.i.f. plus duties in row 37
Availability of import matrix: Not reproduced

Total number of rows: 47
Statistical unit of quadrant 1: Industry

Total number of columns: 53
Statistical unit of quadrant 1: Industry

Fourth quadrant: Not occupied

Input-Output Table of Burundi for the Year 1970

BURUNDI 1970   FLOWS in millions of Burundi Francs of Y 1970   PRODUCERS CURRENT PRICES

INDUSTRY:

	1 Agriculture	2 Agriculture for Export	3 Livestock	4 Fishing - Traditional	5 Fishing - Industrial	6 Forestry Prods (Wood)
DOMESTIC TRANSACTIONS * INDUSTRY						
1 Agriculture	817	0				
2 Agriculture for Export	0	0	0	0	0	0
3 Livestock	0	0	0	0	0	0
4 Fishing - Traditional	0	0	0	0	0	0
5 Fishing - Industrial	0	0	0	0	0	0
6 Forestry Products (Wood)	0	0	0	0	0	0
7 Prim. Proc. of Agric. Prods.	0	0	0	0	0	0
8 Food Products - Domestic Use	0	0	0	0	0	0
9 Food Products - Industrial	0	0	0	0	0	0
10 Textiles,Leather,Basketweavg	0	0	0	0	0	0
11 Wrg. Apparel:Leather,Textile	0	0	0	0	0	0
12 Mining, Energy	0	0	0	0	0	0
13 Wood & Paper Products	7	0	2	0	2	3
14 Mechanics & Repair, Garages	0	0	0	0	4	0
15 Chemicals, Construction Mat.	2	5	2	0	0	0
16 Miscellaneous Manufactures	0	0	0	0	0	0
17 Traditional Dwellings	0	0	0	0	0	0
18 Buildings, Public Works	0	0	0	0	0	0
19 Transport, telecommunications	0	5	0	0	2	0
20 Traditional Trade	0	9	2	9	5	0
21 Modern Trade	2	2	0	0	4	0
22 Traditional Services	0	0	0	0	0	0
23 Modern Services	0	0	0	0	3	0
24 Banking, Insurance	0	0	0	0	0	0
25 General Govt Administration	0	0	0	0	0	0
26 Administration: Econom. Svcs	0	0	0	0	0	0
27 Administration: Education	0	0	0	0	0	0
28 Administration: Health	0	0	0	0	0	0
29 Social Security (INSS)	0	0	0	0	0	0
30 Priv. Non-Prof.Inst:Administr	0	0	0	0	0	0
31 Priv. Non-Prof.Inst:Education	0	0	0	0	0	0
32 Priv. Non-Prof.Inst:Health	0	0	0	0	0	0
33 Foreign Admin: Rural Developm	0	0	0	0	0	0
34 Foreign Admin: Research	0	0	0	0	0	0
35 Foreign Admin: Education	0	0	0	0	0	0
36 Foreign Admin: Miscellaneous	0	0	0	0	0	0
37 Domestic Intermediate Inputs	623.6	36.5	7	8	24	3
38 Imports (c.i.f plus Duties)	8.8	45.8	3	6	8.3	5
39 Local Salaries and Wages	0.0	16.00	0		12.7	0
40 Expatriate Salaries & Wages	0.0	0.0	0		6	0
41 Social Taxes					8	0
42 Indirect Taxes	-2.0	555.3	4	6	0.9	0
43 Subsidies		-58.2	3	4	9	0
45 Depreciation	-58.0			4.4	7.0	0
46 Operating Surplus	9044.3	1062.9	770.3	4.4	0.0	128.0
47 Exceptional Sales	0.0		1.1			
Gross Output	9872.7	1666.0	778.4	49.4	72.2	130.8

36

Input-Output Table of Burundi for the Year 1970

BURUNDI 1970

FLOWS in millions of Burundi Francs of Y 1970

INDUSTRY:	7 Prim. Proc. of Agric. Products	8 Food Products Domestic Use	9 Food Products Industrial	10 Textile,Leather Basketweaving	11 Wearing Apparel Leather,Textile	12 Mining, Energy
* DOMESTIC TRANSACTIONS						
1 Agriculture	45.1	1450.2	5.0	0.0	0.0	0.0
2 Agriculture for Export	1662.7	178.0	2.0	0.0	0.0	0.0
3 Livestock	0.0	0.0	2.0	0.0	0.0	0.0
4 Fishing – Traditional	0.0	0.0	0.0	0.0	0.0	0.0
5 Fishing – Industrial	0.0	0.0	8.0	0.0	7.0	0.0
6 Forestry Products (Wood)	0.0	0.0	6.0	0.0	8.0	0.0
7 Prim. Proc. of Agric. Prods.	0.0	0.0	5.0	0.0	8.0	8.0
8 Food Products – Domestic Use	0.0	0.0	7.0	0.0	0.0	0.0
9 Food Products – Industrial	0.0	0.0	3.0	0.0	3.0	3.0
10 Textiles,Leather,Basketweavg	30.6	0.0	0.0	2.0	0.6	0.0
11 Wrg.Apparel;Leather,Textile	2.0	0.0	8.0	2.0	0.0	0.0
12 Mining, Energy	0.0	0.0	7.0	0.0	6.0	4.0
13 Wood & Paper Products	6.0	0.0	1.0	0.0	0.0	0.0
14 Mechanics & Repair, Garages	0.0	4.0	0.0	0.0	0.0	0.0
15 Chemicals, Construction Mat	0.0	0.0	0.0	0.0	0.0	2.0
16 Miscellaneous Manufactures	0.5	0.0	9.0	0.0	5.0	3.0
17 Traditional Dwellings	2.9	0.0	4.0	0.0	1.0	0.0
18 Buildings, Public Works	0.0	2.0	8.0	0.0	0.0	0.0
19 Transport, Telecommunications	35.0	24.0	9.0	0.0	6.0	2.0
20 Traditional Trade	55.5	2.0	5.0	0.0	3.0	3.0
21 Modern Trade	6.0	2.0	3.0	0.0	6.0	0.0
22 Traditional Services	4.0	2.0	0.0	0.0	3.0	0.0
23 Modern Services	0.2	0.0	0.0	0.0	0.0	0.0
24 Banking, Insurance	0.0	0.0	0.0	0.0	0.0	0.0
25 General Govt. Administration	0.0	0.0	0.0	0.0	0.0	0.0
26 Administration: Econom.Svcs	0.0	0.0	0.0	0.0	0.0	0.0
27 Administration: Education	0.0	0.0	0.0	0.0	0.0	0.0
28 Administration: Health	0.0	0.0	0.0	0.0	0.0	0.0
29 Social Security (INS)	0.0	0.0	0.0	0.0	0.0	0.0
30 Priv.Non-Prof Inst:Administr	0.0	0.0	0.0	0.0	0.0	0.0
31 Priv.Non-Prof Inst:Education	0.0	0.0	0.0	0.0	0.0	0.0
32 Priv.Non-Prof Inst:Health	0.0	0.0	0.0	0.0	0.0	0.0
33 Foreign Admin: Research	0.0	0.0	0.0	0.0	0.0	0.0
34 Forgn Admin: Rural Developm.	0.0	0.0	0.0	0.0	0.0	0.0
35 Forgn Admin: Education	0.0	0.0	0.0	0.0	0.0	0.0
36 Foreign Admin: Miscellaneous	0.0	0.0	0.0	0.0	0.0	0.0
37 Domestic Intermediate Inputs	1815.1	1681.7	153.1	0.4	27.8	14.1
38 Imports (C.i.f plus Duties)	10.6	2.5	256.5	1.4	158.9	32.7
39 Local Salaries and Wages	16.0	0.9	334.6	0.0	15.9	28.6
40 Expatriate Salaries & Wages	14.0	0.0	39.6	0.0	13.5	5.5
41 Social Taxes	0.3	0.1	0.0	0.0	1.1	0.0
42 Indirect Taxes			328.6		0.5	2.0
43 Subsidies	4.5	0.5	36.0	0.0	2.7	2.0
44 Depreciation	25.8	507.8	326.0	28.8	15.0	8.0
45 Operating Surplus				0.0	0.0	0.0
46 Exceptional Sales						
47 Gross Output	1888.4	2173.5	1176.3	31.1	236.8	110.9

37

Input-Output Table of Burundi for the Year 1970

BURUNDI 1970   FLOWS in millions of Burundi Francs of Y 1970   PRODUCERS CURRENT PRICES

INDUSTRY:

		13 Wood & Paper Products	14 Mechanics & Repair, Garages, Constrctn Mat.	15 Chemicals, Constrctn Mat.	16 Miscellaneous Manufacturing	17 Traditional Dwellings	18 Buildings, Public Works
	DOMESTIC TRANSACTIONS *						
	INDUSTRY						
1	Agriculture	0.0	0.0	0.0	0.0	0.0	0.0
2	Agriculture for Export	0.0	0.0	0.0	0.0	0.0	0.0
3	Livestock	0.0	0.0	0.0	0.0	0.0	0.0
4	Fishing - Traditional	0.0	0.0	0.0	0.0	0.0	0.0
5	Fishing - Industrial	0.0	0.0	0.0	0.0	0.0	0.0
6	Forestry Products (Wood)	2.0	0.0	0.0	0.0	7.2	0.0
7	Prim. Proc. of Agric. Prods.	0.0	0.0	0.0	0.0	0.0	0.0
8	Food Products - Domestic Use	0.0	0.0	0.0	0.0	0.0	0.0
9	Food Products - Industrial	0.0	0.0	0.0	0.0	0.0	0.0
10	Textiles,Leather,Basketweavg	0.0	0.0	0.0	4.0	0.0	0.0
11	Wrg. Apparel,Leather,Textile	0.0	0.0	0.0	0.0	0.0	0.0
12	Mining, Energy	8.7	2.5	2.8	0.0	0.0	1.0
13	Wood & Paper Products	4.5	1.5	0.0	0.0	12.6	38.5
14	Mechanics & Repair, Garages	0.0	4.0	0.0	0.0	47.1	54.7
15	Chemicals, Construction Mat.	4.4	5.0	0.0	0.0	22.9	1.0
16	Miscellaneous Manufactures	2.7	2.8	4.0	8.0	2.0	25.9
17	Traditional Dwellings	0.0	1.0	4.3	0.0	1.7	7.9
18	Buildings, Public Works	7.3	2.2	3.3	6.0	2.6	43.3
19	Transport,Telecommunications	3.7	0.9	3.3	5.4	0.0	5.7
20	Traditional Trade	0.0	6.0	1.0	4.0	0.0	3.2
21	Modern Trade	0.0	0.0	0.0	0.0	0.0	0.0
22	Traditional Services	0.0	0.0	0.0	0.0	0.0	0.0
23	Modern Services	0.0	0.0	0.0	0.0	0.0	0.0
24	Banking, Insurance	0.0	0.0	0.0	0.0	0.0	0.0
25	General Govt. Administration	0.0	0.0	0.0	0.0	0.0	0.0
26	Administration: Econom. Svcs	0.0	0.0	0.0	0.0	0.0	0.0
27	Administration: Education	0.0	0.0	0.0	0.0	0.0	0.0
28	Administration: Health	0.0	0.0	0.0	0.0	0.0	0.0
29	Social Security (INSS)	0.0	0.0	0.0	0.0	0.0	0.0
30	Priv. Non-Prof. Inst:Administr	0.0	0.0	0.0	0.0	0.0	0.0
31	Priv. Non-Prof. Inst:Education	0.0	0.0	0.0	0.0	0.0	0.0
32	Priv. Non-Prof. Inst:Health	0.0	0.0	0.0	0.0	0.0	0.0
33	Foreign Admin. Rural Developm.	0.0	0.0	0.0	0.0	0.0	0.0
34	Foreign Admin. Research	0.0	0.0	0.0	0.0	0.0	0.0
35	Foreign Admin. Education	0.0	0.0	0.0	0.0	0.0	0.0
36	Foreign Admin. Miscellaneous	0.0	0.0	0.0	0.0	0.0	0.0
37	Domestic Intermediate Inputs	18.5	63.5	32.6	12.9	16.3	200.0
38	Imports (c.i.f plus Duties)	24.5	125.7	39.9	3.3	38.5	123.6
39	Local Salaries and Wages	13.5	56.7	8.7	8.0	120.4	34.7
40	Expatriate Salaries & Wages	1.0	25.7	1.7	0.0	0.0	34.4
41	Social Taxes	0.8	3.4	1.8	0.3	0.0	3.3
42	Indirect Taxes	0.0	0.0	0.9	0.0	0.0	3.0
43	Subsidies	3.5	4.0	0.9	0.3	0.0	1.9
44	Depreciation	0.4	6.0	3.3	4.0	0.0	0.7
45	Operating Surplus	10.4	41.0	22.3	43.0	100.8	48.0
46	Exceptional Sales	0.0	0.0	0.0	0.0	0.0	0.0
47	Gross Output	72.8	322.2	121.5	68.7	421.0	555.2

38

Input-Output Table of Burundi for the Year 1970

BURUNDI 1970

FLOWS in millions of Burundi Francs of Y 1970

PRODUCERS CURRENT PRICES

INDUSTRY:	19 Transport, Communications	20 Traditional Trade	21 Modern Trade	22 Traditional Services	23 Modern Services	24 Banking, Insurance
* DOMESTIC TRANSACTIONS						
INDUSTRY						
1 Agriculture	0	0	0.0	0.5	0	0
2 Agriculture for Export	0	0	0	0	0	0
3 Livestock	0	0	0	0	0	0
4 Fishing - Traditional	0	0	0	0	0	0
5 Fishing - Industrial	0	0	0	0.5	0	0
6 Forestry Products (Wood)	0	0	0	0.8	0	0
7 Prim Proc. of Agric. Prods.	3.0	0	0	19.0	2	2
8 Food Products - Domestic Use	0	0	0	0	0.0	0
9 Food Products - Industrial	0	0	0	0	9.9	0
10 Textiles,Leather,Basketweavg	1	0	0	0	0	1
11 Wrg. Apparel;Leather,Textile	0.9	0	7.8	0	5.0	2
12 Mining, Energy	2.0	2.5	16.4	0	0	6
13 Wood & Paper Products	37.9	0	0	0	0	0
14 Mechanics & Repair, Garages	0.0	0	2.0	0	7	7
15 Chemicals, Construction Mat.	0.8	5.0	14.3	0	35.7	2
16 Miscellaneous Manufactures	29.2	0	34.0	0	1.0	4
17 Traditional Dwellings	0	0	0	0	0	0
18 Buildings, Public Works	50.9	0	3.0	0	15.9	0
19 Transport,Telecommunications	58.9	17.5	6.2	0	18.8	15.3
20 Traditional Trade	23.0	0	7.8	0	0	0
21 Modern Trade	22.9	0	0	0	9.0	3.0
22 Traditional Services	0	0	0	0	0	0
23 Modern Services	0	0	0	0	0	0
24 Banking, Insurance	0	0	0	0	0	0
25 General Govt Administration	0	0	0	0	0	0
26 Administration: Econom. Svcs	0	0	0	0	0	0
27 Administration: Education	0	0	0	0	0	0
28 Administration: Health	0	0	0	0	0	0
29 Social Security (INSS)	0	0	0	0	0	0
30 Priv Non-Prof Inst:Administr	0	0	0	0	0	0
31 Priv Non-Prof Inst:Education	0	0	0	0	0	0
32 Priv Non-Prof Inst:Health	0	0	0	0	0	0
33 Forgn Admin: Rural Developm	0	0	0	0	0	0
34 Foreign Admin Education	0	0	0	0	0	0
35 Foreign Admin Research	0	0	0	0	0	0
36 Foreign Admin Miscellaneous	0	0	0	0	0	0
37 Domestic Intermediate Inputs	176.0	28.0	248.4	28.8	105.9	37.1
38 Imports (c.i.f plus Duties)	168.8	0.0	43.5	2.2	38.0	117.5
39 Local Salaries and Wages	70.9	0.0	107.9	0	163.7	67.5
40 Expatriate Salaries & Wages	35.8	0.4	112.9	0	74.7	40.2
41 Social Taxes	17.3	0	205.1	0	29.0	22.6
42 Subsidies	0.0	0	-21.8	0	0	0
43 Subsidies	0.0	7.0	-27.2	0	112.4	20.9
44 Depreciation	60.8	0	583.0	5.6	392.3	8.0
45 Operating Surplus	69.2	743.6	0.0	5.0	0	0.0
46 Exceptional Sales	6.2	0.0		0.0	0	0.0
47 Gross Output	802.5	779.0	1313.4	36.6	711.8	252.9

39

Input-Output Table of Burundi for the Year 1970

BURUNDI 1970

FLOWS in millions of Burundi Francs of Y 1970

PRODUCERS CURRENT PRICES

INDUSTRY:

	25 General Govt. Administration: Administration Econom.Services	26 Administration: Econom.Services	27 Administration: Education	28 Administration: Health	29 Social Security (INSS)	30 Priv. Non-Profit Inst. Administr
* DOMESTIC TRANSACTIONS * INDUSTRY						
1 Agriculture						
2 Agriculture for Export						
3 Livestock						
4 Fishing - Traditional						
5 Fishing - Industrial						
6 Forestry products (Wood)						
7 Prim.Proc.of Agric.Prods.						
8 Food Products - Domestic Use						
9 Food Products - Industrial						
10 Textiles,Leather,Basketweavg						
11 Wrg.Apparel;Leather,Textile						
12 Mining,Energy Products						
13 Wood & Paper Products						
14 Mechanics & Repair,Garages						
15 Chemicals,Construction Mat.						
16 Miscellaneous Manufactures						
17 Traditional Dwellings						
18 Buildings,Public Works						
19 Transport,Telecommunications						
20 Traditional Trade						
21 Modern Trade						
22 Traditional Services						
23 Modern Services						
24 Banking,Insurance						
25 General Govt.Administration						
26 Administration:Econom.Svcs						
27 Administration:Education						
28 Administration:Health						
29 Social Security (INSS)						
30 Priv.Non-Prof.Inst:Administr						
31 Priv.Non-Prof.Inst:Education						
32 Priv.Non-Prof.Inst:Health						
33 Foreign Admin.Research						
34 Forgn Admin.Rural Developm.						
35 Foreign Admin:Education						
36 Foreign Admin:Miscellaneous						
37 Domestic Intermediate Inputs	184.1	75.6	59.3	39.7	4.5	31.9
38 Imports(c.i.f plus Duties)	451.8	13.4	10.1	35.2	8.5	8.9
39 Local Salaries and Wages	429.7	160.7	67.3	109.6	8.5	82.9
40 Expatriate Salaries & Wages	100.0	3.8	8.0	20.5	0.5	25.0
41 Social Taxes				2.0		
42 Indirect Taxes						
43 Subsidies						
44 Depreciation						
45 Operating Surplus	-3.0	-0.2				
46 Sundry Sales						
47 Gross Output	872.6	249.3	145.5	187.0	15.8	147.3

40

Input-Output Table of Burundi for the Year 1970

BURUNDI 1970   FLOWS in millions of Burundi Francs of Y 1970   PRODUCERS CURRENT PRICES

INDUSTRY:	31 Priv.Non-Profit Inst: Education	32 Priv.Non-Profit Inst: Health	33 Foreign Admin Research Rural Devel_m	34 Foreign Admin Rural Develop	35 Foreign Admin Education	36 Foreign Admin Miscellaneous
* DOMESTIC TRANSACTIONS * INDUSTRY						
1 Agriculture for Export	18	0	0	0	1	0
2 Agriculture for Export	0	0	0	0	7	0
3 Livestock	0	0	0	0	0	0
4 Fishing - Traditional	0	0	0	0	2	0
5 Fishing - Industrial	0	0	0	3	0	0
6 Forestry Products (Wood)	0	0	0	0	3	0
7 Prim Proc. of Agric. Prods.	9	0	0	0	0	0
8 Food Products - Domestic Use	0	0	0	0	0	0
9 Food Products - Industrial	9	0	0	0	5	0
10 Textiles,Leather,Basketweavg	3	0	0	0	0	0
11 Wrg. Apparel;Leather,Textile	0	0	0	0	5	7
12 Mining, Energy	0	0	1	3	2	2
13 Wood & paper Products	2	0	1	5	4	0
14 Mechanics & Repair, Garages	3	0	2	0	2	2
15 Chemicals, Construction Mat.	2	3	3	0	7	0
16 Miscellaneous Manufactures	0	0	0	0	0	0
17 Traditional Dwellings	0	0	0	0	0	3
18 Buildings, Public Works	2	3	4	5	5	28
19 Transport,Telecommunications	6	0	7	0	0	2
20 Traditional Trade	4	0	0	0	7	0
21 Modern Trade	1	0	6	5	0	2
22 Traditional Services	0	0	0	0	5	5
23 Modern Services	0	0	4	0	6	7
24 Banking, Insurance	0	3	2	5	4	1
25 General Govt. Administration	0	0	0	0	5	0
26 Administration: Econom. Svcs	0	0	0	0	0	0
27 Administration: Education	0	0	0	0	0	0
28 Administration: Health	3	0	0	0	0	0
29 Social Security (INSS)	0	0	0	0	0	0
30 Priv.Non-Prof.Inst:Administr	0	0	0	0	0	0
31 Priv.Non-Prof.Inst:Education	2	0	0	0	0	0
32 Priv.Non-Prof.Inst:Health	0	0	0	0	0	0
33 Foreign Admin.Research	0	0	0	0	0	0
34 Foreign Admin.Rural Develop.	0	0	0	0	0	0
35 Foreign Admin.Education	0	0	0	0	0	0
36 Foreign Admin.Miscellaneous	0	0	0	0	0	0
37 Domestic Intermediate Inputs	32.5	2.3	11.0	13.3	16.3	41.6
38 Imports (c.i.f plus Duties)	20.8	7.9	16.8	13.5	13.8	38.6
39 Local Salaries and Wages	313.1	2.2	5.4	14.3	13.2	12.9
40 Expatriate Salaries & Wages	19.4	10.0	11.9	3.1	53.2	489.9
41 Social Taxes	0.0	0.0	0.0	0.0	0.4	0.0
42 Indirect Taxes	0.0	0.0	0.0	0.0	0.0	0.0
43 Subsidies	0.0	0.0	0.0	0.0	0.0	0.0
44 Depreciation	0.0	0.0	-0.9	0.0	-0.9	0.0
45 Operating Surplus	0.0	0.0	-2.9	0.0	-4.9	0.0
46 Exceptional Sales	0.0	0.0	0.0	0.0	0.0	0.0
47 Gross Output	385.8	22.4	52.3	72.6	82.3	583.0

41

Input-Output Table of Burundi for the Year 1970

BURUNDI 1970   FLOWS in millions of Burundi Francs of Y 1970   PRODUCERS CURRENT PRICES

DOMESTIC TRANSACTIONS	37 Dom. Intermed. Consumption	38 Final Consump. Hsehlds,Non-Cmc	39 Final Consump. Hsehlds,Commrci	40 Final Consump. Gen'l Services	41 Final Consump. Priv.Non-Profit	42 Final Consump. Foreign Svcs
* INDUSTRY						
1 Agriculture	2168.5	6683.0	815.1	0	0	0
2 Agriculture for Export	1666.0	438.3	70.7	0	0	0
3 Livestock - Traditional	200.6	5.300	70.7	0	0	0
4 Fishing - Traditional	0.3	0	44.3	0	0	0
5 Fishing - Industrial		0	71.9	0	0	0
6 Forestry Products (Wood)	48.5	72.5	8.0	0	0	0
7 Prim Prod of Agric.Prods.	14.5	0	57.0	0	0	0
8 Food Products - Domestic Use	58.5	1139.0	1020.4	0	0	0
9 Food Products - Domestic		0	1096.4	0	0	0
10 Textiles Leather Industwal	9.0	0	29.0	0	0	0
11 Wrg. Apparel:Leather,textile	0.7	0	200.0	0	0	0
12 Mining, Energy Prods	60.0	0	230.0	0	0	0
13 Wood & Paper Products	60.4	0	21.8	0	0	0
14 Mechanics & Repair, Garages	248.9	0	24.6	0	0	0
15 Chemicals, Construction Mat.	68.7	0	42.6	0	0	0
16 Miscellaneous Manufactures	41.1	0	18.0	0	0	0
17 Traditional Dwellings		8.0	0	0	0	0
18 Buildings, Public Works	125.6	0	100.0	0	0	0
19 Transport, Telecommunications	280.7	0	300.5	0	0	0
20 Traditional Trade	377.3	0	737.6	0	0	0
21 Modern Trade		0	660.3	0	0	0
22 Traditional Services	326.3	128.0	336.6	0	0	0
23 Modern Services	188.1	0	156.1	0	0	0
24 Banking, Insurance	0	0	250.3	0	0	0
25 General Govt. Administration	0	0	0	672.6	0	0
26 Administration: Econom. Svcs	0	0	0	248.3	0	0
27 Administration: Education	0	0	0	145.5	0	0
28 Administration: Health	0	0	0	186.4	0	0
29 Social Security (INSS)	0	0	0	15.8	0	0
30 Priv. Non-Prof. Inst:Administr	0	0	0	0	147.3	0
31 Priv. Non-Prof. Inst:Education	0	0	0	0	385.8	0
32 Priv. Non-Prof. Inst:Health	0.2	0	0	0	22.2	0
33 Foreign Admin. Research	0	0	0	0	0	52.3
34 Forgn Admin. Rural Developm.	0	0	0	0	0	72.6
35 Foreign Admin. Education	0	0	0	0	0	82.3
36 Foreign Admin. Miscellaneous	0	0	0	0	0	583.0
37 Domestic Intermediate Inputs	5986.6	8475.9	5483.9	1269.6	555.3	790.2
38 Imports (c.i.f plus Duties)	1364.8	0	1092.0	0	0	0
39 Local Salaries and Wages	1953.7	0	0	0	0	0
40 Expatriate Salaries & Wages	993.2	0	0	0	0	0
41 Social Taxes	52.4	0	0	0	0	0
42 Indirect Taxes	1188.4	0	0	0	0	0
43 Subsidies	-80.3	0	0	0	0	0
44 Depreciation	316.0	0	0	0	0	0
45 Operating Surplus	14104.1	0	0	0	0	0
46 Exceptional Sales	0.0	0	0	0	0	0
47 Gross Output	25857.8	8475.9	6575.9	1269.6	555.3	790.2

Input-Output Table of Burundi for the Year 1970

	DOMESTIC TRANSACTIONS INDUSTRY	43 Gr.Fxd.Cap.F Hsehlds,Non-Cmc	44 Gr.Fxd.Cap.F Hsehlds,Commer	45 Gr.Fxd.Cap.F Enterprises	46 Gr.Fxd.Cap.F Gen'l Svcs	47 Gr.Fxd.Cap.F Priv,Non-Profit	48 Gr.Fxd.Cap.F Forgn.Services
1	Agriculture for Export	0.0	0.0	0.0	0.0	0.0	0.0
2	Agriculture	0.0	0.0	0.0	0.0	0.0	0.0
3	Livestock	0.0	0.0	0.0	0.0	0.0	0.0
4	Fishing - Traditional	0.0	0.0	0.0	0.0	0.0	0.0
5	Fishing - Industrial	0.0	0.0	0.0	0.0	0.0	0.0
6	Forestry Products(Wood)	0.0	0.0	0.0	0.0	0.0	0.0
7	Prim.Proc.of Agric.Prods.	0.0	0.0	0.0	0.0	0.0	0.0
8	Food Products - Domestic Use	0.0	0.0	0.0	0.0	0.0	0.0
9	Food Products - Industrial	0.0	0.0	0.0	0.0	0.0	0.0
10	Textiles,Leather,Basketweav	0.0	0.0	0.0	0.0	0.0	0.0
11	Wrg.Apparel,Leather,Textile	0.0	0.0	0.0	0.0	0.0	0.0
12	Mining,Energy	0.0	0.0	0.0	0.0	0.0	0.0
13	Wood & Paper Products	0.0	0.0	0.0	0.0	0.0	0.0
14	Mechanics & Repair,Garages	0.0	0.0	0.0	0.0	0.0	0.0
15	Chemicals,Construction Mat	0.0	0.0	0.0	0.0	0.0	2.3
16	Miscellaneous Manufactures	0.0	0.0	0.0	8.5	0.0	0.0
17	Traditional Dwellings	210.7	205.2	35.1	58.6	78.6	199.0
18	Buildings,Public Works	0.0	58.3	0.5	2.0	0.1	0.2
19	Transport,Telecommunications	0.0	0.0	20.9	6.0	3.9	7.0
20	Traditional Trade	0.0	0.0	0.0	0.0	0.0	0.0
21	Modern Trade	0.0	0.0	0.0	0.0	0.0	0.0
22	Traditional Services	0.0	0.0	0.0	0.0	0.0	0.0
23	Modern Services	0.0	0.0	0.0	5.0	0.0	94.0
24	Banking,Insurance	0.0	0.0	0.0	0.0	0.0	0.0
25	General Govt.Administration	0.0	0.0	0.0	0.0	0.0	0.0
26	Administration:Econom.Svcs	0.0	0.0	0.0	0.0	0.0	0.0
27	Administration:Education	0.0	0.0	0.0	0.0	0.0	0.0
28	Administration:Health	0.0	0.0	0.0	0.0	0.0	0.0
29	Social Security(INSS)	0.0	0.0	0.0	0.0	0.0	0.0
30	Priv.Non-Prof.Inst:Administr	0.0	0.0	0.0	0.0	0.0	0.0
31	Priv.Non-Prof.Inst:Education	0.0	0.0	0.0	0.0	0.0	0.0
32	Priv.Non-Prof.Inst:Health	0.0	0.0	0.0	0.0	0.0	0.0
33	Foreign Admin:Research	0.0	0.0	0.0	0.0	0.0	0.0
34	Foreign Admin:Rural Developm	0.0	0.0	0.0	0.0	0.0	0.0
35	Foreign Admin:Education	0.0	0.0	0.0	0.0	0.0	0.0
36	Foreign Admin:Miscellaneous	0.0	0.0	0.0	0.0	0.0	0.0
37	Domestic Intermediate Inputs	210.7	263.5	56.5	79.0	82.6	302.5
38	Imports(c.i.f plus Duties)	0.0	0.0	131.7	55.3	24.0	58.6
39	Local Salaries and Wages	0.0	0.0	0.0	0.0	0.0	0.0
40	Expatriate Salaries & Wages	0.0	0.0	0.0	0.0	0.0	0.0
41	Social Taxes	0.0	0.0	0.0	0.0	0.0	0.0
42	Indirect Taxes	0.0	0.0	0.0	0.0	0.0	0.0
43	Subsidies	0.0	0.0	0.0	0.0	0.0	0.0
44	Depreciation	0.0	0.0	0.0	0.0	0.0	0.0
45	Operating Surplus	0.0	0.0	0.0	0.0	0.0	0.0
46	Exceptional sales	0.0	0.0	0.0	0.0	0.0	0.0
47	Gross Output	210.7	263.5	188.2	134.3	106.7	361.1

Input-Output Table of Burundi for the Year 1970

BURUNDI 1970   FLOWS in millions of Burundi Francs of Y 1970   PRODUCERS CURRENT PRICES

		49 Stocks	50 Exports (Non-Official)	51 Exports (Official)	52 Final Demand	53 Gross Output
*	DOMESTIC TRANSACTIONS *					
	INDUSTRY					
1	Agriculture	6.0	0.0	0.0	7504.2	9672.7
2	Agriculture for Export	0.0	0.0	0.0	577.8	1666.0
3	Livestock	0.0	55.5	1300.0	49.9	778.4
4	Fishing - Traditional	0.0	0.0	0.0	49.2	49.2
5	Fishing - Industrial	0.0	0.0	0.0	81.9	72.2
6	Forestry Products (Wood)	77.2	0.0	1744.3	1878.9	1806.4
7	Prim. Proc. of Agric. Prods.	0.0	0.0	2.0	2159.0	2173.5
8	Food Products - Domestic Use	0.0	0.0	0.0	1117.0	1176.3
9	Food Products - Industrial	10.9	0.0	10.2	230.1	231.8
10	Textiles,Leather;Basketweavg	13.0	0.0	20.3	250.0	236.9
11	Wearing Apparel;Leather,Textile	0.0	0.0	0.0	75.3	170.6
12	Mining & Energy Products	5.8	0.0	15.9	255.4	322.2
13	Wood & Paper Products	-6.0	0.0	17.6	417.0	321.5
14	Mechan.&Cos.Repair.Garages	0.0	0.0	0.0	46.5	467.0
15	Chemicals & Constr.-Mat.	0.0	0.0	0.0	429.6	505.2
16	Miscellaneous Manufactures	0.0	0.0	200.0	321.7	679.0
17	Traditional Manufactures	0.0	0.3	0.0	737.0	1313.6
18	Buildings, Public Works	0.0	17.8	219.0	936.6	711.8
19	Traditional Dwellings	0.0	0.0	0.0	385.5	252.9
20	Transport,Telecommunications	0.0	0.0	44.5	364.5	672.9
21	Modern Trade	0.0	0.0	0.0	672.9	249.3
22	Traditional Trade	0.0	0.0	0.0	249.3	145.5
23	Modern Services	0.0	0.0	0.0	106.4	187.0
24	Traditional Services	0.0	0.0	0.0	187.0	147.3
25	Banking Insurance	0.0	0.0	0.0	147.3	385.8
26	General Govt Administration	0.0	0.0	0.0	385.8	322.4
27	Administration: Econom.Svcs	0.0	0.0	0.0	322.3	52.3
28	Administration: Education	0.0	0.0	0.0	52.3	72.6
29	Administration: Health	0.0	0.0	0.0	72.6	583.0
30	Social Security (INSS)	0.0	0.0	0.0	583.0	
31	Priv.Non-Prof.Inst:Administr					
32	Priv.Non-Prof.Inst:Education					
33	Priv.Non-Prof.Inst:Health					
34	Foreign Admin: Research					
35	Foreign Admin: Rural Developm.					
36	Foreign Admin: Education					
	Foreign Admin: Miscellaneous					
37	Domestic Intermediate Inputs	96.1	73.6	2131.8	19871.2	25857.8
38	Imports (c.i.f plus Duties)	17.3	0.0	529.6	1908.6	3273.2
39	Local Salaries and Wages	0.0	0.0	0.0	0.0	1993.2
40	Expatriate Salaries & Wages	0.0	0.0	0.0	0.0	52.6
41	Social Taxes	0.0	0.0	0.0	0.0	1166.4
42	Indirect Taxes	0.0	0.0	0.0	0.0	-80.3
43	Subsidies	0.0	0.0	0.0	0.0	316.9
44	Depreciation	0.0	0.0	0.0	0.0	14104.0
45	Operating Surplus	0.0	0.0	0.0	0.0	0.0
46	Exceptional Sales	0.0	0.0	0.0	0.0	
47	Gross Output	113.4	73.6	2661.4	21779.8	47637.6

44

CHILE

The present report is based on *Matriz de Insumo–Producto de la Economía Chilena, 1977,* published by ODEPLAN, Departamento de Contabilidad Social, Presidencia de la República.

A. General information

1.   The latest input-output table available refers to 1977, and was compiled by the Social Accounting Department of the National Bureau of Planning (ODEPLAN). This was the second table compiled in the country, the first one referring to the year 1962. Major differences between the 1962 and 1977 input-output tables include: different classification systems; inclusion of the government sector in the final demand sector only (1962); treatment of the financial system; treatment of import taxes; treatment of trade margins on imports; more narrow scope of the transfer of secondary production in the 1962 table; and the use of the old version of the United Nations system of national accounts (SNA) as the basis of the 1962 table.

2.   One purpose of compiling the 1977 input-output table was to establish a coherent accounting framework which will form the basis of a new series of national accounts with 1977 as reference year.

3.   Major deviations of the Chilean input-output table from the SNA recommendations on input-output include: no make matrix is compiled (para. 4); valuation of transaction at approximate basic values not available (para. 7); activities of private non-profit institutions not recorded separately (para. 10); disaggregation of value added (para. 11); treatment of imports (para. 13); treatment of secondary products (para. 14); definition of output of the transportation sector (para. 19); definition of output of the financial sector (para. 20); and definition of output of the insurance sector (para. 21).

B. Analytical framework

Tables and derived matrices available

4.   Data are presented in three basic tables:

   (i)   Absorption table of total flows at purchasers' prices;
   (ii)   Absorption table of domestic flows at purchasers' prices;
   (iii)   Imports absorption matrix.

5.   On the basis of these data, the following derived matrices were compiled:

   (i′)   Technical coefficients based on table (i);
   (ii′)   Technical coefficients based on table (ii);
   (iii′)   Technical coefficients based on table (iii);

(iv′) Coefficients of distribution based on table (i);

(v′) Coefficients of distribution based on table (ii)

(vi′) Coefficients of distribution based on table (iii);

(vii′) Inverse matrix based on table (i′).

6. All basic tables and derived matrices compiled are presented at a level of disaggregation of 67×67 intermediate sectors. In addition, more aggregated versions of tables (i), (ii) and (iii) with 20 intermediate sectors were also compiled.

Valuation standards

7. All transactions were valued at purchasers' prices. However, information was also compiled on distribution margins and commodity taxes so that a valuation at approximate basic values can be made available at a later stage. Direct imports are valued c.i.f. plus import duties. Indirect imports—i.e., imports through foreign trade channels—are valued at the total cost of purchase by the enterprise which includes internal charges and distribution margins. Exports are valued f.o.b.

Statistical units and classification standards

8. The industry was generally adopted as a statistical unit, due to lack of data at the establishment level. Exceptions to this approach were the agriculture, livestock and forestry sectors, which were defined on a commodity basis, and the trade and private construction sectors, which were defined on an activity basis.

9. A modified version of the International Standard Industrial Classification of all Economic Activities (ISIC) was adopted as classification system. Deviations from this system include:

At the division level

(a) The copper mining sector includes smelting, alloying and refining of copper ores, unlike ISIC, which classifies the processes in the manufacturing division. Lack of data at a more disaggregate level prevented the adoption of the ISIC criterium;

(b) Repair services were assigned to the manufacturing or personal services divisions according to whether major or minor repairs (respectively) were involved;

(c) Sanitary services were included in electricity, gas and water, rather than in community, social and personal services.

At the major group level

(a) Livestock activities were disaggregated from ISIC major group 111 and recorded separately;

(b) Copper and salt mining were treated as separate sectors;

(c) Ownership of dwellings was recorded separately.

10. The classification of the intermediate consumption quadrant differs from SNA recommendations on input-output in that the activities of private non-profit institutions are recorded together with those referring to enterprises. The activities of producers of government services, including public education and health, were recorded in the intermediate consumption quadrant, as recommended in SNA.

11. The SNA presentation of value added was disaggregated as follows: compensation of employees was classified into wages, salaries and employers' contribution to social security and similar schemes; indirect taxes were classified into taxes on value added, taxes on production and other indirect taxes; and operating surplus was divided into that of corporations and net incomes of the self-employed. Components of value added were defined as in SNA.

12. Final demand was disaggregated as in SNA. Private consumption was defined on a national basis. Therefore, it includes expenditure by domestic households on the domestic and foreign markets, and excludes direct purchases in the domestic market by non-resident households. Government consumption was defined as in SNA, i.e., it includes the value of goods and services produced for their own use. Investment was defined as the sum of domestic supply of capital goods during the period plus imports of capital goods, adjusted for change of stocks of capital goods imported. Exports included tourism expenditure in the country and expenditure on the domestic market by diplomats.

13. Contrary to SNA recommendations, no distinction was made in the Chilean input-output table between competitive and complementary imports. All imports have been cross-classified by origin and destination in the import matrix.

Treatment and presentation of selected transactions

14. Due to lack of data, secondary products were not in all instances transferred to their characteristic sectors. However, efforts were made to reallocate secondary outputs belonging to different ISIC divisions. Special attention was given to trade and building rental activities carried out by enterprises other than trade dealers and real estate agencies, since these activities constituted the bulk of secondary production. Both kinds of secondary outputs were recorded as fictitious sales to the characteristic industries, that is, they were recorded as inputs into the trade and real estate sectors, respectively, from the sectors having these activities as secondary production. Lack of information prevented the corresponding transfer of inputs. In the case of large mining enterprises except for copper mining and the industrial subsector of the fishing sector, the reallocation of both output and intermediate inputs corresponding to their manufacturing activities was possible, on the basis of data provided by the enterprises themselves. Similarly, the construction of plants carried out by electricity and water supply industries was transferred to the construction sector, together with their associated inputs.

47

In other cases, such as the ship repair activities carried out by the fishing sector and electricity produced for own consumption, neither output nor input could be reallocated.

15. Scrap sales were included in the trade sector. They were recorded as secondary trade activity of the corresponding sector (in the case of scrap generated by the mining, energy and transport sectors), or as part of direct trade (i.e., transaction of used goods) in the case of second-hand goods mainly consumed by households.

16. Non-monetary output and its associated inputs are recorded together with the monetary components in the corresponding input-output sector. Major types of non-monetary production covered include: own consumption of agriculture products; payments in kind; imputed rents of owner-occupied dwellings; own account gross fixed capital formation; and own account repairs and inputs used and produced in the same establishment.

17. Intra-sector consumption is recorded in the main diagonal of the absorption table and therefore included in the gross output of each input-output sector.

18. Gross output of the trade sector was defined as the sum of: trade margins on agriculture, fishing and manufacturing products; direct trade, i.e., that referring to transactions of used goods; trade margins on imports; commissions received from abroad for trade services; and trade margins which are part of the secondary activities of enterprises included in other input-output sectors. The first component was estimated by comparison of gross outputs of the corresponding sector valued at producers' and purchasers' prices.

19. Gross output of the transportation sector only includes the activity of enterprises mainly engaged in providing transportation services. The remaining transportation activities are recorded as part of the gross output of the enterprises carrying out transportation activities as secondary production.

20. As recommended in SNA, a distinction was made between actual and imputed charges for financial services, the latter being equal to the excess of property income received by banks on loans and other investments, over the interest they paid out on deposits. Only the former were distributed among the intermediate sectors of the table. All imputed charges were recorded as the single input of a fictitious sector (banking imputations), whose value added was set equal to the value of these imputed charges with a minus sign. Lack of data prevented the exclusion from these imputed charges of interest received from investment of the bank's own funds, as recommended in SNA.

21. Gross output of the insurance sector includes: premiums for insurance against risk (lack of data prevented the valuation of premiums net of claims, as recommended in SNA); life insurance premiums minus net additions to actuarial reserves during the year (this value differs from that recommended in SNA in that claims are not deducted); commissions received by agents acting as intermediaries between insurance companies and policy holders.

C. Statistical sources and compilation methodology

22.   Data collection is mainly based on regular sources, special surveys carried out for the purpose of compilation of the input-output table, and on the preliminary results of the 1977 Agriculture and Livestock Census and the 1976 Manufacturing Census.

Gross output, intermediate consumption and value added

Agriculture, livestock and forestry

23.   Data on agriculture, livestock and forestry were obtained as indicated in the following six paragraphs.

24.   The physical volumes of the different commodities produced were estimated on the basis of census data and an analysis of their sectoral destination was carried out so as to obtain a balance of demand and supply in physical terms. The supply of the different commodities was valued at their representative producers' prices, defined as those prevailing in the most usual location of delivery by the producer. Demand was valued at the corresponding purchasers' prices, defined as those at which the final transaction took place (excluding value-added taxes). The commercialization channels, seasonal factors and quality, variety and destination of the quantities demanded of each commodity were taken into account to estimate the purchasers' prices representative of each demand transaction. These data allowed for the estimation of gross output for each one of the three sectors mentioned, i.e., agriculture, livestock and forestry.

25.   An estimate of the total physical quantities of each intermediate input consumed by all three sectors was then obtained. This estimate is based on sales data provided by the corresponding producers. This total was then allocated among the three sectors according to the characteristics of their respective main products. A detailed analysis of the uses of each main intermediate input was thus carried out. This analysis made possible the valuation of intermediate inputs at their representative sales prices to producers. Representative prices were selected taking into account such factors as quality, variety, commercialization channels, and specific destination of each input. Finally, tax on value added was charged so as to obtain a value estimate of intermediate inputs at purchasers' prices.

26.   The components of value added were estimated according to the following procedure. Employment was estimated on the basis of the number of man-days needed in the production process. This total was disaggregated by occupational category in order to determine the man-days corresponding to renumerated work. This disaggregation was based on the results of the Occupational Survey of the National Institute of Statistics and the preliminary results of the Agriculture and Livestock Census. Average wages and salaries per day (including payments in kind) were provided by the results of the IREN Survey. The total value of employers' contribution to social security and similar schemes was provided by the relevant institutions, and was allocated among sectors in proportion to their level of wages and salaries. Net indirect taxes

49

were provided by data compiled for the government sector. Depreciation was estimated by applying coefficients of useful life of each kind of capital good to the value of the stock of the corresponding type of goods. The operating surplus was estimated as residual.

27. In the agricultural sector, the lack of correspondence between the calendar and the agricultural years presented an additional problem. The decision was taken to refer data to the calendar year, which implies that adjustments had to be made for intermediate inputs of products harvested in years other than 1977.

28. The large variety of existing agricultural products also presented a problem. This was dealt with by first classifying all products into "main" and "other", and then extrapolating to the other category the data estimated for the main group.

29. Information on agriculture prices was obtained from the National Institute of Statistics, Empresa de Comercio Agrícola, Oficina de Planificación Agrícola and marketing studies of the agricultural enterprises carried out by a consulting firm.

Fishing

30. In the fishing sector, a distinction was made between the traditional and industrial fishing subsectors, based mainly on the size of the vessels with which the fishing activity was carried out. Data on intermediate and final inputs of the traditional subsector were obtained through surveys conducted for this purpose. Total physical gross output of this subsector and its evaluation at beach prices were obtained from the Fishing Yearbook of the División de Protección Pesquera. Special surveys were also carried out to collect data on physical gross output, beach prices, intermediate inputs and primary inputs of the industrial subsector. The surveyed units were also required to provide separate data on their extractive and manufacturing activities. Data on the sectoral distribution of the physical output of each species were provided by the Agriculture and Livestock Service. The main problem encountered was the influence of regional and destination factors in the prevailing beach prices. To allow for these differences, a distinction was made in the total catch of each fishing area between fish sold for fresh consumption and that sold for further processing. The assumption was made that the output of the traditional sector was mainly sold for fresh consumption, and that the difference between this output and total demand for fresh consumption was provided by the industrial sector. Similarly, in regions where total output of the industrial subsector was inferior to the amount processed, the traditional subsector was assumed to cover the difference. Fish sold for further processing was valued at regional beach prices for industrial fishing. Sales for fresh consumption in each area were further disaggregated into direct sales—which were valued at regional beach prices for traditional fishing—and sales through trade dealers, on the basis of information collected by the surveys. Finally, sales through trade dealers were classified according to the regional location of the final transaction, and were valued according to the retail prices prevailing in Santiago when no information on zonal retail prices was available. A zero trade margin was assumed for direct sales to consumers and for fish sold for further

processing since these sales do not go through distribution channels. Trade margins on the remaining transactions were estimated as the ratio between gross output valued at purchasers' and at producers' prices.

Mining and quarrying

31. The characteristic gross output of the mining sector was obtained as the sum of domestic sales, exports and stock variations. Changes in stocks were estimated as the difference between sales and production both measured in physical terms, and was valued at market prices. Secondary output consists mainly of services provided gratis to employees. Intermediate sales were obtained by deducting from gross output the supply of final demand. Data were obtained from surveys and from the accounts of mining establishments.

Manufacturing

32. In the manufacturing sector, for purposes of data collection, industries were stratified into three groups according to their levels of employment. Data on industries belonging to strata 1 and 2 (i.e., industries with less than 9 and between 10 and 49 employees, respectively) were obtained from the annual reports to the Rol Industrial de la Dirección de Industria y Comercio. This source provides detailed estimates on raw material and products by type of enterprise. The monthly estimates were then inflated into annual estimates. Trends, seasonality and variation of the wholesale price index of each sector were taken into account in the adjustment. For stratum 3 (i.e., industries with over 50 employees), data from the same source were supplemented with the results of the annual Industrial Survey of the National Institute of Statistics and with data obtained directly from the industries.

33. Gross output of the manufacturing sector was estimated from sales data (including indirect taxes) adjusted for variation of stocks of finished and in-process goods. Main statistical sources used were records on tax on value added for several months of 1977, classified by the ISIC four-digit industrial subsector. These data were extrapolated for the whole year of 1977 taking into account trend values, seasonal variations and changes in the wholesale price index of the corresponding industrial subsectors. Total sales, which include those subject to value added tax as well as those exempt from it, were divided into three strata on the basis of their proportion in the sample, and were also compared with the results of the 1967 Industrial Census and the 1977 Industrial Survey. Gross output of each stratum was determined on the basis of the sample ratio between gross value of output and sales.

34. Intermediate inputs of the manufacturing sector data were estimated on the basis of purchases. Adjustments were made to take into account variations of raw material inventory changes. Estimates for each stratum were obtained by expanding the corresponding sample estimates by a factor equal to the ratio of gross output of the universe to gross output of the sample. These estimates were checked against data on corresponding production by the agriculture, fishing, mining and other relevant sectors. Self-consumption was valued at producers' prices. Value-added data were estimated according to the same procedure used for intermediate inputs.

35. Each of the products obtained in the sampled industries was classified by destination into final consumption, intermediate consumption and capital goods, and into goods for the domestic market or goods for exports. To avoid distortions, changes in stocks of finished and in-process goods were proportionally allocated to domestic and exports sales. This classification of commodities by destination was based on the results of the Industrial Survey of the National Institute of Statistics, the 1978 Family Budget Survey, balance of payments data, direct inquiries and the reconciliation of supply and demand for each input-output sector. The producers' and purchasers' prices corresponding to the main destination of each good were determined through marketing surveys and direct inquiries to the enterprises. This analysis required the estimation of the percentages of total output distributed directly and through trade channels. Producers' prices were defined as the average price of cash sales.

Electricity, gas and water

36. Data on output, inputs and distribution of output of the electricity, gas, water and sanitary services sectors were obtained from the accounts, balances, budgets, and direct information of the institutions that produce, supervise and control these activities. Electrical energy output excludes energy production by enterprises for their own use, except in the case of electricity generated by large copper mining enterprises. Estimates of the input structure took into account the marked differences between the hydraulic and thermal technological processes. Water works output excludes production by enterprises for their own consumption and sanitary services.

Construction

37. Because of the wide variety of works included in the construction sector, this sector was disaggregated into five subsectors: housing, non-residential buildings, engineering works, repairs and demolitions. An additional distinction was made in the first 3 subsectors mentioned between works that are carried out by the public and private sectors. For public works, total expenditure in construction was known and the cost structure was estimated as follows:

(a) Data on total expenditure for each public sector project in 1977 were obtained from the institutions and enterprises in charge of the projects;

(b) The most representative projects of each institution were selected;

(c) The budget, unit prices and other data for each project were obtained from the relevant institutions;

(d) Each item of the budget was disaggregated into physical quantities and unit prices;

(e) The expenditure on intermediate consumption and value added was assigned to the corresponding sectors of the input-output table;

(f) This expenditure was valued in terms of the price index corresponding to the first semester of 1977. Different deflators were used for each specific product;

(g) The cost structure thus obtained was applied to the actual expenditures of the institution on each project.

38. Data for works in the first two subsectors of the construction sector carried out by private enterprises were compiled by a consulting firm on the basis of municipal building licences. Licences were first grouped into different typologies, and an analysis was made of the intermediate inputs, value added and market price of each of them. Gross output was estimated as the sum of the products of market price and total area constructed of each type. Market prices were provided by the real estate classified announcements published in newspapers. The area constructed of each type was estimated by applying an estimated expenditure-time curve to the area of each type initiated each month in each "comuna". Intermediate inputs and value added were estimated by first defining a set of unitary construction items (for instance, 1 m² of masonry), and then determining the physical quantities and prices of the corresponding inputs. Adjustments were made for areas constructed without licence on the basis of research carried out in years around 1977.

39. Repairs include only those carried out by enterprises belonging to the construction sector. Housing repairs were estimated by applying to the physical stock of housing units a set of physical repair coefficients mainly determined on the basis of technological considerations.

40. In order to determine the output of demolitions, a coefficient was obtained for the Santiago "comuna" expressing the ratio of demolitions to total stock of housing units. A coefficient equal to half of that obtained for Santiago was assumed for the whole country, since, on average, housing units outside Santiago were of more recent construction.

Trade, restaurants and hotels

41. Data on output, intermediate inputs and value added of the trade sector were obtained from special surveys and other *ad hoc* information. The available data did not allow for the disaggregation of trade margins between those corresponding to wholesale and retail trade.

42. Gross output of restaurants and hotels was estimated as the sum of demand for these services by individuals, intermediate sectors, the Government and tourists on the basis of data provided mainly by the 1978 Households Survey and the results of a survey of tourism hotels carried out by the Instituto Nacional de Estadística and the Servicio Nacional de Turismo. The input structure was obtained as a weighted average of the cost structure of restaurants, tourism hotels and other hotels, which were provided by surveys carried out for this purpose.

Transportation

43. Data for the transportation sector were mainly obtained from general balances, budgets and surveys of transportation firms and special analysis carried out for this purpose. Intermediate consumption data were obtained directly from consumption, rather than purchases, data. This consumption was disaggregated into that of domestic or imported origin mainly on the basis of the currency in which the transaction took place. The interrelationships existing

among enterprises in this sector were taken into account so as to avoid double counting. International freight by Chilean companies was recorded as sales abroad, to obtain data consistent with those of the balance of payments.

Services

44. The finance sector included the institutions forming part of the monetary system and other financial institutions such as savings banks, stock exchange etc. Data on this sector and on the insurance sector were obtained from sample surveys.

45. The real estate sector includes real estate agents and societies and owners of real estate. The universe of the sector was obtained from sources such as tax records, National Confederation of Real Estate Agents, Association of Incorporated Enterprises and telephone books. Data were obtained from sampling surveys and tax records.

46. The business services sector covers the activities described in the corresponding major group of ISIC. Gross output and cost structure were obtained from surveys of the enterprises representative of each type of service. Intermediate and primary inputs were estimated by applying to the gross output of the different activities their corresponding cost structures.

47. The 1978 Family Budget Survey and the 1970 Housing and Population Census were the basic data sources used for estimating gross output of the housing ownership sector. Gross output was estimated as the product of average rent paid per household and the total number of households in the country. The result was compared to other available information, such as tax records. Intermediate inputs include repairs, insurance, commissions paid to real estate agents, maintenance expenditures etc.

48. Activities of the education, health and services sector include those of major division 9 of ISIC except for sanitary services and public administration and defence services. Gross output was generally measured by the amount of gross receipts (in the case of private industries) and by the amount of current expenditures (in the case of public health and education services and of similar services provided by private non-profit institutions). Data sources used were: balance sheets and budgets of the relevant institutions; sampling surveys; physical and financial data of public institutions with centralized information such as the National Association of Education, the National Association of Incorporated Enterprises etc.; and tax records.

49. Gross output of the public administration and defence sector includes the small percentage of output represented by market sales such as rental of real estate, sale of publications, veterinarian services etc. The cost structure of these market sales was estimated separately on the basis of data gathered for the industries having these activities as main production. Data were obtained from the analytical report of the Controller Office, budgets of public institutions, and the Office of Government Supplies. Lack of data prevented the estimation of depreciation charges, which were usually treated as current expenditure. The positive entries recorded in the depreciation and operating surplus rows of the sector correspond mainly to those referring to the market sales mentioned above.

Final demand

50.   Data on final demand categories were obtained by the following method. Private consumption was estimated from the results of the 1978 Family Budget Survey, and from the analysis involved in the process of reconciliation of supply and demand of each input-output sector. Government consumption was estimated as the sum of government services produced for its own consumption recorded in the public education, public health and public administration and defence sectors. Domestic investment data were obtained directly from the accounts of industries included in the construction, mining and agriculture sectors; the analysis of destination of output of the manufacturing sectors; and imported capital goods adjusted for stock changes. Variation of stocks of finished and in-process goods was estimated from information available for each sector of the table; variation of stocks of raw materials was estimated as the residual obtained in the process of balancing supply and demand of each sector; change of stock of imported goods was determined exogenously, assuming an average turnover period of 30 to 60 days. Data on exports of goods were based on customs data and information from the main exporting sectors. Exports of services were estimated on the basis of central bank data. Tourism expenditure was estimated through a special survey, and expenditure by foreign diplomats was estimated also on the basis of survey information.

51.   The basic statistical sources used in estimating imports were the imports registry, tax records and customs data. The first and second sources mentioned provided a classification of imports of goods by origin and destination. On the basis of these data, a preliminary c.i.f. imports matrix was calculated, which was then disaggregated into direct imports and imports-through-trade matrices, so as to make the data comparable to that provided by customs and the balance of payments. Customs data provided information on import duties paid by sector of origin. Aggregate value taxes were then estimated for both matrices. Imports of services by sector of origin were based on statistics on invisible trade provided by the central bank. Their allocation to demand sectors was done on the basis of the nature of the services.

Chile

Reference year: 1977

Entries in table: Domestic flows

Source: Oficina de Planificación Nacional (Odeplan), Presidencia de la República, *Matriz de insumo–producto de la economía chilena, 1977* (Santiago, 1980)

Computerized: Deutsches Institut für Wirtschaftsforschung, Berlin

Currency units: Pesos of Y 1977

Scale factor: 1,000

Pricing system: Purchasers' current prices

Intermediate sectors: 67 × 68

Treatment of trade margins: Inputs in sector 45
Total trade margins for imports in final demand
components

Treatment of imports: Row 69

Availability of import matrix: Not available

Total number of rows: 78

Statistical unit of quadrant 1: Industry

Total number of columns: 77

Statistical unit of quadrant 1: Industry

Fourth quadrant: Not occupied

Note: Quadrant 1 is not symmetric

Input-Output Table of Chile for the Year 1977

CHILE 1977   FLOWS in thousands of Pesos of Y 1977   PURCHASERS CURRENT PRICES

INDUSTRY:	Agriculture 1 - Crops	Agriculture 2 - Livestock	Agricultural 3 Services	Forestry 4 Lumber	Fishing 5	Copper 8 Mining
DOMESTIC TRANSACTIONS INDUSTRY						
1 Agriculture - Crops	1800157	2364197	0	8666	11737	5207
2 Agriculture - Livestock	66435	337355	0	10452	730	
3 Agricultural Services	250039	5977	0	2077	1380	
4 Forestry, Lumber	32592	12972	0	0	211492	37460
5 Fishing	0	0	0	0	0	2205870
6 Copper Mining	0	0	0	0	0	844
7 Iron Ore Mining	0	0	0	1	0	60204
8 Phosphate Mining	382745	0	0	0	0	
9 Petroleum, Natural Gas	0	0	0	0	0	79956
10 Coal Mining	0	0	0	107	0	
11 Stone, Sand Quarrying	4987	268	0	0	96303	66676
12 Other Mineral Extraction	4034	1426663	0	0	1787	39206
13 Food Manufacturing	0		0	0	0	
14 Beverages	0		0	0	0	
15 Tobacco	0		0	826	67930	2996
16 Textile Manufacturing	50220	730	0	0	2301	54861
17 Manuf. of Wearing Apparel	129		0	0	230	18485
18 Leather Manufacturing	0		0	0	0	6436
19 Footwear Manufacturing	0		145	8745	9823	80155
20 Wood, Cork Manufacturing	185127	7959	404	0	107	4510
21 Furniture & Accessories	0		3977	652	579	30651
22 Paper & Paper Products	5041	7152		847	19856	123949
23 Printing, Publishing, etc.	43214		417	1023	290875	475840
24 Industrial Chemicals	46663	178863	42086	66374	8996	2458742
25 Other Chemical Products	128169	92523	1302	22407	18138	73428
26 Petroleum Refining	140919	3356	5538	18964		65107
27 Products of Petrol. & Coal	147184	19455			149	7367
28 Rubber Products	75242					151
29 Plastic Products n.e.s	0		0	184	25	2291
30 Clay, China, Porcelain Prods	8536	459	83	808	1122	302406
31 Glass & Glass Products	39247	2019		147		551788
32 Oth. Non-Met Minerals Prods	6848	368		25	10037	58572
33 Iron & Steel Manufacturing	-183	64	153	23899	23511	539351
34 Non-Ferrous Metal Manufact.	130812	51323	4283	8729	180	1436696
35 Metal Products n.e.s	109735	13158	18203	801	550	73682
36 Non-Elec Products Machnry	56682	12759	175	18812	154131	976231
37 Electric Construction Mach.	54410	18421	1093		271	3528
38 Transport Equipment Mach.	0		1198	104	1625	18079
39 Profnl Equipment & Others	4818	259	133	7390	591	1780002
40 Other Manufactured Products	109303	77796	265		334	229
41 Electricity	0				370	
42 Gas	0					
43 Hydr. Sys. for Water Dist.	0					
44 Construction	7219891	824178	10390	68238	921392	373138
45 Trade	32563	16277	3	2437	3370	23054
46 Restaurants and Hotels	34778	112890	15946	147319		130199
47 Railway Transport	17166			701	3128	150801
48 Freight Transport	112890			56	10808	256005
49 Passenger Transport	4773	1432	0	23	15233	190017
50 Maritime Transport	1901	159				28734
51 Air Transport	1318				120	

57

Input-Output Table of Chile for the Year 1977

CHILE 1977

FLOWS in thousands of Pesos of Y 1977

PURCHASERS CURRENT PRICES

INDUSTRY:	Agriculture 1 Crops	Agriculture 2 Livestock	Agricultural 3 Services	Forestry 4 Lumber	Fishing 5	Copper 6 Mining
52 Oth. Transportation Services	1733	1605			1096	3274
53 Communications	3225		1591	249	900	3551
54 Financial Institutions	31755	15910	596	2335	2939	8243
55 Insurance	2737	6733	3785	934	2010	
56 Real Estate	12702		8078	1508		42488
57 Business Services	40176	17819				310690
58 Dwellings						
59 Public Education	3811	1909		280		1597
60 Private Education	1270	636		94		1508
61 Public Health						
62 Private Health						
63 Recreation Services						31
64 Repair Services	28259	5212	15864	9007	437	2173
65 Laundry Services		7954				
66 Misc. Services	1299				28	
67 Public Admin. & Defence		73802		1107		
68 Domest. Intermediate Inputs	12998801	5734374	135710	1047208	1953475	11772146
69 Imports at Purchasers Prices	1008571	722078	17652	54272	107784	3088653
70 Wages	594228	193920	102380	58817	180629	3510060
71 Salaries	2145401	699998	29893	300742	293915	1978414
72 Social Contributions	850479	277549	40627	11563	102790	1281418
73 Indirect Taxes	1459575	277419	39859	-42460	2563	-34771
74 Subsidies	-22966	-44291		-108735		-261175
75 Consumption of Fixed Capital	3117020	300768	58235	677637	153907	2661175
76 Operating Surplus	8117005	7467368	-74637	677510	718795	8604023
77 Gross Value Added	16314742	9172718	196357	1152994	1452599	18126192
78 Gross Output at Consumer Prc	30412114	15629168	349719	2254474	3513858	32989191

Input-Output Table of Chile for the Year 1977

CHILE 1977   FLOWS In thousands of Pesos of Y 1977

INDUSTRY:	7 Iron Ore Mining	8 Phosphate Mining	9 Petroleum, Natural Gas	10 Coal Mining	11 Stone, sand Quarrying	12 Other Mineral Extraction
DOMESTIC TRANSACTIONS *						
INDUSTRY						
1 Agriculture - Crops	0	0	0	0	0	0
2 Agriculture - Livestock	0	0	0	0	0	0
3 Agricultural Services	150	0	6950	24850	0	998
4 Forestry, Lumber	0	0	0	0	0	0
5 Fishing	0	0	0	0	0	0
6 Copper Mining	250208	0	191087	0	0	0
7 Iron Ore Mining	0	0	0	2061	0	0
8 Phosphate Mining	82	0	0	0	0	0
9 Petroleum, Natural Gas	68986	1163	7074	0	0	3969
10 Coal Mining	0	0	0	0	0	0
11 Stone, Sand Quarrying	0	0	0	0	0	0
12 Other Mineral Extraction	0	0	0	0	0	0
13 Food Manufacturing	7138	573	345	207	0	425
14 Beverages	1516	82	100	0	0	511
15 Tobacco Manufacturing	2393	5256	0	0	0	0
16 Textile Manufacturing	477	1140	502	0	0	0
17 Manuf. of Wearing Apparel	288	3640	5348	5728	0	0
18 Leather Manufacturing	2650	409	0	0	0	810
19 Footwear Manufacturing	4833		1525	2040	1928	1564
20 Woodcork Manufacturing	7042	2873	5278	2200	5784	100
21 Furniture & Accessories	61980	12524	6386	23053	12276	28949
22 Paper & Paper Products	32792	14807	10574	22657	449	14122
23 Printing, Publishing, etc.	149494	360623	490	12546	1	450
24 Industrial Chemicals	4650	35694	989	390		311
25 Other Chemical Products	15516	1812	37190	8714		100
26 Petroleum Refining	1313	8988	65918			
27 Products of Petrol. & Coal	15	14568	14023	8803	974	268
28 Rubber Products	1737	5205	4704	1728		
29 Plastic Products n.e.s.	695	3371		11313		
30 Clay, China, Porcelain Prods	21338	26941	2283	698	21692	21146
31 Glass & Glass Products	18491	4969	3090	595		
32 Oth. Non-Met. Mineral Prods.	8724	10068		10178	1157	13489
33 Iron & Steel Manufacturing	4164			624		
34 Non-Ferrous Metal Manufact.	7043	1666		6721		
35 Metal Products	9318	7788		61964		
36 Non-Elec. Construc. Machnry	715	19578				
37 Electl. Construction Mach.	6492					
38 Transport Equipment & Others	27347		184	7336	97	590
39 Profnl. Equipment & Others	0					280
40 Other Manufactured Products	5342	20	5704	7733	313159	5281
41 Electricity	0	26482	21238	6030		794
42 Gas	775	29830	213085	21060		
43 Hydr. Sys. for Water Dist.		38514		21388		
44 Construction	101815			78790		
45 Trade	52949					
46 Restaurants and Hotels						
47 Railway Transport						
48 Freight Transport						
49 Passenger Transport						
50 Maritime Transport	5959					
51 Air Transport						

Input-Output Table of Chile for the Year 1977

CHILE 1977   FLOWS in thousands of Pesos of Y 1977   PURCHASERS CURRENT PRICES

INDUSTRY:	7 Iron Ore Mining	8 Phosphate Mining	9 Petroleum, Natural Gas	10 Coal Mining	11 Stone, Sand Quarrying	12 Other Mineral Extraction
52 Oth. Transportation Services	9068	27224	6964	17411	0	1207
53 Communications	422	3985	0	3896	0	505
54 Financial Institutions		54		84	0	0
55 Insurance	2863	1346	6653	594	0	125
56 Real Estate	2748	1917		2060	0	0
57 Business Services	54135	1105	5993	21891	3856	15536
58 Dwellings Services	0	0	0	0	0	0
59 Public Education	0	0	0	0	0	0
60 Private Education	0	0	0	919	0	0
61 Public Health	0	0	0	0	0	0
62 Private Health	0	0	0	0	0	0
63 Recreation Services	0	0	0	3390	0	1505
64 Repair Services	1460	0	0	821	0	0
65 Laundry Services	0	0	0	0	0	0
66 Misc. Services	1706	0	0	396	0	0
67 Public Admin. & Defence	0	0	0	0	0	0
68 Domest. Intermediate Inputs	1057399	674215	634168	375274	361373	160335
69 Imports at Purchasers Prices	249467	205078	742518	49086	3551	18873
70 Wages	327126	242538	285544	381725	25033	94769
71 Salaries	83524	183898	150065	441749	9715	95248
72 Social Contributions	123664	155422	74391	278118	9183	42195
73 Indirect Taxes	-19303	20209	2532	187822	6621	106342
74 Subsidies	-91476	-308468		-230511		-27148
75 Consumption of Fixed Capital	98198	163467	494347	130571	28074	64185
76 Operating Surplus	70927	-38402	1229355	-187086	68727	167425
77 Gross Value Added	731266	418714	2101234	1012388	146153	623018
78 Gross Output at Consumer Prc	2038132	1298007	3477918	1438748	511177	802228

60

Input-Output Table of Chile for the Year 1977

CHILE 1977   FLOWS in thousands of Pesos of Y 1977   PURCHASERS CURRENT PRICES

INDUSTRY:	13 Food Manufacturing	14 Beverages	15 Tobacco	16 Textile Manufacturing	17 Manufacture of Wearing Apparel	18 Leather Manufacturing
* DOMESTIC TRANSACTIONS * INDUSTRY						
1 Agriculture - Crops	8162556	2231587	208505	333907	290	180
2 Agriculture - Livestock	10292809	0	150	0	11578	0
3 Agricultural - Services	0	0	382	278	0	0
4 Forestry, Lumber	59304	0	54	7	28	458
5 Fishing	1538668	0	0	0	12	9
6 Copper Mining	0	0	0	0	0	0
7 Iron Ore Mining	0	0	0	0	0	0
8 Phosphate Mining	0	0	0	0	0	0
9 Petroleum Natural Gas	10927	7172	4518	16007	231	882
10 Coal Mining	0	5	597	0	0	0
11 Stone, Sand Quarrying	231851	18645	0	24	0	473
12 Other Mineral Extraction	5	244314	0	6981	2140	480297
13 Food Manufacturing	49510	2148825	9973	0	0	0
14 Beverages	7749363		0	2047960	1884274	36437
15 Tobacco	2975	5654	1057	0	0	777
16 Textile Manufacturing	165088	1184	0	4543	22329	427706
17 Manuf. of Wearing Apparel	11744	547	8216	1157	2589	254
18 Leather Manufacturing	2856	337	95474	4415	2320	336
19 Footwear Manufacturing	3052		22981	65	0	0
20 Wood, Cork Manufacturing	173313	76805	25756	17918	24348	4045
21 Furniture & Accessories	7505	1444	6903	20309	27458	984
22 Printing, Publishing, etc.	41205	11324	408	23693	62176	78152
23 Paper & Paper Products	466268	37040	1132	121666	28249	83327
24 Industrial Chemicals	106268	83172	1073	205897	23494	30605
25 Other Chemical Products	202698	71860	773		0	1485
26 Petroleum Refining	756291	112631	342	23286	5035	0
27 Products of Petrol. & Coal	0	3331	3	21035	14360	21408
28 Rubber Products	22129	6293	1360	411	0	0
29 Plastic Products n.e.s.	301963	28864	6064	631	434	200
30 Clay, China, Porcelain Prods	463		4395	2246	0	1348
31 Glass & Glass Products	18051	151386	12386	30137	4529	3591
32 Oth. Non-Met. Mineral Prods.	5541	289	388	8750	7418	9239
33 Iron & Steel Manufacturing	13940	441	4342	35228	21362	32073
34 Non-Ferrous Metal Manufact.	4489	140	12332	1500	5238	1803
35 Metal Products	476451	99936	5200	2152	3469	5444
36 Non-Elec. Construc. Machnry	78176	53367	470	225417	9219	1907
37 Elect. Construction Mach.	139511	21097	326367	155	27316	0
38 Transport Equipment	15923	1475	3272	3368	736	6588
39 Profnl Equipment & Others	1479	7265	498	1505857	3135	15268
40 Other Manufactured Products	55006	88650	32160	34624	2016359	291
41 Electricity	365815	38547	6552	498	14219	1536
42 Gas	68014		6915	65517	0	93082
43 Hydr. Sys. for Water Dist.	29429	5235		14504	27510	7951
44 Construction	1672			7118	10542	0
45 Trade	6704330	2555532		572	2666	22070
46 Restaurants and Hotels	94084	34624			0	4835
47 Railway Transport	12634	20558				834
48 Freight Transport	790289	400982				75
49 Passenger Transport	55538	7220				
50 Maritime Transport	92807	1667				
51 Air Transport						

61

Input-Output Table of Chile for the Year 1977

CHILE 1977   FLOWS in thousands of Pesos of Y 1977   PURCHASERS CURRENT PRICES

INDUSTRY:	13 Food Manufacturing	14 Beverages	15 Tobacco	16 Textile Manufacturing	17 Manufacture of Wearing Apparel	18 Leather Manufacturing
52 Oth. Transportation Services	71685	2538	1393	10837	3284	1259
53 Communications	165758	37194	8035	39873	40345	1622
54 Financial Institutions	117453	53480	2852	76375	6816	3977
55 Insurance	145318	18736	8271	31242	15277	5994
56 Real Estate	121581	11894	4234	30106	22969	
57 Business Services	250492	37204	14064	92545	140530	17254
58 Dwellings	0	0	0	0	0	
59 Public Education	2107	0	0	818	0	
60 Private Education	0	12	0	0	3	14
61 Public Health	11195	0	0	0	0	0
62 Private Health	0	0	482	0	0	
63 Recreation Services	1829	78333	18850	50118	11439	1543
64 Repair Services	187531	480	130	677	2012	355
65 Laundry Services	39269	0	0	0	134	
66 Misc. Services	1424	0	0	6148	1018	0
67 Public Admin. & Defence	2762	0	0	0	0	
68 Domest. Intermediate Inputs	38944540	8660925	893304	5126565	4517515	1420922
69 Imports at Purchasers Prices	6767673	457254	301917	2163066	677919	241862
70 Wages	2224407	626340	104511	783657	277469	64182
71 Salaries	1771422	409514	40984	742602	373800	140085
72 Social Contributions	945403	222460	33931	355125	163216	46664
73 Indirect Taxes	2278018	912471	1803096	758973	283612	83333
74 Subsidies	-242709	-30842	-4505	-17538	-8948	-4597
75 Consumption of Fixed Capital	1367496	523480	63511	554601	127435	31181
76 Operating Surplus	7461403	957589	733345	728961	674840	114050
77 Gross Value Added	15807440	3621012	2853873	3904381	1891424	475738
78 Gross Output at Consumer Prc	61519653	12739191	4049094	11194014	7066858	2138522

62

Input-Output Table of Chile for the Year 1977

CHILE 1977   FLOWS in thousands of Pesos of Y 1977   PURCHASERS CURRENT PRICES

INDUSTRY:

	19 Footwear Manufacturing	20 Wood, Cork Manufacturing	21 Furniture & Accessories	22 Paper & Paper Products	23 Printing, Publishing, etc	24 Industrial Chemicals
* DOMESTIC TRANSACTIONS * INDUSTRY						
1 Agriculture - Crops	4040	774	0	155	0	28
2 Agriculture - Livestock	0	0	161	0	0	0
3 Agricultural Services	0	0	72	0	0	0
4 Forestry, Lumber	84	755677	72	726889	200	108
5 Fishing	17	15	0	4	0	10519
6 Copper Mining	0	0	0	0	0	585499
7 Iron Ore Mining	0	0	0	0	0	0
8 Phosphate Mining	0	0	0	0	0	1364
9 Petroleum, Natural Gas	0	0	0	5582	439	0
10 Coal Mining	174	6590	113	539	69	2980
11 Stone, Sand Quarrying	2016	68	0	1803	0	1133
12 Other Mineral Extraction	2953	3368	0	2711	0	1705
13 Food Manufacturing	0	0	0	274	0	0
14 Beverages						
15 Tobacco						
16 Textile Manufacturing	140542	17411	105159	329	10944	1179
17 Manuf. of Wearing Apparel	180266	3017	468	508	1030	691
18 Leather Manufacturing	865	853	4955	282	393	0
19 Footwear Manufacturing	3162	852	238138	17249	1512	195
20 Wood, Cork Manufacturing	21130	901296	551	960		3097
21 Furniture & Accessories	70105	4758	9665	1750667	1251815	8298
22 Paper & Paper Products	8037	4565	3254	15442	117866	1601
23 Printing, Publishing, etc	41790	43990	32678	146686	30733	157780
24 Industrial Chemicals	60266	95990	4678	190013	97140	47092
25 Other Chemical Products	17788	115840		488689	26379	224484
26 Petroleum Refining	104581	3285	16347	15178	810	6663
27 Products of Petrol. & Coal	14994	9512	13718	15295	805	6311
28 Rubber Products			1648	18347	14265	14916
29 Plastic Products n.e.s			1740		19	53
30 Clay, China, Porcelain Prods	430	4841	2826	863	35	23726
31 Glass, & Glass Products	5588	8168	22926	11534	2475	4523
32 Oth. Non-Met Mineral Prods	983	10032	28152	1540	1888	35809
33 Iron & Steel Manufacturing	27530	604	28261	789	4745	7055
34 Non-Ferrous Metal Manufact	18724	52518	1889	326	781	36113
35 Metal Products	2467	16938	2542	11952	8681	3742
36 Non-Elec. Construc Machnry	830	36570		2061	27745	7923
37 Electric Consruc Mach.	14197	636	5071	3149	1714	3797
38 Transpor Equipment & Others	22259	12294	11731	13744	1142	1214
39 Other Manufactured Products	194	94073	1301	220562	1854	6924
40 Electricity	770	270	819	181	27474	57111
41 Gas		3717		4765	1113	291
42 Hydr. Sys. for Water Dist.					3164	3482
43 Construction				184359	2520	
44 Trade	249288	41738	298476	224642	525603	22054
45 Restaurants and Hotels	16043	23393	1171	25188	11898	7355
46 Railway Transport				131702		
47 Freight Transport	15745	335422	12102	565843	58457	62449
48 Passenger Transport	50106	75540	902	10516	9509	5768
49 Maritime Transport	894	85	30	60801	1180	18820
50 Air Transport	874			1420	0	0

Input-Output Table of Chile for the Year 1977

CHILE 1977   FLOWS in thousands of Pesos of Y 1977   PURCHASERS CURRENT PRICES

INDUSTRY:	19 Footwear Manufacturing	20 Wood Cork Manufacturing	21 Furniture & Accessories	22 Paper & Paper products	23 Printing, Publishing, etc	24 Industrial Chemicals
52 Oth. Transportation Services	1361	23668	309	21031	1795	9254
53 Communications	17029	33765	5663	14868	29590	23826
54 Financial Institutions	1379	-1684	2122	32843	9830	24153
55 Insurance	5891	26388	7183	40283	15740	10507
56 Real Estate	2225	21952	7013	19594	22372	18793
57 Business Services	12381	87799	11889	24350	63667	72391
58 Dwellings Services	0	0	0	0	0	0
59 Public Education	0	0	0	0	0	0
60 Private Education	4	3	2	1347	415	0
61 Public Health	0	0	0	29	1	0
62 Private Health	0	421	0	12456	1	0
63 Recreation Services	11319	0	770	0	204	0
64 Repair Services	474	807	0	209	1853	78
65 Laundry Services	0	0	0	3780	0	0
66 Misc. Services	243	363	903	5420	460	507
67 Public Admin. & Defence	0	2366	0	0	0	0
68 Domest. Intermediate Inputs	4330238	3333152	863769	5045970	2392236	1568182
69 Imports at Purchasers Prices	295605	182500	35661	587975	398465	62105
70 Wages	161813	355462	123478	427317	646320	244271
71 Salaries	208527	546685	119951	218486	186602	75309
72 Social Contributions	145264	232680	65567	159321	198393	76606
73 Indirect Taxes	171311	248067	144896	251873	513842	127784
74 Subsidies	-5903	-639968	-3379	-149008	-130083	-9301
75 Consumption of Fixed Capital	41820	236758	11173	438824	-12288	44577
76 Operating Surplus	474282	539684	253271	1556959	1506445	583051
77 Gross Value Added	1196914	2075968	806957	2903732	3150605	1502297
78 Gross Output at Consumer Prc	5822757	5591620	1706387	8537677	5941306	3693564

Input-Output Table of Chile for the Year 1977

CHILE 1977 FLOWS in thousands of Pesos of Y 1977 PURCHASERS CURRENT PRICES

INDUSTRY:

* DOMESTIC TRANSACTIONS *

#	INDUSTRY	25 Other Chemical Products	26 Petroleum Refining	27 Petroleum & Coal Products	28 Rubber Products	29 Plastic Products n.e.s	30 Clay, China, Porcelain Prods
1	Agriculture - Crops	1072	542	0	0	0	0
2	Agriculture - Livestock	121	117	0	0	0	0
3	Agricultural Services	0	0	109	0	5	0
4	Forestry, Lumber	2368	67	0	14	9	35
5	Fishing	28	117	0	0	0	0
6	Copper Mining	0	0	0	0	0	0
7	Iron Ore Mining	0	0	0	0	0	0
8	Phosphate Mining	0	0	0	0	0	0
9	Petroleum, Natural Gas	26702	2260963	2314	0	0	0
10	Coal Mining	0	0	0	0	0	0
11	Stone, Sand Quarrying	12133	0	5497	83	102	287
12	Other Mineral Extraction	1535	2154	7099	0	0	6854
13	Food Manufacturing	17461	0	0	3927	1894	22353
14	Beverages	66644	0	0	8	1000	0
15	Tobacco	0	0	0	0	0	0
16	Textile Manufacturing	2846	921	2740	1243	2700	564
17	Manuf of Wearing Apparel	19448	0	194	0	1736	331
18	Leather Manufacturing	1340	0	0	0	1224	0
19	Footwear Manufacturing	505	54	55	356676	2708	94
20	Wood, Cork Manufacturing	30041	1909	0	4717	2764	552
21	Furniture & Accessories	1768	0	0	4228	0	0
22	Paper & Paper Products	109514	8794	2052	226	17774	9859
23	Printing, Publishing, etc.	287057	23626	0	1459	8687	4106
24	Industrial Chemicals	139382	3873	463	3767	124583	2867
25	Other Chemical Products	123642	8289	3482	3143	135597	3878
26	Petroleum Refining	11552	579587	228724	9063	12172	30060
27	Products of Petrol. & Coal	9284	4689	1883	3922	0	935
28	Rubber Products	183599	15391	0	512113	0	0
29	Plastic Products n.e.s	2438	0	550	1215	125360	30
30	Clay, China, Porcelain Prods	96725	8678	0	149	3304	64
31	Glass & Glass Products	8579	19924	15163	2504	1593	21064
32	Oth. Non-Met. Mineral Prods	2472	0	0	781	739	4717
33	Iron & Steel Manufacturing	103616	55808	7470	16	1225	29
34	Non-ferrous Metal Manufact.	9657	19971	5442	2238	5691	423
35	Metal Products	34354	0	1106	7913	1242	44884
36	Non-Elec. Construc. Machnry	11958	2269	5881	29818	2130	182
37	Electl. Construction Mach.	958	27637	0	355	4230	91
38	Transport Equipment	42598	0	0	4915	834	0
39	Profnl Equipment & Others	27787	389	423	23272	1244	726
40	Other Manufactured Products	10962	18905	266	23326	6337	13144
41	Electricity	3700	7240755	691	4648	43191	2930
42	Gas	0	22470	39206	0	372	363
43	Hydr. Sys. for Water Dist.	0	5994	29710	0	2592	0
44	Construction	1150235	55657	7139	574370	339285	216280
45	Trade	672233	51297	54819	6189	7383	0
46	Restaurants and Hotels	67374	184086	19469	246	246	16277
47	Railway Transport	143918	0	400	30368	27085	0
48	Freight Transport	46313	0	0	7545	6895	0
49	Passenger Transport	8468	0	0	2624	1038	0
50	Maritime Transport	8990	0	0	60	85	0
51	Air Transport	0	0	0	0	0	0

Input-Output Table of Chile for the Year 1977

CHILE 1977   FLOWS in thousands of Pesos of Y 1977   PURCHASERS CURRENT PRICES

INDUSTRY:	25 Other Chemical Products	26 Petroleum Refining	27 Petroleum & Coal Products	28 Rubber Products	29 Plastic Products n.e.s	30 Clay, China, Porcelain Prods
52 Oth. Transportation Services	12054	17841	248	3993	1578	309
54 Communications	47171	20205	4850	25707	15247	11574
55 Financial Institutions	22418	41245	300	68450	16380	29933
56 Insurance	29715	21446	1924	31043	9800	1079
57 Real Estate	31812	2360	4475	8302	9039	4722
58 Business Services	124101	1453	2200	42579	30671	19400
59 Dwellings	0	0	0	0	0	0
60 Public Education	1994	0	0	0	0	0
61 Private Education	0	0	0	1835	5	0
62 Public Health	0	0	5235	0	0	0
63 Private Health	0	0	0	0	0	0
64 Recreation Services	164512	1495	0	7	221	204
65 Repair Services	3701	1045	0	659	389	0
66 Laundry Services	0	0	0	549	517	0
67 Misc. Services	31824	8450	0	0	0	0
Public Admin. & Defence						
68 Domest. Intermediate Inputs	3738982	10747808	857382	1815568	975350	470981
69 Imports at Purchasers Prices	2390288	914518	27248	871514	461281	22437
70 Wages	1124185	423212	65368	187514	193350	90203
71 Salaries	324007	34458	35153	187109	73304	49924
72 Social Contributions	297034	87158	19506	158421	176692	53604
73 Indirect Taxes	648264	1580116	59530	150247		4266
74 Subsidies	-16347	-17578	-2749	-7179	-2865	-29816
75 Consumption of Fixed Capital	269249	497889	43346	260242	270075	29816
76 Operating Surplus	1741017	-637205	181723	76270	276036	110832
77 Gross Value Added	4387409	1987052	401870	1054145	959983	392142
78 Gross Output at Consumer Prc	10516679	21849378	1288500	3752242	2402609	885560

Input-Output Table of Chile for the Year 1977

CHILE 1977   FLOWS in thousands of Pesos of Y 1977   PURCHASERS CURRENT PRICES

INDUSTRY:

	31 Glass & Glass Products	32 Oth. Non-Met Mineral Prods	33 Iron & Steel Manufacturing	34 Non-Fer. Metal Manufacturing	35 Metal Products	36 Non-Electrical Construc. Mach.
DOMESTIC TRANSACTIONS						
INDUSTRY						
1 Agriculture - Crops	0	921	5603	394	1554	0
2 Agriculture - Livestock	0	0	374	26	9	0
3 Agricultural Services	114	0	0	0	642	127
4 Forestry, Lumber	0	3679	404	37	31	0
5 Fishing	0	25	179	12	14876	0
6 Copper Mining	0	0	385	1445865	0	0
7 Iron Ore Mining	261	224	146463	7	222	0
8 Phosphate Mining	0	0	281	0	0	0
9 Petroleum, Natural Gas	0	0	0	0	0	0
10 Coal Mining	9078	204029	293695	2534	4557	3932
11 Stone, Sand Quarrying	6942	31817	3252	1135	7940	167
12 Other Mineral Extraction	12892	330255	58621	1526	16375	25987
13 Food Manufacturing	0	4034	21795	0	4382	2624
14 Beverages	0	240	0	0	0	0
15 Tobacco	0	0	0	0	0	0
16 Textile Manufacturing	4	4320	1307	2285	11997	4020
17 Manuf. of Wearing Apparel	699	1069	2667	1678	7066	0
18 Leather Manufacturing	0	0	19	0	1142	84
19 Footwear Manufacturing	113	39	1098	545	2765	0
20 Wood Cork Manufacturing	787	12366	7721	1121	27318	6759
21 Furniture & Accessories	0	0	74	69	2201	0
22 Paper & Paper Products	3825	141864	6464	2467	65241	2468
23 Printing, Publishing, etc.	997	7418	10055	220	10255	28418
24 Industrial Chemicals	7125	15885	15906	4487	149571	10706
25 Other Chemical Products	1431	104078	11474	5658	67755	28659
26 Petroleum Refining	54355	61452	239037	32991	77555	21577
27 Products of Petrol. & Coal	1684	699	5492	0	1073	0
28 Rubber Products	972	2254	5674	9233	9873	4978
29 Plastic Products n.e.s	411	30	936	8655	17034	17598
30 Clay, China, Porcelain Prods	0	7	7187	0	1930	0
31 Glass & Glass Products	59610	4785	191	1360	16556	6820
32 Oth. Non-Met Mineral Prods.	16661	129444	38605	1104	82439	6670
33 Iron & Steel Manufacturing	748	15131	937566	32781	250091	103505
34 Non-Ferrous Metal Manufact.	217	14294	16856	6955	5518	37507
35 Metal Products	2745	17502	28318	4038	54892	50508
36 Non-Elec. Construc. Machnry	245	10780	18426	6002	39428	5764
37 Electl. Construction Mach.	0	34509	2636	3429	7076	1390
38 Transport Equipment	141	2744	7076	7615	5764	316
39 Profnl. Equipment & Others	92	1448	359	1297	1390	24906
40 Other Manufactured Products	17998	109408	150986	49273	16434	1718
41 Electricity	2578	22578	795	1068	72702	1331
42 Gas	580	0	0	0	7110	0
43 Hydr. Sys. for Water Dist.	0	2616	11975	2735	11410	0
44 Construction	178102	295	289650	61669	90	852376
45 Trade	250	270023	41746	718	551981	5683
46 Restaurants and Hotels	7249	18838	44312	4960	19781	5929
47 Railway Transport	85	41375	22035	25978	12389	20494
48 Freight Transport	17	112909	24565	75	53279	7001
49 Passenger Transport		16739	258740	3966	13545	2138
50 Maritime Transport		2090	4433	2295	12610	812
51 Air Transport					277	

67

Input-Output Table of Chile for the Year 1977

CHILE 1977   FLOWS in thousands of Pesos of Y 1977   PURCHASERS CURRENT PRICES

INDUSTRY:	Glass & Glass Products 31	Oth. Non-Met Mineral Prods 32	Iron & Steel Manufacturing 33	Non-Fer. Metal Manufacturing 34	Metal Products 35	Non-Electrical Construc Mach 36
52 Oth. Transportation Services	557	3648	0	8161	4005	3032
53 Communications	10046	16195	15354	18520	40418	8842
54 Financial Institutions	2050	12695	16177	9749	44970	11077
55 Insurance	1999	7578	31001	1711	12991	5565
56 Real Estate	5504	12184	15626	1851	14459	10009
57 Business Services	24996	70948	63809	11256	81196	32873
58 Dwellings	0	0	0	0	0	0
59 Public Education	0	852	6004	49	788	0
60 Private Education	0	-116	5745	289	-17	115
61 Public Health	0	928	0	0	151	0
62 Private Health	0	77	0	207	0	0
63 Recreation Services	0	313	0	0	221	8792
64 Repair Services	0	1423	1372	297	35	1383
65 Laundry Services	0	0	0	0	16250	0
66 Misc. Services	0	2789	5931	670		3184
67 Public Admin. & Defence	0	0	0	0	0	0
68 Domest. Intermediate Inputs	445042	1861965	2978398	1790444	2636300	1303987
69 Imports at Purchasers Prices	128564	247484	1018372	182492	416796	455283
70 Wages	116154	312647	730224	180067	527244	313983
71 Salaries	72271	127570	51081	90239	380460	137051
72 Social Contributions	40257	111104	175968	68960	200686	99424
73 Indirect Taxes	80508	261528	34145	54043	338220	199808
74 Subsidies	-1823	-8492	-24996	-38851	-164180	-16287
75 Consumption of Fixed Capital	51068	235847	37348	72968	232280	132588
76 Operating Surplus	132748	101087	-81505	103239	376972	98854
77 Gross Value Added	491183	1141291	1638265	530663	1891682	965441
78 Gross Output at Consumer Prc	1064789	3250740	5633035	2503599	4944778	2724711

68

Input-Output Table of Chile for the Year 1977

CHILE 1977 — FLOWS in thousands of Pesos of Y 1977 — PURCHASERS CURRENT PRICES

INDUSTRY:	37 Electrical Construc. Mach	38 Transport Equipment	39 Professional Equipmt &Others	40 Other Manufacturing	41 Electricity	42 Gas
* DOMESTIC TRANSACTIONS INDUSTRY *						
1 Agriculture - Crops	2292	3494	0	2831	1676	0
2 Agriculture - Livestock	0	0	515	0	0	0
3 Agricultural Services	42	0	0	119		9
4 Forestry, Lumber	69	97	0	0	2823	0
5 Fishing					42	
6 Copper Mining	17	0	0	0	8142	0
7 Iron Ore Mining						
8 Phosphate Mining		422				
9 Petroleum, Natural Gas			0	0	0	0
10 Coal Mining	1351				8923	37954
11 Other Mineral Extraction	24415	17315	47	263	405370	
12 Stone, Sand Quarrying	8915	663	620	93	30	57
13 Food Manufacturing		276	16	2589	5866	0
14 Beverages		10887		2225		
15 Tobacco		2				
16 Textile Manufacturing	6283	46675	18095	59486	1703	208
17 Manuf. of Wearing Apparel	4182	3242	335	2051	3021	845
18 Leather Manufacturing	1198			4987	1395	643
19 Footwear Manufacturing	1637	4976	131	1395	577	
20 Wood, Cork Manufacturing	9735	46694		1814	2705	185
21 Furniture & Accessories			119	21992	1246	
22 Paper & Paper Products	24073	12446	5703	249	1296	76
23 Printing, Publishing, etc.	14503	10188	186	48681	8895	3248
24 Industrial Chemicals	25531	45374	1122	12201	8703	3427
25 Other Chemical Products	87452	174540	1750	9001	15014	3623
26 Petroleum Refining	46724	77329	5029	45066	1275570	86924
27 Products of Petrol. & Coal	1063	4088		5880	6554	953
28 Rubber Products	16219	87593	115	1208	4618	142
29 Plastic Products n.e.s	20535	47915	2600	17066	1014	90
30 Clay, China, Porcelain Prods	2198				715	36
31 Glass & Glass Products	10153	32159	1842	4763	947	90
32 Oth. Non-Met. Mineral Prods	138835	16682	187	1892	13283	36
33 Iron & Steel Manufacturing	254737	776619	1144	42503	22491	6606
34 Non-Ferrous Metal Manufact	176944	133186	12804	100993	11647	11630
35 Metal Products	206302	92219	2599	98421	33230	1310
36 Non-Elec. Construc. Machnry	146153	20518	2538	2694	25493	1117
37 Electr. Construction Mach.	2207	44378		10588	25667	2661
38 Transport Equipment	8696	253208	1583	10580	13009	1394
39 Profnl. Equipment & Others		88527	6597	247	1875	251
40 Other Manufactured Products	38480	100848	3012	6472	852	230
41 Electricity	4140	2855	772	10643	1792489	9508
42 Gas				855	840	859
43 Hydr. Sys. for Water Dist.				879	3147	800
44 Construction					5557	
45 Trade	872598	790750	175601	373390	1211	13
46 Restaurants and Hotels	22689	17715	324	951	237	707
47 Freight Transport	22242	23685				3773
48 Passenger Transport	44770	95633	3215	6291	5910	14835
49 Maritime Transport	18500	9843	2299	6449	5428	3047
50 Air Transport	7709	4922		1490		0
51 Air Transport	5275	7979	0	124	2821	0

Input-Output Table of Chile for the Year 1977

CHILE 1977   FLOWS in thousands of Pesos of Y 1977   PURCHASERS CURRENT PRICES

INDUSTRY:	37 Electrical Construc Mach	38 Transport Equipment	39 Professional Equipmt &Others	40 Other Manufacturing	41 Electricity	42 Gas
52 Oth.Transportation Services	9864	7499	278	2022	1247	850
53 Communications	39203	52495	2497	6970	22601	2891
54 Financial Institutions	64772	40681	158	3974	3169	153
55 Insurance	20153	28085	4236	5113	2399	877
56 Real Estate	28290	18292	1737	4757	4387	224
57 Business Services	97378	113093	5695	28895	11632	18329
58 Public Education	0	0	0	0	0	0
59 Private Education	2281	10318	0	2638	151	0
60 Public Health	0	0	0	0	0	0
61 Private Health	0	0	0	0	4087	0
62 Recreation Services	2247	2207	27	563	749	0
63 Laundry Services	1229	4437	0	0	0	0
64 Misc Services	8710	21477	769	1170	0	0
65 Public Admin.& Defence	1127	0	0	0	0	0
68 Domest.Intermediate Inputs	2098630	3337024	270406	980089	385022	216328
69 Imports at Purchasers Prices						
70 Wages	1590909	1630142	71937	140386	117814	5134
71 Salaries	525233	907198	40196	98288	1040310	69440
72 Social Contributions	189654	685524	18051	90355	90363	22551
73 Indirect Taxes	-469200	295397	14430	37579	24727	29288
74 Subsidies		-429645	35040	88355	1589146	74227
75 Consumption of Fixed Capital	206680		-1291	-7083	0	22945
76 Operating Surplus	702331	682088	121056	224218	1547812	17612
77 Gross Value Added	2368724	3390853	244358	558370	1066530	
78 Gross Output at Consumer Prc	5879263	8368319	586711	1678845	5610688	236063
					9563524	457525

Input-Output Table of Chile for the Year 1977

CHILE 1977 FLOWS in thousands of Pesos of Y 1977 PURCHASERS CURRENT PRICES

INDUSTRY:

* DOMESTIC TRANSACTIONS *

INDUSTRY	43 Water Distrib.& Sanit. Svcs	44 Construction	45 Trade	46 Restaurants and Hotels	47 Railway Transport	48 Freight Transport
1 Agriculture - Crops	576	0	6032	711955	0	25921
2 Agriculture - Livestock	0	0	0	180955	0	0
3 Agricultural Services	0	59358	0	0	0	0
4 Forestry, Lumber	58	16033	0	11201	0	0
5 Fishing	0	0	0	0	0	0
6 Copper Mining	0	0	0	0	0	0
7 Iron Ore Mining	0	0	0	0	0	0
8 Phosphate Mining	0	0	2660	0	0	0
9 Petroleum, Natural Gas	0	0	0	0	0	0
10 Coal Mining	1-0	1078	0	0	114873	0
11 Stone, Sand Quarrying	2329	431205	0	0	733	0
12 Other Mineral Extraction	1888	17231	0	0	276	0
13 Food Manufacturing	3	0	425942	2603809	184	55582
14 Beverages	5630	0	109676	656415	0	0
15 Tobacco	14555	0	191334	95721	1394	0
16 Textile Manufacturing	5144	48589	102861	13604	211	28101
17 Manuf. of Wearing Apparel	4297	26427	1128	0	1029	0
18 Leather Manufacturing	143	426	9459	3042	0	0
19 Footwear Manufacturing	114	31095	181803	0	7118	2839
20 Wood, Cork Manufacturing	4270	1763411	342	3498	117	5155
21 Furniture & Accessories	23661	149	416209	76410	1275	0
22 Paper & Paper Products	13845	29294	1061807	22411	1795	0
23 Printing, Publishing, etc.	30461	95219	51644	41182	2716	0
24 Industrial Chemicals	34700	32219	185139	78791	4876	2839
25 Other Chemical Products	1711	94478	405881	21210	4297	5155
26 Petroleum Refining	225	315153	13087	24721	137446	2885013
27 Products of Petrol. & Coal	242	143577	124480	3390	479	235580
28 Rubber Products	975	116993	708840	763	1447	86616
29 Plastic Products n.e.s.	77	28205	3623	0	1481	0
30 Clay, China, Porcelain Prods	1293	278010	15478	292	97	9524
31 Glass & Glass Products	28434	105667	3844	4496	485	0
32 Oth. Non-Met. Mineral Prods.	1624	1258168	15303	4613	1815	0
33 Iron & Steel Metal Manufact.	10712	407690	81	0	61963	2345
34 Non-Ferrous Metal Manufact.	64855	842151	92454	149	3635	2018
35 Metal Products	3660	98024	52510	14608	7991	88602
36 Non-Elec. Construc. Machnry	6464	188804	632708	149231	618	1451316
37 Electl. Construction Mach.	168050	3624	343436	29908	2755	0
38 Transport Equipment	208	9087	24058	38126	8536	6510
39 Profnl. Equipment & Others	0	26621	557756	81213	149	1413
40 Other Manufactured Products	0	93661	1740	0	2070	349
41 Electricity	683	625	9856	1204	106582	897
42 Gas	21278	17096	356399	0	411	0
43 Hydr. Sys. for Water Dist.	0	22610	113106	10580	9996	0
44 Construction	0	126379	39992	12660	349	0
45 Trade	0	13417	3636925	1243	1128	359388
46 Restaurants and Hotels	0	477972	5795613	0	101862	0
47 Railway Transport	1146	24671	5198864	0	9042	0
48 Freight Transport	0	0	48356	0	0	0
49 Passenger Transport	1037	0	0	10580	0	0
50 Maritime Transport	1266	0	0	12660	500	4510
51 Air Transport	0	0	0	991	0	0

71

Input-Output Table of Chile for the Year 1977

CHILE 1977   FLOWS in thousands of Pesos of Y 1977   PURCHASERS CURRENT PRICES

INDUSTRY:	43 Water Distrib.& Sanit. Svcs.	44 Construction	45 Trade	46 Restaurants and Hotels	47 Railway Transport	48 Freight Transport
52 Oth. Transportation Services	0	14229	335148	6354	341	186
53 Communications	7090	8595	393328	124905	9049	159275
54 Financial Institutions	207	10000	466068	26748	3702	
55 Insurance		18982	364811	52999	377	89194
56 Real Estate	2352	94217	1414032	309358	7547	16370
57 Business Services	40320	518864	744191	132318		76370
58 Dwellings	0	0	0	0	0	0
59 Public Education	0	12936	0	0	0	0
60 Private Education	0	5545	23011	0	0	0
61 Public Health	0	0	2615	0	0	0
62 Private Health	0	0	0	0	0	0
63 Recreation Services	0	0	14223	2732	204	82
64 Repair Services	0	5375	231296	28079		0
65 Laundry Services	0	0	48262	13857	1544	0
66 Misc. Services	72	0	1942	0	0	0
67 Pusc. Public Admin.& Defence	0	130	5472	0	0	0
68 Domesti. Intermediate Inputs	527202	1050301	14857542	5785185	622563	6397932
69 Imports at Purchasers Prices	210744	986661	541299	157524	68869	517649
70 Wages	170821	1015865	5324393	372779	833394	1173562
71 Salaries	59660	3019848		1002290	46398	
72 Social Contributions	108444	1338501		294614	204405	945319
73 Indirect Taxes	-187438	-125307	8901601	336944	117611	91583
74 Subsidies	-834498	-130944		9005	-17849	
75 Consumption of Fixed Capital	-569984	480157	2690045	-12649	175729	788812
76 Operating Surplus		8693517	2601095	1716090	-220721	-685147
77 Gross Value Added	630161	11706386	44843956	3982613	1159967	2394129
78 Gross Output at Consumer Prc	1175607	23737348	60112797	9905322	1850399	9309710

Input-Output Table of Chile for the Year 1977

FLOWS in thousands of Pesos of Y 1977

PURCHASERS CURRENT PRICES

* DOMESTIC TRANSACTIONS *

INDUSTRY:	49 Passenger Transport	50 Maritime Transport	51 Air Transport	52 Oth. Transport Services	53 Communications	54 Financial Institutions
1 Agriculture - Crops	421	5605	8188	69	70	29443
2 Agriculture - Livestock	0	1366	785	0	0	1548
3 Agricultural Services	0	894	0	0	0	135
4 Forestry, Lumber	0	975	79	2	0	722
5 Fishing	0	0	0	0	0	0
6 Copper Mining	0	0	0	0	0	0
7 Iron Ore Mining	0	0	0	0	0	0
8 Phosphate Mining	0	0	0	0	0	0
9 Petroleum, Natural Gas	0	0	0	0	0	0
10 Coal Mining	4	579	0	196	0	82
11 Stone, Sand Quarrying	0	20931	27922	1308	39	0
12 Other Mineral Extraction	101	8329	2342	5192	815	100171
13 Food Manufacturing	1145	58	245	299	70	3679
14 Beverages	27929	14168	1747	639	410	0
15 Tobacco	681	6941	2322	93	2767	7308
16 Textile Manufacturing	12	1138	319	3828	235	20651
17 Manuf. of Wearing Apparel	188	2663	471	725	738	76
18 Leather Manufacturing	40	6757	25	8178	194	41560
19 Footwear Manufacturing	32458	4518	725	14562	15669	15596
20 Wood & Cork Manufacturing	102	12303	1809	329	16868	58583
21 Furniture & Accessories	3367	55	44	8886	1248	249424
22 Paper & Paper Products	1793376	7009	64517	15177	10895	4343
23 Printing, Publishing, etc.	146956	86966	284517	496	16315	97755
24 Industrial Chemicals	471741	2206	8045	292	2154	34583
25 Other Chemical Products	35	1899	6962	201	6963	1254
26 Petroleum Refining	157	267	28	287	1063	3273
27 Products of Petrol. & Coal	17477	233	163	207	1173	806
28 Rubber Products	14	1174	449	0	738	555
29 Plastic Products n.e.s	59	5059	0	583	7245	9565
30 China, Porcelain Prods	98	357	5806	4727	3846	9344
31 Glass & Glass Products	58877	10672	2539	7653	6234	708
32 Other Non-Met. Mineral Prods.	4831	7888	2825	18443	7802	42459
33 Iron & Steel Manufact.	756626	5967	5642	121	5847	4519
34 Non-Ferrous Metal Manufact.	1259325	58659	22	7218	223	57249
35 Metal Products	168	142	1723	27748	4905	41235
36 Non-Elec. Construc. Machnry	9068	3280	4373	653	33812	833
37 Electr. Construction Mach.	30279	17760	259	11025	1731	245639
38 Transport Equipment	2347	727	518	0	6114	85768
39 Profnl Equipment & Others	2424	8134	6837	0	0	20055
40 Other Manufactured Products	15038	19685	0	22348	60582	3227
41 Electricity	0	0	24808	0	9264	4065
42 Gas	0	0	0	0	55283	0
43 Hydr. Sys. for Water Dist.	0	0	0	0	1082	16756
44 Construction	77103	21879	2151	9108	1730	3373
45 Trade	0	3084	7448	6672	31127	18447
46 Restaurants and Hotels	382	2253	570	24640	0	42248
47 Railway Transport	1227	1227	0	0	0	43732
48 Freight Transport	11276	41398	0	0	0	44660
49 Passenger Transport	0	4811	0	0	0	0
50 Maritime Transport	0	0	0	0	0	0
51 Air Transport	0	0	0	0	0	0

Input-Output Table of Chile for the Year 1977

CHILE 1977   FLOWS in thousands of Pesos of Y 1977   PURCHASERS CURRENT PRICES

INDUSTRY:	49 Passenger Transport	50 Maritime Transport	51 Air Transport	52 Oth. Transport Services	53 Communications	54 Financial Institutions
52 Oth. Transportation Services	3783	38431	72544	40690	248	4571
53 Communications	19867	26767	15412	35128	76419	364177
54 Financial Institutions	19738	22289	818	4663	909	271230
55 Insurance	18725	48184	29280	13245	7542	97914
56 Real Estate	54008	9404	3623	18947	34441	110889
57 Business Services			10207	52186	36688	377011
58 Dwellings Services	150		0	0	0	0
59 Public Education		690		14	0	7307
60 Private Education	690	1088	612	13	3998	
61 Public Health			0	0		2374
62 Private Health	423	1630			2429	0
63 Recreation Services	739	5160	706	1417	549	4931
64 Repair Services	160424	909	0	0	0	25163
65 Laundry Services		243	15		638	9466
66 Misc. Services	9247		194	1738	3598	0
67 Public Admin. & Defence	5675			12085		299
68 Domest. Intermediate Inputs	4498977	920704	562693	373773	543739	2648312
69 Imports at Purchasers Prices	411108	3109423	890002	6930	99573	297546
70 Wages	1379499	367391	421187	282894	1254198	3368633
71 Salaries		817217	254492	76656	32098	
72 Social Contributions	376472	421804	75227	85007	294658	1277560
73 Indirect Taxes	73196	148682	66365	170027	687510	
74 Subsidies	-4884	-2783	-450	-18093		-21197
75 Consumption of Fixed Capital	1111850	860180	220341	75329	1043173	341309
76 Operating Surplus	748354	531665	-17580	257712	62287	3243327
77 Gross Value Added	3684493	3144156	791582	929605	3373927	8630551
78 Gross Output at Consumer Prc	8594578	7174283	2244277	1310308	4017239	11571869

Input-Output Table of Chile for the Year 1977

CHILE 1977   FLOWS in thousands of Pesos of Y 1977   PURCHASERS CURRENT PRICES

* DOMESTIC TRANSACTIONS *

INDUSTRY:	55 Insurance	Real Estate 56	57 Business Services	Dwellings 58	59 Public Education	Private 60 Education
1 Agriculture – Crops	87		10	3141	21825	33916
2 Agriculture – Livestock	0		0	0	1455	2105
3 Agricultural Services	0		0	0		30714
4 Forestry, Lumber	0		0	0	1119	
5 Fishing, Lumber	0		0	0		1737
6 Copper Mining	0		0	0		0
7 Iron Ore Mining	0		0	0		0
8 Phosphate Mining	0		0	0		0
9 Petroleum, Natural Gas	0		0	0		1045
10 Coal Mining	0		0	0		0
11 Stone, Sand Quarrying	0		0	0		9
12 Other Mineral Extraction	330		390	0	343	131988
13 Food Manufacturing	0	1044	29	579	87466	3259
14 Beverages	0	2262		312	325	
15 Tobacco	14		1097		19842	7074
16 Textile Manufacturing	239		4619		3563	2610
17 Manuf. of Wearing Apparel			5	1855	1691	568
18 Leather Manufacturing	1477	1059	299		63	297
19 Footwear Manufacturing	0		3742		6873	13587
20 Wood, Cork Manufacturing	6748	4500	121	6921	318	3093
21 Furniture & Accessories	24052	35871	113435	3250	9212	33674
22 Paper & Paper Products	52	1826	222619	15736	72909	280916
23 Printing, Publishing, etc	703	13833	1410	1286	4121	3608
24 Industrial Chemicals	65		75255		10364	39958
25 Other Chemical Products			42315		28293	59958
26 Petroleum Refining	1	130	6890	25	547	6057
27 Products of Petrol. & Coal	0		10579		1022	6366
28 Rubber Products	7		8258	2938	3206	2070
29 Plastic Products n.e.s.	880		14	25	3786	1084
30 Clay, China, Porcelain Prods	1008		165		1824	1732
31 Glass & Glass Products	0		104		3054	2840
32 Oth. Non-Met. Mineral Prods	0				3212	9993
33 Iron & Steel Manufacturing	0					107
34 Non-Ferrous Metal Manufact	1639	1354	28959	1390	16938	30366
35 Metal Products	546		10572	349	2994	5380
36 Non-Elec. Construc. Machnry	8768	1491	21738	13890	26923	27915
37 Electl. Construction Mach.	0		2695		1807	10365
38 Transport Equipment	3470	9961	58787	5488	100	555
39 Profnl. Equipment & Others	8726	5529	59491	10023	9008	49494
40 Other Manufactured Products	1394		3156	7935	46216	77055
41 Electricity	0				6870	6863
42 Gas	0	1529	3808		3613	10908
43 Hydr. Sys. for Water Dist.	1228	10450		2988284	48384	192147
44 Construction		4803	93604		16260	29291
45 Trade	0	157	558		26800	42318
46 Restaurants and Hotels	168		29273		29273	
47 Railway Transport	7101		43168	312	2159	1403
48 Freight Transport	28	1984	23173		21089	32864
49 Passenger Transport	94	0		0	16738	8392
50 Maritime Transport						
51 Air Transport						

Input-Output Table of Chile for the Year 1977

CHILE 1977   FLOWS in thousands of Pesos of Y 1977   PURCHASERS CURRENT PRICES

INDUSTRY:	55 Insurance	56 Real Estate	57 Business Services	58 Dwellings	59 Public Education	60 Private Education
52 Oth. Transportation Services	42	7701	1551	0	1124	0
53 Communications	15930	7180	17334	0	21145	7272
54 Financial Institutions	11267	8353	1990	680	894	21998
55 Insurance	3898	84790	20742	53593	1915	15270
56 Real Estate	35173	34856	206280	18639	15596	85165
57 Business Services		20210	219350	3062	13474	38163
58 Dwellings	2407	0	9050	0	0	0
59 Public Education	0	1984	10135	0	0	0
60 Private Education	0	0	0	0	250	0
61 Public Health						
62 Private Health						
63 Recreation Services	16657	2433	21732	0	1092	20905
64 Repair Services	693	2008	3545	270	15119	13734
65 Laundry Services	138	1303	1017	0	1374	3356
66 Misc. Services	4844		82558	3810	737	1958
67 Public Admin. & Defence	0		5568		748	2863
68 Domest. Intermediate Inputs	173244	259202	1580453	3144254	604463	1466432
69 Imports at Purchasers Prices	363816	7390	272261	13716	41710	91570
70 Wages	237878	70643	1829932	195969	7133134	3200360
71 Salaries	32703	39274	52727	123248	245574	214423
72 Social Contributions	57734	18612	193621	56390	1302955	712531
73 Indirect Taxes	104380	458723	367269	1161275	203	-8078
74 Subsidies			-7332		0	-48370
75 Consumption of Fixed Capital	15208	344578	232641	7788020	-26898	22958
76 Operating Surplus	1086058	2448188	1997106	11217238	-98194	807572
77 Gross Value Added	1480759	3380018	4665984	20542190	8612370	4687852
78 Gross Output at Consumer Prc	2017819	3643210	6518678	23700160	9258543	6245854

76

Input-Output Table of Chile for the Year 1977

CHILE 1977   FLOWS in thousands of Pesos of Y 1977   PURCHASERS CURRENT PRICES

* DOMESTIC TRANSACTIONS *

INDUSTRY:	61 Public Health	62 Private Health	63 Recreation Services	64 Repair Services	65 Laundry Services	66 Misc Services
1 Agriculture - Crops	58009	20916	2523	2900	68	45491
2 Agriculture - Livestock	4033	5016	168			5229
3 Agricultural Services		121				0
4 Forestry, Lumber	10579	2628	383		1123	5229
5 Fishing		4997		79	2	0
6 Copper Mining						
7 Iron Ore Mining						
8 Phosphate Mining						
9 Petroleum, Natural Gas						
10 Coal Mining						
11 Stone, Sand Quarrying			303	2320		430
12 Other Mineral Extraction						
13 Food Manufacturing	132150	79208	10114	11638	353	11345
14 Beverages		1013	1218	418	156	11036
15 Tobacco						
16 Textile Manufacturing	36961	12401	4090	8188	1706	19755
17 Manuf. of Wearing Apparel	3792	22532	8828	1568	99	28354
18 Leather Manufacturing	153	1070	3321	8160		10903
19 Footwear Manufacturing		1237				
20 Wood, Cork Manufacturing	2819	1405	7478	24117		82769
21 Furniture & Accessories		368	1271	1046		4832
22 Paper & Paper Products	9099	551				
23 Printing, Publishing, etc	34952	16861	19156	2679	1328	55643
24 Industrial Chemicals	29270	54398	3394	18679	1599	24155
25 Other Chemical Products		33165	13545	44051	18739	108206
26 Petroleum Refining	263366	405466	35	28457	23324	35132
27 Products of Petrol. & Coal	138634	64265		218492	21458	
28 Rubber Products	1452	4341	1485	153559	780	5331
29 Plastic Products n.e.s	3977	5606	2497	331	8	35129
30 Clay, China, Porcelain Prods	3059	8538				
31 Glass & Glass Products	44383	420	475	37485		6855
32 Oth. Non-Met. Mineral Prods	820	360	297	570		5598
33 Iron & Steel Manufacturing	107					1590
34 Non-Ferrous Metal Manufact.						
35 Metal Products	1339	8646	2539	7013	2015	37873
36 Non-Elec. Construc. Machnry	12919	4721	5688	1520	3	31960
37 Electric Construction Mach.	10626	10437	3672	42210	2	31879
38 Transpor. Equipment & Others		544		27278		37288
39 Proffl Manufactured Products	49660	58230	1877	23967	1936	1462
40 Other Manufactured Products	47476	15943	17143	660	493	2066
41 Electricity	65352	67004	34012	9221	67	34033
42 Gas	13622	18024	8016	35094		56602
43 Hydr. Sys. for Water Dist.	15012	17100	8073	1662	496	17575
44 Construction	37388	32442	18786	1769	1838	29154
45 Trade					18316	
46 Restaurants and Hotels	30677	6808	84381	7594	5163	86895
47 Railway Transport					75	3234
48 Freight Transport	2750	2013	5753	10269		10294
49 Passenger Transport	27797	43825	30829	5238	1516	18685
50 Maritime Transport		468				
51 Air Transport	0	3920	20204	0	0	511

Input-Output Table of Chile for the Year 1977

CHILE 1977   FLOWS in thousands of Pesos of Y 1977   PURCHASERS CURRENT PRICES

INDUSTRY:	61 Public Health	62 Private Health	63 Recreation Services	64 Repair Services	65 Laundry Services	66 Misc Services
52 Oth. Transportation Services	2604	8166	2886	5441	0	85
53 Communications	22880	72583	63748	25943	3347	2105
54 Financial Institutions	0	2224	30625	0	0	50
55 Insurance	1243	3805	5562	4460	0	124
56 Real Estate	2648	232873	35826	52047	1290	47683
57 Business Services	22684	113055	118212	103137	1460	36189
58 Dwellings Service	0	0	0	0	0	0
59 Public Education	1280	21898	24051	0	0	0
60 Private Education	0	0	0	0	0	15
61 Public Health	122356	159208	0	0	0	0
62 Private Health	0	0	238	7	0	22
63 Recreation Services	0	48	162545	0	0	41
64 Repair Services	45622	4150	2173	0	491	20010
65 Laundry Services	15904	6362	1298	0	0	27917
66 Misc Services	0	3117	824	0	0	201
67 Public Admin. & Defence	0	0	17689	0	0	0
68 Domest. Intermediate Inputs	1338455	1663838	944789	923004	121418	111851
69 Imports at Purchasers Prices	365472	226410	298848	105159	10980	39307
70 Wages	3042105	972437	438106	146379	39963	700439
71 Salaries	86615	212461	69179	163308	45427	2546090
72 Social Contributions	527782	286132	102467	108825	26370	431204
73 Indirect Taxes	1593	106759	260488	214133	57185	7568
74 Subsidies	0	-619	-17018	0	0	-8940
75 Consumption of Fixed Capital	0	219869	79483	35564	20527	14675
76 Operating Surplus	0	3754421	39009	770112	93517	271393
77 Gross Value Added	3658095	5531460	1324714	1438321	282989	4030546
78 Gross Output at Consumer Prc	5362023	7421708	2568351	2466484	415387	5188369

78

Input-Output Table of Chile for the Year 1977

CHILE 1977 FLOWS in thousands of Pesos of Y 1977 PURCHASERS CURRENT PRICES

INDUSTRY:	Public Admin. & Defence 67	Banking Taxes 68	Intermediate Demand 69	Private Consumption 70	General Govt. Consumption 71	Gross Fixed Capital Form. 72
* DOMESTIC TRANSACTIONS * INDUSTRY						
1 Agriculture – Crops	189787	0	13983389	12083652	0	1698769
2 Agriculture – Livestock	17658	0	11264603	3540506	0	322394
3 Agricultural Services	17663	0	1341489	0	0	6230
4 Forestry, Lumber	14143	0	1341193	117373	0	330692
5 Fishing	0	0	1911001	1452501	0	0
6 Copper Mining	0	0	4265634	285903	0	0
7 Iron Ore Mining	0	0	398246	0	0	0
8 Phosphate Mining	0	0	485394	0	0	0
9 Petroleum, Natural Gas	0	0	2460978	-1	0	281366
10 Coal Mining	0	0	756177	0	0	0
11 Other Mineral Extraction	11777	0	519177	59898	0	0
12 Stone, Sand Quarrying	322164	0	15307584	0	0	0
13 Food Manufacturing	56739	0	308442	42307307	0	0
14 Beverages	0	0	46773	8934303	0	0
15 Tobacco	0	0	5750428	3973626	0	0
16 Textile Manufacturing	18880	0	477600	4719247	0	23527
17 Manuf. of Wearing Apparel	66856	0	172361	6184546	0	0
18 Leather Manufacturing	962	0	120948	257751	0	0
19 Footwear Manufacturing	23884	0	420810	516711	0	0
20 Wood, Cork Manufacturing	38028	0	5068677	598754	0	23109
21 Furniture & Accessories	87	0	4291804	1531682	0	113000
22 Paper & Paper Products	232818	0	2158977	445972	0	0
23 Printing, Publishing, etc.	365796	0	5523000	1533475	0	0
24 Industrial Chemicals	0	0	16798971	449972	0	0
25 Other Chemical Products	10895	0	1091586	5113282	0	0
26 Petroleum Refining	58968	0	2972108	5504605	0	0
27 Products of Petrol. & Coal	632830	0	334566	687662	0	47
28 Rubber Products	28495	0	7482245	573174	0	0
29 Plastic Products n.e.s.	5363	0	3068790	407141	0	0
30 Clay, China, Porcelain Prods	9737	0	5194803	343767	0	0
31 Glass & Glass Products	12490	0	1426986	52592	0	0
32 Oth. Non-Met. Mineral Prods	31637	0	3577628	34594	0	10700
33 Iron & Steel Manufacturing	28187	0	929641	621984	0	0
34 Non-Ferrous Metal Manufact	0	0	5544734	1401646	0	0
35 Metal Products	33501	0	191746	2601208	0	280781
36 Non-Elec. Construc. Machnry	51631	0	9105460	1516480	0	335350
37 Electl. Construction Mach.	42501	0	7936829	265357	0	306152
38 Transport Equipment	601911	0	160028	465202	0	999863
39 Profnl. Equipment & Others	3982	0	302459	1608736	0	62181
40 Other Manufactured Products	58114	0	5141054	297499	0	2492
41 Electricity	16884	0	2479703	872545	0	0
42 Gas	20216	0	8912762	0	0	0
43 Hydr. Sys. for Water Dist.	24723	0	8945982	0	0	0
44 Construction	526446	0	1139964	0	0	18593235
45 Trade	1736	0	2173697	40755804	0	0
46 Restaurants and Hotels	549500	0	3842210	5974197	0	0
47 Railway Transport	37244	0		63071	0	0
48 Freight Transport	40000	0		131711	0	86180
49 Passenger Transport	55543	0		7095981	0	0
50 Maritime Transport	21786	0		42484	0	0
51 Air Transport	122798	0		953256	0	0

Input-Output Table of Chile for the Year 1977

CHILE 1977   FLOWS in thousands of Pesos of Y 1977   PURCHASERS CURRENT PRICES

INDUSTRY:	Public Admin. & Defence 67	Banking Taxes 68	Intermediate Demand 69	Private Consumption 70	General Govt. Consumption 71	Gross Fixed Capital Form 72
52 Oth. Transportation Services	14044	0	855155	220374	0	0
53 Communications	207518	0	2724246	1082280	0	0
54 Financial Institutions	12000	9151717	10844758	64141	0	0
55 Insurance	15892	0	1754112	145374	0	0
56 Real Estate	77705	0	3429433	690619	0	0
57 Business Services	461497	0	5454035	0	0	279292
58 Dwellings	0	0	0	23587354	0	0
59 Public Education	28141	0	101484	375402	8781657	0
60 Private Education	8914	0	163883	607474	0	0
61 Public Health	0	0	132175	467651	4762197	0
62 Private Health	0	0	194728	721669	0	0
63 Recreation Services	34135	0	1118288	1289532	0	0
64 Repair Services	77058	0	581028	187715	0	0
65 Laundry Services	25657	0	119614	267725	0	0
66 Misc. Services	18737	0	275132	4904997	0	0
67 Public Admin. & Defence	86084	0	382863	80774	28395107	0
68 Domest. Intermediate Inputs	8952529	9151717	232610790	179777576	41938961	23735360
69 Imports at Purchasers Prices	3644107	0	50191374	29729254	0	14610616
70 Wages	14150165	0	67506264	0	0	0
71 Salaries	1877151	0	25860461	0	0	0
72 Social Contributions	2018582	0	20125855	0	0	0
73 Indirect Taxes	6893	0	31836312	0	0	0
74 Subsidies	0	-9151717	-45066288	0	0	0
75 Consumption of Fixed Capital	14497	0	33696792	0	0	0
76 Operating Surplus	212674	0	99260143	0	0	0
77 Gross Value Added	18274562	-9151717	273778539	0	0	0
78 Gross Output at Consumer Prc	28871198	0	556581703	209506830	41938961	38345976

Input-Output Table of Chile for the Year 1977

CHILE 1977 FLOWS in thousands of Pesos of Y 1977 PURCHASERS CURRENT PRICES

* DOMESTIC TRANSACTIONS INDUSTRY	73 Change in Stock	74 Exports	75 Final Demand	76 Trade Margin on Imports	77 Gross Output at Purchasr Prices
1 Agriculture - Crops	35268	2611036	16428725	0	30412114
2 Agriculture - Livestock	161936	339729	4364565	0	15529768
3 Agricultural - Services			6230	0	349479
4 Forestry, Lumber	-50125	115341	503281	0	3534858
5 Fishing		150356	1602857	0	3259858
6 Copper Mining	84853	27580125	28703886	0	32038132
7 Iron Ore Mining	-130638	1870535	1613886	0	2038132
8 Phosphate Mining		445300	1816940	0	1298007
9 Petroleum, Natural Gas	29266		1018940	0	3477918
10 Coal Mining	-9282		-33920	0	511177
11 Stone, Miscel. Quarrying		75066	45254	0	802226
12 Food, Miscel. Extraction	-29812	4140144	46212069	0	61519653
13 Food Manufacturing	420782	365681	9672069	0	12739191
14 Beverages	-203789		4027321	0	4049094
15 Tobacco	26674	2071	400232	0	1149094
16 Textile Manufacturing	597907	102903	5443586	0	7086858
17 Manuf. of Wearing Apparel	-84740	59972	6609258	0	2188522
18 Leather Manufacturing	105028	63328	286161	0	58227757
19 Footwear Manufacturing	-14928	35670	570180	0	5591620
20 Wood, Cork Manufacturing	-10811	1346502	1457956	0	1706387
21 Furniture & Accessories	-6667	25762	1663777	0	8537677
22 Paper & Paper Products	21891	28105937	3466800	0	5941306
23 Printing Publishing, etc	-51553	1594919	1649502	0	3693564
24 Industrial Chemicals, etc	-174696	92015	1534587	0	21849378
25 Other Chemical Products	-745442	300364	4993679	0	1286500
26 Petroleum Refining	-11316	25774	5059507	0	3752242
27 Products of Petrol. & Coal	-22128	70346	199914	0	2402609
28 Rubber Products	-1359	2520	780136	0	885560
29 Plastic Products n.e.s.	102862	40991	574382	0	1064789
30 Clay, China, Porcelain Prods	-36628	9405	550994	0	3250740
31 Glass & Glass Products	33855	88618	310544	0	2503599
32 Oth. Non-Met. Mineral. Prods	-33787	419427	181950	0	5633035
33 Iron & Steel Manufacturing	-107401	598316	438232	0	4444778
34 Non-Ferrous Metal Manufact.	-13931	2225242	1076613	0	2724711
35 Metal Products	-167168	1255571	1361150	0	5679263
36 Non-Elec. Construc. Machnry	352167	325571	1795070	0	8336319
37 Electi. Construction Mach.	-19329	20980	3385101	0	586711
38 Transport Equipment	46447	292444	2821685	0	1678845
39 Profnl Equipment & Others	8161	9959	394965	0	9583524
40 Other Manufactured Products	0		768299	0	457525
41 Electricity	0		1646695	0	1175607
42 Gas	0		297499	0	2373348
43 Hydr. Sys. for Water Dist.	0	603	871148	0	6012797
44 Construction	0	3059	18596294	0	9905322
45 Trade	0	1368908	1620640	17736353	1850399
46 Restaurants and Hotels	0	1451422	7425619	0	9307710
47 Railway Transport	0	1304566	937637	0	8594578
48 Freight Transport	0	146728	364619	0	717283
49 Passenger Transport	0	395023	7456614	0	2244277
50 Maritime Transport	0	4958102	5000586	0	
51 Air Transport	0	906811	1860067	0	

81

Input-Output Table of Chile for the Year 1977

CHILE 1977   FLOWS in thousands of Pesos of Y 1977   PURCHASERS CURRENT PRICES

		73 Change in Stock	74 Exports	75 Final Demand	76 Trade Margin on Imports	77 Gross Output at Purchasr Prices
52	Oth. Transportation Services	0	234779	455153	0	1310308
53	Communications	0	210713	1292993	0	4017239
54	Financial Institutions	0	79970	727111	0	11571869
55	Insurance	0	118833	263707	0	2017819
56	Real Estate	0	213777	23777	0	3643210
57	Business Services	0	94732	1064643	0	6518678
58	Dwellings	0	112806	23700160	0	23700160
59	Public Education	0		9157059	0	9258543
60	Private Education	0	3497	6081971	0	6245854
61	Public Health	0		7226980	0	5362023
62	Private Health	0		5229848	0	7421708
63	Recreation Services	0	10289	1450063	0	2568351
64	Repair Services	0	16051	1885456	0	2466484
65	Laundry Services	0	9741	2955773	0	415387
66	Misc. Services	0	8240	4913237	0	5188369
67	Public Admin. & Defence	0	12254	28488335	0	28871198
68	Domest. Intermediate Inputs	1444544	59338119	306234560	17736353	556581703
69	Imports at Purchasers Prices	1718754	0	46058624	0	96249998
70	Wages	0	0	0	0	67506264
71	Salaries	0	0	0	0	25860461
72	Social Contributions	0	0	0	0	20125855
73	Indirect Taxes	0	0	0	0	31836312
74	Subsidies	0	0	0	0	33506288
75	Consumption of Fixed Capital	0	0	0	0	99286793
76	Operating Surplus	0	0	0	0	99261241
77	Gross Value Added	0	0	0	0	273779539
78	Gross Output at Consumer Prc	3163298	59338119	352293184	17736353	926611240

82

CONGO

Reference year: 1967

Entries in table: Total flows

Source: Congo, Coordination générale des services de planification, Mission de planification, Sedes; *Tableau d'échanges industriels* (Congo 1967)

Computerized: Deutsches Institut für Wirtschaftsforschung, Berlin

Currency units: CFA francs of Y 1967
Scale factor: 1,000,000

Pricing system: Purchasers' current prices
Intermediate sectors: 20 × 20
Treatment of trade margins: Trade margins in columns 29 and 30

Treatment of imports: Column 32 in final demand
Availability of import matrix: Not available

Total number of rows: 30
Statistical unit of quadrant 1: Industry

Total number of columns: 33
Statistical unit of quadrant 1: Industry

Fourth quadrant: Not occupied

Input-Output Table of Congo for the Year 1967

CONGO 1967   FLOWS In millions of CFA Francs of Y 1967   PURCHASERS CURRENT PRICES

INDUSTRY:	1 Tradit.Agricul. Livest.,Fishng	2 Industrialized Agriculture	3 Forestry	4 Mining & Quarrying Petrol Products	5 Energy, Water	6 Food Industry excl.Beverages
* TOTAL TRANSACTIONS *						
INDUSTRY						
1 Trad.Agric.Livestock Fishng	27.1	0.0	0.0	0.0	0.0	758.0
2 Industrialized Agriculture	0.0	0.0	0.0	0.0	0.0	490.9
3 Forestry	0.0	3.0	0.0	0.0	0.0	0.0
4 Mining & Quarrying	0.0	0.0	0.0	0.0	0.0	0.0
5 Energy,Water & Petrol. Prod.	61.2	100.0	375.0	12.0	83.4	217.7
6 Food Industry exc. Beverages	58.0	0.0	0.0	0.0	0.0	141.5
7 Beverages and Tobacco	0.0	0.0	0.0	0.0	0.0	0.0
8 Footwr. Text. &Wrg. Appar.l	0.0	0.4	0.0	0.0	0.0	0.0
9 Wood	31.7	3.1	48.0	0.0	0.2	472.9
10 Rubber,Paper,Cnemical Indust	0.0	0.0	6.0	0.0	0.0	0.0
11 Mineral & Non-Mineral Prods.	41.1	26.3	537.4	0.0	108.0	41.7
12 Metal Products,Electrical M.	73.2	9.5	139.9	33.2	46.0	39.8
13 Transport Equipment & Repair	19.5	8.0	19.5	26.3	2.0	5.6
14 Various Manufactures	55.6	0.0	62.8	6.7	5.3	0.0
15 Construction (Bldgs. Roads)	12.2	1.0	670.2	4.7	28.6	15.2
16 Banking, Insur., Real Estate	42.6	4.0	856.2	69.0	54.2	60.7
17 Transport	76.8	2.0	67.5	40.0	0.0	315.4
18 Other Services	24.0	0.0	22.0	0.0	3.0	0.0
19 Ownership of Dwellings						
20 Trade						25.5
21 Total Intermediate Inputs	506.3	96.1	2199.5	193.0	360.1	4061.0
22 Wage Income - Afric. Hshlds	83.7	89.1	652.5	32.4	170.7	631.4
23 Duty Charges (African)	18.7	135.0	124.6	1.8	30.3	270.7
24 Wage Income - Expat. Hshlds	82.5	0.0	314.6	17.8	105.1	178.1
25 Duty Charges (Expatriates)	16.4	0.0	62.8	0.9	18.7	68.1
26 Indirect Taxes & Custom Duty	33.9	47.6	173.8	9.2	130.0	63.1
27 Depreciation	29.5	0.0	410.2	3.7	134.0	339.7
28 Operating Surplus	4682.0	776.0	209.9	85.1	454.5	762.2
29 Gross Value Added	4948.7	926.2	1947.7	353.1	1044.0	2854.7
30 Total Inputs	5455.0	1022.3	4117.2	546.1	1404.1	6915.7

84

Input-Output Table of Congo for the Year 1967

CONGO 1967 FLOWS in millions of CFA Francs of Y 1967 PURCHASERS CURRENT PRICES

INDUSTRY:	7 Beverages, Tobacco	8 Footwear & Textiles	9 Wood Industry	10 Rubber, Paper, Chemicals	11 Mining & Non-Mineral Prods.	12 Metal Products
* TOTAL TRANSACTIONS *						
INDUSTRY						
1 Trad.Agric.,Livestock,Fishng	98.5	0.0	0.0	0.0	0.0	0.0
2 Industrialized Agriculture	273.5	0.0	0.0	0.0	0.0	0.0
3 Forestry	0.0	0.0	68.0	0.0	0.0	0.0
4 Mining & Quarrying	0.0	0.0	0.0	0.0	0.0	0.0
5 Energy,Water & Petrol. Prod.	59.0	6.0	68.0	15.8	1.5	20.0
6 Food Industry exc. Beverages	34.5	0.0	0.0	0.0	0.0	0.0
7 Beverages and Tobacco	45.2	0.0	0.0	0.0	0.0	2.7
8 Footwr. Text. &Wrg. Appar1	40.9	45.9	23.1	5.5	0.3	30.7
9 Wood			35.3	237.8	0.0	
10 Rubber,Paper,Chemical Indust	38.7	9.5	102.4	20.1	19.9	29.2
11 Mineral & Non-Mineral Prods.	0.0	0.0	1.2	4.6	3.1	4.0
12 Metal Products,Electrical M.	49.1	22.7	19.0	8.5	1.2	12.0
13 Transport Equipment & Repair	14.3	0.0	31.6	17.5	2.5	33.6
14 Various Manufactures	82.6	46.7	55.3	26.3	4.5	39.9
15 Construction (Bldgs. Roads)	20.1	1.8	141.8	26.5	15.1	27.0
16 Banking,Insur., Real Estate	58.5	55.3	36.8	0.0	0.0	8.0
17 Transport	140.0	57.9	9.7			
18 Other Services	110.8	9.7	0.0			
19 Ownership of Dwellings	41.2	0.0				
20 Trade	0.0	0.0				
21 Total Intermediate Inputs	1066.6	223.0	1217.1	376.9	78.1	474.5
22 Wage Income - Afric. Hsehlds	125.9	34.2	162.0	48.9	29.8	80.4
23 Duty Charges - (African)	44.1	17.1	36.3	45.1	6.7	13.6
24 Wage Income - Expat.Hsehlds	99.5	19.0	130.9	47.4	5.9	72.6
25 Duty Charges - (Expatriates)	34.8	0.0	29.3	5.3	0.3	12.2
26 Indirect Taxes & Custom Duty	953.6	53.8	78.2	98.9	7.5	138.0
27 Depreciation	224.5	10.0	90.4	21.4	12.0	29.0
28 Operating Surplus	439.8	157.8	79.3	24.3		66.5
29 Gross Value Added	1922.0	285.7	606.4	249.1	70.4	412.3
30 Total Inputs	2988.6	508.7	1823.5	626.0	148.5	886.8

Input-Output Table of Congo for the Year 1987

CONGO 1967   FLOWS in millions of CFA Francs of Y 1967   PURCHASERS CURRENT PRICES

INDUSTRY:	13 Transport Equip & Repair	14 Various Manufactures	15 Construction	16 Banking, Insur. Real Estate	17 Transport	18 Other Services
* TOTAL TRANSACTIONS *						
INDUSTRY						
1 Trad.Agric.,Livestock,Fishng	0.0	0.0	0.0	0.0	0.0	12.8
2 Industrialized Agriculture	0.0	0.0	0.0	0.0	0.0	0.0
3 Forestry	0.0	0.0	2.0	0.0	0.0	0.0
4 Mining & Quarrying	52.2	18.7	338.5	13.0	0.0	30.8
5 Energy,Water & Petrol. Prod.	0.0	0.0	0.0	0.0	581.5	17.0
6 Food Industry exc. Beverages	0.0	0.0	0.0	0.0	0.0	37.5
7 Beverages and Tobacco	0.0	6.7	0.4	0.0	2.4	0.0
8 Footwr.,Text.,&Wrg. Apparl	0.0	7.7	4.4	0.0	14.9	3.0
9 Wood	50.2	0.0	314.5	0.0	90.4	31.0
10 Rubber,Paper,Chemical Indust	50.0	67.0	921.2	0.0	19.4	45.1
11 Mineral & Non-Mineral Prods.	78.8	9.0	741.7	0.0	58.8	16.7
12 Metal Products,Electrical M.	53.5	3.5	361.3	4.0	581.9	16.2
13 Transport Equipment & Repair	21.5	3.9	44.7	63.0	156.2	13.4
14 Various Manufactures	30.0	0.3	183.6	5.7	308.7	24.2
15 Construction(Bldgs.,Roads)	61.3	2.4	462.8	154.7	667.5	54.9
16 Banking,Insur.,Real Estate	173.4	1.7	404.8	153.9	667.5	82.7
17 Transport	50.4	7.0	468.8	15.0	100.0	4.0
18 Other Services	9.8	0.0				
19 Ownership of Dwellings	0.0					
20 Trade						
21 Total Intermediate Inputs	566.6	134.1	4309.6	327.4	3623.9	443.3
22 Wage Income - (Afric. Hsehlds	133.0	27.8	1345.5	252.0	2448.1	189.0
23 Duty Charges - (African)	34.8	25.8	624.6	252.3	715.2	30.0
24 Wage Income - Expat.Hsehlds	188.0	26.0	624.7	221.4	972.2	107.2
25 Duty Charges - Expat(rates)	52.0	16.0	246.7	106.8	294.6	14.7
26 Indirect Taxes & Custom Duty	75.0	6.8	755.0	86.9	369.0	89.6
27 Depreciation		10.2		233.8	3052.4	82.1
28 Operating Surplus	189.8	128.9	2240.5		-219.2	401.8
29 Gross Value Added	726.3	222.9	5588.1	983.4	7632.8	907.4
30 Total Inputs	1312.9	357.0	9897.7	1310.8	11256.5	1350.7

Input-Output Table of Congo for the Year 1967

CONGO 1987

FLOWS in millions of CFA Francs of Y 1967

PURCHASERS CURRENT PRICES

INDUSTRY:	19 Ownership of Dwellings	20 Trade	21 Total Intermdt Demand	22 Public Consumption	23 Government G.Fix.Capit.Con	24 Private G.Fix.Capit.Con
* TOTAL TRANSACTIONS *						
INDUSTRY:						
1 Trad.Agric.Livestock.Fishng	0.0	0.0	896.4	79.7	0.0	0.0
2 Industrialized Agriculture	0.0	0.0	769.4	0.0	0.0	0.0
3 Forestry	0.0	0.0	681.2	0.0	0.0	0.0
4 Mining & Quarrying	0.0	0.0	18.7	323.2	0.0	0.0
5 Energy Water & Petrol. Prod.	25.0	350.2	2341.1	18.7	0.0	0.0
6 Food Industry exc. Beverages	.0	.0	244.1	134.6	0.0	0.0
7 Beverages and Tobacco	0.0	0.0	39.5	50.5	0.0	0.0
8 Footwr. Text. &Wrg. Apparl	33.0	138.0	106.3	175.8	0.0	0.0
9 Wood	0.0	140.0	635.3	107.3	0.0	0.0
10 Rubber.Paper.Chemical Indust	30.0	85.2	1826.5	460.5	0.0	4557.1
11 Mineral & Non-Mineral Prods.	0.0	0.0	1028.0	90.5	288.0	3108.6
12 Metal Products.Electrical M.	0.0	260.5	3210.2	382.4	120.1	0.0
13 Transport Equipment & Repair	0.0	144.6	1660.0	338.5	0.0	0.0
14 Various Manufactures	177.6	269.6	653.7	289.8	1254.3	7021.7
15 Construction (Bldgs. Roads)	0.0	0.0	1253.3	337.9	0.0	0.0
16 Banking. Insur.. Real Estate	0.0	253.7	1042.2	18.5	0.0	0.0
17 Transport	12.0	1259.3	5524.7	432.5	156.7	1233.4
18 Other Services	0.0	598.3	2143.1	232.5	0.0	0.0
19 Ownership of Dwellings	0.0	100.7	479.0	43.0	0.0	0.0
20 Trade	0.0	0.0	0.0	0.0	0.0	0.0
21 Total Intermediate Inputs	277.6	3807.9	24362.6	3525.7	1819.1	15920.8
22 Wage Income - Afric. Hsehlds	27.0	1322.4	7851.9	0.0	0.0	0.0
23 Duty Charges - (African) Hsehlds	.0	174.8	1858.5	0.0	0.0	0.0
24 Wage Income - (Expat.) Hsehlds	13.0	1159.8	4374.8	0.0	0.0	0.0
25 Duty Charges (Expatriates)	.0	144.2	968.3	0.0	0.0	0.0
26 Indirect Taxes & Custom Duty	15.0	924.4	4171.4	0.0	0.0	0.0
27 Depreciation	2840.0	411.4	8474.4	0.0	0.0	0.0
28 Operating Surplus	94.4	3320.0	14240.1	0.0	0.0	0.0
29 Gross Value Added	2797.4	7456.8	41935.2	0.0	0.0	0.0
30 Total Inputs	3075.0	11264.7	66297.8	3525.7	1819.1	15920.8

Input-Output Table of Congo for the Year 1967

CONGO 1967   FLOWS in millions of CFA Francs of Y 1967   PURCHASERS CURRENT PRICES

	Private Traded Consumption 25	Private Own-Consumption 26	Exports 27	Change in Stock 28	Trade Margins on Imports 29	Trade Margins on Domest.Prod. 30
* TOTAL INDUSTRY TRANSACTIONS *						
1 Trad.Agric.,Livestock,Fishng	3451.3	2785.0	975.6	0.0	-280.0	-1250.0
2 Industrialized Agriculture	64.4	130.0	492.2	0.0	-48.0	-170.0
3 Forestry	0.0	0.0	4322.5	0.0	0.0	-856.5
4 Mining & Quarrying	0.0	0.0	4335.9	100.3	-857.0	0.0
5 Energy,Water & Petrol. Prod.	1301.6	0.0	159.2	120.0	-1005.0	0.0
6 Food Industry exc. Beverages	4171.7	140.0	4369.5	180.0	-558.0	-180.0
7 Beverages and Tobacco	4308.6	0.0	1410.8	0.0	-450.0	-659.0
8 Footwr.,Text. &Wrg. Apparl	5765.6	0.0	1479.4	0.0	-1700.0	-70.0
9 Wood	143.4	0.0	1163.2	60.0	-70.0	-50.0
10 Rubber,Paper,Chemical Indust	1523.0	0.0	1351.2	-20.0	-245.0	-60.0
11 Mineral & Non-Mineral Prods.		0.0	156.9	102.8	-240.0	0.0
12 Metal Products,Electrical M.	558.4	0.0	652.3	-48.0	-1300.0	0.0
13 Transport Equipment & Repair	739.1	0.0	388.3	-65.0	-689.2	0.0
14 Various Manufactures	332.5	0.0	94.4		-275.0	-18.0
15 Construction (Bldgs. Roads)		0.0	30.5			
16 Banking,Insur.,Real Estate	91.0	0.0	158.4			
17 Transport	756.3	0.0	484.7			
18 Other Services	742.3	0.0	42.7			
19 Ownership of Dwellings	466.0	2060.0	26.0			
20 Trade					7951.2	3313.5
21 Total Intermediate Inputs	24415.1	5115.0	24052.8	639.1	0.0	0.0
22 Wage Income - Afric. Hsehlds	0.0	0.0	0.0	0.0	0.0	0.0
23 Duty Charges - (African)	0.0	0.0	0.0	0.0	0.0	0.0
24 Wage Income - (Expat. Hsehlds	0.0	0.0	0.0	0.0	0.0	0.0
25 Duty Charges (Expatriates)	0.0	0.0	0.0	0.0	0.0	0.0
26 Indirect Taxes & Custom Duty	0.0	0.0	0.0	0.0	0.0	0.0
27 Depreciation	0.0	0.0	0.0	0.0	0.0	0.0
28 Operating Surplus	0.0	0.0	0.0	0.0	0.0	0.0
29 Gross Value Added	0.0	0.0	0.0	0.0	0.0	0.0
30 Total Inputs	24415.1	5115.0	24052.8	639.1	0.0	0.0

Input-Output Table of Congo for the Year 1967

CONGO 1967   FLOWS in millions of CFA Francs of Y 1967   PURCHASERS CURRENT PRICES

		31 Duties & Taxes on Imports	32 Imports (c.i.f.)	33 Total Output
*	TOTAL TRANSACTIONS *			
	INDUSTRY			
1	Trad.Agric.Livestock.Fishng	-125.0	-1078.0	5455.0
2	Industrialized Agriculture	-8.2	-207.1	1022.2
3	Forestry	-0.0	-0.05	4147.2
4	Mining & Quarrying	-0.2	-2988.8	546.1
5	Energy,Water & Petrol. Prod.		-1816.8	1404.1
6	Food Industry exc.Beverages	-353.7	-1174.0	6915.7
7	Beverages and Tobacco	-1194.7	-598.5	2988.6
8	Footwr.,Text.,&Wrg. Appar.	-1270.6	-277.5	508.7
9	Wood	-8.0	-88.9	1823.5
10	Rubber,Paper,Chemical Indust	-602.3	-247.0	626.0
11	Mineral & Non-Mineral Prods.	-155.4	-833.2	148.5
12	Metal Products,Electrical M.	-1013.0	-8313.0	886.5
13	Transport Equipment & Repair	-690.1	-389.0	1312.8
14	Various Manufactures	-150.1	-570.3	357.7
15	Construction (Bldgs. Roads)	0.0	0.0	9897.7
16	Banking,Insur.,Real Estate	0.0	0.0	1310.5
17	Transport	0.0	0.0	11256.5
18	Other Services	0.0	-300.0	1350.7
19	Ownership of Dwellings	0.0	0.0	3075.0
20	Trade	0.0	-320.0	11264.7
21	Total Intermediate Inputs	-5571.9	-27980.5	66297.8
22	Wage Income - Afric. Hsehlds	0.0	0.0	7851.9
23	Duty Charges (African)	0.0	0.0	1856.5
24	Wage Income - Expat.Hsehlds	0.0	0.0	4374.8
25	Duty Charges (Expatriates)	5571.8	0.0	966.3
26	Indirect Taxes & Custom Duty	0.0	0.0	9743.4
27	Depreciation	0.0	0.0	8474.4
28	Operating Surplus	0.0	0.0	14240.1
29	Gross Value Added	5571.9	0.0	47507.1
30	Total Inputs	0.0	-27980.5	113804.9

GHANA

Reference year: 1968

Entries in table: Total flows

Source: Central Bureau of Statistics of Ghana

Computerized: Not available

Currency units: Cedis of Y 1968
Scale factor: 1,000,000

Pricing system: Producers' current prices
Intermediate sectors: 38 × 37
Treatment of trade margins: Inputs, row 30

Treatment of imports: Column 45, after final demand
Availability of import matrix: Not available

Total number of rows: 41
Statistical unit of quadrant 1: Industry

Total number of columns: 46
Statistical unit of quadrant 1: Industry

Fourth quadrant: Not occupied

Input-Output Table of Ghana for the Year 1968

GHANA 1968   FLOWS in millions of Cedis of Y 1968   PRODUCERS CURRENT MARKET PRICES

INDUSTRY:	1 Agriculture	2 Cocoa Beans	3 Forestry	4 Fishing	5 Mining and Quarrying	6 Food Processing
* TOTAL TRANSACTIONS * INDUSTRY						
1 Agriculture	44	0	0	0	0	84
2 Cocoa Beans	0	0	0	0	0	0
3 Forestry	0	0	0	0	0	75
4 Fishing	0	0	0	0	0	15
5 Mining & Quarrying	0	0	0	0	0	0
6 Food Processing	70	0	0	2	0	0
7 Cocoa Products	0	0	0	0	0	0
8 Beverages	0	0	0	0	0	0
9 Tobacco Products	0	0	0	0	0	0
10 Textiles	0	0	0	24	0	0
11 Leather & Footwear	0	0	0	0	15	0
12 Clothing	1	2	0	1	12	2
13 Timber & Furniture	2	2	0	0	3	0
14 Paper & Printing	3	0	7	3	0	0
15 Chemicals	0	0	0	0	0	3
16 Mineral Oil Refining	0	0	0	7	0	0
17 Cement	0	0	0	0	0	0
18 Blocks, Tiles etc.	0	0	10	0	50	0
19 Glass Products	4	29	0	3	0	0
20 Packing Mat., Jute, Plastic	1	12	0	0	0	0
21 Iron & Steel	0	0	0	0	4	0
22 Aluminium Smelting	0	0	0	0	0	0
23 Non-Ferr. Metal Products	0	0	0	0	0	3
24 Electrical Engineering	0	0	0	2	1	0
25 Boat Building & Repair	0	0	0	0	0	0
26 Motor Vehicles	1	4	0	9	3	20
27 Other Manufacturing	2	0	0	5	25	0
28 Electricity	0	5	0	0	0	0
29 Construction	0	13	8	0	0	0
30 Distributive Trade	54	56	0	0	2	0
31 Hotels & Eating Places	8	2	0	0	0	0
32 Transport	0	4	0	0	0	0
33 Communications	0	3	0	0	100	0
34 Banking & Insurance	0	0	0	0	0	0
35 Real Estate	0	0	0	0	0	0
36 Miscellaneous Services	0	0	0	0	0	0
37 Government Services	0	0	0	0	0	0
38 Sales by Final Buyers	0	0	0	0	0	0
39 Total Goods & Services	250	140	25	78	138	211
40 Gross Value Added	4440	1770	635	184	422	126
41 Total Inputs	4690	1910	660	262	560	337

Input-Output Table of Ghana for the Year 1968

GHANA 1968   FLOWS in millions of Cedis of Y 1968   PRODUCERS CURRENT MARKET PRICES

INDUSTRY:	7 Cocoa Products	8 Beverages	9 Tobacco Products	10 Textiles	11 Leather & Footwear	12 Clothing
* TOTAL TRANSACTIONS *						
INDUSTRY						
1 Agriculture	0	32	6	13	0	0
2 Cocoa Beans	246	0	0	0	0	0
3 Forestry	0	0	0	0	0	0
4 Fishing	0	0	0	0	0	0
5 Mining & Quarrying	0	0	0	-1	0	0
6 Food Processing	0	23	0	0	0	0
7 Cocoa Products	0	0	0	0	0	0
8 Beverages	0	16	0	0	0	0
9 Tobacco Products	0	0	18	0	0	0
10 Textiles	0	0	0	106	0	76
11 Leather & Footwear	0	0	0	0	17	0
12 Clothing	0	0	10	0	0	0
13 Timber & Furniture	0	4	0	0	0	0
14 Paper & Printing	0	3	3	0	0	0
15 Chemicals	2	2	0	28	3	3
16 Mineral Oil Refining	0	0	0	2	0	0
17 Cement	0	13	0	0	0	0
18 Blocks, Tiles etc.	0	0	0	0	0	0
19 Glass Products	0	0	0	0	0	0
20 Packing Mat., Jute, Plastic	2	0	0	0	-1	-1
21 Iron & Steel	0	0	0	18	0	0
22 Aluminium Smelting	0	0	0	0	0	0
23 Non-Ferr. Metal Products	0	0	0	0	0	2
24 Electrical Engineering	0	0	0	0	0	0
25 Boat Building & Repair	0	0	0	0	0	0
26 Motor Vehicles	0	0	0	0	0	0
27 Other Manufacturing	0	0	0	0	0	2
28 Electricity	2	0	0	3	0	-1
29 Construction	0	0	0	0	0	0
30 Distributive Trade	0	27	3	23	3	26
31 Hotels & Eating Places	0	0	0	0	0	0
32 Transport	0	8	0	3	0	2
33 Communications	0	0	0	0	0	0
34 Banking & Insurance	0	0	0	0	0	0
35 Real Estate	0	5	0	4	1	4
36 Miscellaneous Services	0	8	0	0	0	0
37 Government Services	0	0	3	0	0	0
38 Sales by Final Buyers	0	0	0	0	0	0
39 Total Goods & Services	258	141	43	199	24	113
40 Gross Value Added	39.	222.	214.	220.	24.	132.
41 Total Inputs	295.	383.	257.	419.	48.	245.

Input-Output Table of Ghana for the Year 1968

GHANA 1968   FLOWS in millions of Cedis of Y 1968

PRODUCERS CURRENT MARKET PRICES

INDUSTRY:

* TOTAL TRANSACTIONS *

INDUSTRY	13 Timber & Furniture	14 Paper and Printing	15 Chemicals	16 Mineral Oil Refining	17 Cement	18 Blocks Tiles etc.
1 Agriculture	0	0	0	0	0	0
2 Cocoa Beans	0	0	0	0	0	0
3 Forestry	79	0	0	0	0	8
4 Fishing	0	0	0	0	0	0
5 Mining & Quarrying	0	0	0	136	27	0
6 Food Processing	0	0	0	0	0	0
7 Cocoa Products	0	0	0	0	0	0
8 Beverage Products	0	0	0	0	0	0
9 Tobacco Products	0	0	0	0	0	0
10 Leather & Footwear	3	0	0	0	0	0
11 Clothing	0	0	1	0	0	0
12 Timber & Furniture	2	0	2	0	5	0
13 Paper & Printing	1	55	9	0	0	0
14 Chemicals	5	6	3	2	2	6
15 Mineral Oil Refining	0	0	3	0	0	0
16 Cement	0	0	0	0	3	0
17 Blocks, Tiles etc.	0	0	0	0	0	0
18 Glass Products	0	0	0	0	0	0
19 Packing Mat. Jute, Plastic	8	0	0	0	0	0
20 Iron & Steel	0	2	0	2	0	0
21 Aluminium Smelting	0	0	0	0	0	0
22 Non-Ferr. Metal Products	0	0	0	0	0	0
23 Electrical Engineering	4	0	0	0	0	0
24 Boat Building & Repair	6	0	0	0	0	0
25 Motor Vehicles	2	2	2	0	2	0
26 Other Manufacturing	3	0	0	1	1	3
27 Electricity	8	1	2	1	0	0
28 Construction	6	2	0	0	6	4
29 Distributive Trade	8	0	2	3	2	0
30 Hotels & Eating Places	0	0	0	0	0	0
31 Transport	0	4	0	1	1	0
32 Communications	0	0	0	0	0	0
33 Banking & Insurance	0	0	0	0	0	0
34 Real Estate	0	0	0	0	0	0
35 Miscellaneous Services	0	0	0	0	0	0
36 Government Services	0	0	0	0	0	0
38 Sales by Final Buyers	0	0	0	0	0	0
39 Total Goods & Services	193	86	140	149	47	21
40 Gross Value Added	208	123	87	256	16	8
41 Total Inputs	401	209	227	405	63	29

93

Input-Output Table of Ghana for the Year 1968

GHANA 1968 FLOWS in millions of Cedis of Y 1968 PRODUCERS CURRENT MARKET PRICES

INDUSTRY:	19 Glass Products	20 Packng Mat. of Jute & Plastic	21 Iron & Steel	22 Aluminium Smelting	23 Non-Ferr. Metal Products	24 Electrical Engineering
* TOTAL TRANSACTIONS *						
1 Agriculture	0	13	0	0	0	0
2 Cocoa Beans	0	0	0	0	0	0
3 Forestry	0	0	0	0	0	0
4 Fishing	0	0	0	0	0	0
5 Mining & Quarrying	0	0	3	0	0	0
6 Food Processing	0	0	0	0	0	0
7 Cocoa Products	0	0	0	0	0	0
8 Beverages	0	0	0	0	0	0
9 Tobacco Products	0	0	0	0	0	0
10 Textiles	0	0	0	0	0	0
11 Leather & Footwear	0	0	0	0	0	0
12 Clothing	0	0	0	0	0	0
13 Timber & Furniture	0	0	0	0	0	0
14 Paper & Printing	0	0	0	0	0	0
15 Chemicals	0	0	2	0	0	0
16 Mineral Oil Refining	2	2	1	186	1	0
17 Cement	0	0	2	54	7	0
18 Blocks, Tiles etc.	0	0	0	0	0	0
19 Glass Products	0	0	0	0	0	0
20 Packing Mat. Jute, Plastic	0	0	0	0	0	0
21 Iron & Steel	0	0	25	1	17	19
22 Aluminium Smelting	0	0	2	0	0	0
23 Non-Ferr. Metal Products	0	0	0	0	0	0
24 Electrical Engineering	0	0	0	0	0	0
25 Boat Building & Repair	0	0	0	0	0	0
26 Motor Vehicles	3	0	2	50	0	2
27 Other Manufacturing	0	0	2	0	0	0
28 Electricity	0	1	1	2	0	0
29 Construction	0	0	0	0	0	0
30 Distributive Trade	0	0	5	0	0	0
31 Hotels & Eating Places	0	0	0	0	0	0
32 Transport	0	0	2	3	0	0
33 Communications	0	0	0	0	0	0
34 Banking & Insurance	0	1	2	0	0	1
35 Real Estate	0	0	0	0	0	0
36 Miscellaneous Services	0	0	2	2	2	0
37 Government Services	0	0	0	0	0	0
38 Sales by Final Buyers	0	0	0	0	0	0
39 Total Goods & Services	9	18	51	308	20	25
40 Gross Value Added	5	22	46	247	14	8
41 Total Inputs	14	40	97	555	34	33

94

Input-Output Table of Ghana for the Year 1968

GHANA 1968   FLOWS in millions of Cedis of Y 1968   PRODUCERS CURRENT MARKET PRICES

INDUSTRY:	25 Boat Building & Repair	26 Motor Vehicles	27 Other Manufacturing	28 Electricity	29 Construction	30 Distributive Trade
* TOTAL TRANSACTIONS *						
1 Agriculture	0	0	0	0	0	48
2 Cocoa Beans	0	0	0	0	23	0
3 Forestry	0	0	0	0	0	0
4 Fishing	0	0	0	0	17	-0
5 Mining & Quarrying	0	0	0	0	0	0
6 Food Processing	0	0	0	0	0	0
7 Cocoa Products	0	0	0	0	0	0
8 Beverages	0	0	0	0	0	0
9 Tobacco Products	0	0	0	0	0	0
10 Textiles	0	0	0	0	0	5
11 Leather & Footwear	0	0	0	0	116	0
12 Clothing & Footwear	-0	0	0	-1	3	12
13 Timber & Furniture	-0	0	0	0	25	0
14 Paper & Printing	0	0	0	0	3	8
15 Chemicals	0	-1	3	5	8	0
16 Mineral Oil Refining	0	0	0	5	70	100
17 Cement	0	0	0	0	51	0
18 Blocks, Tiles etc.	0	0	0	0	-1	0
19 Glass Products	0	0	0	0	0	0
20 Packing Mat., Jute, Plastic	0	0	2	0	99	0
21 Iron & Steel	2	0	5	0	32	0
22 Aluminium Smelting	0	0	0	7	0	7
23 Non-Ferr. Metal Products	0	0	0	3	0	6
24 Electrical Engineering	0	0	9	0	0	13
25 Boat Building & Repair	0	35	3	0	0	-0
26 Motor Vehicles	-1	0	8	4	86	2
27 Other Manufacturing	-1	0	0	0	68	406
28 Electricity	0	0	0	0	0	8
29 Construction	0	0	0	2	0	56
30 Distributive Trade	0	0	0	2	0	54
31 Hotels & Eating Places	0	0	0	0	0	29
32 Transport	0	0	0	0	0	0
33 Communications	0	0	0	0	0	3
34 Banking & Insurance	0	0	0	0	0	
35 Real Estate						
36 Miscellaneous Services						
37 Government Services						
38 Sales by Final Buyers						
39 Total Goods & Services	6	44	30	24	600	687
40 Gross Value Added	6	128	64	168	729	2281
41 Total Inputs	12	172	94	192	1329	2968

95

Input-Output Table of Ghana for the Year 1968

GHANA 1968   FLOWS in millions of Cedis of Y 1968   PRODUCERS CURRENT MARKET PRICES

INDUSTRY:	31 Hotels & Eating Places	32 Transport	33 Communications	34 Banking & Insurance	35 Real Estate	36 Miscellaneous Services
* TOTAL TRANSACTIONS * INDUSTRY						
1 Agriculture	102	0	0	0	0	0
2 Cocoa Beans	4	0	0	0	0	0
3 Forestry	0	0	0	0	0	0
4 Fishing	54	0	0	0	0	0
5 Mining & Quarrying	57	4	0	0	0	0
6 Food Processing	18	8	2	0	0	2
7 Cocoa Products	0	0	0	0	0	0
8 Beverages	0	0	0	0	0	0
9 Tobacco Products	0	0	0	0	0	0
10 Textiles	0	0	0	0	0	0
11 Leather & Footwear	0	0	0	0	0	0
12 Clothing	1	7	0	0	0	0
13 Timber & Furniture	0	8	0	0	0	0
14 Paper & Printing	0	7	0	0	0	6
15 Chemicals	0		3	2	0	14
16 Mineral Oil Refining	0	200	0	0	0	
17 Cement	0	0	2	1	0	4
18 Blocks, Tiles etc.	0	0	0	0	0	0
19 Glass Products	0	0	0	2	0	0
20 Packing Mat.; Jute, Plastic	0	0	0	0	0	0
21 Iron & Steel	0	29	1	0	0	1
22 Aluminium Smelting	0	0	0	0	0	0
23 Non-Ferr. Metal Products	0	2	0	0	0	0
24 Electrical Engineering	0	0	7	0	0	0
25 Boat Building & Repair	0	9	0	0	0	4
26 Motor Vehicles	0	1	2	0	0	0
27 Other Manufacturing	1	0	0	0	0	0
28 Electricity	3	5	2	2	0	2
29 Construction	2	1	0	0	93	4
30 Distributive Trade	64	106	0	1	0	0
31 Hotels & Eating Places	0	22	0	0	0	0
32 Transport	15	126	1	4	0	0
33 Communications	0	64	2	166	0	2
34 Bank, Eg. & Insurance	0	15	0	100	0	4
35 Real Estate	2	5	0	9	0	0
36 Miscellaneous Services	0	5	0	1	0	0
37 Government Services						
38 Sales by Final Buyers						
39 Total Goods & Services	323	704	32	219	93	38
40 Gross Value Added	96	623	44	243	1025	181
41 Total Inputs	419	1327	76	462	1118	219

Input-Output Table of Ghana for the Year 1968

GHANA 1968   FLOWS in millions of Cedis of Y 1968   PRODUCERS CURRENT MARKET PRICES

* TOTAL TRANSACTIONS *

INDUSTRY:	37 Government Services	38 Total Intermed. Output	39 Consumer Expenditures	40 Government Expenditures	41 Gross Fixed Capital Form	42 Stocks
1 Agriculture	0	342	4416	53	0	-32
2 Cocoa Beans	0	246	0	0	0	-192
3 Forestry	0	108	388	0	0	0
4 Fishing	0	129	225	0	0	-54
5 Mining & Quarrying	0	199	20	17	0	-34
6 Food Processing	0	180	490	0	0	-38
7 Cocoa Products	0	0	0	10	0	-1
8 Beverages	0	32	334	0	0	-1
9 Tobacco Products	0	0	240	9	0	94
10 Textiles	0	206	453	8	0	25
11 Leather & Footwear	0	20	30	0	0	23
12 Clothing	0	0	225	10	0	-4
13 Timber & Furniture	0	165	99	0	20	-18
14 Paper & Printing	0	139	89	83	0	45
15 Mineral Oil Refining	0	473	171	76	0	-42
16 Chemicals	0	339	32	88	0	0
17 Cement	0	0	0	0	0	200
18 Blocks, Tiles etc.	0	59	15	0	0	0
19 Glass Products	0	53	0	0	0	0
20 Packing Mat., Jute, Plastic	0	57	0	21	0	-4
21 Iron & Steel	0	339	0	0	326	0
22 Aluminium Smelting	0	51	25	0	0	0
23 Non-Ferr. Metal Products	0	35	20	0	150	35
24 Electrical Engineering	0	1	0	3	13	0
25 Boat Building & Repair	0	155	101	1	162	-0
26 Motor Vehicles	0	49	60	1	0	0
27 Other Manufacturing	0	0	46	30	0	-3
28 Electricity	0	132	0	103	0	1
29 Construction	0	551	0	176	1081	0
30 Distributive Trade	0	525	2241	11	0	0
31 Hotels & Eating Places	0	746	383	44	0	0
32 Transport	0	18	624	15	0	0
33 Communications	0	311	43	4	0	0
34 Banking & Insurance	0	78	130	47	0	0
35 Real Estate	0	112	993	74	0	0
36 Miscellaneous Services	0	0	183	2004	0	0
37 Government Services	0	14	0	-67	0	0
38 Sales by Final Buyers	0		53			
39 Total Goods & Services	0	5485	12130	2853	1752	49
40 Gross Value Added	2004	17060	0	0	0	0
41 Total Inputs	2004	22545	0	0	0	0

Input-Output Table of Ghana for the Year 1968

GHANA 1968   FLOWS in millions of Cedis of Y 1968

		43 Exports	44 Total Final Demand	45 Imports	46 Total Output
	* TOTAL TRANSACTIONS *				
	INDUSTRY				
1	Agriculture	39	4540	-192	4690
2	Cocoa Beans	1856	1664	0	1910
3	Forestry	164	552	0	660
4	Fishing	0	171	-38	282
5	Mining & Quarrying	553	539	-178	560
6	Food Processing	2	557	-400	337
7	Cocoa Products	290	285	0	295
8	Beverages	0	343	-1	363
9	Tobacco Products	0	257	0	257
10	Textiles	0	557	-344	419
11	Leather & Footwear	0	258	-27	48
12	Clothing	0	246	-18	245
13	Timber & Furniture	128	298	0	401
14	Paper & Printing	0	299	-120	209
15	Chemicals	7	139	-491	227
16	Mineral Oil Refining	17		-93	405
17	Cement	0		-16	63
18	Blocks, Tiles etc.	0	2	0	29
19	Glass Products	0	15	-20	40
20	Packing Mat., Jute, Plastic	0		-17	97
21	Iron & Steel	3	346	-588	40
22	Aluminium Smelting	555	555	0	555
23	Non-Ferr. Metal Products	0	526	-43	31
24	Electrical Engineering	0	205	-207	34
25	Boat Building & Repair	0	-13	0	3
26	Motor Vehicles	0	293	-276	172
27	Other Manufacturing	40	121	-76	94
28	Electricity	0	76	0	192
29	Construction	0	1197	0	1329
30	Distributive Trade	0	2417	0	2968
31	Hotels & Eating Places	0	394	0	419
32	Transport	204	872	-29	1327
33	Communications	0	58	0	76
34	Banking & Insurance	17	151	0	462
35	Real Estate	0	1040	0	1118
36	Miscellaneous Services	71	328	0	1219
37	Government Services	0	2004	-221	2004
38	Sales by Final Buyers	0	-14	0	0
39	Total Goods & Services	3981	20745	-3685	22545
40	Gross Value Added	0	0	0	0
41	Total Inputs	0	0	0	0

IVORY COAST

Reference year: 1976

Entries in table: Total flows, absorption matrix

Source: Côte d'Ivoire, Ministère de l'économie, des finances et du Plan, Direction de la statistique, *Comptes de la nations, 1976*

Computerized: Not available

Currency units: CFA francs of Y 1976
Scale factor: 1,000,000

Pricing system: Producers' current market prices
Intermediate sectors: 31 × 33
Treatment of trade margins: Trade margins are treated as resource below row of gross output (row 44-row 49)

Treatment of imports: Imports c.i.f. row 41, duties and taxes on imports row 42
Availability of import matrix: Not available

Total number of rows: 50
Statistical unit of quadrant 1: Commodity

Total number of columns: 44
Statistical unit of quadrant 1: Industry

Fourth quadrant: Not occupied

Input-Output Table of Ivory Coast for the Year 1976

IVORY COAST 1976   FLOWS in millions of CFA francs of Y 1976   PRODUCERS CURRENT MARKET PRICES

INDUSTRY:

#	* COMMODITY *	Agric. Prodn. & Livestock 1	Agric. Products for Ind. & Export 2	Forestry & Forest Prodn 3	Fishing 4	Ore & Mineral Mining 5	Grain & Flour Manufacturing 6
	* TOTAL TRANSACTIONS *						
1	Agric. Products & Livestock	14357	160	0	0	0	16402
2	Agric. Prods - Export & Ind.	0	0	0	0	0	0
3	Forestry Products	0	0	0	0	0	110
4	Fishing Products	0	0	0	239	0	0
5	Mining	0	3425	0	0	0	0
6	Grain & Flour Products	81	0	0	0	0	8949
7	Food Products, Prep. & Pres.	0	0	0	800	0	0
8	Beverages & Ice Cream	87	0	0	0	0	0
9	Edible Oils & Fats	720	0	0	40	0	455
10	Food Prods n.e.c. & Tobacco	0	2	0	542	0	458
11	Textiles	100	948	3787	46	800	32
12	Leather Products & Footwear	0	8770	1567	0	171	276
13	Wood Products	717	191	0	0	232	1150
14	Petroleum Products	0	23	0	380	0	128
15	Chemicals	50	0	4242	150	612	28
16	Rubber	0	1117	5828	0	332	0
17	Non-Metallic Minerals	0	1037	566	100	-1	339
18	Basic Metals	700	623	848	0	34	814
19	Transport Machinery	40	108	1424	224	68	364
20	Elec. & Mech. Prods. n.e.c.	0	154	14178	0	601	574
21	Other Manufacturing	200	382	330	58	-1	32
22	Electricity, Gas & Water	300	103	382	525	0	863
23	Construction & Public Works	0	626	3582	0	0	221
24	Transport & Communications	63	249	130	60	0	1112
25	Construction Services, Admin.	0	990	0	0	0	204
26	Other Services	0	0	0	0	0	36
27	Banking Services	0	0	0	0	0	0
28	Insurance	0	0	0	0	0	0
29	Public Administration Srvc.	0	0	0	0	0	0
30	Private Administration Srvc.	0	0	0	0	0	0
31	Household Services	0	0	0	0	0	0
32	Total Intermediate Input	17240	17518	35053	2670	2879	30115
33	Gross Salaries & Wages	1110	17912	12774	1671	985	3198
34	Employer's Social Contrib.		587	848	163	140	281
35	Nominal Emplyr's Soc. Contr.				224		
36	Taxes Linked to Production	2500	-432	14618		630	
37	Subsidies	-185	-2950				-483
38	Gross Operating Surplus	12580	93201	12604	5909		-8924
39	Gross Added Value	126818	109182	40844	7967	1673	9124
40	Gross Output	144058	126700	75897	10637	4552	34287
41	Imports C.i.f on Imports	17829	1800	126	357	38743	1104
42	Duties & Taxes on Imports	223	904	44	12	128	316
43	Change in Stocks	1806	1806	0		98	4388
44	Trade Margin Interm. Inputs	1213	155	491	2777	229	986
45	Trade Margin Hsehld. Consm.	27094	1305	0	0	0	2301
46	Trade Margin Gr.Fxd. CDD.Fo	0	0	0	0	0	-2028
47	Trade Margin Gr.Fxt.CDD.Fo	0	0	0	0	0	0
48	Trade Margin Stocks	151541	151541	0	0	0	0
49	Total Trade Margin	28307	153375	491	2777	229	1259
50	Total Resources	193007	284585	76560	13783	43750	41364

Input-Output Table of Ivory Coast for the Year 1976

IVORY COAST 1978

FLOWS in millions of CFA francs of Y 1978

PRODUCERS CURRENT MARKET PRICES

INDUSTRY:

#	TOTAL COMMODITY TRANSACTIONS	7 Food Preserving & Preparation	8 Beverages & Ice Cream Manuf.	9 Man. of Edible Oils & Fats	10 Food Prods nec & Tobacco Ind	11 Textile & Wrg Apparel Indus.	12 Leather &Footwr Manufacturing
1	Agric. Products & Livestock	13113	53	0	142	0	0
2	Agric. Prods.- Export &Ind.	22020	115	7075	4632	5280	0
3	Forestry Products	581	0	0	0	0	0
4	Fishing	5592	0	0	17	0	0
5	Mining	0	19	97	0	0	188
6	Grain & Flour Products	3420	28	0	0	0	0
7	Food Products, Prep.& Pres.		89	0	0	0	0
8	Beverages & Ice Cream	131	1048	0	0	0	0
9	Edible Oils & Fats	1389	0	3287	0	0	0
10	Food Prods n.e.c.& Tobacco	332	960	206	515	0	0
11	Textiles		0	0	4	14108	118
12	Leather Products & Footwear			0		33	270
13	Wood Products	494	27	241	336	853	1
14	Petroleum Products	269	259	517	296	2948	713
15	Chemicals	440	428	46	38	48	539
16	Rubber	8	65	430	0	17	512
17	Non-Metallic Minerals	8	620	0	0	0	
18	Basic Metals						4
19	Transport Machinery	128	186	587	188	127	77
20	Elec.& Mech. Prods. n.e.c.	3587	482	1414	466	1714	78
21	Other Manufacturing	2400	336	493	1398	521	146
22	Electricity, Gas & Water	511	26	205	90	157	83
23	Construction & Public Works	83	177	250	282	77	8
24	Transport & Communications	713	28	178	472	893	68
25	Construction Services.Admin.	76		134	475	65	74
26	Other Services	1425	306	1591	269	1980	124
27	Banking Services	92	300	90	280	172	8
28	Insurance	38	9	47		175	5
29	Public Administration Srvc	0	0	0	0	0	0
30	Private Administration srvc	0	0	0	0	0	0
31	Household Services	0	0	0	0	0	0
32	Total Intermediate Input	58528	5482	16868	9242	30591	2433
33	Gross Salaries & Wages	2494	1604	3650	1120	7337	644
34	Employer's Social Contrib.	225	237	330	178	902	64
35	Nominal Emplyr's Soc. Contr.						
36	Taxes Linked to Production	1714	1550	-1121	4425	1911	228
37	Subsidies			-2665	2031	-18	629
38	Gross Operating Surplus	5800	2825	-3441	7854	11779	1585
39	Gross Added Value	10233	6216	5877	16896	21911	3998
40	Gross Output	68761	11698	22745		52502	
41	Imports, C.i.f.on Imports	12896	8190	761	13277	19074	3480
42	Duties & Taxes on Imports	3050	7399	118	3674	9399	1686
43	Change in Stocks			2	5	-28	64
44	Trade Margin: Interm. Inputs	598	238	92	1197	3950	19
45	Trade Margin: Hsehld. Consm.	9829	1205	1813	9186	15178	3574
46	Trade Margin: Gr.Fxd.Cap.Fo	97		168	0	1219	0
47	Trade Margin: Exports	8	8		0	0	0
48	Trade Margin: Stocks						
49	Total Trade Margin	10322	12297	2073	10363	20345	3583
50	Total Resources	93134	37584	25699	44235	101292	12831

Input-Output Table of Ivory Coast for the Year 1976

IVORY COAST 1976 FLOWS in millions of CFA francs of Y 1976

PRODUCERS CURRENT MARKET PRICES

INDUSTRY:

	TOTAL COMMODITY TRANSACTIONS	13 Wood Manufacturing	14 Petroleum Refining	15 Chemical Manufacturing	16 Rubber	17 Non-Metallic Minerals	18 Basic Metal Industry
1	Agric. Products & Livestock	0	0	231	0	0	0
2	Agric. Prods. Export & Ind.	0	0	86	2826	0	0
3	Forestry Products	8140	0	0	0	0	0
4	Fishing	0	0	124	0	0	0
5	Mining	0	37440	0	0	284	0
6	Grain & Flour Products	0	0	0	0	0	0
7	Food Products.Prep.& Pres.	0	0	0	0	0	0
8	Beverages & Ice Cream	0	0	0	0	0	0
9	Edible Oils & Fats	0	0	2336	54	0	0
10	Food Prods n.e.c. & Tobacco	0	0	5	0	0	0
11	Textiles	57	0	10	0	0	0
12	Leather Products & Footwear	0	0	0	0	0	0
13	Wood Products	4908	0	72	0	0	0
14	Petroleum Products	1758	1883	369	87	195	27
15	Chemicals	1162	1324	1236	103	6	2
16	Rubber	1126	22	3	17	0	0
17	Non-Metallic Minerals	0	1	455	0	5462	0
18	Basic Metals	321	0	146	54	359	1278
19	Transport Machinery	1449	37	1073	246	354	5
20	Elec.& Mech. Prods. n.e.c.	221	1108	587	66	916	21
21	Other Manufacturing	248	59	585	113	556	25
22	Electricity,Gas & Water	478	79	299	48	62	28
23	Construction & Public Works	564	28	67	0	0	0
24	Transport & Communications	69	157	1333	105	385	52
25	Construction Services.Admin.	787	610	99	0	3	0
26	Other Services	104	48	38	2	0	48
27	Banking Services	56	10	0	0	0	0
28	Insurance Services	0	0	0	0	0	0
29	Public Administration Srvc.	0	0	0	0	0	0
30	Private Administration Srvc	0	0	0	0	0	0
31	Household Services	0	0	0	0	0	0
32	Total Intermediate Input	21442	42809	20331	3705	8897	1491
33	Gross Salaries & Wages	5207	716	2888	328	854	143
34	Employer's Social Contrib.	5510	52	337	34	80	10
35	Nominal Emplyr's Soc.Contr.	52					
36	Taxes Linked to Production	1695	15742	1572	187	1007	355
37	Subsidies	0	0	-765	-67	0	0
38	Gross Operating Surplus	4839	1155	4347	462	1135	377
39	Gross Added Value	12251	17665	8177	4167	3076	886
40	Gross Output	33693	60474	28508	8497	11773	2377
42	Imports & C.i.f on Imports	1306	7827	32842	4311	10295	20138
43	Duties & Taxes on Imports	471	1477	9783	201	2855	3127
43	Change in Stocks	0	454	845		192	0
44	Trade Margin: Interm. Inputs	366	12808	5022	2554	2924	3405
45	Trade Margin: Hsehld. Consm.	203	5163	10342	870	448	1556
46	Trade Margin: Er.Fxd.Cap.Fo.	0	0	0	0	0	0
47	Trade Margin: Exports	0	0	0	0	0	0
48	Trade Margin: Stocks	0	0	0	0	0	0
49	Total Trade Margin	569	17769	15364	3424	3372	4961
50	Total Resources	36039	88069	87342	18600	28487	30603

Input-Output Table of Ivory Coast for the Year 1978

IVORY COAST 1976 | FLOWS in millions of CFA francs of Y 1976 | PRODUCERS CURRENT MARKET PRICES

INDUSTRY:

COMMODITY	19 Constrn &Repair of Transport M.	20 Elec. & Mechan. Prods., n.e.c.	21 Other Manufacturing	22 Electricity,Gas Water Producn.	23 Construction & Public Works	24 Transport & Communications
* TOTAL TRANSACTIONS *						
1 Agric. Products & Livestock	0	0	0	0	0	0
2 Agric. Prods.- Export &Ind.	0	0	0	0	0	0
3 Forestry Products	0	0	0	0	0	0
4 Fishing	0	0	0	0	0	0
5 Mining	0	0	0	0	4620	0
6 Grain & Flour Products	0	0	0	0	0	0
7 Food Products, Prep. & Pres.	0	0	0	0	0	0
8 Beverages & Ice Cream	0	0	0	0	0	0
9 Edible Oils & Fats	0	0	0	0	0	0
10 Food Prods n.e.c. & Tobacco	0	0	2	0	26	52
11 Textiles	3	70	21	0		7
12 Leather Products & Footwear	0	0	0	0	0	0
13 Wood Products	127	68	38	38	10555	
14 Petroleum Products	347	272	92	92	5604	22481
15 Chemicals	621	1138	1150	1150	7310	162
16 Rubber	329	9	5	5	996	6228
17 Non-Metallic Minerals	291	9877	617	617	16771	35
18 Basic Metals	651	146	330	218	7350	50
19 Transport Machinery	18787	2447	3818	1706	2578	15563
20 Elec. & Mech. Prods. n.e.c.	694	272	149	430	1238	2433
21 Other Manufacturing	208	248	36	389	1693	1081
22 Electricity, Gas & Water	457	494	146	157	16047	1664
23 Construction & Public Works	461	134	125	492	436	530
24 Transport & Communications	401	1360	731	1061	9576	17274
25 Other Services.Admin.	1709	56	6	250	15	436
26 Banking Services	97	24	0	240	0	9230
27 Insurance Services	30	0	0	0	0	253
28 Private Administration Srvc.	0	0	0	0	0	848
29 Public Administration Srvc.	0	0	0	0	0	0
30 Household Services	0	0	0	0	0	0
32 Total Intermediate Input	25116	16679	7334	10990	112068	79732
33 Gross Salaries & Wages	6853	3502	1885	4882	39122	45713
34 Employer's Social Contrib	818	365	173	800	2079	2395
35 Nominal Employr's Social Contr.						
36 Taxes Linked to Production	1908	1931	552	3160	10595	8208
37 Subsidies				-7		-1768
38 Gross Operating Surplus	5873	4209	2908	5835	21675	31413
39 Gross Added Value	15254	10007	5451	14453	73806	85957
40 Gross Output	40370	26686	12785	25443	185674	165689
41 Imports, c.i.f.	50864	74808	14717	882	1113	19734
42 Duties & Taxes on Imports	17789	16892	3195			
43 Change in Stocks	112	55	1883			
44 Trade Margin: Interm. Inputs	12554	12599	3981	0	0	0
45 Trade Margin: Hsehld. Consm.	2162	7451	1764	0	0	0
46 Trade Margin: Gr.Fxd.Cap.Fo.	6516	8360	0	0	0	0
47 Trade Margin: Exports	0	0	293	0	0	0
48 Trade Margin: Stocks	0	0	0	0	0	0
49 Total Trade Margin	21232	28410	8018	0	0	0
50 Total Resources	130047	148849	38598	28325	186787	185423

Input-Output Table of Ivory Coast for the Year 1978

IVORY COAST 1978   FLOWS in millions of CFA francs of Y 1978   PRODUCERS CURRENT MARKET PRICES

INDUSTRY:

	25 Construction Svcs. Admin.	26 Other Services	27 Trade	28 Banking Services	29 Prodn. Attrib. to Banking Svc	30 Insurance
* TOTAL TRANSACTIONS * COMMODITY						
1 Agric. Products & Livestock	0	0	0	0	0	0
2 Agric. Prods. - Export & Ind.	0	0	0	0	0	0
3 Forestry Products	0	0	0	0	0	0
4 Fishing	0	0	0	0	0	0
5 Mining	0	0	0	0	0	0
6 Grain & Flour Products	0	0	3045	0	0	0
7 Food Products, Prep. & Pres.	0	0	0	0	0	0
8 Beverages & Ice Cream	0	0	0	0	0	0
9 Edible Oils & Fats	0	0	0	9	0	0
10 Food Prods n.e.c. & Tobacco	127	127	142	19	0	2
11 Textiles	600				0	5
12 Leather Products & Footwear	557				0	8
13 Wood Products	549	510	1397	38	0	0
14 Petroleum Products		993			0	0
15 Chemicals	105	41	212	30	0	0
16 Rubber		34	108		0	0
17 Non-Metallic Minerals	79	510	1585	95	0	22
18 Basic Metals	28	868	2824	1118	0	27
19 Transport Machinery n.e.c.	182	1664	3473	288	0	161
20 Elec. & Mech. Prods. n.e.c.	1416	1894	3523	600	0	67
21 Other Manufacturing	629	1090		402	0	18
22 Electricity, Gas & Water	2214				0	93
23 Construction & Public Works					0	0
24 Transport & Communications	2567	8370	35095	1450	0	240
25 Construction Services. Admin.					0	0
26 Other Services	578		17959		0	2758
27 Banking Services		90	1635	45	16226	854
28 Insurance Administration Srvc.			300		0	0
29 Public Administration Srvc.	0	0	0	0	0	0
30 Household Services	0	0	0	0	0	0
32 Total Intermediate Input	10848	18570	82945	4260	16226	4056
33 Gross Salaries & Wages	2500	15122	53120	7088	0	588
34 Employer's Social Contrib.	130	1274	22282	800	0	559
35 Nominal Emplyr's Soc. Contir.			30141		0	
36 Taxes Linked to Production	2317	5748	108902	6156	0	183
37 Subsidies	-887	-751			0	
38 Gross Operating Surplus	30674	6499	69180	4504	-16226	-2163
39 Gross Added Value	34754	27892	283625	18346	-16226	-1353
40 Gross Output	45600	46462	346570	22606	0	2703
41 Imports, c.i.f.	2343	44240	0	0	0	854
42 Duties & Taxes on Imports			0	0	0	
43 Change in Stocks	0	0	0	0	0	0
44 Trade Margin: Interm. Inputs	0	0	-64668	0	0	0
45 Trade Margin: Hsehld. Consm.	0	0	-113800	0	0	0
46 Trade Margin: Gr.Fxd.Cap.Fo.	0	0	-11478	0	0	0
47 Trade Margin: Exports	0	0	-151290	0	0	0
48 Trade Margin: Stocks	0	0	-1930	0	0	0
49 Total Trade Margin	0	0	-348570	0	0	0
50 Total Resources	47943	90702	0	22606	0	3357

Input-Output Table of Ivory Coast for the Year 1976

IVORY COAST 1976   FLOWS in millions of CFA francs of Y 1976   PRODUCERS CURRENT MARKET PRICES

INDUSTRY:	31 Public Administ Services	32 Private Admin. Services	33 Household Services	34 Total Intermed. Consumption	35 Public Services	36 Private Services
* TOTAL TRANSACTIONS * COMMODITY						
1 Agric. Products & Livestock	0	0	0	44298	0	0
2 Agric. Prods. Export &Ind.	0	0	0	4807	0	0
3 Forestry Products	0	0	0	9907	0	0
4 Fishing Products	0	0	0	9609	0	0
5 Mining	0	0	0	4504	0	0
6 Grain & Flour Products	728	0	0	10041	0	0
7 Food Products. Prep. & Pres.	667	10	0	4433	0	0
8 Beverages & Ice Cream	610	8	0	1903	0	0
9 Edible Oils & Fats	508	7	0	658	0	0
10 Food Prods n.e.c. & Tobacco	2341	0	0	458	0	0
11 Textiles	136	30	0	2167	0	0
12 Leather Products & Footwear	0	0	0	1411	0	0
13 Wood Products	1951	26	0	1911	0	0
14 Petroleum Products	4023	68	0	54177	0	0
15 Chemicals	2074	28	0	45315	0	0
16 Rubber	588	0	0	11568	0	0
17 Non-Metallic Minerals	403	0	0	24915	0	0
18 Basic Metals	0	0	0	20247	0	0
19 Transport Machinery	8192	90	0	57063	0	0
20 Elec. & Mech. Prods. n.e.c.	7364	85	0	62210	0	0
21 Other Manufacturing	9752	108	0	31629	0	0
22 Electricity, Gas & Water	4333	58	0	20339	0	0
23 Construction & Public Works	6222	63	0	31039	0	0
24 Transport & Communications	11698	109	0	92568	0	0
25 Construction Services, Admin.	10874	138	0	275513	0	0
26 Other Services	8296	54	0	77872	0	0
27 Banking Services	0	0	0	21011	0	0
28 Insurance	106	0	0	3254	0	0
29 Public Administration Srvc.	0	0	0	0	177217	0
30 Private Administration Srvc.	0	0	0	0	0	3039
31 Household Services	0	0	0	0	0	0
32 Total Intermediate Input	78861	900	0	793678	177217	3039
33 Gross Salaries & Wages	90190	3982	4205	342949	0	0
34 Employer's Social Contrib.	1998	197	195	18014	0	0
35 Nominal Emplyr's Soc. Contr.	3578	0	0	13578	0	0
36 Taxes Linked to Production	2592	0	0	121360	0	0
37 Subsidies	0	0	0	89806	0	0
38 Gross Operating Surplus	0	0	0	449612	0	0
39 Gross Added Value	98355	4159	4400	1025319	0	0
40 Gross Output	177217	5059	4400	1818997	0	0
41 Imports, C.i.f.	0	0	0	403807	0	0
42 Duties & Taxes on Imports	0	0	0	88638	0	0
43 Change in Stocks	0	0	0	12567	0	0
44 Trade Margin: Interm. Inputs	0	0	0	0	0	0
45 Trade Margin: Hsehld. Consm.	0	0	0	0	0	0
46 Trade Margin: Gr.Fxd.Cap.Fo.	0	0	0	0	0	0
47 Trade Margin: Exports	0	0	0	0	0	0
48 Trade Margin: Stocks	0	0	0	0	0	0
49 Total Trade Margin	0	0	0	0	0	0
50 Total Resources	177217	5059	4400	2324009	0	0

Input-Output Table of Ivory Coast for the Year 1976

IVORY COAST 1976   FLOWS in millions of CFA francs of Y 1976   PRODUCERS CURRENT MARKET PRICES

COMMODITY TOTAL TRANSACTIONS	37 Subsistence Hsehld. Cons.	38 Commercial Hsehld. Cons.	39 Total Final Consumption	40 Total Fixed Capital Formtn.	41 Change in Stocks	42 Exports, f.o.b.
1 Agric. Products & Livestock	96582	50373	146955	0	1259	495
2 Agric. Prods.- Export &Ind.	1976	3187	5163	0	539	236975
3 Forestry Products	2579	882	3281	0	101	63281
4 Fishing Products	3399	4868	8067	0	35	72
5 Mining	0	0	0	0	593	593
6 Grain & Flour Products	0	28484	28484	0	521	2378
7 Food Products, Prep.& Pres.	0	49190	49190	0	738	38773
8 Beverages & Ice Cream	0	35202	35202	0	193	228
9 Edible Oils & Fats	0	9381	9381	0	468	9334
10 Food Prods n.e.c. & Tobacco	0	37720	37720	0	1057	900
11 Textiles	2110	63421	65531	0	288	14288
12 Leather Products & Footwear	0	11744	11744	0		676
13 Wood Products	0	1679	1679	0	159	15245
14 Petroleum Products	0	15072	15072	0	1719	18593
15 Chemicals	0	34978	34978	0	127	5330
16 Rubber	0	3787	3787	0	61	3120
17 Non-Metallic Minerals	0	1902	1902	0		1264
18 Basic Metals	0	0	0	0	9092	1609
19 Transport Machinery	0	0	0	44078	130	3820
20 Elec. & Mech. Prods. n.e.c.	0	23758	23758	48387	3669	5820
21 Other Manufacturing	0	28543	28543	0	10	2381
22 Electricity, Gas & Water	0	4570	4570	0		421
23 Construction & Public Works	0	5565	5565	154718		532
24 Transport & Communications	0	5500	5500	0		35864
25 Transport & Communications.Admin	0	57193	57193	0		1120
26 Other Services	0	19310	19310	0		207
27 Banking Services	0	10759	10759	0		
28 Insurance	0	1595	1595	0		
29 Public Administration Srvc.	0	103	103	0		
30 Private Administration Srvc.	0	0	0	0		
31 Household Services	0	2020	2020	0		
	0	4400	4400	0		
32 Total Intermediate Input	106646	509784	816430	247181	21485	484979
33 Gross Salaries & Wages	0	0	0	0	0	0
34 Employers Social Contrib.	0	0	0	0	0	0
35 Nominal Emply'rs Soc.Contr.	0	0	0	0	0	0
36 Taxes Linked to Production	0	0	0	0	0	0
37 Subsidies	0	0	0	0	0	0
38 Gross Operating Surplus	0	0	0	0	0	0
39 Gross Added Value	0	0	0	0	0	0
40 Gross Output	0	0	0	0	0	0
41 Imports C.i.f.	0	0	0	0	0	0
42 Duties & Taxes on Imports	0	0	0	0	0	0
43 Change in Stocks	0	0	0	0	0	0
45 Trade Margin: Interm. Inputs	0	0	0	0	0	0
46 Trade Margin: Hsehld Consm.	0	0	0	0	0	0
47 Trade Margin: Gr.Fxd.Cap.Fo	0	0	0	0	0	0
48 Trade Margin: Stocks	0	0	0	0	0	0
49 Total Trade Margin	0	0	0	0	0	0
50 Total Resources	0	0	0	0	0	0

IVORY COAST 1976   FLOWS in millions of CFA francs of Y 1976   PRODUCERS CURRENT MARKET PRICES

		43 Total Final Demand	44 Total Resources
	* TOTAL TRANSACTIONS *		
1	Agric. Products & Livestock	148709	193007
2	Agric. Prods Export &Ind.	242277	284585
3	Forestry Products	66643	76560
4	Fishing	8184	43783
5	Mining		43750
6	Grain& Flour Products	30885	91364
7	Food Products Prep. & Pres.	86521	93734
8	Beverages & Ice Cream	35821	37584
9	Edible Oils & Fats	19981	25584
10	Food Prods n.e.c. & Tobacco	39677	44299
11	Textiles	80105	101292
12	Leather Products & Footwear	12420	12631
13	Wood Products	18924	36039
14	Petroleum Products	33024	88005
15	Chemicals	42027	87342
16	Rubber	7034	18600
17	Non-Metallic Minerals	3572	28487
18	Basic Metals	10358	30603
19	Transport Machinery	72984	130047
20	Elec.& Mech. Prods. n.e.c.	86439	148649
21	Other Manufacturing	5988	38598
22	Electricity, Gas & Water	5966	26325
23	Construction & Public Works	155748	168787
24	Transport & Communications	92857	185423
25	Construction Services, Admin.	20430	47943
26	Other Services	12830	90702
27	Banking Services	1595	22606
28	Insurance	103	3357
29	Public Administration Srvc.	177217	177217
30	Private Administration Srvc.	5059	5059
31	Household Services	4400	4400
32	Total Intermediate Input	1530331	2324009
33	Gross Salaries & Wages	0	0
34	Employer's Social Contrib.	0	0
35	Nominal Emplyr's Soc. Contr.	0	0
36	Taxes Linked to Production	0	0
37	Subsidies	0	0
38	Gross Operating Surplus	0	0
39	Gross Added Value	0	0
40	Gross Output	0	0
41	Imports, C.i.f.	0	0
42	Duties & Taxes on Imports	0	0
43	Change in Stocks	0	0
44	Trade Margin: Interm. Inputs	0	0
45	Trade Margin: Hsehld. Consm.	0	0
46	Trade Margin: Gr.Fxd.Cap.Fo.	0	0
47	Trade Margin: Exports	0	0
48	Trade Margin: Stocks	0	0
49	Total Trade Margin	0	0
50	Total Resources	0	0

KENYA

The present report is based on *Input-Output Tables for Kenya, 1976,* published by the Central Bureau of Statistics of the Ministry of Economic Planning and Community Affairs in October 1979, and on *Sources and Methods Used for the National Accounts of Kenya,* published by the Central Bureau of Statistics of the Ministry of Finance and Planning in December 1977.

A. General information

1.   Input-output tables for Kenya have been compiled approximately every five years since 1967 by the Central Bureau of Statistics of Kenya, with technical assistance provided by the Chr. Michelsen Institute of Bergen, Norway. The latest table available refers to 1976. A similar basic methodology has been followed in the compilation of the 1967, 1971 and 1976 tables. In fact, the 1976 table has been obtained by updating the 1971 table according to a special variant of the RAS method developed by the Chr. Michelsen Institute. The only difference between the 1971 and 1976 tables refers to the number of intermediate sectors which in the 1976 table has been increased from 30 to 37. The new sectors are formed by disaggregating government services into 5 sectors and by setting up petroleum products, water supply and communications as separate sectors. The non-monetary sectors of previous tables have been replaced by a separate traditional sector which excludes all agricultural activities, and includes non-monetary output of forestry, fishing, building and construction and ownership of dwellings. All output of this traditional sector is assumed to be produced and consumed by the same units.

2.   Consistency checks were made between the figures used in the input-output tables and the corresponding aggregates in the national accounts. For some sectors recent revisions effected in the national accounts were incorporated in the input-output tables. However, national accounts figures published in the 1979 Economic Survey included other revisions carried out after the aggregates for the input-output tables had been finalized so that minor differences still remain between the aggregates of the two sources. These differences affect mainly private final consumption which was estimated as a residual in the input-output tables. Further, imports in the input-output tables are net of re-exports, whereas those published in the national accounts include the value of goods imported but subsequently re-exported.

3.   The main discrepancies between the Kenya input-output table and SNA recommendations on input-output include the following: inclusion of two dummy sectors (para. 11); treatment of the activities of private non-profit institutions (para. 11); treatment of the public sector health and education services (para. 11); disaggregation of final demand in tables (ii) and (iii) (para. 13); breakdown of value added (para. 14); treatment of imports (para. 15); treatment of by-products and scrap (para. 16); and no separate information on commodity taxes (para. 8).

B. Analytical framework

Tables and derived matrices available

4. The following basic tables were compiled:

    (i) Input-output table of total flows valued at producers' prices;

    (ii) Input-output table for domestic flows valued at producers' prices;

    (iii) Import matrix;

    (iv) End-use analysis of imports. This table is a more condensed version of the final demand quadrant of table (iii) and identifies separately, within the same classification, the distribution of import duties with respect to end uses.

5. On the basis of the data mentioned in para. 4, the following derived matrices were compiled:

    (i′) Technical coefficients, based on table (i);

    (ii′) Technical coefficients, based on table (ii);

    (iii′) Technical coefficients, based on table (iii);

    (iv′) Inverse matrix based on table (i′);

    (v′) Inverse matrix based on table (ii′);

    (vi′) Inverse matrix based on table (iii′).

6. It should be noted that different assumptions underlie the inverse matrix (iv′) and the inverse matrices (v′) and (vi′). In matrix (iv′) products are assumed to be identical regarding their use as intermediate products, no matter whether they are domestically produced or imported. In this case, imports represent a mere expansion of the existing domestic production of a particular commodity, i.e., the assumption is made that it is always possible to expand production without any adverse effects on the balance of payments. However, the adverse effects on the balance of payments are made explicit in the case of inverse matrices based on table (v′) and (vi′). For those tables unit increases in final demand for domestic products are assumed to be met in fixed proportions from increased domestic production (matrix v′) and from increased imports (matrix vi′).

7. All basic tables and derived matrices are presented at a level of disaggregation of 37×37 intermediate sectors.

Valuation standards

8. All basic tables are valued at producers' prices. Producers' prices are defined to exclude distribution margins which are treated as payments for services rendered by the distribution sectors. Imports are valued c.i.f. plus import duties. Exports are valued at ex-factory prices, which are obtained by deducting estimated distribution margins from their f.o.b. prices. Contrary to SNA recommendations, commodity taxes are not recorded separately.

Statistical units and classification standards

9.   The establishment is the statistical unit adopted for all columns of tables (i), (ii) and (iii), and commodities are the statistical units adopted for the rows of all tables mentioned in para. 4.

10.   The overall classification of input-output sectors adopted generally follows the ISIC, except for minor variations.

11.   The classification of the intermediate consumption quadrant differs from SNA recommendations in the following respects:

  (a)   Two dummy sectors are included in the table, namely ownership of business premises and unspecified. Output of the unspecified sector includes commodity flows for which there is little reliable data, as well as the imputed service charges of financial institutions (see para. 19);

  (b)   No distinction is made between activities of the industries and activities of private non-profit institutions;

  (c)   Health and education services provided by the Government are distributed together with the same kind of services provided by private industries.

12.   Intermediate and primary inputs of the dummy sectors are incorporated into the structure of production of the remaining sectors of the table and therefore all entries in the columns of these sectors are 0. It should also be noted that since total output of the non-dummy sectors includes gross earnings from rental and unspecified activities, while deliveries from these sectors excludes deliveries from the dummy sectors, a discrepancy should appear in the total of rows and columns of all sectors of the table except for the dummy sectors. However, this discrepancy is not shown in the table because private consumption of each input-output sector has been estimated as a residual. The resulting over-estimation of total private consumption is compensated by recording negative entries in the private consumption of the dummy sectors.

13.   Final demand is disaggregated according to SNA recommendations in table (i). However, in tables (ii) and (iii), private consumption is combined with the changes in stocks to form a single column.

14.   The breakdown of value added adopted differs from that recommended in SNA in that operating surplus is disaggregated into profits and interest paid. Other categories of value added are defined as in SNA.

15.   Imports are classified by commodity and distributed together with domestic production in table (i). In addition, imports are cross-classified by origin and destination in table (iii) (see para. 4). In table (iii), imports are defined net of re-exports, and therefore no exports column is recorded in this table. Contrary to SNA recommendations, no distinction is made between complementary and competitive imports.

Treatment and presentation of selected transactions

16.   Efforts were made to reallocate secondary activities of the establishments to their corresponding characteristic sectors, but only in those cases in which

110

establishments engaged 50 or more employees in these activities. By-products, that is, secondary products technologically linked to the production of characteristic products, and scrap generated in the production process were not transferred to their characteristic sectors.

17.   Non-monetary output and its corresponding inputs are generally recorded together with monetary output and inputs in the corresponding input-output sectors except in the case of forestry, fishing, building and construction, and ownership of dwellings. For the latter sectors, non-monetary output is included in a separate sector called traditional sector, as mentioned in para. 1.

18.   Output is generally defined on a gross basis, i.e., it includes intra-sector consumption of characteristic and non-characteristic goods and services.

19.   Output of the financial sector is defined and distributed as recommended in the SNA. The corresponding dummy sector showing the value of imputed service charges is incorporated into the unspecified sector (see para. 11).

20.   Output of the government services sectors includes the activities of the central Government and of firms with 50 per cent or more of the capital owned by the Government. These activities are recorded in the intermediate consumption quadrant. Activities of the East African Community Corporation and of firms which are 50 per cent or less owned by the Government are recorded together with similar activities carried out by private enterprises. This procedure is in agreement with SNA recommendations. The value of output and corresponding inputs of the East African Commodity Corporation has been allocated amongst the partner states in proportion to the value of output obtained in each partner state.

Statistical sources and compilation methodology

21.   The 1976 input-output table was obtained by updating the 1971 table according to a special variant of the RAS method. This model has been developed solely to estimate the elements of the intermediate consumption quadrant. All primary inputs and final uses, as well as the row and column totals of intermediate uses, are treated by the program as exogenous variables. Information on statistical sources and compilation methodology of these exogenous variables is given below (paras. 29 through 64). The elements of the intermediate consumption quadrant of the basic year (that is, the corresponding elements of the 1971 input-output table) are also exogenous variables of the programme. However, the decision to expand the number of intermediate sectors in the 1976 input-output table required an extensive re-aggregation exercise of the unpublished 59 sectors of the basic 1971 table.

22.   The basic assumption on which the RAS model relies may be summarized as follows: all variations that have affected the matrix of intermediate uses between the base year and the updating year are on the whole the results of certain uniformity operating price and volume changes and these can be represented by simple price and volume indices. The price effect index is assumed to represent the price increase (or decrease) which has affected the intermediate uses of products originating from each sector. The price effects are assumed to vary between the sectors of origin, but to be uniform within each

sector of origin, in other words all products that a sector delivers to other sectors are subject to one and the same price effect. The volume effect index is assumed to represent the increase (or decrease) in the volume of production of each sector. As in the previous case, the volume effects are assumed to vary between production sectors but to be uniform within each production sector, that is, all intermediate goods and services which the sector uses in its production process are affected by one and the same volume effect.

23. The basic assumption just described implies that, in general, the model assumes the non-existence of substitution between different intermediate production factors. However, the model does not entirely exclude the possibility of introducing substitution effects. Such effects are incorporated into the model by a predefinition mechanism. The application of this mechanism is limited by the access to relevant data, and the modest breakdown of intermediate uses by type of goods. Apart from the agricultural sector, which is fully determined exogenously, only the use by manufacturing sectors of transport services and water are based on direct knowledge of elements. In addition to these direct predefinitions some elements have been adjusted between successive runs of the RAS programme.

24. The values of the volume and price indexes are not known *a priori*, and their estimation, which in practice may prove to be quite difficult, is not carried out by the programme. This, however, is of no importance, since the above-mentioned assumption of individual but uniform price and volume effects provide enough information for the calculation of the one set of values of the elements of the intermediate consumption quadrant which conforms to these assumptions.

25. The Kenyan input-output tables are three dimensional, each element of the intermediate consumption quadrant being split between use of imports and use of domestic products. Row and column totals are, however, calculated according to the modified RAS method for the total dimension only, i.e., for the aggregate of imports and domestic products.

26. The disaggregation of the total supply matrix into two matrices for imports and domestic production is carried out as follows. Deliveries of imports to intermediate and final demand sectors are based mainly on the end-use analysis of imports matrix (table (iv), para. 4) and the domestic elements are calculated as residuals. In cases where no information is available on end-use totals of table (iv), import matrix elements are estimated from the total supply matrix (table (i), para. 4) elements on the assumption that the 1971 import fractions, adjusted for import price effects, still hold.

27. The assumption concerning the relative constancy of import fractions implies that this model assumes no substitution between imports and domestic products. However, the programme does not entirely rule out the possibility of introducing substitution effects, for it would be a rare case indeed if no such changes in production techniques occurred over the years. Such changes, whether they be due to substitution, new production lines, etc., are incorporated into the model by a predefinition mechanism. The predefinition mechanism may also, if the necessary data are available, be used to give special treatment of the largest or most important of the intermediate uses, thereby increasing the quality of the final results.

112

28.   The calculations of both the technical and the full input coefficients are computerized. These calculation routines are incorporated with the main RAS program in a complete updating program package. Hence, all calculations of elements and coefficients may be carried out directly when all the exogenous variables are given.

Gross output, intermediate consumption and value added

Agriculture, forestry and fishing

29.   Total agricultural output includes the following: sales of crops, fruits and vegetables to marketing boards, co-operations and processing factories; home-grown seed; output sold in local markets, home-consumed, fed to livestock or given free to employees; growth in immature permanent crops; and land improvement.

30.   The Annual Survey of Employees and Self-Employed Persons is the source of information on wages and salaries paid by the agricultural sector. Subtraction of wages and salaries from total value added yields the operating surplus, including consumption of fixed capital. Total value added is estimated as the difference between value of output and intermediate consumption.

31.   As mentioned above (para. 1), the traditional sector covers non-monetary output of forestry, fishing, building and construction and ownership of dwellings. This output is estimated as indicated in the next four paragraphs.

32.   Firewood, poles and posts are the products of non-monetary output of forestry. Production of firewood is based on the number of rural households outside pastoral areas, the estimated number of working days per year devoted to collecting firewood—presently assumed to be 42—and the opportunity cost of such labour. The opportunity cost—that is, the wage rate available in alternative employment—is taken as the wage rate for casual female labour on small farms and settlement schemes based on data obtained from the 1971-1972 Census of Small Farms. This wage rate is assumed to rise at the same rate as that on large farms obtained from the annual survey of employees and self-employed persons. Intermediate consumption is nil.

33.   Non-monetary output of fishing consists of fishing undertaken for own consumption. The value of this output, in the absence of any information, is arbitrarily put at 10 per cent of that of monetary output of fishing. Value added is the same as value of output since no inputs are consumed in this production.

34.   Non-monetary output of building and construction consists of "hut" building, i.e., all traditional residential buildings outside the boundaries of municipal and local authority areas. Value of this non-monetary output is taken to be equal to the product of new huts built and building costs. These data are taken from a special study undertaken in 1967. Inputs consist of posts and poles from forestry output and inputs from the manufacturing sector. The former is put at 9 per cent of the value of output and the latter at 10 per cent. These percentages are based on *ad hoc* inquiries. Subtraction of intermediate consumption from the value of total output provides the estimate of value added.

35.   Non-monetary output of ownership of dwellings consists of actual and imputed huts rental. Few, if any, huts in rural areas are in fact rented. An imputed rental for owner-occupied huts has therefore to be derived indirectly. The imputed rental, it is assumed, must be sufficient to account for maintenance costs, consumption of fixed capital, and still yield a normal return on capital, that is, on the current value of the stock of huts. Maintenance costs are assumed to be equal to 25 per cent of the value of new huts constructed. Consumption of fixed capital is estimated as being equal to the aggregate value of all traditional dwellings that are replaced during the year. The interest on capital is estimated at an assumed rate of return based on the rate of interest offered on post office deposit accounts of 4 per cent.

36.   Total output of the forestry sector includes that obtained by the Forestry Department of the Kenyan Public Sector and forestry activities of private firms. A special problem exists with regard to the measurement of the forestry output by the Forestry Department. In countries where planting has been going on regularly for some time the value of output can be satisfactorily measured by the value of trees felled. But in Kenya, where many of the forests—which take 35 years to mature—are newly planted, this does not seem appropriate. If the value of output is measured solely by the value of trees felled, then for a newly planted forest the value of output will be nil for 34 years and a large figure in the thirty-fifth year when the trees are felled. To avoid this, the value of output of forests planted and maintained by the Forestry Department is measured not only by the value of timber—both mature trees and thinnings—felled, but also by the value of the increase in standing timber or work in progress. Included too in the value of output of the Forestry Department are expenditures on new planting and royalties except outlays on new planting of trees during the current year.

37.   The Forestry Department supplies each year information on the distribution of its planted forests by years to maturity. From this information it is possible to make at any given time an estimate of the increase in the number of hectares of planted forests detailed by "vintage". The physical increase, or decrease, so obtained for each vintage in terms of hectares is then valued. A discount factor of 8 per cent is applied to the value of timber on one mature hectare to obtain the then current value of immature timber on a hectare of planted forest for all the vintages to the year of maturity. This enables the value of the physical increase in each vintage to be calculated.

38.   Information on the forestry activities in the planted and natural forests of large farms is similarly lacking. Estimates, however, of the area of planted and of natural forests are available. For planted forests, the area is multiplied by an assumed annual offtake of 14 cubic metres per hectare to obtain an estimate of the value of the annual offtake. The prices obtained from the Forestry Department are used to value this annual offtake. A similar method is used for natural forests. A base year figure on the value of the offtake per hectare was estimated by the Forestry Department. The value of intermediate consumption of large farms for forestry is included with their intermediate consumption for agriculture. Their total intermediate consumption is allocated between agriculture and forestry in proportion to the value of output from these activities.

39.   Output estimates of logging within the forestry reserves are based on licences issued by the Forestry Department to private firms. Information on the

114

number of persons so employed is supplied by the Forestry Department. The total wage bill is derived by multiplying this number by the average wage for casual labour in sawmills obtained from the Annual Survey of Employees and Self-Employed Persons. The ratio of the value of output to the wage bill, and that of intermediate consumption to the wage bill, were calculated from an *ad hoc* inquiry. These ratios are applied to the current wage bill to obtain the required estimates of the value of output and intermediate consumption. A similar method is applied to obtain estimates for logging outside forestry reserves.

40. The Fisheries Department provides estimates on the value and quantities of the commercial catches brought on shore at the various landing points both on inland waters and the sea. The value of other marine products is added to obtain the total value of output. Inputs consist of nets, cork and glass buoys, diesel fuel, and the cost of repair and maintenance of boats. The cost of nets is obtained from import figures and from output figures on local production. These are duly adjusted to purchaser prices by adding import duty and transport and distribution margins. The quantity of diesel fuel used is taken as a fixed percentage of the value of output at constant prices; this figure is then raised in line with the rise in the price of diesel fuel. Maintenance and repair costs are obtained by multiplying the estimated average cost per boat by the number of boats. The average cost per boat is increased annually in line with the landed prices of imported paint.

Mining and quarrying

41. The Annual Survey of Mining and Quarrying is the main source of data for this sector. The survey covers all establishments with 50 or more employees, and a 25 per cent sample of establishments with 20 to 49 employees. Information on the value of output, intermediate consumption and value added is obtained. Comparable information for establishments with 5 to 19 employees was obtained in the 1972 Census of Industry. The output of these small-sized establishments is calculated on the assumption that the rate of growth of their output is the same as that of establishments with 20 to 49 employees. The Annual Survey of Employees and Self-Employed Persons provides information on salaries and wages of establishments with under 20 employees. This information—together with the assumption that the ratios of the other components of value added to labour costs remain as in the census year—enables an estimate of value added to be made. Intermediate consumption for these small-sized establishments is the difference between the value of output and value added.

Manufacturing

42. The manufacturing sector consists of the following three main categories of establishments: urban and large rural private establishments, small rural private establishments, and public establishments. The latter include parastatal bodies undertaking enterprise activities in the manufacturing sector, manufacturing enterprises in which the public sector has a majority holding in their equity capital, enterprise activities of the central Government and local authorities using technological processes similar to those used by the private

115

sector, and the manufacturing activities of the East African Community corporations that occur in Kenya.

43. Data on urban and large rural private establishments are obtained from the 1972 Census of Industry which fully covered all manufacturing establishments with five or more employees in urban areas and all large establishments in rural areas which are included in the Directory of Industries held by the Central Bureau of Statistics. In addition, a 25 per cent sample of urban establishments with less than five employees was also covered in the census. Among other information, details on sales, the value of increase in stocks of manufactured but unsold goods, the changes in stocks of raw materials and work in progress, intermediate consumption, labour costs, the consumption of fixed capital and the number of employees were obtained from each establishment covered in the census. The information obtained from the census is updated through the *Annual Survey of Manufacturing Industry*. This survey covers all establishments employing 50 or more persons and a 25 per cent sample of the establishments employing 20 to 49 persons. The survey collects information similar to that obtained from the census. Hence, for establishments in these size groups, estimates can be made of the value of output, intermediate consumption, and value added and its components. For establishments with less than 20 employees, which were covered in the census but are not covered in the annual survey, it is assumed that the annual percentage increase in the value of their output is the same as that for establishments with 20 to 49 employees. The Annual Survey of Employees and Self-Employed Persons provides the wage bill for such establishments. A further assumption made is that the other components of value added, for establishments with under 20 employees, have the same ratio to their labour costs as in the census year. Intermediate consumption of these establishments is obtained as a residual, that is, as the difference between the estimated value of output and value added.

44. Bench-mark data on small rural private manufacturing except the manufacture of indigenous beers were obtained from the survey of Small Scale Rural Enterprises held in 1972, which included information on sales and the value of inputs. These data were updated with an index of gross domestic output of the traditional economy. Bench-mark estimates of output and production of indigenous beer were based on the results of the Central Province Household Survey undertaken in 1963 which indicated that an average of 10 Kenyan shillings per household per week was spent on traditional alcoholic beverages. Multiplication of this figure by the number of rural households provided an estimate of the value of output. Intermediate consumption was assumed to be equal to 25 per cent of the value of output. The number of persons engaged in making beer was derived from the estimated volume of production and an assumed production of 3,550 litres per person per year. An average price of 90 Kenyan cents per litre was used to calculate the volume of output. Only 20 per cent of the persons engaged in the industry were assumed to be paid employees. The average wage of casual employees in agriculture—obtained from the Annual Survey of Employees and Self-Employed Persons—was used to calculate the labour cost of paid employees. Subtraction of this figure from value added provided an estimate of operating surplus. As with other sectors and activities, the consumption of fixed capital is included in the operating surplus. These various estimates—of the value of output, intermediate consumption and labour costs—are extrapolated annually in line with the index of the estimated gross domestic product of the traditional economy

mentioned above. The estimates for this subsector are of poor quality and may be too low. Household surveys recently undertaken will, it is hoped, give some clues on the extent of this underestimate.

45. The required information for parastatal bodies and for firms with a majority holding of equity capital by the public sector are obtained directly from the enterprises themselves, and that for the Government Printer and the Ministry of Works from the published accounts of the central Government. The Ministry of Works also supplies supplementary information on an annual basis. The sources of information on the East African Community corporations are their annual reports and the data provided by answers to a special national accounts questionnaire which they complete each year.

Construction

46. Data on building and construction of the private sector are taken from the 1972 Census of Industry which covered all establishments of building and construction contractors employing five or more persons and a 25 per cent sample of those employing less than five persons. Detailed information is given in the census about value of output, intermediate consumption, labour costs, and other aggregates related to production. There is always a possibility of duplication in the information on production supplied by the contractors, as contractors sub-contract out work to other contractors. Information on the value of work sub-contracted was specifically obtained by the census to obviate this. In addition, each year the survey of building contractors collects information similar to that collected in the census from all contractors with 50 or more employees, and from a 25 per cent sample of contractors with 20 to 49 employees. Accordingly, for contractors in these size groups, estimates can be made of the value of output, intermediate consumption, value added, and the components of value added. For contractors having less than 20 employees, it is assumed that the percentage change in the value of their output since the census year is the same as that of contractors with 20 to 49 employees. The wage bill of these small contractors is supplied by the Annual Survey of Employees and Self-Employed Persons. The assumption is also made that the other components of their value added remain in the same ratio to their labour costs as in the census year. Intermediate consumption for these small contractors is obtained as the difference between the estimates of the value of output and value added. Also included is the value of residential and non-residential building and other construction work undertaken on large farms as reported in the annual census of large farms. Excluded from the latter is the value of building work undertaken on large farms by contractors to avoid double counting. It was assumed that, of the total building and construction work undertaken on large farms, 14 per cent was contracted out. This figure is based on an *ad hoc* inquiry made with large farms. Expenditure by large farms on maintenance of building and construction works is assumed to be 10 per cent of their annual account expenditure on building and construction. Labour costs are estimated as being equal to 20 per cent of the value of own account construction. This figure is based on the proportion of contractors' labour costs to the value of output for similar construction work. Intermediate consumption of large farms is calculated as the difference between their value of output and labour costs, i.e., the assumption is made that operating surplus is nil.

47.   Data on the public subsector of the building and construction sector are obtained as outlined below. The East African Power and Lighting Company annually provides the information needed on the value of its own account building and construction activities. For the Ministry of Works, the source of information is the accounts of the central Government supplemented by special information from the Ministry of Works itself. The value of output—equal to total expenditures on goods and services and personal emoluments—is obtained from the recurrent and development accounts. The value of output is then broken down by economic activity into the value of manufacturing output, the value of building and construction, and the value of new purchases of machinery and equipment. This is done by allocating all recognizable expenditure to one of these categories and prorating the headquarters expenditure on personal emoluments and other non-specific expenditures in proportion to the value of the expenditures already allocated. From the value of building and construction so derived is deducted the value of building and construction work contracted out in order to obtain the value of output on own account. To this value of output of own account building are added two imputed values, namely, the contribution of the employer to pensions and the value of consumption of fixed capital. The latter is based on the average replacement cost of lorries and road building equipment during the previous three years. Further, an analysis of the relevant expenditures, together with some additional prorations, enables the value of output to be split between expenditures on residential and non-residential building on the one hand, and on roads and other construction works on the other. The estimates of the value of own account building and construction work undertaken by the Forestry Department are made from the information supplied annually by the Department. All local authorities are requested to provide annual information on the value of residential and non-residential buildings and other construction work undertaken and labour costs. Maintenance expenditure is assumed to be equal to 10 per cent of the value of such capital expenditure. The two together give the total value of output of building and construction by local authorities. The value of work contracted out is estimated at 56.8 per cent of the value of output; this is deducted from the total output to obtain the value of output of own account work. This percentage deduction is based on an *ad hoc* inquiry. Intermediate consumption is calculated as the difference between the value of own account output and labour costs. No imputations are made for the consumption of fixed capital.

48.   The value of output so derived obviously needs to tie in with the estimate of capital expenditures on building and construction obtained from the expenditure side. In fact, there always is a discrepancy. The first step in eliminating the discrepancy is to estimate the maintenance component in the value of output of building and construction, since it is impossible for building contractors and others engaged in this activity to subdivide realistically their output into its maintenance and capital formation components. Hence, alternative means are adopted to estimate the maintenance component. The value of maintenance of residential buildings is taken to be equal to the maintenance input into ownership of dwellings (see para. 59). Maintenance expenditure on roads and non-residential buildings owned by the central Government is obtained from its accounts. The only missing estimate then left to be computed is the value of maintenance on private non-residential building which is assumed to be equal to 2 per cent of the estimated replacement cost on

these buildings. The various estimates of maintenance—on residential and non-residential buildings and on other construction works—are then added to obtain the overall estimate of the value of maintenance. This estimate of maintenance is added to the estimate of capital formation in buildings and construction works obtained from the expenditure side. The estimates of capital formation from the expenditure side are adopted since they are believed to be more reliable than those from the production side. The final step is to revise the original estimates of intermediate consumption and value added. These are multiplied by the ratio of the revised value of the output of building and construction to their original value.

Electricity and water supply

49.   All data on the electricity sector—value of output, intermediate consumption, personal emoluments, consumption of fixed capital etc.—are provided by the two enterprises undertaking generation and distribution of electricity in the country.

50.   In the monetary economy, the collection, processing and distribution of water is mainly a public sector activity undertaken by the Ministry of Water Development, the Mombasa Water Supply, the Mombasa Pipeline Board, and by the water departments of various local authorities. A small amount of activity is also undertaken by private enterprises. The relevant information on the operation of the public sector institutions and enterprises engaged in this activity is readily available from their published accounts. The private concerns are covered by the Annual Survey of Employees and Self-Employed Persons, from which information about their total labour costs is obtained. It is assumed that the ratios of the value of output and of intermediate consumption to labour costs prevailing for the water departments of municipal councils are also relevant to these private concerns. For the traditional economy, the value of output is based on the number of rural households outside pastoral areas, the estimated number of woman-hours per household spent a year in drawing water, and the opportunity cost of such labour. The alternative to drawing water is taken to be farm work; and the average wage for casual adult females working on small farms and settlement schemes—the same rate as used for firewood collection—is taken to measure the opportunity cost. Since intermediate consumption is irrelevant, value added equals the value of output. The imputation is only made for rural households living in non-pastoral areas, since in pastoral areas no alternative employment is thought to exist.

Trade, hotels, cafes and restaurants

51.   Data on wholesale and retail trade (other than petrol and oil products) were obtained from the 1971 Survey of Distribution, the National Accounts Questionnaire and the annual Trade Report of the East African Customs and Excise Department. The annual estimates of output and value added are based in the breakdown of expenditure of trade enterprises in four categories of throughputs namely, domestic manufactured goods, domestic agricultural products, imports from Uganda and United Republic of Tanzania and imports from the rest of the world. Estimates are calculated as follows. First, the ratio of each throughput to its total domestic production of import are estimated for the base year. These ratios are then applied to the relevant 1976 totals of flows

of goods to obtain the value of each of these throughputs in that year. Next, these 1976 values are aggregated and the aggregate is adjusted for the value of the change in stocks in 1976 obtained from the quarterly Business Expectations Enquiry. The base year ratio of value added to the value of aggregate throughputs is then applied to the adjusted value of aggregate throughputs for 1976 to provide an estimate of value for that year. This estimate is then subdivided into its components—personal emoluments and operating surplus—using the proportion composition of the base year. Finally, output is estimated using the base year ratio of value added to output. These calculations are all based on the assumption that the base year ratios remain unchanged.

52. Data on wholesale distribution of petroleum and oil products are provided directly by the small number of firms engaged in this activity. For the firms engaged in retail distribution of petrol and oil products, base year figures on the value of their output, intermediate consumption, value added, and the components of value added were obtained in the 1971 Survey of Distribution. The base year estimate of value added is extrapolated forward on the basis of the value of petroleum and oil products entering the Kenya market in 1976. This is estimated as the sum of the total value of imports of final products, plus domestic production, less the value of transfers to Uganda and to the United Republic of Tanzania, plus import duties and sales tax on the value of products entering the Kenya market. Value added is subdivided into its components on the assumption that the composition of value added remains proportionally the same as in the base year. Similarly, output is estimated on the assumption that the ratio of the value of output to value added remains the same as in the base year.

53. The 1975 Survey of Services provided the bench-mark information on cafes and restaurants in urban areas and also for the larger cafes and restaurants in rural areas. The data was analysed separately for hotels, restaurants and cafes with 50 or more employees, 20 to 49 employees, and 0 to 19 employees; and the value of output, intermediate consumption, value added and the wage bill were determined for each size class. The Annual Survey of Employees and Self-Employed Persons provides figures on the wage bill in 1976. Again, 1975 base year ratios—of the wage bill to value added and of value added to the value of output—for each size class are applied to the 1976 wage bill to estimate the relevant aggregate for that year.

Transport, storage and communication

54. Data on railway, ocean and coastal water, inland water, and air transport are obtained directly from the public and private enterprises engaged in these activities. Data on urban, suburban and interurban highway passenger transport are mainly obtained from an annual survey of firms with 20 or more employees operating taxis, minibuses and passenger carrying utility vans. For each type of vehicle, figures are obtained on the value of output, intermediate consumption and labour costs. Ratios of the value of output and intermediate consumption to labour costs are then calculated and these are applied to the estimated labour costs of unsurveyed firms in each category. Labour cost estimates are derived from the number of such vehicles registered, the number of operators per vehicle, and an average wage rate supplied by the Annual Survey of Employees and Self-Employed Persons. The numbers of operators

120

per taxi, minibus and lorry are put at 1.04, 1.10 and 1.40 respectively. These averages are based on information collected in a bench-mark inquiry a few years earlier. The sum of the value of the surveyed and unsurveyed firms, and similarly of their intermediate consumption, provides the needed estimates for the activity. Value added is derived as the difference between the value of output and intermediate consumption. Beforehand, however, 25 per cent of the labour costs of the unsurveyed enterprises is deducted from the total labour costs of all enterprises to take account of the number of operators thought to be self-employed. It is this adjusted labour cost that is deducted from value added to obtain the operating surplus. An almost identical method is applied to obtain the estimates of output and value added of private enterprises engaged in freight transport by road.

55. Data on supporting services to water and air transport provided by local offices of foreign enterprises are obtained through an annual questionnaire. Ratios of the value of output and intermediate consumption to their labour costs are calculated from it. These ratios are then applied to the estimated labour costs of the unsurveyed offices, which are obtained from the Annual Survey of Employees and Self-Employed Persons. The local offices of foreign shipping lines are treated as agents of their foreign principals. Accordingly, value added consists of wages and salaries only. Consumption of fixed capital is assumed to be insignificant in value.

56. All private booking and travel agencies with 20 or more employees are covered in an annual survey which provides information on their operations. The usual ratios of the value of output and intermediate consumption to labour costs are calculated and then applied to the labour costs of the unsurveyed firms obtained from the Annual Survey of Employees and Self-Employed Persons.

57. The required information on storage and warehousing enterprises with 20 or more employees in this activity is obtained directly. The estimates on the operations of the smaller enterprises are derived by applying the usual ratios, calculated from the information supplied by the large enterprises, to their labour costs obtained through the Annual Survey of Employees and Self-Employed Persons. Data on the communication sector are provided by the East African Posts and Telecommunications Corporation, by far the largest contributor to the value of this activity.

Services

58. Data on financial institutions, insurance, real estate and business services are obtained from the following sources: special questionnaire circulated by the central bank among commercial banks, Annual Survey of Employees and Self-Employed Persons, income tax statistics, annual survey of insurance companies, and the 1975 Survey of Services, the results of which are extrapolated forward in line with the ratio of the 1976 labour bill to that of 1975.

59. The ownership of dwellings sector is subdivided into two subsectors —monetary and traditional—to facilitate the computation of output, intermediate consumption and value added. Output of the monetary sector is provided by the results of an annual rent survey. Rental values of owner-occupied dwellings are considered to be equal to the average rent paid on

equivalent rented properties in the same locality. Intermediate consumption of this monetary sector covers maintenance expenditures which are put at 10 per cent of aggregate rental for privately owned dwellings and 5 per cent for those owned by the central Government, municipalities and the East African Community. Non-monetary output for owner-occupied huts was described in para. 35.

60. Data on the social and personal services sector are obtained from the 1975 Survey of Services which provides information on salaries and wages, employment, intermediate consumption and capital expenditures. These data are updated to 1976 by multiplying, on a service-by-service basis, the 1975 estimates by the ratio of the 1976 wage bill to that in 1975. Information on the 1976 wage bill is provided by the Annual Survey of Employees and Self-Employed Persons. Data on services in the rural sector was based on the 1972 Survey of Small-scale Rural Enterprises, which are updated to 1976 on the assumption that their rate of growth is two thirds that of the corresponding activities in urban areas.

61. Government services cover general administration, education, health and defence. General administration includes the National Social Security Fund as well as the Government Agricultural Service, while education and health also embraces the private enterprises engaged in these fields. The main sources of information are the accounts of the central Government, local authorities, the East African Community (General Fund Services) and the relevant Statutory Boards.

62. The value of output of government services is mainly for the use of the Government itself, and to that extent is included in general government consumption. Some part, however, is used by industry as intermediate consumption or is purchased by households and therefore included as private consumption. Households, for example, make purchases of education and health services.

Final demand

63. Gross fixed capital formation is classified by sector of origin. The end-use analysis of imports provides estimates of imports of capital goods. The locally produced element of capital formation is estimated from details of production of various commodities. The value of land improvement, plantation development and increase in cattle herds is included, while the increase in forest reserves is treated as an addition to stocks.

64. The total value of private consumption is derived as the residual when all other end-use categories and intermediate deliveries have been calculated. Sector specific information has been made available for the changes in stocks through special studies. However, it has not been possible to undertake satisfactory breakdowns of these figures into imported and domestically

produced goods mainly because of the possibility that changes of opposite signs in these two categories may occur in the same sector. Therefore, in the import and domestic production tables changes in stocks are recorded together with private consumption. In the table on the total supply of goods and services joint estimates of sector-specific private consumption and intermediate use are derived residually after the other components of end-uses have been completed. The allocation of the output of each sector to each one of these two categories has been made possible by combining all relevant information from published and unpublished sources. For a few sectors, however, the allocation was based on the nature of its products.

65.   The Annual Trade Report and the balance of payment estimates are the sources of information for exports and imports. Exports are reduced from f.o.b. values to ex-factory prices by deducting estimated distribution margins, which are obtained on the basis of survey results.

Kenya

Reference year: 1976

Entries in table: Total flows, import matrix

Source: Ministry of Economic Planning and Community Affairs, Central Bureau of Statistics, *Input-Output Tables for Kenya, 1976* (Nairobi, 1979)

Computerized: Wirtschaftsuniversität, Vienna

Currency units: Kenya pounds of Y 1976
Scale factor: 100,000

Pricing system: Producers' current prices
Intermediate sectors: 37 × 37
Treatment of trade margins: Intermediate inputs, row 24

Treatment of imports: Separate import matrix
Availability of import matrix: Available

Total number of rows: 88
Statistical unit of quadrant 1: Industry

Total number of columns: 45

Statistical unit of quadrant 1: Industry

Fourth quadrant: Not occupied

Input-Output Table of Kenya for the Year 1976 (Revised)

KENYA 1976

FLOWS In hundred thousand Kenya pounds of Y 1976

PRODUCERS CURRENT PRICES

INDUSTRY:	1 Traditional Economy	2 Agriculture	3 Fishing & Forestry	4 Mining & Quarrying	5 Food Preparation	6 Food Bakery Products Sweets
* TOTAL TRANSACTIONS *						
1 Traditional Economy	86.00	0.00	0.00	0.00	0.00	0.31
2 Agriculture	13.81	212.72	0.00	0.00	1038.04	0.00
3 Fishing & Forestry	10.00	0.00	0.13	10.06	4.96	0.00
4 Mining & Quarrying	0.00	0.79	0.00	0.00	4.35	109.83
5 Food Preparation	0.00	60.38	0.00	0.00	81.00	0.01
6 Bakery, Sweets	0.00	0.00	0.00	0.00	0.00	0.00
7 Beverages & Tobacco	0.00	0.00	5.03	3.28	0.01	0.00
8 Textile Raw Materials	0.00	0.17	0.00	0.00	9.01	0.00
9 Finished Textiles	0.00	27.34	0.00	0.02	0.25	0.00
10 Garments, Knitwear	25.31	0.00	0.00	0.03	0.17	0.00
11 Footwear, Leather	0.00	0.00	0.00	0.18	0.54	1.67
12 Wood Products, Furniture	0.00	8.12	0.07	1.50	107.23	0.84
13 Paper Printing, Publishing	0.00	0.00	0.00	1.76	39.76	0.05
14 Petroleum Products	0.00	50.12	4.07	0.87	0.19	0.00
15 Rubber Products	22.41	0.00	0.17	0.04	0.51	0.45
16 Paint, Detergent, Soap	18.00	139.08	0.02	5.21	10.41	0.31
17 Other Chemicals	0.00	9.82	0.02	5.09	2.83	0.12
18 Non-Metal. Mineral Prods	0.00	0.02	0.10	3.11	82.65	0.31
19 Metallic Prods, Machinery	0.00	10.02	0.36	0.00	2.00	0.31
20 Transport Equipment	0.00	0.55	0.00	0.59	2.90	0.00
21 Electricity	0.00	0.29	0.00	2.94	2.90	0.08
22 Water Supply	8.14	85.29	0.88	4.03	133.89	0.19
23 Building & Construction	0.00	87.62	0.00	10.81	24.53	0.21
24 Trade	0.00	0.65	0.01	0.23	3.99	0.02
25 Transport	0.00	0.00	0.00	0.00	0.32	0.04
26 Communications	0.00	0.00	0.00	0.00	0.00	0.01
27 Restaurants, Hotels	0.00	0.00	0.00	7.00	0.00	0.00
28 Ownership in Dwellings	0.00	4.30	0.00	2.00	51.23	0.99
29 Financial Services	0.00	32.56	0.00	0.00	8.99	0.11
30 Misc. Services	0.00	0.00	0.00	0.00	0.81	0.00
31 Govt. Public Adminstration	0.00	0.00	0.00	0.00	0.00	0.00
32 Govt. Education	0.00	3.08	0.00	0.00	0.00	0.00
33 Govt. Health	0.00	3.00	0.00	0.00	0.00	0.00
34 Govt. Agriculture	0.00	0.00	0.00	0.00	5.47	0.11
35 Govt. Other Services	0.00	0.00	0.00	1.58	0.00	0.00
36 Business Premises	0.00	0.22	0.00	5.54	13.88	0.90
37 Unspecified incl. Hunting	0.00					
38 Total Intermediate Inputs	173.49	650.82	12.54	85.98	2292.78	118.81

125

Input-Output Table of Kenya for the Year 1976 (Revised)

KENYA 1976 FLOWS in hundred thousand Kenya pounds of Y 1976 PRODUCERS CURRENT PRICES

INDUSTRY:	1 Traditional Economy	2 Agriculture	3 Fishing & Forestry	4 Mining & Quarrying	5 Food Preparation	6 Food Bakery Products Sweets
* IMPORT TRANSACTIONS *						
39 Traditional Economy	0.00	0.25	0.00	0.00	0.00	0.00
40 Agriculture	0.00	14.25	0.00	0.00	33.03	0.00
41 Fishing & Forestry	0.00	0.00	0.00	0.00	0.00	0.00
42 Mining & Quarrying	0.00	0.79	0.00	0.00	4.32	0.00
43 Food Preparations	0.00	0.36	0.00	0.00	36.74	0.12
44 Bakery, Sweets	0.00	0.00	0.00	0.00	0.00	0.04
45 Beverages & Tobacco	0.00	0.00	0.00	0.00	0.00	0.00
46 Textile Raw Materials	0.00	0.14	0.00	0.00	0.00	0.00
47 Finished Textiles	0.00	0.00	0.87	0.02	0.17	0.00
48 Garments, Knitwear	0.00	12.79	0.00	0.02	0.00	0.00
49 Footwear, Leather	0.00	0.00	0.00	0.07	0.00	0.00
50 Wood Prods, Furniture	0.00	0.02	0.00	0.00	3.55	0.08
51 Paper, Printing, Publishing	0.00	0.00	0.00	0.17	0.56	0.02
52 Petroleum Products	0.00	4.58	0.43	0.28	0.00	0.00
53 Rubber Products	0.00	0.00	0.00	0.00	0.00	0.35
54 Paint, Detergent, Soap	0.00	0.04	0.14	0.01	0.00	0.00
55 Other Chemicals	0.00	94.04	0.02	3.05	78.34	0.02
56 Non-Metallic Mineral Prods	0.00	0.00	0.00	0.18	0.32	0.01
57 Metallic Prods, Machinery	3.55	4.52	0.02	2.34	32.82	0.00
58 Transport Equipment	3.39	0.05	0.04	2.06	0.02	0.00
59 Electricity	0.00	0.00	0.00	0.00	0.00	0.00
60 Water Supply	0.00	0.00	0.00	0.00	0.00	0.00
61 Building & Construction	0.00	0.00	0.00	0.29	0.02	0.00
62 Trade	0.00	0.00	0.00	0.03	0.08	0.00
63 Transport	0.00	8.54	0.00	0.84	4.80	0.00
64 Communications	0.00	0.00	0.00	0.00	0.00	0.00
65 Restaurants, Hotels	0.00	0.00	0.00	0.00	0.00	0.00
66 Ownership in Dwellings	0.00	0.00	0.00	0.00	0.00	0.00
67 Financial Services	0.00	0.00	0.00	0.00	0.00	0.00
68 Misc. Services	0.00	0.00	0.00	0.00	0.00	0.00
69 Govt. Public Adminstration	0.00	0.00	0.00	0.00	0.00	0.00
70 Govt. Education	0.00	0.00	0.00	0.00	0.00	0.00
71 Govt. Health	0.00	0.00	0.00	0.00	0.00	0.00
72 Govt. Agriculture	0.00	0.00	0.00	0.00	0.00	0.00
73 Govt. Other Services	0.00	0.00	0.00	0.00	0.00	0.00
74 Business Premises	0.00	0.00	0.00	0.00	0.00	0.00
75 Unspecified, incl. Hunting	0.00	0.00	0.00	0.00	0.00	0.00
76 Total Imported Inputs	4.94	140.64	2.33	10.13	208.23	1.93
78 Gross Fixed Capital Conspt.	0.00	270.90	4.90	7.15	52.07	3.14
79 Compensation of Employees	8.70	514.04	82.35	18.54	117.03	11.65
80 Indirect Taxes	0.00	27.20	-0.15	8.41	82.75	5.38
81 Subsidies	0.00	-0.48		0.00		
82 Operating Surplus	688.40	3852.02	18.75	8.40	133.87	5.31
83 Gross Value Added	688.10	4660.68	86.34	35.50	385.72	25.48
Statistical Differences	0.01	0.00	0.02	30.00	0.02	-0.04
84 Gross Output	871.60	5311.31	98.90	121.46	2678.52	144.03
85 Imports CIF	0.00	105.70	4.04	943.18	145.51	1.04
86 Import Duties	0.00	3.70	0.53	186.74	19.55	0.20
87 Imports incl. Duties	0.00	109.40	4.57	1129.92	165.06	1.24
88 Total Resources	871.60	5420.71	103.47	1251.38	2843.58	145.27

Input-Output Table of Kenya for the Year 1976 (Revised)

KENYA 1976   FLOWS in hundred thousand Kenya pounds of Y 1976   PRODUCERS CURRENT PRICES

INDUSTRY:	7 Beverages & Tobacco	8 Textile Raw Materials	9 Finished Textiles	10 Garments, Knitwear	11 Footwear, Leather	12 Wood Products, Furniture
* TOTAL TRANSACTIONS *						
INDUSTRY						
1 Traditional Economy	0.00	0.00	0.00	0.00	0.00	0.00
2 Agriculture	11.23	21.08	0.00	2.78	7.54	0.24
3 Fishing & Forestry	0.02	0.00	0.00	0.00	0.00	8.64
4 Mining & Quarrying	0.94	0.00	0.00	0.00	0.00	8.07
5 Food Preparation	92.25	0.00	0.00	0.00	24.92	0.00
6 Bakery, Sweets	29.75	0.00	0.00	0.07	0.00	0.00
7 Beverages & Tobacco	0.00	3.22	18.29	0.47	0.53	2.61
8 Textile Raw Materials	0.00	0.03	17.35	119.47	2.52	5.10
9 Finished Textiles	0.05	0.02	0.02	14.55	8.20	5.09
10 Garments, Knitwear	0.02	0.86	0.56	0.04	7.46	0.00
11 Footwear, Leather	0.76	0.85	3.25	1.99	5.34	47.58
12 Wood Products, Furniture	10.06	0.05	3.05	3.47	0.52	24.17
13 Paper Printing, Publishing	13.41	2.25	26.84	0.24	10.76	-1.43
14 Petroleum Products	0.58	2.06	0.10	3.02	0.52	15.18
15 Rubber Products	0.10	3.82	0.45	0.06	10.76	10.69
16 Paint, Detergent, Soap	10.74	0.29	0.37	1.41	-0.13	28.83
17 Other Chemicals	3.64	0.42	0.62	3.64	0.24	26.23
18 Non-Metall. Mineral Prods	12.79	0.48	1.43	0.32	0.07	2.90
19 Metallic Prods, Machinery	2.62	3.26	0.54	0.85	-0.3	0.08
20 Transport Equipment	4.50	0.25	0.45	25.11	5.12	-0.27
21 Electricity	4.55	0.00	0.61	0.10	-1.8	19.76
22 Water Supply	0.90	3.02	0.25	1.45	0.00	2.36
23 Building & Construction	30.44	0.00	0.00	0.45	0.82	0.80
24 Trade	10.21	0.00	9.49	27.42	0.59	0.05
25 Transport	0.84	0.10	0.86	27.99	0.00	14.51
26 Communications	0.28	0.65	0.00	0.00	0.00	1.84
27 Restaurants, Hotels	0.00		0.00	0.00	0.00	0.00
28 Ownership in Dwellings	10.85		0.00	0.00	0.00	0.00
29 Financial Services	20.83		0.00	0.00	0.00	0.00
30 Misc. Service	0.39		0.00	0.00	0.00	0.00
31 Govt: Public Administration	0.00		0.00	0.00	0.00	2.96
32 Govt: Education	0.00		0.51	2.40	1.00	0.93
33 Govt: Health	0.00		0.65	18.00	1.22	
34 Govt: Agriculture	0.00					
35 Govt: Other Services						
36 Business Premises	1.26					
37 Unspecified, incl. Hunting						
38 Total Intermediate Inputs	281.27	43.95	98.74	249.42	82.72	191.49

Input-Output Table of Kenya for the Year 1976 (Revised)

KENYA 1976 FLOWS in hundred thousand Kenya pounds of Y 1976 PRODUCERS CURRENT PRICES

INDUSTRY:	7 Beverages & Tobacco	8 Textile Raw Materials	9 Finished Textiles	10 Garments, Knitwear	11 Footwear, Leather	12 Wood Products, Furniture
* IMPORT TRANSACTIONS *						
39 Traditional Economy	8.37	13.13	0.00	0.00	0.00	0.19
40 Agriculture	0.00	0.00	0.00	2.35	3.85	0.48
41 Fishing & Forestry	0.04	0.00	0.00	0.00	0.00	0.00
42 Mining & Quarrying	12.23	0.00	0.00	0.00	0.00	0.00
43 Food Preparations		0.00	0.00	0.00	0.00	0.00
44 Bakery, Sweets	4.52	0.00	0.07	0.00	0.00	0.02
45 Beverages & Tobacco	0.00	0.77	17.35	0.00	2.53	1.09
46 Textile Raw Materials	0.02	1.21	17.01	12.40	0.01	0.00
47 Finished Textiles	0.02	0.03	0.00	2.00	0.04	0.44
48 Garments, Knitwear	0.99	0.02	0.10	0.00	0.18	0.17
49 Footwear, Leather	1.26	0.03	0.28	0.08	0.05	2.19
50 Wood Prods, Furniture	0.22	0.02	0.02	0.28	0.91	0.55
51 Paper, Printing, Publishing	0.06	0.18	0.53	2.31	0.79	0.25
52 Petroleum Products	8.61	0.72	18.98	0.72	0.77	1.20
53 Rubber Products	4.02	0.03	0.01	0.03	0.01	0.00
54 Paint, Detergent, Soap	-1.00	0.01	0.00	7.05	0.00	0.00
55 Other Chemicals	2.27	0.58	0.48	0.00	0.95	0.89
56 Non-Metallic Mineral Prods	0.00	0.00	0.00	0.00	0.00	0.00
57 Metallic Prods, Machinery	0.00	0.00	0.02	0.10	0.00	0.13
58 Transport Equipment	0.00	0.00	0.00	0.00	0.00	0.00
59 Electricity	0.00	0.00	0.00	1.05	0.00	0.00
60 Water Supply	0.00	0.00	0.00	0.00	0.00	0.00
61 Building & Construction	0.00	0.00	0.00	0.00	0.00	0.00
62 Trade	0.00	0.00	0.00	0.00	0.00	0.00
63 Transport	0.00	0.00	0.00	0.00	0.00	0.00
64 Communications	0.00	0.00	0.00	0.00	0.00	0.00
65 Restaurants, Hotels	0.00	0.00	0.00	0.00	0.00	0.00
66 Ownership, Dwellings	0.00	0.00	0.00	0.00	0.00	0.00
67 Financial Services	0.00	0.00	0.00	0.00	0.00	0.00
68 Misc. Services	0.00	0.00	0.00	0.00	0.00	0.00
69 Govt. Public Adminstration	0.00	0.00	0.00	0.00	0.00	0.00
70 Govt. Education	0.00	0.00	0.00	0.00	0.00	0.00
71 Govt. Health	0.00	0.00	0.00	0.00	0.00	0.00
72 Govt. Agriculture	0.00	0.00	0.00	0.00	0.00	0.00
73 Govt. Other Services	0.00	0.00	0.00	0.00	0.00	0.00
74 Business Premises	0.00	0.00	0.00	0.00	0.00	0.00
75 Unspecified, incl. Hunting	0.00	0.00	0.00	0.00	0.01	0.00
76 Total Imported Inputs	44.06	17.66	44.60	128.20	22.90	37.58
77 Gross Fixed Capital Conspt.						
78 Compensation of Employees	66.00	5.10	27.95	9.35	2.28	7.87
79 Indirect Taxes	68.00	0.89	38.62	28.43	11.30	37.80
80 Subsidies	336.86	0.00	0.00	0.00	-1.22	11.97
81 Operating Surplus	128.57	4.80	4.04	26.20	11.08	15.50
82 Gross Value Added	547.81	20.84	70.12	102.53	35.86	72.74
83 Statistical Differences	0.00	0.84	0.01	0.01	-0.03	0.01
84 Gross Output	808.90	85.57	170.65	335.86	118.55	264.24
85 Imports CIF	19.43	10.19	149.58	99.29	17.13	16.54
86 Import Duties	19.86	2.01	54.58	34.74	6.48	2.47
87 Imports incl. Duties	39.39	12.20	203.93	134.03	23.61	19.01
88 Total Resources	848.29	77.77	374.78	485.99	142.16	283.25

Input-Output Table of Kenya for the Year 1976 (Revised)

KENYA 1976

FLOWS in hundred thousand Kenya pounds of Y 1976

INDUSTRY:	13 Paper, Printing, Publishing	14 Petroleum Products	15 Rubber Products	16 Paint, Detergent & Soap	17 Other Chemicals	18 Non-Metallic Mineral Prods
* TOTAL TRANSACTIONS INDUSTRY						
1 Traditional Economy	0.00	0.00	0.00	0.00	0.00	0.00
2 Agriculture	0.00	0.00	2.34	0.00	64.21	0.05
3 Fishing & Forestry	0.00	0.00	0.00	0.16	0.47	0.43
4 Mining & Quarrying	0.00	1099.64	0.32	0.32	0.23	24.00
5 Food Preparation	0.00	0.00	0.00	80.30	46.07	0.00
6 Bakery Sweets	0.00	0.00	0.00	0.00	0.00	0.00
7 Beverages & Tobacco	0.70	0.00	0.00	0.00	0.81	0.27
8 Textile Raw Materials	0.00	0.00	0.00	0.00	0.08	0.01
9 Finished Textiles	0.83	0.00	2.53	0.00	0.03	0.07
10 Garments, Knitwear	0.05	0.00	0.03	0.00	0.00	0.00
11 Footwear, Leather	0.13	0.00	0.00	0.00	2.13	0.40
12 Wood Products, Furniture	0.03	0.00	0.15	0.00	10.49	8.63
13 Paper, Printing, Publishing	236.96	0.71	1.87	7.00	7.05	44.04
14 Petroleum Products	0.43	5.85	0.87	3.18	0.36	0.19
15 Rubber Products	0.31	0.00	22.55	0.08	0.69	2.15
16 Paint, Detergent, Soap	0.00	10.06	10.23	0.63	125.82	18.80
17 Other Chemicals	23.59	6.38	5.18	28.82	16.68	20.59
18 Non-Metall. Mineral Prods	14.88	0.22	1.37	2.58	18.68	16.80
19 Metallic Prods, Machinery	1.40	4.88	0.57	2.46	1.82	13.77
20 Transport Equipment	3.03	0.71	0.28	0.51	2.86	4.07
21 Electricity	0.25	15.71	0.47	0.33	0.47	12.04
22 Water Supply	23.59	0.63	0.28	5.07	24.84	1.91
23 Building & Construction	24.88	22.50	0.24	5.70	5.66	0.84
24 Trade	23.73	0.50	0.39	3.49	1.33	0.31
25 Transport	30.58	0.00	0.00	0.06	0.35	1.91
26 Communications	0.47	0.00	0.00	0.00	0.00	0.84
27 Restaurants, Hotels	0.00	0.47	4.08	3.14	18.61	0.31
28 Ownership in Dwellings	19.00	6.97	0.45	2.48	8.53	5.84
29 Financial Services	19.42	2.46	0.00	0.00	0.00	1.47
30 Misc. Service	4.40	3.02	0.00	0.00	0.00	0.00
31 Govt. Public Adminstration	0.00	0.00	0.00	0.00	0.00	0.00
32 Govt. Education	0.00	0.00	0.00	0.00	0.00	0.00
33 Govt. Health	0.00	0.00	0.00	0.00	0.00	0.00
34 Govt. Agriculture	0.00	0.00	0.00	0.00	0.00	0.00
35 Govt. Other Services	5.91	0.00	0.91	0.00	2.82	13.13
36 Business Premises	4.85	2.28	0.91	0.01	0.38	13.85
37 Unspecified, incl. Hunting			2.63	0.22		
38 Total Intermediate Inputs	357.12	1182.21	84.77	142.37	347.13	190.75

Input-Output Table of Kenya for the Year 1976 (Revised)

KENYA 1976 FLOWS in hundred thousand Kenya pounds of Y 1976 PRODUCERS CURRENT PRICES

INDUSTRY:

* IMPORT TRANSACTIONS *	13 Paper,Printing, Publishing	14 Petroleum Products	15 Rubber Products	16 Paint,Detergent & Soap	17 Other Chemicals	18 Non-Metallic Mineral Prods
39 Traditional Economy	0.00	0.00	0.00	0.00	0.00	0.00
40 Agriculture	0.00	0.00	0.00	0.00	8.98	0.00
41 Fishing & Forestry	0.00	0.00	0.00	0.00	0.47	0.92
42 Mining & Quarrying	0.00	1099.64	0.01	0.06	1.23	17.92
43 Food Preparations	0.00	0.00	0.00	0.00	5.53	0.00
44 Bakery Sweets	0.02	0.00	0.98	0.00	0.00	0.00
45 Beverages & Tobacco	0.03	0.00	0.00	0.10	0.08	0.03
46 Textile Raw Materials	0.02	0.00	0.00	0.00	0.01	0.03
47 Finished Textiles	0.03	0.01	0.32	0.00	0.00	0.11
48 Garments, Knitwear	0.01	0.00	0.00	0.00	0.00	0.13
49 Footwear, Leather	0.00	0.00	2.53	0.00	0.60	4.39
50 Wood Prods, Furniture	7.28	0.00	0.00	0.05	1.02	0.70
51 Paper, Printing, Publishing	4.10	0.00	0.28	0.29	0.65	8.37
52 Petroleum Products	0.00	0.00	0.00	0.03	0.41	8.02
53 Rubber Products	0.00	0.00	2.00	0.36	0.00	0.13
54 Paint, Detergent, Soap	0.00	8.06	8.05	2.09	99.83	0.00
55 Other Chemicals	15.08	2.69	2.17	0.04	60.79	0.00
56 Non-Metallic Mineral Prods	8.27	0.00	0.02	0.02	0.07	0.00
57 Metallic Prods, Machinery	0.07	0.00	0.00	0.00	0.00	0.08
58 Transport Equipment	0.00	0.00	0.00	0.00	0.00	0.00
59 Electricity	0.00	0.00	0.00	0.00	0.00	0.00
60 Water Supply	0.00	0.00	0.00	0.00	0.00	0.00
61 Building & Construction	0.00	0.00	0.00	0.00	2.00	0.00
62 Trade	0.04	0.48	0.24	0.38	0.04	0.08
63 Transport	0.00	0.00	0.00	0.00	0.00	0.00
64 Communications	0.04	0.00	0.00	0.00	3.51	0.77
65 Restaurants, Hotels	2.32	0.00	0.00	0.00	0.00	0.00
66 Ownership in Dwellings	0.00	0.00	0.00	0.00	0.00	0.00
67 Financial Services	0.00	0.00	0.00	0.00	0.00	0.00
68 Misc. Service	0.00	0.00	0.00	0.00	0.00	0.00
69 Govt. Public Adminstration	0.00	0.00	0.00	0.00	0.00	0.00
70 Govt. Education	0.00	0.00	0.00	0.00	0.00	0.00
71 Govt. Health	0.00	0.00	0.00	0.00	0.00	0.00
72 Govt. Agriculture	0.00	0.00	0.00	0.00	0.00	0.00
73 Govt. Other Services	0.00	0.00	0.00	0.00	0.00	0.00
74 Business Premises	0.00	0.00	0.00	0.00	0.00	0.00
75 Unspecified, incl. Hunting	0.00	0.00	0.00	0.00	0.00	0.00
76 Total Imported Inputs	96.53	1113.55	25.04	35.28	130.57	39.77
77 Gross Fixed Capital Conspt.	21.85	8.96	5.43	1.75	54.66	17.89
78 Compensation of Employees	74.05	8.07	1.29	11.13	51.95	35.24
79 Indirect Taxes	28.17	65.22	10.27	25.42	30.00	8.46
80 Subsidies	0.00	0.00	0.00	0.00	0.00	0.00
81 Operating Surplus	50.78	34.32	13.81	35.43	58.99	58.08
82 Gross Value Added	172.63	116.57	40.80	94.23	159.93	120.47
83 Statistical Differences	0.00	0.02	0.00	0.01	0.00	0.02
84 Gross Output	529.75	1278.80	105.57	238.81	507.08	311.20
85 Imports CIF	104.90	83.86	37.33	9.87	461.10	35.51
86 Import Duties	15.52	5.87	4.73	2.95	35.58	7.38
87 Imports incl. Duties	120.42	89.73	42.06	12.82	496.68	42.89
88 Total Resources	650.17	1368.53	147.63	249.43	1003.72	354.09

Input-Output Table of Kenya for the Year 1976 (Revised)

KENYA 1976   FLOWS in hundred thousand Kenya pounds of Y 1976   PRODUCERS CURRENT PRICES

INDUSTRY:	19 Metallic Prods, Machinery	20 Transport Equipment	21 Electricity	22 Water Supply	23 Building Construction	24 Trade
* TOTAL INDUSTRY TRANSACTIONS *						
1 Traditional Economy	0.00	0.00	0.00	0.00	0.00	0.00
2 Agriculture	0.52	0.00	0.00	0.00	0.00	0.00
3 Fishing & Forestry	0.00	0.00	0.00	0.00	69.06	0.00
4 Mining & Quarrying	4.29	0.00	0.00	0.42	0.00	0.00
5 Food Preparation	5.78	0.00	0.00	0.00	0.00	0.00
6 Bakery, Sweets	0.00	0.00	0.00	0.00	0.01	8.92
7 Beverages & Tobacco	4.08	0.00	0.04	0.00	0.00	0.00
8 Textile Raw Materials	0.00	0.78	0.04	0.07	0.23	0.04
9 Finished Textiles	0.70	0.20	0.28	0.07	0.09	0.64
10 Garments, Knitwear	0.18	0.93	3.11	0.05	42.28	26.84
11 Footwear, Leather	0.00	1.91	0.50	5.94	150.78	38.19
12 Wood Products, Furniture	2.69	19.83	0.09	0.27	150.27	6.84
13 Paper Printing, Publishing	16.83	9.12	0.31	0.02	10.84	-1.08
14 Petroleum Products	22.62	4.67	1.34	0.98	22.95	-0.90
15 Rubber Products	1.30	5.36	2.58	0.00	28.08	13.72
16 Paint, Detergent, Soap	5.48	108.18	18.18	0.63	139.40	19.48
17 Other Chemicals	73.48	58.99	0.29	3.29	254.46	5.05
18 Non-Metall Mineral Prods	480.88	0.18	14.59	1.41	223.31	2.40
19 Metallic Prods, Machinery	9.06	0.14	0.05	5.28	8.24	0.00
20 Transport Equipment	8.00	25.46	5.85	0.00	0.00	28.88
21 Electricity	57.01	3.02	2.18	0.57	193.13	107.85
22 Water Supply	5.73	3.08	0.51	0.20	76.15	29.59
23 Building & Construction	3.44	0.51	40.70	0.00	27.46	0.84
24 Trade	0.87	18.00	12.02	0.00	3.08	0.00
25 Transport	40.69	18.89	2.89	0.03	18.33	191.68
26 Communications	8.71	0.00	0.00	0.22	48.17	6.39
27 Restaurants, Hotels	0.00	0.00	1.91	0.00	4.38	0.00
28 Ownership, Dwellings	0.00	0.00	0.00	0.00	0.00	0.00
29 Financial Services	0.00	0.00	0.00	0.00	0.00	0.00
30 Misc. Services	0.00	0.00	0.00	0.00	0.00	0.00
31 Govt. Public Administration	0.00	0.00	0.00	0.00	0.00	0.00
32 Govt. Education	0.00	0.00	0.00	0.00	0.00	0.00
33 Govt. Health	0.00	0.00	0.00	0.00	0.00	0.00
34 Govt. Agriculture	0.00	0.00	2.04	0.00	7.80	71.50
35 Govt. Other Services	6.81	13.35	3.87	0.79	16.75	22.02
36 Business Premises						
37 Unspecified incl. Hunting	3.63	3.41		3.16		
38 Total Intermediate Inputs	762.83	355.20	99.58	38.49	1160.25	571.91

131

Input-Output Table of Kenya for the Year 1976 (Revised)

KENYA 1976   FLOWS in hundred thousand Kenya pounds of Y 1976   PRODUCERS CURRENT PRICES

INDUSTRY:	19 Metallic Prods, Machinery	20 Transport Equipment	21 Electricity	22 Water Supply	23 Building Construction	24 Trade
* IMPORT TRANSACTIONS *						
39 Traditional Economy	0	0	0	0	0	0
40 Agriculture	1.28	0.00	0.00	0.00	0.00	0.00
41 Fishing & Forestry	0.00	0.00	0.00	0.00	0.00	0.00
42 Mining & Quarrying	4.29	0.00	0.00	0.00	1.24	0.00
43 Food Preparations	0.30	0.00	0.00	0.00	0.00	0.00
44 Bakery, Sweets	0.00	0.00	0.00	0.00	0.00	0.00
45 Beverages & Tobacco	0.00	0.00	0.00	0.00	0.00	0.00
46 Textile Raw Materials	1.89	0.00	0.00	0.00	0.00	0.00
47 Finished Textiles	0.69	0.00	0.00	0.00	0.24	0.70
48 Garments, Knitwear	0.08	0.78	0.00	0.00	0.00	0.00
49 Footwear, Leather	0.00	0.16	0.02	0.03	0.10	0.02
50 Wood Prods, Furniture	0.07	0.03	0.00	0.00	0.09	0.00
51 Paper, Printing, Publishing	1.81	0.14	0.00	0.00	2.80	0.36
52 Petroleum Products	2.09	0.10	0.04	0.00	2.38	2.59
53 Rubber Products	0.49	1.87	2.82	0.54	13.09	3.51
54 Paint, Detergent, Soap	1.51	3.78	0.19	0.11	4.12	2.44
55 Other Chemicals	51.90	2.70	0.00	0.00	0.60	0.00
56 Non-Metallic Mineral Prods	3.21	2.26	0.00	0.75	6.70	0.51
57 Metallic Prods, Machinery	307.45	3.17	0.01	0.08	15.89	0.00
58 Transport Equipment	0.24	34.22	3.90	2.09	93.63	7.12
59 Electricity	0.00	93.85	0.05	0.05	0.92	0.37
60 Water Supply	0.00	0.00	4.33	0.00	0.00	0.00
61 Building & Construction	0.00	0.00	0.00	0.00	0.00	0.00
62 Trade	0.00	0.00	0.00	0.00	0.00	0.00
63 Transport	0.23	0.00	0.00	0.00	0.00	0.00
64 Communications	0.00	0.00	0.70	0.15	0.77	2.62
65 Restaurants, Hotels	0.14	0.18	0.00	0.00	0.00	0.00
66 Ownership in Dwellings	0.00	0.00	0.18	0.02	0.45	0.14
67 Financial Services	0.00	0.00	0.00	0.00	0.00	0.00
68 Misc. Services	5.14	1.89	1.04	0.00	3.00	26.95
69 Govt. Public Adminstration	0.00	0.00	0.00	0.12	2.15	3.69
70 Govt. Education	0.00	0.00	0.00	0.00	0.00	0.00
71 Govt. Health	0.00	0.00	0.00	0.00	0.00	0.00
72 Govt. Agriculture	0	0	0	0	0	0
73 Govt. Other Services	0	0	0	0	0	0
74 Business Premises						
75 Unspecified, incl. Hunting	0.00	0.00	0.00	0.00	0.00	0.00
76 Total Imported Inputs	382.99	144.93	13.28	3.92	145.17	51.02
77 Gross Fixed Capital Conspt.	23.93	19.00	18.84	2.78	60.49	75.96
78 Compensation of Employees	118.40	101.70	14.80	37.50	378.20	531.60
79 Indirect Taxes	147.70	72.31	4.44	0.29	4.34	25.14
80 Subsidies	0.00	0.00	0.00	-0.10	0.00	0.00
81 Operating Surplus	74.96	44.80	45.06	23.24	23.31	584.51
82 Gross Value Added	364.99	237.81	82.94	63.89	466.34	1217.21
83 Statistical Differences	-0.02	0.01	0.02	0.01	-0.05	-0.01
84 Gross Output	1127.80	593.02	182.54	102.19	1826.54	1789.11
85 Imports CIF	1208.34	336.49	4.73	0.44	10.00	18.56
86 Import Duties	154.65	97.41	0.00	0.00	0.00	0.00
87 Imports incl. Duties	1362.99	433.90	4.73	0.44	10.00	18.56
88 Total Resources	2490.79	1026.92	187.27	102.63	1836.54	1807.67

Input-Output Table of Kenya for the Year 1976 (Revised)

KENYA 1976   FLOWS in hundred thousand Kenya pounds of Y 1976   PRODUCERS CURRENT PRICES

INDUSTRY:

	25 Transport	26 Communications	27 Restaurants Hotels	28 Dwellings	29 Financial Services	30 Miscel. Services
* TOTAL TRANSACTIONS *						
INDUSTRY						
1 Traditional Economy	0.00	0.00	0.00	0.00	0.00	0.00
2 Agriculture	0.15	0.00	5.10	0.00	0.00	0.00
3 Fishing & Forestry	0.00	0.00	5.08	0.00	0.00	0.00
4 Mining & Quarrying	12.04	0.00	0.05	0.00	0.00	0.39
5 Food Preparation	8.81	0.00	263.85	0.00	0.00	10.28
6 Bakery, Sweets	5.42	0.00	112.75	0.00	0.00	0.00
7 Beverages & Tobacco	0.32	0.00	0.00	0.00	0.00	0.04
8 Textile Raw Materials	1.04	0.00	0.76	0.00	0.00	0.07
9 Finished Textiles	0.07	0.00	0.25	0.00	0.00	21.27
10 Garments, Knitwear	0.00	0.00	0.04	0.00	0.00	16.08
11 Footwear, Leather	14.99	7.76	2.77	0.00	1.00	0.00
12 Wood Products, Furniture	240.00	4.83	2.09	0.00	5.66	6.44
13 Paper Printing, Publishing	16.39	0.41	6.28	0.00	8.03	0.04
14 Petroleum Products	2.32	0.00	0.47	0.00	0.00	5.35
15 Rubber Products	0.29	0.00	3.07	0.00	0.00	5.58
16 Paint, Detergent, Soap		0.00	2.49	0.00	0.00	3.51
17 Other Chemicals	27.78	33.01	1.33	0.00	13.25	3.87
18 Non-Metall. Mineral Prods	172.54	2.06	1.35	0.00	2.20	23.03
19 Metallic Prods, Machinery	17.74	0.73	1.95	0.00	1.33	25.36
20 Transport Equipment	18.43	0.74	2.86	0.00	1.29	0.00
21 Electricity	0.20	0.87	8.32	49.78	2.05	23.49
22 Water Supply	43.99	0.00	0.32	0.00	2.80	0.00
23 Building & Construction	388.40	28.21	0.96	0.00	6.79	16.15
24 Trade	50.84	88.84	1.07	0.00	8.58	0.00
25 Transport	151.84	0.00	0.33	0.00	10.07	0.00
26 Communications	8.21	0.00	6.31	0.00	111.97	32.30
27 Restaurants, Hotels	0.00	0.08	0.87	0.00	1.40	19.20
28 Ownership, Dwellings	0.00	0.40	0.00	0.00	0.00	0.00
29 Financial Services	0.00	0.00	0.00	0.00	0.00	0.00
30 Misc. Service Administration	0.00	0.00	0.00	0.00	0.00	0.00
31 Govt. Education	0.28	0.28	0.00	0.00	0.00	0.24
32 Govt. Health						
33 Govt. Agriculture	34.60	4.48	320.95	0.00	24.96	32.30
34 Govt. Other Services	3.40	5.92	0.38	0.00	4.59	19.20
35 Govt. Business Premises						
36 Unspecified incl. Hunting						
38 Total Intermediate Inputs	1231.19	180.40	489.10	49.78	206.40	201.88

Input-Output Table of Kenya for the Year 1976 (Revised)

KENYA 1976   FLOWS in hundred thousand Kenya pounds of Y 1976   PRODUCERS CURRENT PRICES

INDUSTRY:

	25 Transport	26 Communications	27 Restaurants Hotels	28 Dwellings	29 Financial Services	30 Miscel. Services
* IMPORT TRANSACTIONS *						
39 Traditional Economy	0.000	0.000	0.000	0.000	0.000	0.000
40 Agriculture	0.000	0.000	0.77	0.000	0.000	0.000
41 Fishing & Forestry	0.000	0.000	0.28	0.000	0.000	0.000
42 Mining & Quarrying	0.033	0.000	0.10	0.000	0.000	0.000
43 Food Preparations	0.000	0.000	3.63	0.000	0.000	0.98
44 Bakery, Sweets	0.000	0.000	9.04	0.000	0.000	0.00
45 Beverages & Tobacco	-0.37	0.000	9.24	0.000	0.000	0.02
46 Textile Raw Materials	0.53	0.000	0.76	0.000	0.000	0.05
47 Finished Textiles	0.32	0.000	0.04	0.000	1.04	0.02
48 Garments, Knitwear	0.24	0.000	0.07	0.000	1.84	0.23
49 Footwear, Leather	0.07	0.000	0.21	0.000	0.04	0.02
50 Wood Prods, Furniture	0.00	0.62	0.17	0.000	0.54	0.65
51 Paper Printing, Publishing	0.42	0.04	0.57	0.000	0.38	0.81
52 Petroleum Products	33.25	0.000	0.15	0.000	0.000	0.58
53 Rubber Products	8.19	0.000	0.87	0.000	0.000	0.02
54 Paint, Detergent, Soap	0.07	0.000	0.62	0.000	0.000	0.99
55 Other Chemicals	0.79	0.000	0.16	0.000	8.04	0.02
56 Non-Metallic Mineral Prods	-0.71	0.93	0.04	0.000	8.89	0.01
57 Metallic Prods, Machinery	10.95	0.000	0.000	0.000	0.75	0.04
58 Transport Equipment	2.48	0.000	0.000	0.000	0.000	0.00
59 Electricity	0.00	0.000	0.000	0.000	0.000	0.00
60 Water Supply	0.00	0.000	0.05	0.000	0.000	0.14
61 Building & Construction	0.00	0.000	0.03	0.000	0.000	0.00
62 Trade	49.24	26.37	0.42	0.000	0.000	0.00
63 Transport	28.88	0.000	0.000	0.000	0.000	0.00
64 Communications	0.00	0.000	0.000	0.000	0.000	0.00
65 Restaurants, Hotels	4.48	0.000	0.000	0.000	0.50	0.00
66 Ownership in Dwellings	0.000	0.000	0.000	0.000	0.98	0.00
67 Financial Services	0.000	0.000	0.000	0.000	39.96	0.00
68 Misc. Services	0.000	0.000	0.000	0.000	0.75	18.000
69 Govt: Public Adminstration	0.000	0.000	0.000	0.000	0.00	0.00
70 Govt: Education						
71 Govt: Health						
72 Govt: Agriculture						
73 Govt: Other Services						
74 Business Premises	0.000	0.000	0.000	0.000	0.000	0.00
75 Unspecified incl. Hunting	0.00	0.00	0.00	0.00	0.00	0.00
76 Total Imported Inputs	141.43	43.96	20.04	0.00	54.90	30.22
77 Gross Fixed Capital Conspt.	108.23	5.83	25.88	0.00	.17	26.33
78 Compensation of Employees	358.00	52.40	123.10	0.00	320.71	258.21
79 Indirect Taxes	-8.38	0.41	15.51	65.84	22.88	-7.85
80 Subsidies					0.00	-3.87
81 Operating Surplus	142.29	20.11	103.52	498.37	34.36	31.09
82 Gross Value Added	618.05	80.85	268.01	564.01	704.12	319.81
83 Statistical Differences				0.00	0.01	0.01
84 Gross Output	1849.45	242.25	737.11	613.79	910.52	521.70
85 Imports CIF	221.40	26.00	65.72	5.44	87.18	95.23
86 Import Duties		0.00	0.00	0.00	0.00	0.22
87 Imports Incl. Duties	221.40	26.00	65.72	5.44	87.18	95.45
88 Total Resources	2070.85	268.25	802.83	619.23	997.70	617.15

134

Input-Output Table of Kenya for the Year 1976 (Revised)

KENYA 1976   FLOWS in hundred thousand Kenya pounds of Y 1976   PRODUCERS CURRENT PRICES

INDUSTRY:

	31 Govt. Public Administration	32 Govt. Education	33 Govt. Health	34 Govt. Agriculture	35 Govt. Oth. Services	36 Business Premises
* TOTAL TRANSACTIONS *						
TOTAL INDUSTRY						
1 Traditional Economy	0.00	0.00	0.00	0.00	2.17	0.00
2 Agriculture	0.00	0.14	0.74	0.44	0.08	0.00
3 Fishing & Forestry	0.00	0.03	0.02	0.00	0.00	0.00
4 Mining & Quarrying	59.41	45.41	27.66	20.01	22.45	0.00
5 Food Preparation	0.00	0.15	0.06	0.01	0.04	0.00
6 Bakery Sweets	0.19	0.00	0.00	0.00	0.03	0.00
7 Beverages & Tobacco	0.12	0.00	0.43	0.35	0.02	0.00
8 Textiles Raw Materials	0.59	0.28	0.22	0.16	0.76	0.00
9 Finished Textiles	2.15	0.20	1.06	0.24	0.06	0.00
10 Garments, Knitwear	2.58	0.06	1.00	0.20	0.01	0.00
11 Footwear, Leather	0.16	33.77	0.80	1.20	0.12	0.00
12 Wood Products, Furniture	0.45	7.29	2.95	0.20	2.00	0.00
13 Paper Printing, Publishing	23.19	0.58	0.44	1.00	4.90	0.00
14 Petroleum Products	0.77	0.00	0.19	0.00	0.05	0.00
15 Rubber Products	0.40	0.00	0.95	4.17	2.31	0.00
16 Paint, Detergent, Soap	0.00	2.63	0.12	0.89	5.98	0.00
17 Other Chemicals	0.00	0.17	1.00	0.21	2.58	0.00
18 Non-Metall. Mineral Prods	2.00	0.91	4.69	8.14	0.44	0.00
19 Metallic Prods. Machinery	12.83	0.53	0.51	0.28	10.29	0.00
20 Transport Equipment	4.70	14.80	1.30	0.22	1.04	0.00
21 Electricity	3.43	5.89	7.47	3.00	0.89	0.00
22 Water Supply	4.91	8.48	2.95	0.17	2.87	0.00
23 Building & Construction	101.88	8.47	4.87	3.00	0.00	0.00
24 Trade	1.38	2.74	0.99	0.00	9.24	0.00
25 Transport	84.04	20.00	0.89	2.24	0.00	0.00
26 Communications	24.96	0.00	0.00	0.15	0.00	0.00
27 Restaurants, Hotels	0.00	0.75	1.42	0.00	0.06	0.00
28 Ownership in Dwellings	0.00	0.00	0.00	0.34	0.02	0.00
29 Financial Services	4.86	0.00	0.00	0.00	0.07	0.00
30 Misc. Service	0.34	0.00	0.00	0.00	0.00	0.00
31 Govt. Public Administration	0.00	0.00	0.00	0.00	0.03	0.00
32 Govt. Education	0.00	0.00	0.00	0.00	0.01	0.00
33 Govt. Health	0.00	0.00	0.00	0.18	0.08	0.00
34 Govt. Agriculture	0.15	0.00	1.36	1.05	1.63	0.00
35 Govt. Other Services	52.51	2.30	3.68	1.95	13.63	0.00
36 Business Premises	17.42	2.72				0.00
37 Unspecified, incl. Hunting						
38 Total Intermediate Inputs	404.11	163.97	87.41	85.04	105.18	0.00

135

Input-Output Table of Kenya for the Year 1978 (Revised)

KENYA 1978   FLOWS in hundred thousand Kenya pounds of Y 1978   PRODUCERS CURRENT PRICES

INDUSTRY:	31 Govt. Public Administration	32 Govt. Education	33 Govt. Health	34 Govt. Agriculture	35 Govt. Oth. Services	36 Business Premises
* IMPORT TRANSACTIONS *						
38 Traditional Economy	0.00	0.00	0.00	0.00	0.00	0.00
39 Agriculture	0.00	0.00	0.00	0.00	0.00	0.00
40 Fishing & Forestry	0.00	0.00	0.00	0.00	0.00	0.00
41 Mining & Quarrying	0.37	0.18	0.53	0.13	0.14	0.00
42 Food Preparations	0.00	0.00	0.00	0.00	0.00	0.00
43 Bakery, Sweets	0.02	0.00	0.00	0.00	0.01	0.00
44 Beverages & Tobacco	0.08	0.00	0.21	0.00	0.02	0.00
45 Textile Raw Materials	0.59	0.26	0.10	0.05	0.06	0.00
46 Finished Textiles	0.31	0.11	0.09	0.05	0.00	0.00
47 Garments, Knitwear	0.55	0.15	0.06	0.17	0.10	0.00
48 Footwear, Leather	0.01	0.47	0.06	0.67	0.24	0.00
49 Wood Prods, Furniture	2.71	0.86	0.28	0.66	0.89	0.00
50 Paper, Printing, Publishing	0.30	0.22	0.07	0.00	0.01	0.00
51 Rubber Products	0.02	0.00	0.05	0.17	0.00	0.00
52 Petroleum Products	0.00	0.82	6.31	2.90	0.47	0.00
53 Paint, Detergent, Soap	5.68	2.07	2.05	2.07	0.86	0.00
54 Other Chemicals	0.75	0.00	2.47	0.30	0.02	0.00
55 Non-Metallic Mineral Prods	0.00	0.00	0.00	0.01	0.00	0.00
56 Metallic Prod, Machinery	0.02	0.00	0.00	0.07	0.01	0.00
57 Transport Equipment	0.04	0.50	0.32	0.07	0.00	0.00
58 Electricity	0.67	0.00	0.00	0.24	0.00	0.00
59 Water Supply	0.78	0.06	0.03	0.00	0.09	0.00
60 Building & Construction	0.00	0.00	0.00	0.00	0.00	0.00
61 Trade	0.94	0.00	0.00	0.00	0.06	0.00
62 Transport	2.04	0.88	0.06	0.03	0.00	0.00
63 Communications	0.00	0.00	0.00	0.00	0.00	0.00
64 Restaurants, Hotels	0.00	0.00	0.00	0.00	0.00	0.00
65 Ownership in Dwellings	0.00	0.00	0.00	0.00	0.00	0.00
66 Financial Services	0.00	0.00	0.00	0.00	0.00	0.00
67 Misc. Services	0.00	0.00	0.00	0.00	0.00	0.00
68 Govt. Public Administration	0.00	0.00	0.00	0.00	0.00	0.00
69 Govt. Education	0.00	0.00	0.00	0.00	0.00	0.00
70 Govt. Health	0.00	0.00	0.00	0.00	0.00	0.00
71 Govt. Agriculture	0.00	0.00	0.00	0.00	0.00	0.00
72 Govt. Other Services	0.00	0.00	0.00	0.00	0.00	0.00
73 Business Premises	0.00	0.00	0.00	0.00	0.00	0.00
74 Unspecified incl. Hunting	0.30	0.00	0.00	0.00	0.00	0.00
76 Total Imported Inputs	22.60	8.95	10.78	9.58	15.46	0.00
77 Gross Fixed Capital Conspt.	0.00	0.00	0.00	0.00	0.00	0.00
78 Compensation of Employees	520.41	825.38	172.87	107.38	20.92	0.00
79 Indirect Taxes	-0.96	0.73	-1.27	0.41	0.59	0.00
80 Subsidies	0.00	0.00	0.00	0.00	-0.75	0.00
81 Operating Surplus	0.00	0.75	0.00	0.07	-0.00	0.00
82 Gross Value Added	529.08	828.25	175.58	114.01	205.13	0.00
83 Statistical Differences	0.02	0.00	-0.01	0.00	0.00	0.00
84 Gross Output	933.21	892.24	262.98	199.05	310.32	0.00
85 Imports CIF	0.05	61.74	0.21	0.00	0.00	0.00
86 Import Duties	0.00	0.00	0.00	0.00	0.00	1.30
87 Imports incl. Duties	0.05	61.74	0.21	0.00	0.00	1.30
88 Total Resources	933.26	1053.98	263.19	199.05	310.32	1.30

Input-Output Table of Kenya for the Year 1978 (Revised)

KENYA 1978   FLOWS in hundred thousand Kenya pounds of Y 1978   PRODUCERS CURRENT PRICES

* TOTAL TRANSACTIONS *

INDUSTRY:	37 Unspecified & Hunting	38 Total Intermdt. Consumption	39 Priv. Conspt. + Chngs. in Stock	40 Government Consumption	41 Gross Fixed Capital Form.	42 Exports
1 Traditional Economy	0.00	86.00	555.48	0.00	230.14	0.00
2 Agriculture	0.00	1372.65	2804.19	0.00	52.51	139.37
3 Fishing & Forestry	0.00	25.93	57.14	0.00	0.00	20.48
4 Mining & Quarrying	0.00	1216.84	1044.25	0.00	0.00	315.68
5 Food Preparation	0.00	1463.51	139.51	0.00	0.00	
6 Bakery, Sweets	0.00	2.50	676.11	0.00	0.00	13.24
7 Beverages & Tobacco	0.00	159.74		0.00	0.00	6.75
8 Textile Raw Materials	0.00	84.63	211.65	0.00	0.00	1.73
9 Finished Textiles	0.00	51.39	398.51	0.00	0.00	37.99
10 Garments, Knitwear	0.00	49.51	109.42	0.00	0.00	32.92
11 Footwear, Leather	0.00	10.22	71.52	0.00	0.00	22.53
12 Wood Products, Furniture	0.00	137.05	21.77	0.00	28.84	46.52
13 Paper, Printing, Publishing	0.00	808.24	91.25	0.00	0.00	52.06
14 Petroleum Products	0.00	92.14	49.52	0.00	0.00	468.81
15 Rubber Products	0.00	41.69	184.26	0.00	0.00	6.01
16 Paint, Detergent, Soap	0.00	65.49	175.64	0.00	0.00	23.48
17 Other Chemicals	0.00	222.71	325.70	0.00	0.00	175.61
18 Non-Metall. Mineral Prods	0.00	155.49	152.83	0.00	0.34	81.94
19 Metallic Prods, Machinery	0.00	444.01	133.26	0.00	918.48	90.09
20 Transport Equipment	0.00	151.42	31.34	0.00	386.80	43.29
21 Electricity	0.00	69.20		0.00	0.00	2.59
22 Water Supply	0.00	445.24		0.00	0.00	2.08
23 Building & Construction	0.00	882.17	532.05	0.00	1187.07	0.00
24 Trade	0.00	746.42	656.84	0.00	93.30	499.53
25 Transport	0.00	196.59	458.65	0.00	0.00	704.80
26 Communications	0.00	131.05	592.62	0.00	0.00	15.00
27 Restaurants, Hotels	0.00		501.07	0.00	0.00	188.96
28 Ownership in Dwellings	0.00	792.70	365.77	0.00	0.00	27.04
29 Financial Services	0.00	141.32		0.00	7.02	83.91
30 Misc. Services	0.00		100.65	0.00	0.00	103.12
31 Govt. Public Adminstration	0.00	6.42		905.26	0.00	0.26
32 Govt. Education	0.00	0.07		210.55	0.00	8.71
33 Govt. Health	0.00	3.27	5.88	189.10	0.00	0.04
34 Govt. Agriculture	0.00	0.98	14.54	294.80	0.00	0.00
35 Govt. Other Services	0.00	304.81	8.57	0.00	0.00	0.00
36 Business Premises	0.00	427.34	-365.05	0.00	0.00	1.50
37 Unspecified, Incl. Hunting	238.80		-450.57			42.90
38 Total Intermediate Inputs	238.80	12917.47	9135.20	2537.91	2904.30	4515.57

137

Input-Output Table of Kenya for the Year 1976 (Revised)

KENYA 1976 — FLOWS in hundred thousand Kenya pounds of Y 1978 — PRODUCERS CURRENT PRICES

INDUSTRY:

* IMPORT TRANSACTIONS *	37 Unspecified & Hunting	38 Total Intermdt Consumption	39 Priv. Consp + Chngs. in Stock	40 Government Consumption	41 Gross Fixed Capital Form.	42 Exports
39 Traditional Economy	0.00	88.38	19.58	0.00	0.00	0.00
40 Agriculture	0.00	86.39	3.18	0.00	0.45	0.00
41 Fishing & Forestry	0.00		3.00	0.00	0.00	0.00
42 Mining & Quarrying	0.00	1129.92	93.37	0.00	0.00	0.00
43 Food Preparations	0.00	171.70	1.12	0.00	0.00	0.00
44 Bakery, Sweets	0.00	18.12	23.27	0.00	0.00	0.00
45 Beverages & Tobacco	0.00	16.94	0.25	0.00	0.00	0.00
46 Textile Raw Materials	0.00	144.36	59.56	0.00	0.00	0.00
47 Finished Textiles	0.00	3.52	117.03	0.00	0.00	0.00
48 Garments, Knittwear	0.00		20.09	0.00	0.00	0.00
49 Footwear, Leather	0.00		18.81	0.00	0.00	0.00
50 Wood Prods, Furniture	0.00	101.81	18.61	0.00	2.53	0.00
51 Paper, Printing, Publishing	0.00	85.70	4.03	0.00	0.00	0.00
52 Petroleum Products	0.00	35.62	6.45	0.00	0.00	0.00
53 Rubber Products	0.00		31.91	0.00	817.90	0.00
54 Paint, Detergent, Soap	0.00	464.69	0.37	0.00	278.48	0.00
55 Other Chemicals	0.00	535.25	152.31	0.00	0.00	0.00
56 Non-Metallic Mineral Prods	0.00	592.77	50.98	0.00	0.00	0.00
57 Metal Prods, Machinery	0.00	101.44	0.39	0.00	0.00	0.00
58 Transport Equipment	0.00	0.05	0.13	0.00	0.00	0.00
59 Electricity	0.00		148.83	0.00	100.38	0.00
60 Water Supply	0.00	71.58	32.21	0.00	0.00	0.00
61 Trading & Construction	0.00	26.58	5.44	0.00	0.00	0.00
62 Transport	0.00	33.50	12.35	0.00	0.00	0.00
63 Communications	0.00	66.91	6.05	0.00	0.00	0.00
64 Restaurants, Hotels	0.00	83.10	0.74	0.00	0.03	0.00
65 Ownership, Dwellings	0.00		0.21	0.00	0.00	0.00
66 Financial Services	0.00	0.00		0.00	0.00	0.00
67 Misc. Services	0.00	0.00		0.00	0.00	0.00
68 Govt. Public Adminstration	0.00	0.00		0.00	0.00	0.00
69 Govt. Education	0.00			0.00	0.00	0.00
70 Govt. Health	0.00			0.00	0.00	0.00
71 Govt. Agriculture	0.00			0.00	0.00	0.00
72 Govt. Other Services	0.00			0.00	0.00	0.00
73 Business Premises	0.00			0.00	0.00	0.00
74 Unspecified incl. Hunting	4.00	4.01	15.20	0.00	0.00	0.00
75 Total Imported Inputs	4.00	3207.15	923.04	0.00	911.11	0.00
76 Gross Fixed Capital Conspt.	0.00	873.94	0.00	0.00	0.00	0.00
77 Compensation of Employees	0.00	5245.00	0.00	0.00	0.00	0.00
78 Indirect Taxes	0.49	1097.70	0.00	0.00	0.00	0.00
79 Subsidies						
80 Operating Surplus	-238.80	8812.48				
81 Gross Value Added	-238.31	1405.01	0.00	0.00	0.00	0.00
82 Statistical Differences						
83 Gross Output	0.49	28989.19	0.00	0.00	0.00	0.00
84 Imports CIF	16.57	4383.87	0.00	0.00	0.00	0.00
85 Import Duties	2.84	657.59	0.00	0.00	0.00	0.00
86 Imports incl. Duties	19.21	5041.26	0.00	0.00	0.00	0.00
87 Total Resources	19.70	32010.45	0.00	0.00	0.00	0.00

Input-Output Table of Kenya for the Year 1976 (Revised)

KENYA 1976   FLOWS in hundred thousand Kenya pounds of Y 1976   PRODUCERS CURRENT PRICES

INDUSTRY	43 Total Final Demand	44 Statistical Diffrences	45 Total Resources
* TOTAL TRANSACTIONS *			
1 Traditional Economy	785.80	0.00	871.60
2 Agriculture	4048.07	-0.01	5420.47
3 Fishing & Forestry	77.55	-0.01	103.41
4 Mining & Quarrying	34.55	-0.01	125.38
5 Food Preparation	1360.00	0.00	2843.58
6 Bakery, Sweets	142.77	0.00	145.29
7 Beverages & Tobacco	688.55	0.01	849.77
8 Textile Raw Materials	13.13	0.01	37.78
9 Finished Textiles	223.38	-0.02	405.99
10 Garments, Knitwear	436.50	0.02	485.16
11 Footwear, Leather	131.99	0.00	186.25
12 Wood Products, Furniture	146.99	0.00	260.17
13 Paper Printing, Publishing	560.08	0.01	1366.53
14 Petroleum Products	149.63	0.01	149.63
15 Rubber Products	207.74	-0.01	243.43
16 Paint, Detergent, Soap	351.40	-0.02	1003.72
17 Other Chemicals	335.09	-0.02	350.09
18 Non-Metal Mineral Prods	1334.77	-0.03	2490.79
19 Metal Prods, Machinery	582.92	-0.01	1022.92
20 Transport Equipment	33.42	-0.01	187.27
21 Electricity	1191.41	-0.01	1636.54
22 Water Supply	1125.48	-0.02	1807.67
23 Building & Construction	1322.44	0.00	2070.85
24 Trade	671.68	-0.02	288.25
25 Transport	671.78	0.00	802.83
26 Communications	819.23	-0.01	819.23
27 Restaurants, Hotels	184.92	-0.01	977.70
28 Ownership in Dwellings	475.91	-0.01	617.15
29 Financial Services	930.94	0.00	933.26
30 Misc. Services	1047.56	0.00	1053.98
31 Govt. Public Adminstration	263.19	0.00	283.19
32 Govt. Education	195.38	0.00	199.05
33 Govt. Health	-309.34	0.00	310.32
34 Govt. Agriculture	-383.52	0.01	1.30
35 Govt. Other Services	-407.87	0.03	19.70
38 Total Intermediate Inputs	19092.88	0.00	32010.45

139

Input-Output Table of Kenya for the Year 1976 (Revised)

KENYA 1976   FLOWS in hundred thousand Kenya pounds of Y 1976

* IMPORT TRANSACTIONS *	43 Total Final Demand	44 Statistical Differences	45 Total Resources
39 Traditional Economy	21.03	-0.01	109.40
41 Agriculture	3.08	-0.00	129.52
42 Fishing & Forestry	3.90	0.00	165.04
43 Mining & Quarrying	93.17	-0.00	39.39
44 Food Preparations	23.17	0.00	12.20
45 Bakery Sweets	0.25	-0.00	134.03
46 Beverages & Tobacco	59.56	-0.01	-23.61
47 Textiles Raw Materials	117.03	-0.01	-19.01
48 Finished Textiles	120.09	0.00	120.42
49 Garments, Knitwear	18.61	0.00	189.73
50 Footwear, Leather	8.03	-0.01	42.06
51 Wood Prods Furniture	0.45	0.00	496.86
52 Paper Printing Publishing	8.91	-0.01	42.89
53 Petroleum Products	37.65	-0.01	1362.99
54 Rubber Products	770.21	-0.01	433.90
55 Paint, Detergent, Soap	332.46	-0.00	4.73
56 Other Chemicals	0.37	0.00	10.00
57 Non-Metallic Mineral Prods	0.39	0.00	18.56
58 Metallic Prods. Machinery	10.00	-0.00	226.40
59 Transport Equipment	149.83	-0.01	65.72
60 Electricity	32.00	0.01	67.18
61 Water Supply	5.44	-0.00	95.45
62 Building & Construction	0.27	-0.00	60.21
63 Trade	12.38	-0.03	
64 Transport	61.74	0.00	
65 Communications	0.21	0.00	
66 Restaurants, Hotels			
67 Ownership in Dwellings			
68 Financial Services			
69 Misc. Services			
70 Govt. Public Administration			
71 Govt. Education			
72 Govt. Health			
73 Govt. Agriculture			
74 Govt. Other Services	0.00	0.00	-9.30
75 Business Premises			
Unspecified, incl. Hunting	15.20	0.00	19.21
76 Total Imported Inputs	1834.15	-0.04	5041.26
77 Gross Fixed Capital Conspt	0.00	0.00	0.00
78 Compensation of Employees	0.00	0.00	0.00
79 Indirect Taxes	0.00	0.00	0.00
80 Subsidies	0.00	0.00	0.00
81 Operating Surplus	0.00	0.00	0.00
82 Gross Value Added	0.00	0.00	0.00
83 Statistical Differences	0.00	0.00	0.00
84 Gross Output	0.00	0.00	0.00
85 Imports CIF	0.00	0.00	0.00
86 Import Duties	0.00	0.00	0.00
87 Imports incl. Duties	0.00	0.00	0.00
88 Total Resources	0.00	0.00	0.00

MADAGASCAR

Reference year: 1973

Entries in table: Total flows, import matrix

Source: Madagascar, Institut national de la statistique et de la recherche économique

Computerized: UNIDO

Currency units: Malagasy francs of Y 1973
Scale factor: 10,000,000

Pricing system: Producers' current prices
Intermediate sectors: 30 × 30
Treatment of trade margins: Trade margins for domestic production in row 70 and for imports in row 74

Treatment of imports: Import matrix
Availability of import matrix: Available

Total number of rows: 77
Statistical unit of quadrant 1: Commodity

Total number of columns: 38
Statistical unit of quadrant 1: Industry

Fourth quadrant: Not occupied

Input-Output Table for Madagascar for the Year 1973 (Revised)

MADAGASCAR 1973   FLOWS in hundred million Malagasy francs of Y 1973   PRODUCERS CURRENT MARKET PRICES

INDUSTRY:	1 Agriculture	2 Livestock Fishing,Hunting	3 Forestry Basket-Weaving	4 Agro-Industries	5 Mining Quarrying	6 Energy & Water
COMMODITY						
1 Agricultural Products	13.27	25.07	0.86	4.95	0.00	0.00
2 Livestock,Fishing, Hunting	44.95	3.34	0.09	0.00	0.12	0.00
3 Forestry Products	0.21	0.07	5.00	0.26	0.00	0.02
4 Agro-Industry	0.07	0.00	0.00	0.74	0.00	0.00
5 Minerals	0.04	0.49	0.00	3.06	3.70	39.92
6 Electricity,Water,Petr.Prds	4.60	3.24	0.72	3.43	3.00	3.00
7 Food Products	0.00	0.00	0.00	0.00	0.00	0.00
8 Beverages	0.00	0.00	0.00	0.00	0.30	2.82
9 Tobacco	0.00	0.98	0.00	1.94	0.56	0.00
10 Oils and Fats	0.00	0.95	0.00	0.64	0.00	0.00
11 Chemical & Pharmac. Prods.	7.94	0.61	0.78	0.17	0.00	3.94
12 Textiles, Wearing	1.28	0.01	0.00	0.05	0.92	3.93
13 Leather, Footwear	0.01	0.00	0.05	2.66	0.38	5.04
14 Wood and Furniture	0.38	0.68	0.00	0.06	0.03	0.68
15 Constr Matrls & Misc.Miner	0.59	0.00	0.03	0.46	0.88	0.85
16 Metals Prod.,Mech.Machinery	7.52	0.00	0.02	0.10	0.17	0.51
17 Electrical Equipment	0.07	0.00	0.01	0.83	0.39	20.26
18 Transport Equipment	3.33	0.44	0.06	0.15	0.63	0.62
19 Paper, Paperprd,Printing	0.16	0.71	0.38	0.48	0.00	4.08
20 Misc.Manufactured Goods	0.71	0.10	0.08	0.15	0.82	0.56
21 Buildings		0.02		0.01	0.00	0.00
22 Transport (Products)	0.81	0.00	0.06	0.07	0.39	0.49
23 Transport (Passenger)	0.17	0.00	0.06	0.00	0.63	0.30
24 Post, Telecommunications		0.33	0.30	0.07	0.80	
25 Trade	0.81		0.08	0.00	0.82	
26 Banking, Insurance Services	0.78					
27 Services to Enterprises	0.00					
28 Household Services	3.98					
29 Other Misc.Services	3.75					
30 Non-Marketable Services						
31 Total Intermediate Inputs	91.13	40.37	8.07	24.89	15.97	66.00

Input-Output Table for Madagascar for the Year 1973 (Revised)

MADAGASCAR 1973   FLOWS In hundred million Malagasy francs of Y 1973   PRODUCERS CURRENT MARKET PRICES

INDUSTRY:	1 Agriculture	2 Livestock Fishing.Hunting	3 Forestry Basket-Weaving	4 Agro-Industries	5 Mining Quarrying	8 Energy & Water
* IMPORT TRANSACTIONS *						
32 Agricultural Products	1.38	0.00	0.00	0.00	0.00	0.00
33 Livestock,Fishing,Hunting	0.00	0.00	0.00	0.00	0.00	0.00
34 Forestry Products	0.00	0.00	0.00	0.00	0.00	0.00
35 Agro-Industry	0.04	0.17	0.05	0.06	0.19	0.09
36 Minerals	0.65	0.00	0.00	0.58	0.00	35.09
37 Electrcty,Water,Petroleum	0.00	0.00	0.00	0.00	0.00	0.00
38 Food Products	0.00	0.00	0.00	0.00	0.00	0.00
39 Beverages	0.00	0.00	0.00	0.00	0.00	0.00
40 Tobacco	0.00	0.00	0.00	0.00	0.00	0.00
41 Oils and Fats	7.39	0.95	0.00	1.51	0.82	0.76
42 Chemical & Pharmac. Prods.	0.39	0.74	0.00	0.20	0.20	0.00
43 Textiles, Wearing	0.00	0.00	0.00	0.00	0.00	0.00
44 Leather, Footwear	0.00	0.00	0.00	0.00	0.00	0.00
45 Wood and Furniture	6.76	0.68	0.37	2.06	0.44	3.94
46 Constr. Matrls &Misc.Minera	0.52	0.00	0.00	0.46	0.38	0.93
47 Metal Prds.Mech.Machinery	0.07	0.00	0.00	0.00	0.16	0.85
48 Transport Equipment	0.06	0.00	0.00	0.09	0.00	0.30
49 Electrical Machinery	0.00	0.00	0.00	0.00	0.00	0.00
50 Paper,Paperbd.,Printing	0.00	0.00	0.00	0.00	0.19	0.55
51 Misc.Manufactured Goods	0.00	0.00	0.00	0.00	0.00	0.00
52 Buildings	0.00	0.00	0.00	0.00	0.00	0.00
53 Transport (Products)	0.00	0.00	0.00	0.00	0.00	0.00
54 Transport (Passenger)	0.00	0.00	0.00	0.00	0.00	0.00
55 Post,Telecommunications	0.00	0.00	0.00	0.00	0.00	0.00
56 Trade	0.30	0.00	0.00	0.42	0.09	0.72
57 Banking & Insurance Servic.	0.00	0.00	0.00	0.00	0.00	0.00
58 Business Services	0.00	0.00	0.00	0.00	0.00	0.00
59 Household Services	0.00	0.00	0.00	0.00	0.00	0.00
60 Other Misc. Services	0.00	0.00	0.00	0.00	0.00	0.00
61 Non-Marketable Services	0	0	0	0	0	0
62 Total Imported Inputs	17.58	2.54	0.42	5.99	3.47	45.14
63 Gross Fixed Capital Conspt	9.60	2.71	0.19	17.54	5.54	10.48
64 Compensation of Employees	22.67	2.47	2.22	19.84	5.77	18.28
65 Indirect Taxes	25.97	2.00	0.87	14.78	0.49	43.46
66 Subsidies	0.00	0.00	0.00	-0.15	0.00	0.00
67 Operating Surplus	479.88	347.81	74.96	-4.42	5.28	17.28
68 Gross Value Added	529.73	354.32	78.24	46.41	17.08	89.48
69 Change in Stocks	16.14	14.54	0.00	0.00	0.00	5.81
70 Distribution Margins	130.23	25.84	13.24	20.33	8.97	49.88
71 Gross Output	767.23	435.07	99.55	91.63	42.02	210.95
73 Imports (c.i.f.)	4.70	0.13	0.22	0.08	0.73	42.91
74 Import Duties on Imports	0.31	0.08	0.07	0.01	0.13	3.01
75 Distrib Margins on Imports	0.68	0.04	0.01	0.02	0.08	21.28
75 Change in Stocks of Imports	0.00	0.00	0.00	0.00	0.00	0.00
76 Imports incl.Duties & Margin	5.69	0.19	0.30	0.11	0.94	67.20
77 Total Resources	772.92	435.28	99.85	91.74	42.96	278.15

143

Input-Output Table for Madagascar for the Year 1973 (Revised)

MADAGASCAR 1973   FLOWS in hundred million Malagasy francs of Y 1973   PRODUCERS CURRENT MARKET PRICES

INDUSTRY:	7 Food Industry	8 Beverage Industry	9 Tobacco Industry	10 Oils & Fats Industry	11 Chemical & Pharmac. Ind.	12 Textiles Wearing
* TOTAL TRANSACTIONS *						
* COMMODITY *						
1 Agricultural Products	241.31	2.97	7.94	8.98	0.01	19.25
2 Livestock,Fishing,Hunting	317.71	1.55	0.02	0.01	0.24	0.15
3 Forestry Products	2.06	0.93	0.00	0.64	0.04	0.04
4 Agro-Industry	0.36	0.89	0.25	2.64	0.40	0.00
5 Minerals		0.15	0.00		0.68	8.49
6 Electricity,Water,Petr.Prds	4.39	0.00	0.00	7.00	0.97	0.00
7 Food Products	23.35	0.00	0.00	0.00	0.00	0.00
8 Beverages		0.00	0.00	0.32	0.00	0.00
9 Tobacco	2.41	0.00	0.08	0.14	0.00	0.00
10 Oils and Fats	2.83	0.85	0.00	1.82	5.08	0.71
11 Chemical & Pharmac. Prods.	0.04	0.41	0.12	0.34	0.00	82.40
12 Textiles, Wearing	5.08	0.04	0.00	0.00	0.73	0.00
13 Leather, Footwear	0.00	0.26	0.00	0.00	0.00	0.00
14 Wood and Furniture	3.04	0.07	0.32	0.59	0.12	5.18
15 Constr. Matrls & Misc.Minerl	0.21	0.47	0.05	0.14	0.42	0.00
16 Metal Prods.,Mech. Machinery	0.68	0.83	0.13		0.15	0.54
17 Transport Equipment	0.86	0.17	0.06	0.09	0.21	0.29
18 Electrical Machineries	1.81	0.17	0.07	0.09	0.16	0.26
19 Paper, Paperbd.; Printing	4.12	0.22	0.43	0.36	0.36	0.83
20 Misc. Manufactured Goods	0.00	0.35	0.29	0.28	0.49	1.78
21 Buildings	2.97	0.78	0.18	0.22	0.00	0.88
22 Transport (Products)	0.00	0.26	0.00	0.00	0.33	2.58
23 Transport (Passenger)		0.00			0.00	0.00
24 Post, Telecommunications						
25 Trade						
26 Banking, Insurance Services						
27 Services to Enterprises						
28 Household Services						
29 Other Misc.Services						
30 Non-Marketable Services						
31 Total Intermediate Inputs	615.08	12.78	12.04	22.09	12.47	112.88

144

Input-Output Table for Madagascar for the Year 1973 (Revised)

MADAGASCAR 1973   FLOWS in hundred million Malagasy francs of Y 1973   PRODUCERS CURRENT MARKET PRICES

#	IMPORT TRANSACTIONS	7 Food Industry	8 Beverage Industry	9 Tobacco Industry	10 Oils & Fats Industry	11 Chemical & Pharmac. Ind	12 Textiles Wearing
32	Agricultural Products	0.00	1.76	1.09	1.21	0.01	0.00
33	Livestock, Fishing, Hunting	0.00	0.00	0.00	0.00	0.04	0.13
34	Forestry Products	0.00	0.00	0.00	0.00	0.00	0.00
35	Agro-Industry	0.00	0.00	0.00	0.00	0.26	0.00
36	Minerals	0.00	0.17	0.00	0.84	0.48	1.65
37	Electrcty,Water,Petroleum	0.22	0.48	0.00	6.82	0.00	0.00
38	Food Products	14.52	0.00	0.00	0.00	0.00	0.00
39	Beverages	0.00	0.00	0.00	0.00	0.00	0.00
40	Tobacco	0.00	0.00	0.00	0.00	0.00	0.00
41	Oils and Fats	1.69	0.34	0.00	1.09	0.00	0.00
42	Chemical & Pharmac. Prods.	1.86	0.00	0.02	1.29	3.63	0.00
43	Textiles, Wearing	0.00	0.00	0.00	0.00	3.04	7.36
44	Leather, Footwear	0.00	0.00	0.00	0.00	0.00	20.80
45	Wood and Furniture	0.00	0.00	0.00	0.00	0.00	0.00
46	Constr. Matrls.&Misc.Minera	0.00	0.18	0.00	0.22	0.54	5.15
47	Metal Prds.Mach.Machinery	1.38	0.00	1.02	0.00	0.00	0.00
48	Transport Equipment	0.07	0.07	0.00	0.00	0.00	0.00
49	Electrical Machinery	0.34	0.00	0.00	0.00	0.00	0.03
50	Paper,Paperbd.,Printing	0.87	0.28	0.84	0.00	0.45	0.87
51	Misc. Manufactured Goods	0.03	0.00	0.00	0.00	0.16	0.00
52	Buildings	0.00	0.00	0.00	0.00	0.00	0.00
53	Transport (Products)	0.00	0.00	0.00	0.00	0.00	0.00
54	Transport (Passenger)	0.00	0.00	0.00	0.00	0.00	0.00
55	Post, Telecommunications	0.00	0.00	0.00	0.00	0.00	0.00
56	Trade	0.10	0.00	0.00	0.00	0.00	0.00
57	Banking & Insurance Servic.	0.00	0.00	0.00	0.00	0.00	0.00
58	Business Services	0.00	0.00	0.00	0.00	0.00	0.00
59	Household Services	0.00	0.00	0.00	0.00	0.00	0.00
60	Non-Marketable Services	0.00	0.00	0.00	0.00	0.00	0.00
62	Total Imported Inputs	20.01	3.35	2.97	11.51	5.61	3.99
63	Gross Fixed Capital Conspt.	4.82	1.30	0.72	1.38	0.15	14.82
64	Compensation of Employees	24.50	2.95	2.28	2.95	3.28	20.36
65	Indirect Taxes	6.52	6.28	18.24	1.90	2.57	0.36
66	Subsidies	-0.01	0.01	0.00	1.00	1.07	0.00
67	Operating Surplus	80.68	3.24	7.36	3.95	0.05	48.39
68	Gross Value Added	116.51	13.77	28.61	10.18	8.73	88.73
69	Change in Stocks	1.40	0.00	0.00	0.00	0.00	0.00
70	Distribution Margins	41.40	10.14	20.13	7.57	8.51	39.14
71	Gross Output	772.97	38.89	60.78	39.84	29.03	238.55
72	Imports (c.i.f.)	76.77	11.53	1.55	4.25	66.86	33.60
73	Import Duties	9.18	12.87	0.08	1.29	17.73	13.58
74	Distrib. Margins on Imports	49.89	7.80	3.34	2.00	29.82	39.34
75	Change in Stocks of Imports	0.00	0.00	1.07	0.00	0.00	12.31
76	Imports incl.Duties & Margin	135.84	32.20	6.04	8.31	114.41	98.83
77	Total Resources	908.61	68.89	66.82	48.15	143.44	337.38

Input-Output Table for Madagascar for the Year 1973 (Revised)

MADAGASCAR 1973   FLOWS in hundred million Malagasy francs of Y 1973   PRODUCERS CURRENT MARKET PRICES

INDUSTRY:	13 Leather Leather Tanning	14 Wood Industry	15 Construction Matl. Ceramics	16 Metal Industry Mech. Machinery	17 Transport Equipment	18 Electrical Industry
* TOTAL TRANSACTIONS * COMMODITY						
1 Agricultural Products	0.00	0.00	0.00	0.00	0.00	0.00
2 Livestock,Fishing, Hunting	0.00	0.00	0.00	0.00	0.00	0.00
3 Forestry Products	0.00	5.74	2.03	0.06	0.85	0.00
4 Agro-Industry	0.00	0.00	0.00	0.02	0.00	0.00
5 Minerals	0.16	0.07	1.48	0.68	0.20	0.58
6 Electricity,Water,Petr.Prds	2.33	0.00	1.86	0.00	0.00	0.00
7 Food Products	0.00	0.00	0.00	0.00	0.00	0.00
8 Beverages	0.00	0.00	0.00	0.00	0.00	-1.00
9 Tobacco	0.00	-0.34	0.00	-0.03	0.54	0.00
10 Oil and Fats	2.98	0.00	-0.14	0.43	0.00	0.84
11 Chemical & Pharmac. Prods.	0.87	-0.80	0.00	0.00	0.33	0.00
12 Textiles, wearing	0.83	0.00	0.00	0.39	0.00	0.00
13 Leather, Footwear	-1.63	-0.20	0.00	0.04	0.62	0.84
14 Wood and Footwear	0.25	0.00	0.67	24.55	-1.17	7.15
15 Constr.Matrl & Misc.Miner)	0.00	0.85	0.78	0.29	0.21	0.32
16 Metal Prods.Mech.Machinery	0.00	0.00	0.13	0.39	0.03	0.16
17 Transport Equipment	0.00	0.00	0.02	0.44	0.16	0.09
18 Electrical Equipment	0.07	0.07	0.00	0.12	0.09	0.03
19 Paper, Paper & printing	0.09	0.07	0.00	0.78	0.03	0.12
20 Misc. Manufactured Goods			0.04	0.43	0.04	
21 Buildings	0.19	0.19	0.17	0.36	0.12	0.32
22 Transport (Products)	0.08	0.11	0.19	0.68	0.13	0.21
23 Transport (Passenger)			0.04		0.08	
24 Post Telecommunications	0.22	0.17	0.10	0.00	0.02	0.24
25 Trade	0.54	0.25		0.85		0.00
26 Banking, Insurance Services	0.50	0.10				
27 Services to Enterprises	0.09	0.03				
28 Household Services	0.00	0.00				
29 Other Misc. Services	0.00					
30 Non-Marketable Services						
31 Total Intermediate Inputs	9.72	12.22	7.23	32.47	14.24	12.16

146

Input-Output Table for Madagascar for the Year 1973 (Revised)

MADAGASCAR 1973   FLOWS in hundred million Malagasy francs of Y 1973   PRODUCERS CURRENT MARKET PRICES

INDUSTRY:

* IMPORT TRANSACTIONS *	13 Leather Tanning	14 Wood Industry	15 Construction Matl, Ceramics	16 Metal Industry Mech. Machinery	17 Transport Equipment	18 Electrical Industry
32 Agricultural Products	.00	.00	.00	.00	.00	.00
33 Livestock, Fishing, Hunting	.00	.00	.00	.00	.00	.00
34 Forestry Products	.00	.02	.00	.00	.00	.00
35 Agro-Industry	.00	.00	.02	.01	.00	.00
36 Minerals	.03	.02	.75	.05	.04	.16
37 Electrcty,Water,Petroleum	.00	.00	.00	.00	.00	.00
38 Food Products	.00	.00	.00	.00	.00	.00
39 Beverages	.00	.00	.00	.00	.00	.00
40 Tobacco	.00	.00	.00	.00	.31	.96
41 Oils and Fats	2.70	.00	.00	.47	.00	.00
42 Chemical & Pharmac. Prods.	.84	.38	1.00	.00	.00	.00
43 Textiles, Wearing	.89	.72	.00	.00	.00	.00
44 Leather, Footwear	.00	.00	.00	.00	.00	.84
45 Wood and Furniture	.00	1.20	.36	.01	.00	-.15
46 Constr Matrls & Misc.Minera	.25	.55	.77	19.41	.23	.32
47 Metal Prds, Mech.Machinery	.00	.00	.00	.00	.00	.00
48 Transport Equipment	.00	.00	.13	.29	10.69	.00
49 Electr'cal Machinery	.00	.00	.51	.00	.00	7.00
50 Paper,Paperbd.,Printing	.00	.00	.00	.16	.00	.00
51 Misc. Manufactured Goods	.00	.00	.00	.00	.00	.16
52 Buildings	.00	.00	.00	.00	.00	.00
53 Transport (Products)	.00	.00	.00	.00	.00	.00
54 Transport (Passenger)	.00	.00	.00	.00	.00	.00
55 Post, Telecommunications	.00	.00	.00	.00	.00	.00
56 Trade	.00	.00	.00	.00	.00	.00
57 Banking & Insurance Servic.	.00	.00	.00	.00	.00	.00
58 Business Services	.00	.00	.00	.00	.00	.00
59 Household Services	.00	.00	.00	.00	.00	.00
60 Other Services	.00	.00	.00	.00	.00	.00
80 NonMarketable Services	.00	.00	.00	.00	.00	.00
62 Total Imported Inputs	3.91	3.89	2.88	20.50	11.27	10.59
83 Gross Fixed Capital Conspt.	1.23	0.54	0.71	1.25	0.51	0.72
84 Compensation of Employees	2.95	3.30	7.88	13.14	1.31	0.99
85 Indirect Taxes	0.47	0.18	0.25	0.88	.04	.14
86 Subsidies	.00	.00	-0.87	-0.01	.00	.00
87 Operating Surplus	2.32	5.69	10.60	3.66	.87	2.27
68 Gross Value Added	6.97	9.71	18.57	20.03	2.53	5.12
89 Change in Stocks	.00	.00	.00	.00	.00	.00
70 Distribution Margins	4.55	2.22	22.16	10.62	4.55	3.49
71 Gross Output	21.24	24.15	47.98	63.12	21.32	20.71
72 Imports(c.i.f.)	1.83	1.40	6.48	97.39	61.28	44.18
73 Import Duties	1.14	0.73	0.17	20.59	12.42	14.01
74 Distrib. Margins on Imports	3.27	0.34	9.69	20.37	10.38	8.49
75 Change in Stocks of Imports	2.14	.00	8.73	14.85	0.00	0.00
76 Imports incl.Duties & Margin	8.38	3.47	26.07	153.20	85.08	66.68
77 Total Resources	29.62	27.62	74.03	216.32	106.40	87.45

Input-Output Table for Madagascar for the Year 1973 (Revised)

MADAGASCAR 1973   FLOWS in hundred million Malagasy francs of Y 1973   PRODUCERS CURRENT MARKET PRICES

INDUSTRY: COMMODITY	19 Paper, Printing & Publishing	20 Miscellaneous Industries	21 Buildings & Public Works	22 Transportation - Merchand Gds	23 Transportation Passenger	24 Telecommunications & Post
* TOTAL TRANSACTIONS						
1 Agricultural Products	0.00	0.00	-.14	0.41	0.00	0.00
2 Livestock, Fishing, Hunting	0.00	0.15	0.00	0.33	0.00	0.00
3 Forestry Products	0.00	0.27	22.97	0.08	-.17	0.00
4 Agro-Industry	0.00	0.07	-.03	-.00	0.00	0.00
5 Minerals	0.00	0.07	1.03	0.07	0.00	0.00
6 Electricity,Water,Petr.Prds	0.00	0.18	19.30	0.91	58.79	0.87
7 Food Products	2.03	0.00	0.00	0.54	0.15	0.00
8 Beverages	0.00	0.00	0.00	0.15	0.53	0.00
9 Tobacco	0.00	0.00	0.00	0.00	0.04	0.00
10 Oils and Fats	0.00	0.00	0.16	0.08	0.00	0.00
11 Chemical & Pharmac. Prods.	3.98	0.16	5.74	1.34	1.70	0.00
12 Textiles, Wearing	3.03	0.00	0.00	0.20	-.81	0.65
13 Leather, Footwear	0.00	0.00	0.00	0.43	0.17	0.32
14 Wood and Furniture	0.00	0.00	0.00	0.57	0.00	0.05
15 Constr. Matrls & Misc.Minerl	0.00	0.31	8.88	3.55	0.57	0.25
16 Metal Prods.Mech. Machinery	0.95	0.68	44.27	3.69	0.40	0.92
17 Transport Equipment	0.17	0.00	2.46	0.01	4.54	0.89
18 Electrical Machineries	0.00	0.04	3.46	-.1	4.21	-.04
19 Paper, Paperbd., Printing	6.25	0.00	3.31	0.56	4.22	0.99
20 Misc. Manufactured Goods	0.19	2.00	0.07	0.54	0.85	-.08
21 Buildings	0.00	0.00	0.00	0.00	0.64	0.00
22 Transport (Products)	0.20	0.05	0.83	7.83	0.00	0.32
23 Transport (Passenger)	0.21	0.06	0.71	0.29	2.75	0.41
24 Post, Telecommunications	0.00	0.00	0.00	0.00	2.09	0.00
25 Trade	0.66	0.15	5.14	6.28	0.00	0.48
26 Banking, Insurance Services	0.48	0.05	0.89	0.22	2.11	0.36
27 Services to Enterprises	0.00	0.00	0.00	0.48	2.64	0.00
28 Household Services	0.48	0.63	12.41	8.65	1.60	0.09
29 Other Misc. Services	0.00	0.00	0.00	0.00	23.90	0.09
30 Non-Marketable Services	0.00	0.00	0.00	0.00	1.39	0.00
31 Total Intermediate Inputs	15.90	4.80	191.98	77.12	154.31	10.29

148

Input-Output Table for Madagascar for the Year 1973 (Revised)

MADAGASCAR 1973 — FLOWS in hundred million Malagasy francs of Y 1973 — PRODUCERS CURRENT MARKET PRICES

INDUSTRY:	19 Paper, Printing & Publishing	20 Miscellaneous Industries	21 Buildings & Public Works	22 Transportation - Merchand. Gds	23 Transportation - Passenger	24 Telecommunicns. & Post
* IMPORT TRANSACTIONS *						
32 Agricultural Products	0.00	0.00	0.00	0.00	0.00	0.00
33 Livestock, Fishing, Hunting	0.00	0.00	0.00	0.00	0.00	0.00
34 Forestry Products	0.00	0.00	0.00	0.00	0.00	0.00
35 Agro-Industry	0.00	0.07	0.28	0.00	0.00	0.17
36 Minerals	0.21	0.02	3.25	4.01	0.00	0.00
37 Electrcty,Water,Petroleum	0.00	0.00	0.00	0.00	10.68	0.00
38 Food Products	0.00	0.00	0.00	0.00	0.00	0.00
39 Beverages	0.00	0.00	0.00	0.00	0.00	0.00
40 Tobacco	0.00	0.00	0.00	0.00	0.00	0.00
41 Oils and Fats	3.91	0.08	0.43	9.14	10.43	0.34
42 Chemical & Pharmac. Prods.	0.00	0.00	0.00	0.00	0.00	0.25
43 Textiles, Wearing	0.00	0.00	0.00	0.21	0.08	0.00
44 Leather, Footwear	0.00	0.00	0.00	0.00	0.04	0.14
45 Wood and Furniture	0.93	0.16	0.19	0.07	0.21	0.53
46 Constr.Matrls &Misc.Minera	0.17	0.00	29.90	0.30	4.07	0.89
47 Metal Prds.Mech.Machinery	0.10	0.68	29.58	2.90	4.71	0.94
48 Transport Equipment	3.22	0.00	3.46	5.73	2.68	0.24
49 Electrical Machinery	0.00	0.10	0.00	1.52	0.74	0.00
50 Paper.Paperbd., Printing	0.00	0.00	0.07	0.00	0.26	0.09
51 Misc.Manufactured Goods	0.00	0.00	0.00	0.00	0.00	0.00
52 Buildings	0.00	0.00	0.00	0.00	0.00	0.00
53 Transport (Products)	0.00	0.00	0.00	8.78	20.57	0.00
54 Transport (Passenger)	0.00	0.00	0.00	0.00	0.00	0.57
55 Post, Telecommunications	0.00	0.00	0.41	0.00	0.00	0.41
56 Trade	0.00	0.00	0.00	0.00	0.00	0.00
57 Banking & Insurance Servic.	0.00	0.00	0.00	0.00	0.00	0.00
58 Business Services	0.00	0.00	0.00	0.00	0.00	0.00
59 Household Services	0.00	0.00	0.00	0.00	0.00	0.00
60 Other Misc. Services	0.00	0.00	0.00	0.00	0.00	0.00
61 Non-Marketable Services	0.00	0.00	0.00	0.00	0.00	0.00
62 Total Imported Inputs	8.54	2.87	68.13	31.43	56.87	5.00
63 Gross Fixed Capital Conspt.	2.97	0.12	9.15	8.88	15.74	0.89
64 Compensation of Employees	8.28	1.25	58.85	48.25	39.24	17.23
65 Indirect Taxes	0.10	0.30	5.90	3.75	3.01	0.07
66 Subsidies	0.00	0.00	0.00	-1.25	0.00	0.00
67 Operating Surplus	4.60	2.93	27.33	33.42	37.54	7.89
68 Gross Value Added	15.95	4.60	101.23	93.05	95.53	26.08
69 Change in Stocks	4.34	0.00	0.00	0.00	0.00	0.00
70 Distribution Margins	8.31	0.68	0.00	-170.17	0.00	0.00
71 Gross Output	45.10	10.08	293.21	0.00	249.84	36.37
72 Imports (c.i.f.)	18.30	16.71	0.00	0.00	63.80	2.74
73 Import Duties	2.98	6.69	0.00	0.00	0.00	0.00
74 Distrib.Margins on Imports	8.00	4.71	0.00	0.00	0.00	0.00
75 Change in Stocks of Imports	0.00	0.00	0.00	0.00	0.00	0.00
76 Imports incl Duties & Margin	29.28	28.11	0.00	0.00	63.80	2.74
77 Total Resources	74.38	38.17	293.21	0.00	313.64	39.11

Input-Output Table for Madagascar for the Year 1973 (Revised)

MADAGASCAR 1973   FLOWS in hundred million Malagasy francs of Y 1973   PRODUCERS CURRENT MARKET PRICES

INDUSTRY:

COMMODITY	25 Wholesale & Trade	26 Banking Insurance	27 Services to Enterprises	28 Services to Households	29 Other Misc. Services	30 Administration
* TOTAL TRANSACTIONS *						
1 Agricultural Products	0 00	0 00	0 00	0 16	1 34	2 64
2 Livestock, Fishing, Hunting	0 00	0 00	0 00	0 03	0 16	0 06
3 Forestry Products	0 00	0 00	0 00	0 03	0 49	0 06
4 Agro-Industry	0 08	0 07	0 00	0 00	0 00	0 07
5 Minerals	9 98	0 57	0 68	0 91	0 14	
6 Electricity,Water,Petr.Prds	0 00	0 00	0 00	0 40	3 71	27 08
7 Food Products	0 00	0 00	0 00	0 00	4 30	2 22
8 Beverages	0 00	0 00	0 00	0 00	0 67	0 43
9 Tobacco						
10 Oils and Fats	0 46	0 19	0 09	2 67	2 36	4 00
11 Chemical & Pharmac. Prods.	0 89	0 00	0 00	0 00	0 28	5 00
12 Textiles, Wearing	0 43	0 30	0 14	0 97	0 00	0 43
13 Leather, Footwear	0 00	0 00	0 07	0 68	0 87	0 86
14 Wood and Furniture	0 00	0 44	0 07	0 15	7 85	1 04
15 Constr. Matris & Misc.Mineri	0 00	0 81	0 31	0 78	2 28	20 75
16 Metal Prods.,Mech. Machinery	1 31	0 00	0 48	0 40	0 33	0 52
17 Transport Equipment	3 37	0 11	0 25	0 59	9 95	27 35
18 Electrical Machineries	10 25				9 81	27 93
19 Paper, Paperbd.; Printing						
20 Misc. Manufactured Goods		0 00	0 37	0 35	0 95	8 18
21 Buildings	9 11	0 19	0 99	0 37	0 43	8 10
22 Transport (Products)	12 71					
23 Transport (Passenger)	25 59	4 94	0 58	0 78	6 84	3 00
24 Post, Telecommunications	8 42	6 63	2 05	2 05	0 98	0 98
25 Trade	0 44	0 00	0 27	0 13	0 00	0 32
26 Banking, Insurance Services	10 97	3 27	1 59	1 22	0 00	0 05
27 Services to Enterprises	10 67	0 00	0 00	1 00	0 00	15 34
28 Services to Enterprises						
29 Household Services						
30 Non-Marketable Services						
31 Total Intermediate Inputs	116 38	21 72	10 07	12 73	55 87	142 37

150

Input-Output Table for Madagascar for the Year 1973 (Revised)

MADAGASCAR 1973 — FLOWS in hundred million Malagasy francs of Y 1973

PRODUCERS CURRENT MARKET PRICES

INDUSTRY:	25 Wholesale & Trade	26 Banking Insurance	27 Services to Enterprises	28 Services to Households	29 Other Misc. Services	30 Administration
* IMPORT TRANSACTIONS *						
32 Agricultural Products	0.00	0.00	0.00	0.00	0.00	0.03
33 Livestock, Fishing, Hunting	0.00	0.00	0.00	0.00	0.00	0.00
34 Forestry Products	0.00	0.00	0.00	0.00	0.00	0.00
35 Agro-Industry	0.00	0.00	0.00	0.00	0.00	0.00
36 Minerals	0.00	0.00	0.00	0.00	0.00	0.00
37 Electrcty.Water.Petroleum	0.79	0.16	0.05	0.15	0.08	2.81
38 Food Products	0.00	0.00	0.00	0.17	0.49	2.68
39 Beverages	0.00	0.00	0.00	0.00	3.85	0.05
40 Tobacco	0.00	0.00	0.00	0.00	0.00	0.11
41 Oils and Fats	0.00	0.00	0.00	0.05	0.05	0.00
42 Chemical & Pharmac. Prods.	1.07	0.00	0.09	2.51	2.05	0.93
43 Textiles, Wearing	0.00	0.00	0.00	0.05	0.05	0.11
44 Leather, Footwear	0.00	0.00	0.00	0.00	0.00	0.00
45 Wood and Furniture	0.00	0.00	0.00	0.00	0.00	0.00
46 Constr. Matrs.&Misc.Minera	0.00	0.30	0.04	0.97	0.98	0.07
47 Metal Prds. Mech.Machinery	0.00	0.44	0.12	0.68	0.79	0.77
48 Transport Equipment	0.00	0.00	0.07	0.00	7.85	3.51
49 Electrical Machinery	0.00	0.00	0.07	0.05	2.03	1.04
50 Paper,Paperbd. Printing	2.99	0.54	0.83	0.07	0.05	2.01
51 Misc. Manufactured Goods	2.78	0.32	0.48	0.29	0.95	5.01
52 Buildings	0.00	0.00	0.00	0.00	0.00	0.42
53 Transport (Products)	0.00	0.00	0.00	0.00	0.00	0.00
54 Transport (Passenger)	0.00	0.00	0.00	0.00	0.00	0.00
55 Post, Telecommunications	0.00	0.00	0.00	0.00	0.00	0.00
56 Trade	0.00	0.00	0.00	0.00	0.00	0.00
57 Banking & Insurance Servic.	0.00	4.83	2.00	0.00	0.00	0.00
58 Business Services	0.89	0.01	0.05	2.03	2.00	0.00
59 Household Services	0.00	0.00	0.00	0.00	0.00	0.00
60 Other Misc.Services	0.00	0.00	0.00	0.00	0.00	0.00
61 Non-Marketable Services	0.00	0.00	0.00	0.00	0.00	0.00
62 Total Imported Inputs	9.52	7.60	4.03	7.05	20.45	22.08
63 Gross Fixed Capital Conspt	16.03	2.94	1.24	0.98	1.83	0.33
64 Compensation of Employees	107.71	27.78	9.18	42.59	15.41	406.04
65 Indirect Taxes	11.85	0.84	0.38	0.41	-1.75	0.00
66 Subsidies	-27.71	0.00	0.00	0.00	-1.28	0.00
67 Operating Surplus	160.08	28.26	16.13	24.78	131.29	0.00
68 Gross Value Added	387.96	59.82	28.93	69.76	149.00	406.37
69 Change in Stocks	-484.34	0.00	0.00	0.00	0.00	0.00
70 Distribution Margins	-484.34	0.00	0.00	0.00	0.00	0.00
71 Gross Output	0.00	81.54	37.00	82.49	204.87	548.74
72 Imports (c.i.f.)	0.00	0.00	0.00	0.00	0.00	0.00
73 Import Duties (.f.)	0.00	4.83	9.65	2.03	47.71	0.00
74 Distrib.Margins on Imports	0.00	0.00	0.00	0.00	0.00	0.00
75 Change in Stocks of Imports	0.00	0.00	0.00	0.00	0.00	0.00
76 Imports incl.Duties & Margin	0.00	4.83	9.65	2.03	47.71	0.00
77 Total Resources	0.00	86.37	46.65	84.52	252.58	548.74

151

Input-Output Table for Madagascar for the Year 1973 (Revised)

MADAGASCAR 1973   FLOWS in hundred million Malagasy francs of Y 1973   PRODUCERS CURRENT MARKET PRICES

COMMODITY	31 Intermediate Consumption	32 Private Consumption	33 Government Consumption	34 Gross Fixed Capital Formtn.	35 Changes In Stocks	36 Exports
* TOTAL TRANSACTIONS						
1 - Agricultural Products	328.30	191.78	0.00	0.00	1.77	251.07
2 - Livestock, Fishing, Hunting	368.43	37.19	0.00	3.00	0.00	26.26
3 - Forestry Products	42.40	47.27	0.00		1.19	10.18
4 - Agro-Industry	45.08	40.28	0.00	07.45	4.05	35.21
5 - Minerals	3.55	0.00-	0.00	10.00	1.65	17.31
6 - Electricity, Water, Petr. Prds	214.49	42.01-	0.00		17.05	20.58
7 - Food Products	57.21	778.17	0.00		17.12	55.83
8 - Beverages	0.53	57.55	0.00		4.11	0.02
9 - Tobacco		35.91	0.00		12.33	2.05
10 - Oils and Fats	5.22	51.21	0.00		2.73	4.75
11 - Chemical & Pharmac. Prods.	84.45	245.50	0.00		8.03	5.29
12 - Textiles, Wearing	84.27	22.60	0.00		2.32	0.34
13 - Leather, Footwear	2.10	7.60	0.00		0.58	0.57
14 - Wood and Furniture	14.83	11.95	0.00	5.26	0.00-	0.58
15 - Constr. Matrls & Misc. Minerl	85.85	13.64	0.00		6.75	6.51
16 - Metal Prods. Mech. Machinery	123.71	20.26	0.00	87.00	6.64	6.54
17 - Transport Equipment	37.58		0.00	47.00	9.98	4.41
18 - Electrical Machineries	32.53		0.00	24.01-	8.15	0.68
19 - Paper, Paperbd., Printing	55.36	14.39	0.00		6.13	0.00
20 - Misc. Manufactured Goods	17.10		0.00		0.00	0.00
21 - Buildings	60.02		0.00	231.80		
22 - Transport (Products)		204.68	0.00		6.00	52.35
23 - Transport (Passenger)	56.61	5.27	0.00			2.45
24 - Post, Telecommunications	31.39		0.00		0.00	
25 - Trade		3.21	0.00	0.00	0.00	0.23
26 - Banking, Insurance Services	80.93	72.33	0.00	4.09	0.00	5.54
27 - Services to Enterprises	38.69	76.25	0.00		0.00	2.00
28 - Household Services	8.27	162.95	0.00		0.00	0.000
29 - Other Misc. Services	90.37	13.95	0.00		0.000	0.000
30 - Non-Marketable Services	20.43		514.36		0.000	0.00
31 - Total Intermediate Inputs	1935.13	2154.47	514.38	400.78	104.58	503.85

152

Input-Output Table for Madagascar for the Year 1973 (Revised)

MADAGASCAR 1973   FLOWS in hundred million Malagasy francs of Y 1973   PRODUCERS CURRENT MARKET PRICES

* IMPORT TRANSACTIONS *	Intermediate Consumption 31	Private Consumption 32	Government Consumption 33	Gross Fixed Capital Formtn 34	Changes in Stocks 35	Exports 36
32 Agricultural Products	5.56	0.13	0.000	0.000	0.000	0.000
33 Livestock,Fishing,Hunting	0.00	0.19	0.000	0.000	0.000	0.000
34 Forestry Products	0.28	0.02	0.000	0.000	0.000	0.000
35 Agro Industry	0.94	0.10	0.000	0.000	0.000	0.000
36 Minerals	64.14	0.00	0.000	0.000	0.000	0.000
37 Elect.Pcty,Water,Petroleum	28.38	0.01	0.000	0.000	1.05	0.000
38 Food Products	2.73	97.62	0.000	0.000	9.64	0.000
39 Beverages	0.00	27.20	0.000	0.000	2.27	0.000
40 Tobacco	0.00	6.04	0.000	0.000	0.00	0.000
41 Oils and Fats	67.23	8.08	0.000	0.000	8.01	0.000
42 Chemical & Pharmac. Prods	67.88	39.89	0.000	0.000	8.01	0.000
43 Textiles,Weaving	26.04	72.29	0.000	0.000	0.00	0.000
44 Leather,Wearwear	24.71	8.71	0.000	0.000	0.00	0.000
45 Wood and Furniture	96.13	7.40	0.000	0.000	1.05	0.000
46 Const.Matrls &Misc.Minera	23.96	7.23	0.000	0.000	0.00	0.000
47 Metal Prds.Mech.Machinery	36.13	8.03	0.000	53.04	0.28	0.000
48 Transport Equipment	27.36	16.64	0.000	41.85	8.03	0.000
49 Electrical Machinery	10.92	2.96	0.000	20.85	8.15	0.000
50 Paper,Paperbd.,Printing		3.77	0.000	0.000	8.13	0.000
51 Misc.Manufactured Goods		1.08	0.000	0.000	0.00	0.000
52 Buildings			0.000	0.000	0.000	0.000
53 Transport (Products)	27.36	36.44	0.000	0.00	0.00	0.000
54 Transport (Passenger)	1.41	1.33	0.000	0.00	0.00	0.000
55 Post,Telecommunications	0.00	0.00	0.000	0.000	0.000	0.000
56 Trade	4.83	0.00	0.000	0.000	0.000	0.000
57 Banking & Insurance Servic	9.65	47.71	0.000	0.000	0.000	0.000
58 Business Services	2.03	0.00	0.00	0.00	0.00	0.00
59 Household Services	0.00	0	0.00	0.00	0.00	0.00
60 Other Misc. Services	0.00					
81 Non-Marketable Services	0.00					
62 Total Imported Inputs	451.17	392.62	0.00	114.79	42.31	0.00
63 Gross Fixed Capital Conspt.	128.81	0.00	0.00	0.00	0.00	0.00
64 Compensation of Employees	938.90	0.00	0.00	0.00	0.00	0.00
65 Indirect Taxes	260.12	0.00	0.00	0.00	0.00	0.00
66 Subsidies	-39.27	0.00	0.00	0.00	0.00	0.00
67 Operating Surplus	1571.76	0.00	0.00	0.00	0.00	0.00
68 Gross Value Added	2858.32	0.00	0.00	0.00	0.00	0.00
69 Change in Stocks	-40.83	0.00	0.00	0.00	0.00	0.00
70 Distribution Margings	-222.19	0.00	0.00	0.00	0.00	0.00
71 Gross Output	4612.09	2154.47	514.36	400.79	104.58	503.85
72 Imports(c.i.f.)	821.66	0.00	0.000	0.000	0.000	0.000
73 Import Duties on Imports	117.94	0.00	0.000	0.000	0.000	0.000
74 Distrib. Margins on Imports	222.19	0.00	0.000	0.000	0.000	0.000
75 Change in Stocks of Imports	39.10	0.00	0.000	0.000	0.000	0.000
76 Imports incl.Duties & Margin	1000.89	0.00	0.00	0.00	0.00	0.00
77 Total Resources	5812.98	2154.47	514.36	400.79	104.58	503.85

Input-Output Table for Madagascar for the Year 1973 (Revised)

MADAGASCAR 1973   FLOWS in hundred million Malagasy francs of Y 1973

PRODUCERS CURRENT MARKET PRICES

	COMMODITY	37 Total Final Demand	38 Total Resources (Imports)
*	TOTAL TRANSACTIONS *		
1	Agricultural Products	444.62	772.92
2	Livestock, Fishing, Hunting	66.83	435.26
3	Forestry Products	57.45	99.85
4	Agro-Industry	86.66	91.74
5	Minerals	39.41	42.96
6	Electricity,Water,Petr.Prds	83.72	278.15
7	Food Products	851.12	908.61
8	Beverages	61.68	68.89
9	Tobacco	42.93	66.82
10	Oils and Fats	66.29	48.15
11	Chemical & Pharmac. Prods.	253.11	143.44
12	Textiles, Wearing	22.52	337.38
13	Leather, Footwear	1.79	29.62
14	Wood and Furniture	8.18	27.62
15	Constr. Matr's & Misc.Mineral	92.61	74.03
16	Metal Prod.,Mech. Machinery	68.82	216.32
17	Transport Equipment	54.92	106.40
18	Electrical Machineries	19.02	87.45
19	Paper,Paperbd.,Printing	21.07	74.38
20	Misc.Manufactured Goods	233.19	293.21
21	Buildings		238.17
22	Transport (Products)	257.03	313.64
23	Transport (Passenger)	7.72	38.11
24	Post, Telecommunications		
25	Trade	0.44	86.37
26	Banking, Insurance Services	5.96	46.65
27	Services to Enterprises		
28	Household Services	176.25	252.58
29	Other Misc.Services	554.31	548.74
30	Non-Marketable Services		
31	Total Intermediate Inputs	3677.85	5612.98

Input-Output Table for Madagascar for the Year 1973 (Revised)

MADAGASCAR 1973   FLOWS in hundred million Malagasy francs of Y 1973   PRODUCERS CURRENT MARKET PRICES

* IMPORT TRANSACTIONS *	37 Total Final Demand	38 Total Resources (Imports)
32 Agricultural Products	0.13	5.89
33 Livestock,Fishing,Hunting	0.19	0.19
34 Forestry Products	0.02	0.30
35 Agro-Industry	0.11	0.11
36 Minerals	0.00	0.94
37 Elec.Cty,Water,Petroleum	3.00	67.20
38 Food Products	107.26	135.64
39 Beverages	29.47	32.20
40 Tobacco	6.04	6.04
41 Oils and Fats	6.08	8.31
42 Chemical & Pharmac. Prods.	46.53	114.41
43 Textiles, Wearing	72.79	98.83
44 Leather, Footwear	8.79	98.38
45 Wood and Furniture	1.76	3.47
46 Constr.Matrls.&Misc.Minera	1.40	26.07
47 Metal Prds.Mech.Machinery	60.03	153.20
48 Transport Equipment	48.95	85.08
49 Electrical Machinery	47.92	29.08
50 Paper, Paperbd. Printing	17.19	28.11
51 Misc. Manufactured Goods		
52 Buildings	0	0
53 Transport (Products)	36.44	82.80
54 Transport (Passenger)	.33	0.74
55 Post, Telecommunications		
56 Trade	0.00	
57 Banking & Insurance Servic.	0.00	4.83
58 Business Services	0.00	2.85
59 Household Services	0.00	2.03
60 Other Misc. Services	47.71	47.71
61 Non-Marketable Services	0	0
62 Total Imported Inputs	549.72	1000.89
63 Gross Fixed Capital Conspt.	0.00	126.81
64 Compensation of Employees	0.00	938.90
65 Indirect Taxes	0.00	260.12
66 Subsidies	0.00	-39.27
67 Operating Surplus	0.00	1571.76
68 Gross Value Added	0.00	2858.32
69 Change in Stocks	0.00	-40.83
70 Distribution Margings	0.00	-222.19
71 Gross Output	3677.85	8289.94
72 Imports (c.i.f.)	0.00	821.66
73 Import Duties on Imports	0.00	117.94
74 Distrib. Margins on Imports	0.00	222.19
75 Change in Stocks of Imports	0.00	39.10
76 Imports Incl.Duties & Margin	0.00	1000.89
77 Total Resources	3677.85	9290.83

MALTA

Reference year: 1971

Entries in table: Domestic flows

Source: Central Office of Statistics of Malta, *National Accounts of the Maltese Island*

Computerized: Deutsches Institut für Wirtschaftsforschung, Berlin

Currency units: Maltese pounds of Y 1971
Scale factor: 10,000

Pricing system: Producers' current prices
Intermediate sectors: 24 × 24
Treatment of trade margins: —

Treatment of imports: Inputs, row 26
Availability of import matrix: Not available

Total number of rows: 31
Statistical unit of quadrant 1: Industry

Total number of columns: 32
Statistical unit of quadrant 1: Industry

Fourth quadrant: Not occupied

Input-Output Tables of Malta for the Year 1971

FLOWS in ten thousand Maltese pounds of Y 1971

PRODUCERS CURRENT PRICES

INDUSTRY:	1 Agriculture and Fishing	2 Mining and Quarrying	3 Food	4 Flour Mills	5 Beverages	6 Tobacco
DOMESTIC TRANSACTIONS						
1 Agriculture and Fishing	0	0	322	0	1576	0
2 Mining and Quarrying	0	0	10	0	0	0
3 Food	1223	0	775	0	0	0
4 Flour Mills	134	0	12	0	0	0
5 Beverages	0	0	0	0	0	0
6 Tobacco	0	0	0	0	0	0
7 Textiles	0	0	0	0	0	0
8 Footwear Apparel	0	0	0	0	0	0
9 Wearing Apparel	0	0	32	0	42	50
10 Furniture and Fittings	0	0	9	0	24	0
11 Leather	0	0	0	0	0	0
12 Chemicals	0	0	20	0	43	0
13 Non-Metallic Minerals	0	0	17	0	0	0
14 Metals	0	30	10	5	398	0
15 Machinery	59	0	12	0	70	0
16 Transport	54	0	5	0	0	0
17 Construction	0	4	12	0	32	0
18 Other Industries	0	0	5	0	1	3
19 Gas	0	0	43	20	72	0
20 Electricity	0	0	0	0	23	0
21 Water	0	0	0	0	0	0
23 Transp.Trade,Fin'l.Oth Svcs	682	49	461	320	351	281
24 Pub.Svcs.Ownshp of Dwellgs	0	0	0	0	0	0
25 Total Intmdt Domestic Inputs	2102	86	1724	347	2632	335
26 Imports CIF	2299	116	1961	1232	1108	417
27 Compensation of Employees	410	264	547	104	1224	160
28 Indrct.Taxes less Subsidies	12	17	121	-831	-692	1744
29 Operating Surplus	5519	206	850	59	941	181
30 Gross Value Added	5941	487	1518	-668	1473	2085
31 Gross Output	10342	689	5203	911	5213	2837

Input-Output Tables of Malta for the Year 1971

MALTA 1971   FLOWS in ten thousand Maltese pounds of Y 1971   PRODUCERS CURRENT PRICES

INDUSTRY:	7 Textiles	8 Footwear	9 Wearing Apparel	10 Furniture and Fittings	11 Printing	12 Leather
* DOMESTIC TRANSACTIONS * INDUSTRY						
1 Agriculture and Fishing	0	0	0	0	0	21
2 Mining and Quarrying	0	0	0	0	0	0
3 Food	0	0	0	0	0	0
4 Flour Mills	0	0	0	0	0	0
5 Beverages	0	0	0	0	0	0
6 Tobacco	0	0	0	0	0	0
7 Textiles	0	0	20	0	0	0
8 Footwear	0	0	0	0	0	0
9 Wearing Apparel	0	6	0	0	0	0
10 Furniture and Fittings	10	0	0	0	0	0
11 Printing	24	0	13	0	0	0
12 Leather	0	0	0	0	0	0
13 Chemicals	0	0	0	16	0	0
14 Non-Metallic Minerals	0	1	0	32	13	0
15 Metals	7	0	4	24	0	0
16 Machinery	0	0	0	0	13	0
17 Transport	0	0	7	0	0	0
18 Other Industries	2	0	3	9	13	0
19 Construction	0	0	0	0	0	0
20 Gas	0	0	1	0	1	0
21 Electricity	115	0	0	10	16	0
22 Water	6	0	0	0	18	3
23 Transp..Trade.Fin'l.Oth.Svcs	48	60	369	200	202	31
24 Pub.Svcs..Ownshp of Dwellgs	1	0	0	0	0	0
25 Total Intmdt.Domestic Inputs	646	69	428	295	246	55
26 Imports CIF	2392	148	767	491	458	53
27 Compensation of Employees	1228	103	619	544	797	42
28 Indrct.Taxes less Subsidies	102	3	112	52	21	4
29 Operating Surplus	2099	66	387	414	388	41
30 Gross Value Added	3429	172	1118	1010	1204	87
31 Gross Output	6467	389	2313	1796	1908	195

158

Input-Output Tables of Malta for the Year 1971

MALTA 1971   FLOWS in ten thousand Maltese pounds of Y 1971   PRODUCERS CURRENT PRICES

INDUSTRY:	13 Chemicals	14 Non-Metallic Minerals	15 Metals	16 Machinery	17 Transport	18 Other Industries
* DOMESTIC TRANSACTIONS *						
1 Agriculture and Fishing	0	0	0	0	0	0
2 Mining and Quarrying	0	121	0	0	0	0
3 Food	0	0	0	0	0	0
4 Flour Mills	0	0	0	0	0	0
5 Beverages	0	0	0	0	0	0
6 Tobacco	0	0	0	0	0	0
7 Textiles	0	0	0	0	0	0
8 Footwear	17	0	0	0	0	0
9 Wearing Apparel	82	0	0	0	0	0
10 Furniture and Fittings	0	0	0	0	0	6
11 Printing	0	0	0	0	0	0
12 Leather	0	0	0	0	4	0
13 Chemicals	2	0	4	6	0	0
14 Non-Metallic Minerals	-0	14	-0	0	40	80
15 Metals	0	2	34	0	0	8
16 Machinery	-0	-0	100	-0	0	0
17 Transport	0	4	2	4	0	4
18 Other Industries	0	0	5	8	10	14
19 Construction	20	12	9	9	74	3
20 Electricity					2	
21 Gas						
22 Water						
23 Transp.,Trade,Fin'l.Oth.Svcs	258	313	240	260	330	203
24 Pub.Svcs.:Ownshp of Dwellgs	0	0	0	0	0	0
25 Total Intmdt.Domestic Inputs	400	488	306	285	464	240
26 Imports CIF	991	623	526	568	1020	518
27 Compensation of Employees	470	516	296	824	1255	358
28 Indrct.Taxes less Subsidies	89	74	181	70	180	38
29 Operating Surplus	548	333	449	418	1040	296
30 Gross Value Added	1107	923	908	1312	2475	692
31 Gross Output	2498	2034	1738	2165	3959	1450

Input-Output Tables of Malta for the Year 1971

MALTA 1971   FLOWS in ten thousand Maltese pounds of Y 1971   PRODUCERS CURRENT PRICES

INDUSTRY:	19 Construction	20 Gas	21 Electricity	22 Water	23 Transp.,Trade,Fin'l,Oth.Svcs	24 Public Services Ownshp Dwellings
* DOMESTIC TRANSACTIONS *						
1 Agriculture and Fishing	529	0	0	0	44	0
2 Mining and Quarrying	0	0	0	0	10	0
3 Food	0	0	0	0	0	0
4 Flour Mills	0	0	0	0	0	0
5 Beverages	0	0	0	0	0	0
6 Tobacco	0	0	0	0	0	0
7 Textiles	0	0	0	0	0	0
8 Footwear	0	0	0	0	0	0
9 Wearing Apparel	0	0	0	0	0	0
10 Furniture and Fittings	0	0	0	0	0	0
11 Printing	0	0	0	0	558	0
12 Leather	0	0	0	0	0	0
13 Chemicals	195	0	0	0	0	0
14 Non-Metallic Minerals	390	0	0	0	0	0
15 Metals	338	0	0	0	0	0
16 Machinery	51	0	0	0	0	0
17 Transport	0	0	0	0	578	0
18 Other Industries	0	0	0	0	79	0
19 Construction	0	0	0	0	0	0
20 Gas	0	0	0	0	0	0
21 Electricity	9	3	86	93	1019	0
22 Water	3	-1	144	0	105	0
23 Transp.,Trade,Fin'l,Oth.Svcs	2160	63	645	177	0	0
24 Pub.Svcs,Ownshp of Dwellings	0	0	0	0	0	0
25 Total Intmdt.Domestic Inputs	3502	78	875	272	2393	0
26 Imports CIF	1619	181	1022	106	20400	0
27 Compensation of Employees	3005	131	467	850	8948	21425
28 Indrct.Taxes less Subsidies	316	123	0	-524	2457	0
29 Operating Surplus	1590	124	538	-200	13814	4409
30 Gross Value Added	4911	378	1005	126	25219	25834
31 Gross Output	10032	615	2902	504	48012	25834

Input-Output Tables of Malta for the Year 1971

MALTA 1971   FLOWS in ten thousand Maltese pounds of Y 1971   PRODUCERS CURRENT PRICES

	25 Total Intmdt. Consumption	26 Private Consumption	27 Government Consumption	28 Gross Fixed Capital Format	29 Changes in Stocks	30 Exports
* DOMESTIC TRANSACTIONS *						
1 Agriculture and Fishing	1963	7174	88	0	254	863
2 Mining and Quarrying	1671		0	0	-18	503
3 Food	1223	3483	48	0	-54	5
4 Flour Mills	909	14	0	0	-17	438
5 Beverages	12	4637	160	0	-34	137
6 Tobacco	20	2653	27	0	-20	6474
7 Textiles		25	2	0	-52	156
8 Footwear	20	252		0	-21	1577
9 Wearing Apparel		1678	30	0	30	73
10 Furniture and Fittings	70	1467	16	175	-5	434
11 Printing	796	600	40	0	-34	122
12 Leather		81	0		-8	908
13 Chemicals	92	1545	16		0	14
14 Non-Metallic Minerals	423		0	1583	-83	601
15 Metals	795	0	0	460	4	1123
16 Machinery	334		0	814	-118	1949
17 Transport	651	1105	7	292	-106	728
18 Other Industries	90	655	0		-38	577
19 Construction	102		5	10112	-28	23
20 Gas	136	55			-759	53
21 Electricity	1553	1055	241	0	0	33
22 Water	246	28	7	0	0	22990
23 Transp.Trade,Fin'l,Oth.Svcs	7635	13668	862	2857	0	22990
24 Pub.Svcs.,Ownshp of Dwellgs	645	7428	17416	0	0	345
25 Total Intmdt.Domestic Inputs	18266	47317	18989	18273	-943	40124
26 Imports CIF	39908	21141	528	6991	3812	3453
27 Compensation of Employees	44387			0		6135
28 Indrct.Taxes less Subsidies	3669		0	2257	0	309
29 Operating Surplus	34688	6318	0	0	0	0
30 Gross Value Added	82744	6318	0	2257	0	6444
31 Gross Output	140008	75076	19495	25521	2869	50021

161

Input-Output Tables of Malta for the Year 1971

MALTA 1971   FLOWS in ten thousand Maltese pounds of Y 1971

	31 Total Final Demand	32 Gross Output
* DOMESTIC TRANSACTIONS *		
INDUSTRY		
1 Agriculture and Fishing	8379	10342
2 Mining and Quarrying	18	689
3 Food	3980	5203
4 Flour Mills	2	911
5 Beverages	5201	5213
6 Tobacco	2837	2837
7 Textiles	6447	6467
8 Footwear	389	389
9 Wearing Apparel	2313	2313
10 Furniture and Fittings	1726	1736
11 Printing	112	1908
12 Leather	195	195
13 Chemicals	2406	2498
14 Non-Metallic Minerals	1611	2034
15 Metals	843	1738
16 Machinery	1831	2165
17 Transport	3308	3959
18 Other Industries	1360	1450
19 Construction	9930	10032
20 Gas	579	615
21 Electricity	1349	2902
22 Water	258	504
23 Transp.Trade,Fin'l.Oth.Svcs	40377	48012
24 Pub.Svcs.,Ownshp.of Dwellgs	25189	25834
25 Total Intmdt.Domestic Inputs	121740	140006
26 Imports CIF	36823	75219
27 Compensation of Employees	6135	50522
28 Indrct.Taxes less Subsidies	8884	12553
29 Operating Surplus	0	34688
30 Gross Value Added	15019	97763
31 Gross Output	172982	312966

162

MEXICO

The present report is based on volume seven of the *Series de Cuentas Nacionales de México*, entitled *Matriz de Insumo–Producto, Año de 1975*, published by the Secretaría de Programación y Presupuesto de México.

A. General information

1. Input-output tables for Mexico have been compiled for the years 1950, 1960, 1970 and 1975. The present report refers to the 1975 table, which was compiled by the Secretaría de Programación y Presupuesto and the Banco de México, with technical assistance provided by the United Nations Development Programme and the United Nations Regional Commission for Latin America. The 1970 and 1975 tables are not strictly comparable with those for 1950 and 1960 due to different classifications of activities. The differences are the following:

(a) Industrial activities related to agriculture except those that involve cleaning and packing of agricultural products were transferred in the 1970 and 1975 tables from agriculture to manufacturing;

(b) Refining of non-ferrous metallic minerals and carbon were included in the 1970 and 1975 tables in mining together with extraction activities, while in the earlier tables such activities were covered in manufacturing;

(c) The services of repair and maintenance which do not result in the production of parts of machinery and equipment were transferred in the 1970 and 1975 tables from manufacturing to services. To improve comparability of the 1970 and 1975 tables with the earlier tables, the latter ones were adapted to the more recent classification on the basis of a detail of 30 sectors.

2. The compilation of the 1975 input-output table was undertaken as part of a programme aimed at the improvement and updating of the system of National Accounts estimates for 1975 onwards. A complete equivalence exists between the input-output and the national accounts estimates of the corresponding aggregates.

3. The main deviations of the Mexican input-output table from SNA recommendations include: treatment of producers of government services (para. 10); treatment of education and health public services (para. 10); treatment of activities of private non-profit institutions (para. 10); breakdown of value added (para. 12); treatment of imports (para. 13); and commodity taxes not recorded separately, hence no valuation at approximate basic values can be derived.

B. Analytical framework

Tables and derived matrices available

4. The following basic tables were compiled:

(i) Input-output table of domestic transactions valued at producers' prices;

(ii)   Imports matrix;

(iii) Input-output table of total transactions (i.e., domestic production plus imports) valued at producers' prices;

(iv)   Input structure of subgroups of the food, beverages and tobacco sectors;

(v)   Input structure of subgroups of the textile, clothing and leather sectors;

(vi)   Input structure of subgroups of the wood sectors;

(vii) Input structure of subgroups of the paper and printing sectors;

(viii) Input structure of subgroups of the chemicals, petroleum, rubber and plastics sector;

(ix)   Input structure of subgroups of the non-metallic mineral sectors;

(x)   Input structure of subgroups of the basic metal sectors;

(xi)   Input structure of subgroups of the metal products, machinery and equipment goods sectors;

(xii) Input structure of subgroups of the health and education sectors;

(xiii) Input structure of subgroups of the government sector;

(xiv) Imports by type of good and subsectors of final demand categories;

(xv)   Indirect taxes by type of taxes and economic sector of incidence.

5.   On the basis of the data mentioned in para. 4, the following derived matrices were compiled:

(i')   Technical coefficients, based on table (i);

(ii') Inverse matrix of table (i);

(iii') Distribution coefficients based on table (i). Each element of matrix (ii) obtained by dividing the corresponding entry in the row of table (i) by the total demand for output of the relevant sector;

(iv') Technical coefficients, based on table (ii);

(v')   Technical coefficients, based on table (iii).

6.   All basic tables and derived matrices are presented at a level of disaggregation of 72×72 intermediate sectors.

Valuation standards

7.   All basic tables are valued at producers' prices, defined as purchasers' prices less distribution margins. Imports are valued c.i.f. and exports f.o.b.

Statistical units and classification standards

8.   The establishment is the statistical unit generally used in the data collection process. Input-output tables (i) and (iii) are of the industry by industry type.

9.   The overall classification of input-output sectors corresponds to a national classification system, specially devised for the purpose of compilation of the 1975 national accounts and input-output estimates. This special classification system was adopted on a temporary basis, to be used during the

164

process of revision of the Mexican Catalogue of Economic Activities (at present under way), and it generally coincides with the broader aggregates of the ISIC, except for the coal and metallic non-ferrous mining sectors, which, in the Mexican classification system, also include the corresponding manufacturing activities.

10. The classification of the intermediate consumption quadrant differs from SNA recommendations on input-output in the following respects:

   (a) Public health and educational services are recorded together with the same services provided by the private sector;

   (b) The activities of producers of government services—except health and education—are recorded in the final demand quadrant, under the government consumption category;

   (c) The activities of private non-profit institutions are recorded together with the corresponding activities of the private sector.

11. The definition and breakdown of final demand is in agreement with SNA recommendation. Private consumption is defined on a domestic basis.

12. Value added is defined as in SNA, but its breakdown differs from SNA recommendations in that operating surplus in the Mexican table also includes depreciation of fixed capital.

13. Imports are classified by destination only in table (i) (see para. 4). In addition, imports are cross-classified by origin and destination in table (ii). Contrary to SNA recommendations, no distinction is made between complimentary and competitive imports.

Treatment and presentation of selected transactions

14. Secondary products and their associated inputs were not transferred. Secondary outputs were distinguished, however, during the compilation process and allocated to their respective destinations on the basis of market shares per product.

15. Non-monetary output (such as self-consumption of agricultural products, imputed housing rents etc.) and its corresponding inputs were generally recorded together with the monetary output and inputs in the corresponding input-output sector.

16. Second-hand products were restricted to intermediate-type products only, such as metal scrap, glass and paper. Due to data limitations, transactions in second-hand capital goods were not considered. The sales and purchases of second-hand goods are recorded as plus and minus items in the rows of those industries that are the characteristic producers of those products, except for the trade margins which were included as output of the trade sector.

17. Output is generally defined on a gross basis, i.e., it includes intra-sector consumption of goods and services.

18. As recommended in the SNA, output of the financial sector is defined to include imputed service charges, which are defined as the difference between

165

interests received and interests paid. The distribution of output of this sector also follows the SNA recommendations, i.e., imputed services charges were allocated to a dummy sector which forms part of the other-services sector of the input-output table.

19. Output of the insurance sector is defined as in SNA, i.e., it excludes claims paid and includes net addition to the actuarial reserves by life insurance companies.

C. Statistical sources and compilation methodology

20. Data collection is based on existing regular sources, the results of the 1975 Industrial, Trade, Transportation and Services censuses, and special analysis carried out for the purposes of compilation of the table.

21. Although the 1975 table presents a level of disaggregation of 72×72 intermediate sectors, the basic information used for the compilation of the table was available at a much finer level of disaggregation. Output values were based on the analysis of data collected for 197 groups and 353 subgroups of economic activities. In addition, the tabulations used in the 1975 Industrial Census identify some 1,500 main products and raw materials. This high level of disaggregation allowed for the calculation of balances of supply and demand (measured in quantity terms) for the main products as well as for balances of output of each sector and its use by intermediate and final demand sectors. Such balances as well as the 1970 input-output table and the time series data available for the production sectors of the national accounts were used as additional consistency checks of the results of the 1975 input-output table.

Gross output and intermediate consumption

Agriculture, livestock, forestry and fishing

22. Output of the agricultural sector was estimated as the sum of the product of outputs of annual and permanent crops and their corresponding average rural prices. A total of 178 varieties of annual and permanent crops were considered. Most of the total agricultural production is covered in data provided by such agencies as Dirección General de Economía Agrícola, Dirección General de Distritos de Riego, Comisión Nacional de Fruticultura, Unión Nacional de Productores de Azúcar, Instituto Mexicano de Café, etc. The rest is mainly obtained from estimates based on the adjusted results of periodically conducted household surveys.

23. Data on intermediate inputs of the agriculture sector published in regular sources were relatively scarce. Therefore, special studies had to be carried out by the Dirección General de Economía Agrícola and other agencies.

24. Output and intermediate inputs of the livestock sector were obtained from data mainly provided by the Direcciones Generales de Ganadería, Avicultura y Especies Menores, Instituto Nacional de la Leche and the results of the 1968 National Household Surveys. The estimate of gross output of livestock was

based on an estimation of the total animal population needed to satisfy total demand for livestock as obtained in the above-mentioned household surveys. This total demand for livestock was obtained by applying to each one of several types of livestock a model of biological evolution which takes into account the prevailing practices in animal-rearing as well as the impact of known anomalies in the corresponding years. Livestock volumes so calculated were then multiplied by the corresponding average rural prices, which were compared to the extrapolated average prices in 1970 for further consistency of estimates. Two balances of supply and demand, one in quantity terms and another in terms of protein content were also used as consistency checks.

25. Data on gross output and intermediate consumption of the Forestry, Hunting and Fishing sectors were provided by the Subsecretaría Forestal y de la Fauna and the Departamento de Pesca respectively. The special characteristics of the production process in timber-yielding activities were taken into account in the estimation of the input structure of the Forestry sector. Similarly, subgroups of the hunting and fishing sectors were formed to allow for the existing varieties of products in the output of these sectors.

Mining and quarrying

26. Data on the mining sector (except for natural gas and petroleum products) were mainly obtained from the results of the 1975 Industrial Census, mining and metal statistics, and the Comisión de Fomento Minero. Census data include information on output, use of intermediate inputs, compensation of employees and other value added. Census data are valued at average purchasers' prices which were transformed into producers' prices by deducting the corresponding distribution margins (see para. 31). Data on output, and cost structure of the natural gas and petroleum sectors were obtained from the accounting books of the government owned petroleum company Petróleos Mexicanos (PEMEX).

Manufacturing

27. Data on the manufacturing sector (except petroleum refining and petroleum products) were obtained from the results of the 1975 Industrial Census, annual industrial statistics and the Dirección General de Estadística. Only establishments with output values exceeding one million pesos were covered by the Census. Additional surveys were carried out to cover the remaining manufacturing establishments. Census data included estimates on quantity and value of production, intermediate consumption and compensation of employees of each establishment covered. The detailed level of disaggregation at which these data were available (see para. 21) allowed for a consistency analysis of the census estimates of intermediate inputs and the known technical relationships existing between output and amount of raw materials used. Although two types of observation units (namely the establishment and the ancillary unit responsible for administration activities) are used in the census, available data do not permit the separation of industrial and ancillary activities. However, a major improvement could be introduced in the 1975 input-output table with respect to the 1970 table, namely, the disaggregation of the content of such census items as other incomes and other expenditures into their main

167

components (i.e., packing, advertising and repair and maintenance activities). This disaggregation was carried out on the basis of the information provided by direct research on these items.

28. Data on petroleum refining and petroleum products were provided by PEMEX. Output of these sectors was valued at the reported average prices for domestic sales and exports, which include the distribution margins charged by the distribution agencies of PEMEX. Therefore, the inputs of these distribution agencies were also added to the input structure of the petroleum refining and petroleum products sectors. Self-consumption of crude petroleum, natural gas and other products was valued at the prices used for PEMEX to calculate the unit costs of products of the sector.

Construction

29. Gross output of the construction sector was estimated by extrapolating the output of the sector in the 1970 table by means of the combined evolution of the following three indexes: index of quantity used of strategic domestic and imported inputs; index of prices of those inputs; and index of wages. The cost structure of the sector was determined by updating the input coefficients of the sector in 1970, taking into account the evolution of prices of each intermediate input. Estimates so obtained were checked against available data on apparent consumption of strategic inputs.

Electricity, gas and water supply

30. Gross output of this sector was estimated as the sum of net incomes obtained by the Comisión Federal de Electricidad and the Compañía de Luz y Fuerza del Centro from sales of electric power, taxes on electricity consumption and sales of gas and drinking water. Data on output and intermediate consumption were obtained from the accounting records of the agencies mentioned. Not covered are the municipal services of water distribution, which remain included in government consumption.

Trade, hotels and restaurants

31. Gross output of the trade sector was estimated indirectly, by deducting transport margins from the estimated total distribution margins. Total distribution margins of each intermediate sector were obtained as the difference between the purchasers' and producers' prices of their corresponding inter-mediate inputs, on the basis of data on quantity, value and average prices of main products and raw materials collected in the 1975 Industrial Census. The same procedure was applied in the estimation of total distribution margins of government consumption and exports. In the case of private consumption and fixed capital formation, for which original data were collected at producers' prices, total distribution margins were estimated on the basis of data on average mark-ups of importers and trade dealers, provided by the 1970 and 1975 Trade Censuses, registers of controlled prices of the Secretaría de Comercio and direct research on trade in the metropolitan area of Mexico City. Intermediate inputs of the trade sector were estimated on the basis of data provided by the 1970 and 1975 Trade Censuses.

32. Output of hotel services was estimated from data provided by the Secretaría de Turismo, hotel associations and special research carried out by the Fondo Nacional de Fomento al Turismo, which include estimates of numbers of rooms, average annual occupation and average rates charged by category and type of establishment. These estimates were compared to the indicators of tourism activity collected by the Banco de México, Dirección General de Estadística and other agencies. Cost structure estimates were mainly based on the 1970 and 1975 Trade Censuses data and on the results of special research carried out by the Asociación de Hoteles y Moteles de la Ciudad de México for the period 1975-1978.

33. Data on output of restaurants were collected on the basis of the assumption that output of restaurants was a fixed proportion of output of hotel services. This estimate was checked against the expenditure on restaurant services by tourists and resident households obtained in the Tourism and Family Income Expenditure Surveys carried out by the Banco de México, the Centro Nacional de Información y Estadísticas del Trabajo and the Dirección General de Estadística. Cost structure data were obtained from the Trade Census, the above mentioned survey of hotels and motels in Mexico City and a survey of major taxpayers carried out by the Secretaría de Hacienda y Crédito Público for the period 1970-1974.

Transportation, storage, communications

34. Different data collection methods were followed for each one of the two main components of the transportation sector, i.e., public sector transportation enterprises and private sector freight and passenger transportation services. Reasonably good information was available on the public sector transportation, the output and cost structure of which were estimated directly on the basis of data provided by the Transportation Census and the following agencies: Ferrocarriles Nacionales de México, Ferrocarril del Pacífico, Tranvías y Trolebuses, Sistema de Transporte Colectivo (METRO) del D.D.F., Aeronaves de México y Cía. Mexicana de Aviación, Caminos y Puentes Federales de Ingreso y Servicios Conexos; Aeropuertos y Servicios Auxiliares; Servicios a la Navegación en el Espacio Aéreo Mexicano; and Almacenes Nacionales y Generales de Depósito. However, information on the second component of the sector, which represents almost 75 per cent of its total output, had to be obtained through indirect methods involving the estimation of number and types of vehicles licensed. In the case of passenger transportation, use was also made of data on number of days worked, income, expenditure, fuel consumption and number of passengers and of kilometres covered per unit and type of service. These data were provided by the Transportation Census. Since the comparison of census data with data available on licensed vehicles indicated an insufficient coverage of census data, the latter were adjusted by an index of average income and cost per unit, in order to obtain total output and intermediate consumption of this subsector. In the case of private freight, data collection was further complicated by the absence of accurate data on number of vehicles used for this purpose. This number was estimated by applying the annual net increment in number of vehicles registered to the total number of vehicles registered in 1974. This total was distributed among input-output sectors on the basis of an updated index of the 1970 input-output data on physical output of the agriculture, livestock, industrial and service sectors.

Output of this subsector was first estimated at 1970 prices and then expressed in 1975 prices by means of an index of cost per load. This index was a combination of price indexes of the main intermediate inputs, labour and replacement cost of the vehicles, weighted by their relative importance in the 1970 cost structure. Intermediate consumption was estimated on the basis of census data and data obtained from a sample of transportation enterprises.

35. Data on output and cost structure of the communications sector were based on direct information provided by the Teléfonos de México and its subsidiaries, and the Dirección de Correos, Telégrafos y Telecomunicaciones and include an imputation of franchise services which are consumed mainly by the Federal Government. Output was distributed among the input-output sectors on the basis of available global estimates carried out by the same Dirección, and on estimates based on direct inquiries.

Financing and real estate

36. Most activities included in the Financial Services sector are regulated by the Central Bank and the Comisión Nacional Bancaria y de Seguros, which provided the required data on output and intermediate inputs. Data on most activities not covered by this Commission were based on the 1975 Services Census and on direct inquiries with the producers of the services.

37. Gross output of rentals of residential units was obtained by extrapolating the corresponding 1970 output. The extrapolation was based on a value index which combined the evolution of the amount of residential construction with the rent estimates used in the elaboration of the national consumer price index of the Banco de México. The estimate so obtained was compared to estimates of the same variable obtained in the 1975 and 1977 Family Income and Expenditure Surveys. Estimates of intermediate consumption were likewise based on the extrapolation of the 1970 input-output data adjusted by appropriate evolution indicators. Gross output of rentals of non-residential construction was estimated from the demand side by adding up the use of this type of service by each input-output sector. Intermediate consumption of non-residential construction was estimated as in the residential subsector.

Services

38. Various data collection methods were used to estimate the input-output data of the five main groups of services included in the input-output table. Services provided by professionals (except medical doctors) were obtained by extrapolating the output and cost structures of the 1970 input-output table. These data were adjusted with a price index of intermediate inputs and labour and with data collected in the 1975 Services Census. In the case of advertising and notary services, data were supplemented with direct inquiries on income, expenditures and employment to the main advertising agencies and notaries respectively. Data on education services were obtained from the expenditures required to provide them, in the case of public education. Output of private education was obtained by extrapolating the 1970 input-output value according to a combined index of annual growth of the number of students and the evolution of average income per student, provided by direct inquiries to education establishments. The corresponding cost structure was obtained from

the 1975 Services Census. Data on medical services were based on the expenditure required to provide them in the case of public medical services. Output of private medical services was mainly based on an index combining data on income, expenditure, employment and number of patients cared for per day. These data were provided by the Dirección General de Estadística, and the 1975 Services Census. Data on the remaining services were obtained by combining the 1975 Services Census information with statistics on income and expenditures of the main taxpayers compiled by the Secretaría de Hacienda y Crédito Público, demand data on repair and maintenance services and several indexes of the evolution of prices of output and level of activity.

Value added

39.   Value added was generally estimated as the difference between the output of each sector and intermediate consumption. Value added was disaggregated into labour costs and net indirect taxes, and the residual was assigned to operating surplus. Data on net indirect taxes of each sector were compiled by means of special research carried out by the Government and based on data provided by the Federal Government, the Federal District and local and municipal Governments. Data on labour costs were estimated as follows. In the agriculture and livestock sectors, labour costs were obtained as the product of estimated demand for labour and the corresponding average wages. In the fishing and hunting sectors, labour data were obtained by expanding those corresponding to the main species. Labour costs for the construction sector are based on the 1970 input-output table coefficients updated by an index of evolution of minimum wages. In the hotels and restaurants sector, labour costs were based on an estimate of employment per room in different types of establishments. The remaining labour data were generally obtained from the same sources as output and intermediate consumption data.

Final demand and imports

40.   Final demand data were obtained according to the commodity flow method. Private consumption was mainly estimated as a residual. Estimates so obtained were compared to direct data available from the Family Income and Expenditure Surveys referring to 1963, 1968, 1975 and 1977. Use was also made of direct information provided by enterprises in the electricity and communications sectors.

41.   Government consumption data were provided by the Cuenta de la Hacienda Pública Federal, the Cuenta Pública del Distrito Federal and financial statistics of the state and municipal Governments.

42.   Gross fixed capital formation was estimated partly on the basis of direct information from statistical sources and partly by means of the commodity flow method. The direct sources of information are the 1975 censuses of industry and trade, the annual compilations of Mexican trade (as published in the Anuario de Estadística de Comercio Exterior de los Estados Unidos Mexicanos by the Dirección General de Estadística), data compiled on investments by the Federal Government (as published by the Dirección General de Inversiones Públicas, 1975), and finally special surveys of trade outlets of capital goods, conducted in the metropolitan area of Mexico City.

43. Export and import data were provided by the Statistical Yearbook of Foreign Trade and the Balance of Payments, which include separate information on special transactions such as trade of precious metals, direct purchases in the domestic market by non-resident households etc. Import data were also supplemented by direct information on imports of the main public sector agencies, lists of main importers, tariffs of the general import tax and the classification of imports by origin and destination elaborated for the 1970 input-output table.

Mexico (aggregated)

Reference year: 1970

Entries in table: Total flows, import matrix

Source: Secretaría de programación y presupuesto, Banco de México and UNDP, *Matriz de Insumo–Producto de México, 1970,* vol. 1

Computerized: UNIDO

Currency units: Pesos of Y 1970

Scale factor: 1,000,000

Pricing system: Producers' current prices

Intermediate sectors: 24 × 24

Treatment of trade margins: Inputs, row 18

Treatment of imports: Matrix

Availability of import matrix: Available

Total number of rows: 60

Statistical unit of quadrant 1: Industry

Total number of columns: 32

Statistical unit of quadrant 1: Industry

Fourth quadrant: Occupied

Aggregation scheme for Mexico (1970)

Aggregated sector	Original sector	Aggregated sector	Original sector
1. Agriculture	1. Agriculture 2. Livestock 3. Forestry 4. Hunting and fishing		28. Leather and leather products
		8. Wood and wood products	29. Sawmilling including "triplay"
2. Coal mining	5. Coal and coal products		30. Other wood products
3. Crude petroleum	6. Petroleum and gas mining	9. Paper, printing	31. Paper and paper-board
4. Metal ore mining	7. Iron minerals		32. Printing and publishing
5. Other mining	8. Non-ferrous metal mining 9. Quarrying (sand and gravel) 10. Other non-metallic minerals	10. Chemicals	34. Basic petro-chemicals 35. Basic chemicals 36. Fertilizers and manure 37. Resins, synthetic plastics 38. Medicinal products 39. Soap and detergents 40. Other chemical industries 41. Linoleum products 42. Plastic products
6. Manufacture of food	11. Meat and dairy products 12. Fruit and vegetable preservation, processing 13. Grain milling and grain products 14. Corn milling and products 15. Coffee processing 16. Sugar and sugar products 17. Vegetable oil and fats 18. Animal feed 19. Other food products 20. Alcoholic beverages 21. Beer 22. Bottled refreshments 23. Tobacco and tobacco products	11. Petroleum refineries	33. Petroleum refining
		12. Non-metallic mineral products	43. Glass and glass products 44. Cement 45. Other non-metal mineral products
		13. Basic metal industries	46. Basic iron industry 47. Basic non-ferrous metal industry
		14. Metal products, machinery	48. Furniture, metal accessories 49. Structured metal products 50. Other metal products 51. Non-electrical machinery 52. Electrical machinery 53. Electrical house-hold appliances 54. Electronic equipment and apparatus
7. Textiles, clothing	24. Spinning and weaving, soft fibre 25. Spinning and weaving, hard fibre 26. Other textile industries 27. Wearing apparel		

Aggregated sector	Original sector	Aggregated sector	Original sector
	55. Other electrical equipment and apparatus	19. Restaurants and hotels	63. Restaurants, hotels
	56. Automotive vehicles	20. Transport and storage	64. Transportation
	57. Auto bodies and parts	21. Communications	65. Communications
	58. Other transport equipment and materials	22. Finance, insurance	66. Financial services
			67. Real estate
15. Other manufacturing	59. Other manufacturing industries		68. Professional services
		23. Public services	69. Education services
16. Electricity, gas and steam	61. Electricity		70. Medical services
			71. Recreation
17. Construction	60. Construction, installation		72. Other services
18. Trade (distribution)	62. Commerce	24. Imputed banking services	73. Imputed banking services

Aggregated Input-Output Table of Mexico for the Year 1970

MEXICO 1970

FLOWS in millions of pesos of Y 1970

PRODUCERS CURRENT MARKET PRICES

INDUSTRY:

* TOTAL TRANSACTIONS *	1 Agriculture	2 Coal Mining	3 Crude Petroleum	4 Metal Ore Mining	5 Other Mining	6 Manufacture of Food
1 Agriculture	7607.8		0.0	0.0	11.6	33556.0
2 Coal Mining	0.0	224.7	0.0	0.0	74.1	27.9
3 Crude Petroleum	0.0	0.0	539.4	0.0	85.1	27.3
4 Metal Ore Mining	0.0	0.0	0.0	53.0	0.0	3.6
5 Other Mining	63.9	0.0	137.5	0.0	2061.3	45
6 Manufacture of Food	4283.5	0.0	0.0	0.0	34.8	13629.7
7 Textiles, Clothing	288.5	30.0	80.2	0.0	37.5	808.1
8 Wood and Wood Products	312.2	1.8	22.4	1.0	10.5	53
9 Paper and Printing	71.1	3.9	93.5	7.3	168.7	137.4
10 Chemicals	2894.1	53.0	106.9	0.3	103.3	839.3
11 Petroleum Refineries	941.4	0.7	121.7	9.4	32.5	695.1
12 Non-metallic Mineral Prod.	83.4	0.0	254.7	9.9	85.8	664.4
13 Basic Metal Industries	108.6	7.3	546.5	5.3	87.8	85.8
14 Metal Products, Machinery	538.6	0.0	547.2	0.0	0.0	1405.9
15 Other Manufacturing	67.8	0.0	125.3	2.3	119.0	0.0
16 Electricity, Gas and Steam	256.9	0.0	184.1	0.7	0.0	559.2
17 Construction	0.0					
18 Trade (Distribution)	1934.3	34.4	184.3	3.4	529.8	6450.7
19 Restaurants and Hotels	375.6	4.7	190.5	4.0	43.8	167.8
20 Transport and Storage	355.5	4.2	112.2	2.0	45.8	962.8
21 Communications					117.5	119.0
22 Finance, Insurance	247.3	10.8	278.6	9.7	151.0	1311.0
23 Public Service	384.1	13.8		0		1048.7
24 Bank Service Charges						0
25 Total Intermediate Inputs	20464.2	387.4	2784.0	118.6	3728.9	63815.1

Aggregated Input-Output Table of Mexico for the Year 1970

MEXICO 1970   FLOWS in millions of pesos of Y 1970   PRODUCERS CURRENT MARKET PRICES

INDUSTRY:

	1 Agriculture	2 Coal Mining	3 Crude Petroleum	4 Metal Ore Mining	5 Other Mining	6 Manufacture of Food
* IMPORT TRANSACTIONS						
26 Agriculture	81.8	0.0	0.0	0.0	0.0	968.1
27 Coal Mining	0.0	34.2	0.0	0.0	32.6	7.8
28 Crude Petroleum	0.0	0.0	0.0	0.0	47.0	0.0
29 Metal Ore Mining	0.0	0.0	0.0	0.0	4.7	0.0
30 Other Mining	0.0	0.0	0.0	0.0	0.0	0.0
31 Manufacture of Food	79.8	0.0	0.0	0.0	0.0	377.8
32 Textiles, Clothing	0.1	0.0	0.0	0.0	0.0	43.7
33 Wood and Wood Products	0.3	0.0	0.0	0.0	0.0	0.0
34 Paper, Printing	0.0	0.0	0.0	0.0	0.0	62.5
35 Chemicals	40.0	0.0	43.5	0.1	0.0	83.4
36 Petroleum Refineries	0.0	0.0	0.0	0.0	0.0	0.0
37 Non-metallic Mineral Prod.	0.0	0.0	3.2	9.0	0.0	70.5
38 Basic Metal Industries	0.0	0.0	5.2	0.0	0.0	0.0
39 Metal Products, Machinery	37.0	4.0	172.9	0.4	2.0	83.9
40 Other Manufacturing	0.0	0.0	23.8	0.0	0.0	0.0
41 Electricity, Gas and Steam	0.0	0.0	0.0	0.0	0.0	0.0
42 Construction	0.0	0.0	0.0	0.0	0.0	0.0
43 Trade (Distribution)	0.0	0.0	0.0	0.0	0.0	0.0
44 Restaurants and Hotels	0.0	0.0	0.0	0.0	0.0	0.0
45 Transport and Storage	0.0	0.0	0.0	0.0	0.0	0.0
46 Communications	0.0	0.0	0.0	0.0	0.0	0.0
47 Public Services	0.0	0.0	0.0	0.0	0.0	0.0
48 Finance, Insurance	0.0	0.0	0.0	0.0	0.0	0.0
49 Bank Service Charges	0.0	0.0	0.0	0.0	0.0	0.0
50 Tot Merchandize Imports	241.2	78.3	262.3	10.8	113.8	1614.8
51 Imports of Services	0.0	0.0	0.0	0.0	0.0	0.0
52 Cmpns of Sales to tourists	0.0	0.0	0.0	0.0	0.0	0.0
53 Total Imported Inputs	241.2	78.3	262.3	10.8	113.8	1614.8
54 Compensation of Employees	15101.6	167.1	2438.6	79.7	1984.8	8051.3
55 Indirect Taxes less Subsid.	13307.9	243.8	382.1	21.7	378.4	2768.0
56 Gross Operating Surplus	38713.7	247.3	1554.6	498.0	3453.2	18555.4
57 Gross Value added	54123.2	418.2	4355.3	600.4	5816.4	29372.7
58 Gross Output	74587.4	765.6	7118.3	718.0	9545.3	93187.8
59 Imports	1588.4	204.6	56.1	38.7	854.8	1047.7
60 Total Resources	76175.8	990.2	7175.4	757.7	10399.9	94235.5

176

Aggregated Input-Output Table of Mexico for the Year 1970

MEXICO 1970 FLOWS in millions of pesos of Y 1970 PRODUCERS CURRENT MARKET PRICES

INDUSTRY:	7 Textiles, Clothing	8 Wood and Wood Products	9 Paper, Printing	10 Chemicals	11 Petroleum Refineries	12 Non-metallic Mineral Prod.
* TOTAL TRANSACTIONS * INDUSTRY						
1 Agriculture	2398.0	974.9	92.9	330.8	0.0	3.6
2 Coal Mining	0.4	1.9	0.9	35.0	0.4	109.9
3 Crude Petroleum	6.3	0.0	36.2	195.0	5607.9	15.7
4 Metal Ore Mining	5.8	0.0		548.0	0.0	1178.0
5 Other Mining		60.8	30.5	529.4	91.6	11.6
6 Manufacture of Food	408.0	24.3	150.2	314.4	5.0	35.2
7 Textiles, Clothing	9278.0	284.3		46.8	36.9	426.7
8 Wood and Wood Products	486.5	1092.3	200.7	130.9	288.9	305.9
9 Paper, Printing	15.0	21.2	4494.3	7989.3	684.2	234.7
10 Chemicals	3087.4	253.6	476.5	345.2	10.7	480.2
11 Petroleum Refineries	112.4	52.8	49.7	252.5	17.7	63.4
12 Non-metallic Mineral Prod.	47.9	186.5	76.7	231.2	228.4	143.2
13 Basic Metal Industries	247.5	41.9	41.5	487.4	229.9	274.2
14 Metal Products, Machinery	273.6		163.0	24.0	24.0	
15 Other Manufacturing	307.8	40.7		308.0		
16 Electricity, Gas and Steam	307.6	825.0	953.2	3005.7	105.0	665.2
17 Construction		15.9	36.0	280.3	18.6	250.6
18 Trade (Distribution)	3441.6	122.4	230.7	834.2	786.0	285.5
19 Restaurants and Hotels	140.4		12.5	82.7		
20 Transport and Storage	471.5	137.7	238.6	897.0	150.1	338.5
21 Communications	38.5	68.6	149.5	326.0	261.6	180.9
22 Finance, Insurance	692.4					
23 Public Services	260.7					
24 Bank Service Charges						
25 Total Intermediate Inputs	21524.8	4121.8	7514.9	18339.0	8354.7	4820.0

177

Aggregated Input-Output Table of Mexico for the Year 1970

MEXICO 1970 FLOWS in millions of Pesos of Y 1970

PRODUCERS CURRENT MARKET PRICES

INDUSTRY:

IMPORT TRANSACTIONS	7 Textiles, Clothing	8 Wood and Wood Products	9 Paper, Printing	10 Chemicals	11 Petroleum Refineries	12 Non-metallic Mineral Prod.
26 Agriculture	46.4	4.2	4.7	175.4	0	0
27 Coal Mining	0	0	0	5.0	0	0
28 Crude Petroleum	0	0	0	3.0	0	0
29 Metal Ore Mining	0	0	0	2.3	0	4
30 Other Mining	0	0	0	9.7	.2	0
31 Manufacture of Food	0	0	0	.1	0	0
32 Textiles Clothing	803.9	.1	.1	.1	0	0
33 Wood and Wood Products	.4	32.6	17.8	.7	.3	0
34 Paper, Printing	0	0	840.3	1.8	.7	287
35 Chemicals	175.5	1.0	14.3	287.9	89.3	86.7
36 Petroleum Refineries	.1	.2	.1	.7	39.1	.3
37 Non-metallic Minerals Prod.	0	0	0	0	0	107.0
38 Basic Metallic Industries	0	.4	0	0	5.8	.1
39 Metal Products, Machinery	52.3	1.5	.4	11.8	52.6	27.4
40 Other Manufacturing	.0	6.7	.0	2.0	1.0	0
41 Electricity, Gas and Steam	0	.0	0	.0	0	0
42 Construction	0	0	0	0	0	0
43 Trade (Distribution)	0	0	0	0	0	0
44 Restaurants and Hotels	0	0	0	0	0	0
45 Transport and Storage	0	0	0	0	0	0
46 Communications	0	0	0	0	0	0
47 Finance, Insurance	0	0	0	0	0	0
48 Public Services	0	0	0	0	0	0
49 Bank Service Charges	.0	.0	.0	.0	.0	.0
50 Tot.Merchandize Imports	881.5	55.0	901.0	3352.1	200.4	399.2
51 Imports of Services	.0	.0	.0	.0	.0	.0
52 Cmpns.of Sales to Tourists	.0	.0	.0	.0	.0	.0
53 Total Imported Inputs	881.5	55.0	901.0	3352.1	200.4	399.2
54 Compensation of Employees	8417.4	1351.8	2621.8	5590.2	1384.7	2319.8
55 Indirect Taxes less Subsid	451.9	78.4	241.8	897.3	1302.2	245.9
56 Gross Operating Surplus	8650.3	2177.1	2821.4	8040.4	1217.6	3522.5
57 Gross Value added	15519.6	3607.1	5685.0	14527.9	3904.5	6088.0
58 Gross Output	37044.4	7728.9	13199.9	32968.9	12259.2	10908.7
59 Imports	1163.7	257.9	1475.7	4068.9	768.5	258.7
60 Total Resources	38208.1	7986.8	14875.6	37036.0	13027.7	11167.7

Aggregated Input-Output Table of Mexico for the Year 1970

MEXICO 1970

FLOWS in millions of pesos of Y 1970

INDUSTRY:

* TOTAL TRANSACTIONS * INDUSTRY	13 Basic Metal Industries	14 Metal Products, Machinery	15 Other Manufacturing	16 Electricity, Gas and Steam	17 Construction	18 Trade (Distribution)
1 Agriculture	538.0	32.5	137.5	2.5	0.0	0.0
2 Coal Mining		32.9	2.2		0.9	0.0
3 Crude Petroleum	129.0	3.1	6.4	227.0	4.2	72.0
4 Metal Ore Mining	619.0	5.3	0.0		0.8	70.3
5 Other Mining	1176.7	534.9	559.0	9.3	603.8	10.3
6 Manufacture of Food	19.0	142.5	37.4	1.8	22.5	337.9
7 Textiles, Clothing	22.5	398.9	37.6		2304.5	14.0
8 Wood and Wood Products	187.5	468.9	162.5	43.2	1433.0	920.6
9 Paper, Printing	280.3	113.6	165.7		462.0	460.6
10 Chemicals	46.3	140.2	104.6	407.4	6591.0	687.8
11 Petroleum Refineries	6401.3	323.2	120.2	12.4	3889.0	194.6
12 Non-metallic Mineral Prod.	699.9	5112.2	97.3	251.5	2931.9	355.8
13 Basic Metal Industries		10502.5	140.2	4.2	2918.2	90.2
14 Metal Products, Machinery	371.8	287.0	118.9	42.0	149.4	767.0
15 Other Manufacturing		4296.8		102.3	3749.2	1369.4
16 Electricity, Gas and Steam	1452.8	129.0	367.0		12.0	182.0
17 Construction	345.2	727.3	42.0	17.5	1832.0	349.3
18 Trade (Distribution)	320.4	734.3	95.7	65.8	38.4	5837.9
19 Restaurants and Hotels	130.9	611.4	13.4	108.5	782.9	1632.5
20 Transport and Storage	38.0	0			310.1	
21 Communications						
22 Finance, Insurance						
23 Public Service						
24 Bank Service Charges						
25 Total Intermediate Inputs	12840.7	25397.9	2205.7	1312.1	25378.9	13654.4

179

Aggregated Input-Output Table of Mexico for the Year 1970

MEXICO 1970 — FLOWS in millions of pesos of Y 1970 — PRODUCERS CURRENT MARKET PRICES

INDUSTRY:

IMPORT TRANSACTIONS	13 Basic Metal Industries	14 Basic Metal Products, Machinery	15 Other Manufacturing	16 Electricity, Gas and Steam	17 Construction	18 Trade (Distribution)
26 Agriculture	87.0	2.0	-2.0	0.0	6.0	0.0
27 Coal Mining	0.0	0.0	0.0	0.0	0.0	0.0
28 Crude Petroleum	87.0	0.0	0.0	0.0	4.0	0.0
29 Metal Ore Mining	36.0	3.0	0.0	0.0	2.0	0.0
30 Other Mining	159.0	0.0	0.0	0.0	0.0	0.0
31 Manufacture of Food	0.0	0.0	32.5	0.0	180.2	0.0
32 Textiles, Clothing	0.0	0.0	9.0	0.0	7.0	0.0
33 Wood and Wood Products	0.0	25.0	4.4	0.0	0.0	0.0
34 Paper, Printing	0.0	29.0	2.4	0.0	132.4	0.0
35 Chemicals	98.6	59.0	0.0	50.5	23.9	0.0
36 Petroleum Refineries	0.0	0.0	0.0	5.1	3.4	0.0
37 Non-metallic Mineral Prod	188.6	22.0	58.0	1.8	74.8	0.0
38 Basic Metal Industries	48.1	25.0	10.5	24.7	304.1	0.0
39 Metal Products, Machinery	0.0	78.0	8.0	124.3	310.0	0.0
40 Other Manufacturing	0.0	0.0	0.0	4.2	0.0	0.0
41 Electricity, Gas and Steam	0.0	91.0	0.0	0.0	0.0	0.0
42 Construction	0.0	0.0	0.0	0.0	0.0	0.0
43 Trade (Distribution)	0.0	653.0	0.0	0.0	0.0	0.0
44 Restaurants and Hotels	0.0	3886.0	0.0	0.0	0.0	0.0
45 Transport and Storage	0.0	2.0	0.0	0.0	0.0	0.0
46 Communications	0.0	0.0	0.0	0.0	0.0	0.0
47 Finance, Insurance	0.0	0.0	0.0	0.0	0.0	0.0
48 Public Service	0.0	0.0	0.0	0.0	0.0	0.0
49 Bank Service Charges	0.0	0.0	0.0	0.0	0.0	0.0
50 Tot Merchandize Imports	1031.5	4833.8	508.6	153.4	894.8	0.0
51 Imports of Services	0.0	0.0	0.0	0.0	0.0	0.0
52 Capns. or Sales to Tourists	0.0	0.0	0.0	0.0	0.0	0.0
53 Total Imported Inputs	1031.5	4833.9	508.6	153.4	894.8	0.0
54 Compensation of Employees	2262.7	8522.0	748.9	2116.6	14578.1	20575.3
55 Indirect Taxes less Subsid.	190.7	1022.3	148.8	737.2	336.5	8525.3
56 Gross Operating Surplus	3401.4	9287.7	913.4	2292.9	8615.8	72344.0
57 Gross Value added	5854.8	18832.3	1811.1	5146.7	23530.2	101444.7
58 Gross Output	18685.5	44230.2	4016.8	6458.8	48909.0	115099.0
59 Imports	1299.4	16500.1	1352.2	4.2	0.0	0.0
60 Total Resources	19984.9	60730.3	5369.0	6463.0	48909.1	115099.1

180

Aggregated Input-Output Table of Mexico for the Year 1970

MEXICO 1970

FLOWS in millions of pesos of Y 1970

PRODUCERS CURRENT MARKET PRICES

INDUSTRY:	19 Restaurants & Hotels	20 Transport and Storage	21 Communications	22 Finance, Insurance	23 Public Services	24 Imputed Banking Services
* TOTAL TRANSACTIONS *						
INDUSTRY						
1 Agriculture	0.0	9.0	0.0	0.0	144.8	0.0
2 Coal Mining	0.0	7.5	0.0	0.0	0.0	0.0
3 Crude Petroleum	0.0	0.0	0.0	0.0	0.0	0.0
4 Metal Ore Mining	0.0	0.9	0.0	4.0	9.1	0.0
5 Other Mining	0.0	10.3	0.0	5.0	280.0	0.0
6 Manufacture of Food	58.2	23.1	8.0	10.4	490.6	0.0
7 Textiles, Clothing	52.9	68.5	7.0	8.1	46.9	0.0
8 Wood and Wood Products	188.3	169.0	22.9	485.1	481.9	0.0
9 Paper, Printing	88.7	1263.6	29.5	143.7	2772.9	0.0
10 Chemicals	75.0	2616.0	3.0	97.2	305.9	0.0
11 Petroleum Refineries	46.3	40.9	0.0	26.5	489.5	0.0
12 Non-metallic Mineral Prod.	13.0	109.8	103.0	26.5	64.9	0.0
13 Basic Metal Industries	115.0	1818.0	100.1	119.6	3076.9	0.0
14 Metal Products, Machinery	28.7	36.5	13.3	119.6	429.7	0.0
15 Other Manufacturing	153.9	66.7	14.4	146.4	299.5	0.0
16 Electricity, Gas and Steam						
17 Construction	265.4	1448.7	65.0	374.8	2176.4	0.0
18 Trade (Distribution)	241.7	362.5	70.7	216.8	207.7	0.0
19 Restaurants and Hotels	172.4	781.0	71.3	332.5	383.8	0.0
20 Transport and Storage	187.4	128.0	104.5	221.7	195.8	0.0
21 Communications	1352.2	946.5	156.4	987.7	2727.2	0.0
22 Finance Insurance	956.1	796.5		311.0	2285.7	0.0
23 Public Services						5395.5
24 Bank Service Charges	0					0
25 Total Intermediate Inputs	3845.0	10718.5	593.7	6474.3	16949.7	5395.5

181

Aggregated Input-Output Table of Mexico for the Year 1970

MEXICO 1970 FLOWS in millions of pesos of Y 1970 PRODUCERS CURRENT MARKET PRICES

INDUSTRY:

#	IMPORT TRANSACTIONS	19 Restaurants & Hotels	20 Transport and Storage	21 Communications	22 Finance, Insurance	23 Public Services	24 Imputed Banking Services
26	Agriculture	0.0	0.0	0.0	0.0	0.0	0.0
27	Coal Mining	0.0	0.0	0.0	0.0	0.0	0.0
28	Crude Petroleum	0.0	0.0	0.0	0.0	0.0	0.0
29	Metal Ore Mining	0.0	0.0	0.0	0.0	0.0	0.0
30	Other Mining	0.0	0.0	0.0	0.0	0.0	0.0
31	Manufacture of Food	0.0	0.0	0.0	0.0	6.0	0.0
32	Textiles, Clothing	0.0	0.3	0.0	2.0	0.0	0.0
33	Wood and Wood Products	0.0	0.1	0.0	0.0	0.3	0.0
34	Paper, Printing	0.0	8.9	0.0	6.0	14.9	0.0
35	Chemicals	2.0	1.0	0.0	1.2	67.3	0.0
36	Petroleum Refineries	0.0	29.1	0.0	0.8	1.0	0.0
37	Non-metallic Mineral Prod.	0.0	137.9	0.0	0.0	0.9	0.0
38	Basic Metal Industries	0.0	13.5	0.0	0.0	9.0	0.0
39	Metal Products, Machinery	8.0	866.3	0.0	1.0	597.4	0.0
40	Other Manufacturing	0.0	0.6	0.0	0.8	154.0	0.0
41	Electricity, Gas and Steam	0.0	0.0	0.0	0.0	0.0	0.0
42	Construction	0.0	0.0	0.0	0.0	0.0	0.0
43	Trade (Distribution)	0.0	0.0	0.0	0.0	0.0	0.0
44	Restaurants and Hotels	0.0	0.0	0.0	0.0	0.0	0.0
45	Transport and Storage	0.0	0.0	0.0	0.0	0.0	0.0
46	Communications	0.0	0.0	0.0	0.0	0.0	0.0
47	Finance, Insurance	0.0	0.0	0.0	0.0	0.0	0.0
48	Public Service	0.0	0.0	0.0	0.0	39.8	0.0
49	Bank Service Charges	0.0	0.0	0.0	0.0	0.0	0.0
50	Tot Merchandize Imports	1.8	1059.0	3.5	16.4	854.8	0.0
51	Imports of Services	0.0	133.0	0.0	241.0	186.0	0.0
52	Cmprs. of Sales to Tourists	0.0	0.0	0.0	0.0	0.0	0.0
53	Total Imported Inputs	1.6	1192.0	3.8	257.4	1090.8	0.0
54	Compensation of Employees	3893.7	8419.7	1171.2	7799.2	28875.0	0.0
55	Indirect Taxes less Subsid	437.7	67.8	258.2	2386.0	419.3	0.0
56	Gross Operating Surplus	9586.8	10082.7	1358.0	45397.0	16534.4	-5395.5
57	Gross Value added	13718.2	18570.0	2787.4	55582.2	45828.7	-5395.5
58	Gross Output	17563.2	29419.5	3381.1	62297.5	62974.4	0.0
59	Imports	0.0	0.0	0.0	17.9	46.6	0.0
60	Total Resources	17563.2	29419.5	3381.1	62315.4	63021.0	0.0

Aggregated Input-Output Table of Mexico for the Year 1970

MEXICO 1970

FLOWS in millions of pesos of Y 1970

PRODUCERS CURRENT MARKET PRICES

		25 Total Intermdt. Consumption	26 Private Consumption	27 Government Consumption	28 Gross Fixed Capital Form.	29 Changes in Stock	30 Exports
*	TOTAL TRANSACTIONS INDUSTRY						
1	Agriculture	45262.5	23950.5	34.5	1313.0	2555.3	3060.0
2	Coal Mining	941.3	0.0	0.0	0.0	-34.9	14.0
3	Crude Petroleum	7045.6	64.0	0.0	0.0	-26.3	91.4
4	Metal Ore Mining	709.7		0.0	0.0	-48.1	0.0
5	Other Mining	7158.7	21.0	18.0	35.9	287.0	2878.2
6	Manufacture of Food	19223.2	68907.1	39.7	130.4	1963.4	3971.7
7	Textiles. Clothing	12298.6	22132.6	60.4	47.8	1505.3	2183.4
8	Wood and Wood Products	4675.6	2839.4	9.6	126.4	220.5	115.3
9	Paper. Printing	11481.1	1947.3		6.7	627.6	236.8
10	Chemicals	24100.9	9450.0	376.6	187.5	2066.8	929.7
11	Petroleum Refineries	9000.9	3199.8	301.6		109.8	388.1
12	Non-metallic Mineral Prod.	8930.3	1490.8	329.1	0.0	423.2	187.5
13	Basic Metal Industries	16653.4		108.9	27.3	1013.2	403.9
14	Metal Products. Machinery	24024.6	1366.1	30.2	1698.2	1428.2	1629.4
15	Other Manufacturing	1207.6	3049.1	479.7	2800.0		238.3
16	Electricity, Gas and Steam	4468.3	1861.7	40.7	798.0	0.0	0.0
17	Construction	0.0	0.0	313.0	48909.1	30.4	0.0
18	Trade (Distribution)	33799.7	87659.9	310.2	12014.3	0.0	1315.0
19	Restaurants and Hotels	2259.8	15299.9	349.2	1143.4	0.0	0.0
20	Transport and Storage	9324.8	1778.6	218.9	0.0	0.0	819.0
21	Communications	1453.7	1708.5	1771.5	0.0	0.0	0.0
22	Finance. Insurance	23499.7	38039.2				
23	Public Services	13179.5	33585.0	1576.0	422.6	3.0	69.5
24	Bank Service Charges						
25	Total Intermediate Inputs	280697.8	324344.8	19555.9	88660.6	12295.4	18517.5

183

Aggregated Input-Output Table of Mexico for the Year 1970

MEXICO 1970   FLOWS in millions of pesos of Y 1970   PRODUCERS CURRENT MARKET PRICES

* IMPORT TRANSACTIONS	25 Total Intermdt. Consumption	26 Private Consumption	27 Government Consumption	28 Gross Fixed Capital Form	29 Changes in Stock	30 Exports
26 Agriculture	1281.3	118.4	11.0	72.0	105.7	0.0
27 Coal Mining	188.2	100.0	0.0	0.0	16.4	0.000
28 Crude Petroleum	52.1	0.0	0.0	0.0		0.000
29 Metal Ore Mining	36.0	0.0	0.0	0.0	32.7	0.000
30 Other Mining	817.3	0.3	0.0	0.0	37.0	0.000
31 Manufacture of Food	569.9	444.1	0.4	0.0	33.6	0.000
32 Textiles, Clothing	695.1	427.1	0.3	0.0	40.9	0.000
33 Wood and Wood Products	207.4	25.7	0.0	29.2	15.9	0.000
34 Paper, Printing	1133.9	280.1	3.6	0.3	257.5	0.000
35 Chemicals	299.6	174.2	4.4	0.0	286.9	0.000
36 Petroleum Refineries	234.8	445.6	0.0	0.5	22.0	0.000
37 Non-metallic Mineral Prod.	1179.0	6.00	6.6	0.0	18.0	0.000
38 Basic Metal Industries	6759.0	0.0	39.5	8871.0	90.3	0.000
39 Metal Products, Machinery	306.3	506.9	2.4	602.0	324.3	0.000
40 Other Manufacturing	4.2	417.0	0.0	0.0	23.5	0.000
41 Electricity, Gas and Steam	0.0	0.0	0.0	0.0	0.00	0.000
42 Construction	0.0	0.0	0.0	0.0		0.000
43 Trade (Distribution)	0.0	0.0	0.0	0.0		0.000
44 Restaurants and Hotels	0.0	0.0	0.0	0.0		0.000
45 Transport and Storage	0.0	0.0	0.0	0.0		0.000
46 Communications	0.0	0.0	0.0	0.0	0.0	0.0
47 Finance, Insurance	0.0	17.9	0.0	0.0	0.0	0.0
48 Public Services	38.6	0.0	0.0	4.0	3.0	0.0
49 Bank Service Charges						
50 Tot Merchandize Imports	17507.8	2843.8	55.8	9578.1	1084.8	0.0
51 Imports of Services	570.0	-674.0	145.0	0.0	0.0	0.0
52 Cmpns of Sales to Tourists		-5497.0				5497.0
53 Total Imported Inputs	18077.8	-1979.2	204.8	9579.1	1084.8	5497.0
54 Compensation of Employees	146270.8	0.0	12182.7	0.0	0.0	
55 Indirect Taxes less Subsid.	21587.3	0.0	54.2	0.0	0.0	
56 Gross Operating Surplus	263871.0	0.0	305.4	0.0	0.0	
57 Gross Value added	431729.1	0.0	12542.3	0.0	0.0	
58 Gross Output	712998.9	31952.8	32243.2	88660.8	12295.4	24014.5
59 Imports	31075.1	-31075.0	0.0	0.0	0.0	
60 Total Resources	744072.0	31521.8	32243.2	88660.8	12295.4	24014.5

Aggregated Input-Output Table of Mexico for the Year 1970

MEXICO 1970

FLOWS in millions of pesos of Y 1970

PRODUCERS CURRENT MARKET PRICES

		31 Total Final Demand	32 Total Resources (Imports)
*	TOTAL TRANSACTIONS INDUSTRY *		
1	Agriculture	30913.3	76175.8
2	Coal Mining	48.9	990.2
3	Crude Petroleum	130.0	7175.4
4	Metal Ore Mining	324.1	7175.7
5	Other Mining	3241.2	10357.7
6	Manufacture of Food	75909.3	94205.9
7	Textiles, Clothing	25909.5	37306.5
8	Wood and Wood Products	319.5	37306.1
9	Paper, printing	1293.5	14875.8
10	Chemicals	4028.8	37036.6
11	Petroleum Refineries	2237.4	13027.7
12	Non-metallic Mineral Prod.	3311.5	11167.7
13	Basic Metal Industries	36705.7	19964.9
14	Metal Products, Machinery	4161.4	60730.3
15	Other Manufacturing	1994.7	5369.0
16	Electricity, Gas and Steam		6463.0
17	Construction	48909.1	48909.1
18	Trade (Distribution)	81299.1	115099.1
19	Restaurants and Hotels	15303.3	17563.2
20	Transport and Storage	20094.9	29419.5
21	Communications	1927.4	3381.1
22	Finance, Insurance	38816.4	62315.4
23	Public Services	49841.5	63021.0
24	Bank Service Charges	0	
25	Total Intermediate Inputs	463374.2	744072.0

Aggregated Input-Output Table of Mexico for the Year 1970

MEXICO 1970

FLOWS in millions of pesos of Y 1970

PRODUCERS CURRENT MARKET PRICES

	IMPORT TRANSACTIONS	31 Total Final Demand	32 Total Resources (Imports)
26	Agriculture	307.1	1588.4
27	Coal Mining	16.4	204.6
28	Crude Petroleum	4.0	56.7
29	Metal Ore Mining	2.7	38.7
30	Other Mining	37.3	854.7
31	Manufacture of Food	477.8	1047.7
32	Textiles, Clothing	468.6	1163.7
33	Wood and Wood Products	50.5	1257.9
34	Paper, Printing	341.8	1475.1
35	Chemicals	468.9	4169.1
36	Petroleum Refineries	468.9	768.1
37	Non-metallic Mineral Prod.	25.1	259.7
38	Basic Metal Industries	90.1	1269.4
39	Metal Products, Machinery	974.9	16500.1
40	Other Manufacturing	1045.0	1352.2
41	Electricity, Gas and Steam	0.0	4.2
42	Construction	0.0	0
43	Trade (Distribution)	0.0	0
44	Restaurants and Hotels	0.0	0
45	Transport and Storage	0.0	0
46	Communications	0.0	0
47	Finance, Insurance	17.9	17.9
48	Public Services	17.0	46.6
49	Bank Service Charges	0.0	0
50	Tot. Merchandize Imports	13567.3	31075.1
51	Imports of Services	810.0	
52	Cmpns of Sales to Tourists	0.0	1388.0
53	Total Imported Inputs	14386.3	32484.1
54	Compensation of Employees	12182.7	158453.5
55	Indirect Taxes less Subsid.	54.2	21841.4
56	Gross Operating Surplus	305.4	264176.4
57	Gross Value added	12542.3	444271.4
58	Gross Output	476735.5	189732.4
59	Imports	0.0	31075.0
60	Total Resources	476735.5	1220807.4

PAPUA NEW GUINEA

The present report is based on *An Input-Output Matrix for Papua New Guinea 1972/73, Monograph 5* published by the Institute of Applied Social and Economic Research of Papua New Guinea.

A. General information

1. Input-output tables for Papua New Guinea have been compiled for 1969/70 and 1972/73. Different methodologies and data sources were used in each table. The present report refers to the 1972/73 table, which was compiled by the National Statistical Office with technical and financial assistance provided by the United Nations Office for Technical Co-operation.

2. The national accounts series is calculated using an income and consumption approach. A revision of this methodology was implemented in 1974 with the purpose of allowing for a more extensive use of a production based method of calculating GDP estimates. However, the compilation of the 1972/73 input-output table helped to highlight the deficiencies existing in the currently available production data. In general, the methodology followed in the compilation of the input-output table is in line with the methodology followed for the national accounts. However, a number of differences exist between the national accounts and input-output estimates as a result of the production approach and the wider range of sources of data used in the input-output table. A comparison of GDP estimates according to the national accounts and the input-output table shows a 3 per cent under-recording of GDP in the national accounts estimates. This difference is mainly due to the under-evaluation of the national accounts estimates for compensation of employees, private consumption expenditure and imports of goods and services.

3. Major deviations from SNA recommendations on input-output include the following: the treatment of government health, education and welfare services (para. 9); the inclusion of two dummy sectors (para. 9); the disaggregation of final demand and value added (paras. 10 and 11); the treatment and disaggregation of imports (para. 12); the exclusion of intra-industry transactions (para. 16); and the distribution of imputed financial charges (para. 17).

B. Analytical framework

Tables and derived matrices available

4. Data are presented in five basic tables:
   (i) Absorption table at purchasers' prices;
   (ii) Make table valued at purchasers' prices;

(iii) Input-output table of the industry by industry type, valued at purchasers' prices;

(iv) Imports absorption matrix;

(v) Rent matrix. This matrix provides an industry by industry flow analysis of rent paid and received. The reasons for compiling this table are explained in para. 13 below.

No derived matrices have been published.

5. All basic tables compiled are presented at a 68 × 68 level of aggregation of intermediate sectors.

Valuation standards

6. Transactions have been valued at purchasers' prices in all basic tables compiled. However, a research project conducted in an Australian university transformed the 1972/73 input-output table from purchasers' to approximate basic values. The Papua New Guinea statistician currently holds the information required to repeat this transformation whenever this is required. Imports are valued f.o.b. plus the mark-ups applied to derive the purchasers' value of imports. Exports are valued f.o.b.

Statistical units and classification standards

7. Industries are the statistical units adopted for columns of table (i), rows of table (ii), rows and columns of tables (iii) and (v) and columns of table (iv). The statistical unit adopted for rows of table (i), columns of table (ii) and rows of table (iv) is commodities.

8. Industries are classified according to the 1966 Australian Classification of Industries. Commodities follow the classification developed in a 1973 inter-industry study of Papua New Guinea.[1]

9. The classification of the intermediate consumption quadrant differs from SNA recommendations in the following respects:

(a) Health, education and welfare services provided by the Government are distributed together with the same kind of services provided by industries;

(b) Two dummy sectors are included, namely, unallocated rent, which records the minor amount of rental income earned by the goods-producing sectors, and business expenses, which include:

(i) Administrative expenditures which are too small to be allocated directly to the corresponding sector;

(ii) Expenditure on drinks and other entertainment expenses that have not been allocated to the amusements, hotels and cafes sector;

(iii) Expenditures on administrative expenses paid to parent companies overseas.

---

[1]M. L. Parker, *Papua New Guinea—An Inter-industry Study,* Research School of Pacific Studies, Australian National University, Canberra, 1973.

10. The final demand quadrant presents a higher disaggregation than that recommended in SNA. Private consumption is disaggregated into its market and non-market components, and gross fixed capital formation is subdivided into Government and private, with private gross capital formation further disaggregated into market and non-market. In addition, exports are subdivided into exports of commodities f.o.b., exports of services, exports of other commodities (i.e., management and commissions for services provided to overseas buyers and transfers of emigrants' personal and household effects) and direct purchases by non-residents. Private consumption is defined on a national basis. All components of final demand are defined as recommended in SNA.

11. Value added is also disaggregated into a finer breakdown than that recommended in SNA. Compensation of employees is subdivided into its indigenous and non-indigenous components and the operating surplus is subdivided into market and non-market. Indigenous primary producers mainly producing cash crops, as well as their immediate families who assist them in their production activity, are assumed to receive a return for their labour from entrepreneurial income. These labour returns are thus included separately in operating surplus rather than in compensation of employees. This treatment applies both to indigenous smallholders and village industries in the market component of the economy, and to subsistence villagers in the non-market component. It should also be noted that, in agreement with SNA recommendations, compensation of employees includes wages and salaries in kind such as housing provided to government employees at markedly reduced costs. In addition, a housing subsidy has been imputed. This has resulted in an increase of gross output, which has been treated as a sale from the corresponding input-output sectors to the government final consumption expenditure component of final demand.

12. Contrary to SNA recommendations, the Papua New Guinea input-output tables do not present a distinction between competitive and complimentary imports. All imports have been cross-classified by origin and destination in the import matrix, and by destination only in separate rows of the input-output table. Imports in this table have been subdivided into imports of merchandise (at both f.o.b. and c.i.f. values), freight and insurance, other imports services, imports of other commodities (which include repair work done overseas, administrative and management expenses overseas, rent paid overseas and immigrants' personal effects) and imports of other goods and services which include expenditure by Papua New Guinea residents travelling overseas.

Treatment and presentation of selected transactions

13. As mentioned above (para. 4), a pure industry by industry input-output table has been compiled on the basis of the information provided by the absorption and make tables. However, in the case of two types of secondary production, namely rental income and own account capital formation, the corresponding outputs and inputs have been retained in the industry sector in which they are produced. The reasons for adopting this approach is to preserve a direct link between the industry by industry matrix and the industry statistics collected and generally used. The influence of this secondary production is in most instances of such a minor nature that this treatment will probably not

189

impair greatly the value of the pure input-output table. On the other hand, the Papua New Guinea statistician has available enough information to modify this treatment according to the users' convenience. In addition, an industry by industry rent matrix has been compiled describing the origin and destination of this component of secondary production.

14. Sales and purchases of second-hand goods are presented together in a sales-by-final-buyers row of the input-output table, which is added to domestic production and imports to obtain total supply.

15. Non-market output of the agriculture and owner-occupied dwellings sectors have been recorded in separate rows with a single input, namely operating surplus non-market component. Gross output of these sectors has been distributed along their corresponding rows to the private final consumption non-market category component of final demand.

16. Intra-industry transactions have been excluded from the table because of lack of data on this type of transaction. This procedure is in disagreement with SNA recommendations on input-output.

17. Output of the financial and insurance sectors has been defined according to SNA recommendations. Thus, output of financial institutions includes actual service charges as well as the imputed excess of property income received over property income paid for by banks; imputed output of ancillary insurance companies equals premiums less claims; and, for life insurance, a service charge is imputed which is equivalent to the excess of premiums received over the sum of claims paid plus the net addition to actuarial reserves which accrues to policy holders. The distribution of financial output does not conform to SNA recommendations, since the imputed service charges have been allocated to input-output sectors and final demand categories together with actual service charges.

C. Statistical sources and compilation methodology

18. Data collection is mainly based on regular statistical sources and the results of the Agricultural and Pastoral Census, and the Secondary Industries Census.

19. The methodology followed involved a detailed step by step exercise of gathering all the available information on commodity flows, completing a commodity flow analysis for the whole economy and translating this into an inter-industry flow matrix. Work commenced by quantifying all available supplies of goods and services into 100 commodity groups. These were distributed among producing industries and recorded in the make matrix. Concurrently, work progressed on the allocation of commodities as inputs into these industry sectors. This work could only proceed as the total cost of each industry sector was determined and after the primary inputs of compensation of employees, operating surplus, and consumption of fixed capital along with other indirect taxes net of subsidies had been estimated. The allocation of commodity groups to the final demand sectors was undertaken as a separate exercise.

190

Gross output, intermediate consumption and primary inputs

Agriculture

20. Data on the agriculture sectors were mainly obtained from the Agricultural and Pastoral Census, which collects quantity data on agriculture operations. These were supplemented with financial data gathered in the Rural Industries Bulletin and a number of *ad hoc* studies carried out to cover the operations of indigenous producers. The main agricultural sectors associated with exported and domestically consumed commodities such as copra, cocoa, coffee, rubber, tea, oil palm and cattle have been disaggregated into plantation and smallholder types of operations. The main sources of data for the plantation sectors have been the Papua New Guinea Bureau of Statistics, annual Rural Industries Bulletins and International Trade Statistics Bulletins, unpublished details from the Bureau of Statistics Agricultural and Pastoral Census (A and P Census), various *ad hoc* studies conducted into the operations of particular producers, privately collected information from the department of primary industries, and company records and reports.

Mining and quarrying

21. Sources of data on the mining and quarrying sectors include published and unpublished company records, records kept by the Department of Natural Resources, export statistics, cost structure information obtained from the input-output sector of the Australian Bureau of Statistics and direct correspondence with some companies.

Manufacturing

22. Data on the manufacturing sectors are mainly obtained from the Secondary Industries Census. This source presented several problems. The questionnaire used in the Census excludes management, sales and distribution costs and the census results have generally proved to be incompatible with other privately collected data. Therefore, it was necessary to undertake an extensive re-editing and recording of the census questionnaires. This exercise uncovered a number of errors in the published results which had to be corrected. In general, the lack of suitable production statistics was overcome by a heavy reliance upon company records, governmental reports and financial reports of various public authorities and commissions, *ad hoc* studies prepared for particular industries, taxation statistics etc.

Electricity

23. The main sources of data for the electricity sector are the Electricity Commission Annual Report, and cost and receipt records relating to the operation of government owned power houses.

Construction

24. The building and construction sector includes various public sector maintenance and construction operations in addition to private contractors

providing similar services. Output of the sector includes maintenance operations with the imputed value for work performed by free and partially paid labour. Sources of data for public sector operations range from published documents and reports to privately collected confidential files and papers. Private building and construction operations have been estimated indirectly, because of lack of data. An estimate of total demand for private contractors' services was first determined as the difference between total demand for construction services and demand for public sector services. Then, primary inputs were estimated on the basis of taxation statistics and the Department of Labour Employment Census. Finally, the value of intermediate inputs was estimated and checked against a number of indicators.

Transport and communications

25.　Aggregated statistics relating to the transport and storage sector are not available. Therefore, use has been made of a wide variety of data sources including the Department of Transport Road Use and Freight reports, government details of expenditure and receipts, published documents and privately collected company data.

26.　The communications sector is dominated by the activities of the Department of Posts and Telegraphs, although in 1972/73 the Australian Overseas Telecommunications Commission was responsible for telecommunications flowing in and out of the country. In addition to the usual published reports relating to these two organizations, access has also been obtained through the departments concerned to more detailed unpublished financial statements on revenue and operating costs.

Trade

27.　Output of the commerce sector has been derived from the demand in the economy for commercial services. Demand for commercial services has been calculated in a variety of ways depending upon the sector and commodity group involved. For imported goods and much of the supply of domestic goods, retail and wholesale mark-ups have been determined after examination of the maximum mark-up rates set by the Prices Controller and after private discussions with a number of large retailing and wholesaling companies. Included in this sector are the regular wholesale and retail operators, export and import agents, and various traders and distributing branches of larger overseas manufacturers. In calculating the value of operating costs, those parts of the sector (such as export agents) who have peculiar cost structures, have been dealt with separately. Likewise co-operative stores for which some cost information is available, and indigenous trade stores for which a recent unpublished survey has been conducted by the Department of Business Development have been treated individually when determining operating costs. For most wholesale and retail operators it has been necessary to rely upon privately collected company records for some of the largest nation-wide operators. It has also been necessary to draw upon taxation statistics, the Department of Labour Employment Census results (suitably modified for omissions) and the working papers used in the compilation of the 1973 input-output table for Papua New Guinea.

Financial and real estate services

28. Data on financial institutions and the insurance sector are obtained directly from company financial records. Included in this sector are the main trading and savings banks, the Papua New Guinea Development Bank and Investment Corporation, and the Reserve Bank of Australia (which operated as the central bank in Papua New Guinea in 1972/73). Also included are all the insurance (life and general) companies and agencies operating in Papua New Guinea and three main leasing companies.

29. Output of the real estate property and services sector has been calculated mainly in terms of rental income. Unpublished taxation statistics have been used to determine the total rent receipts from Papua New Guinea and overseas. Output in the form of fees charged by real estate agents, stockbrokers, auctioneers etc., could only be derived from the total demand for these types of services by the other sectors of the economy. Both published and unpublished information from taxation statistics and the Department of Labour Employment Census have been used to determine the primary inputs of this sector. Having obtained the value of total intermediate inputs by subtraction, various company records and reports have been used as a guide to the individual intermediate inputs.

30. Estimates of imputed gross rental income from owner-occupied dwellings are based on official national accounts estimates which are derived as follows. A market value has been assigned to the owner-occupied dwellings included in the latest population census and an estimate of current annual rental value has been obtained based on a percentage of the market value of the stock of available houses (the stock being suitably allocated between various high- and low-cost housing groups). The operating costs associated with the estimated gross rental value of the owner-occupied dwellings are estimated using observed operating costs and gross rent ratios from sources of taxation statistics. As estimates of gross rent obtained from the latter sources were slightly higher than the estimate based on the first method, it was necessary to modify the official estimates of operating costs accordingly. In an attempt to retain the same official operating surplus estimate, the adjustment had to be made to intermediate inputs and other value added components only.

Services

31. The education sector is basically composed of government-controlled and -administered education facilities, but also includes the education facilities operated by various missions. Output for this sector, where actual payment received from services is exceeded by expenditure in providing these services, is measured in terms of the total expenditure incurred in providing these services. The difference between total expenditure on these services and the actual cash receipts is treated as part of the final consumption expenditure of either Government (for government-operated facilities) or private households and non-profit making institutions servicing households (for mission-operated activities). The sources of data used in calculating sales of education services and total expenditure by this sector are government income and expenditure records such as the Appropriate Ordinance 1973/74, annual reports from institutions such as universities and the survey of religious organizations conducted by the Bureau of Statistics.

32. The health sector is basically composed of two parts: the operations of government and mission hospitals, aid posts and other assorted health services, on the one hand, and the operations of private doctors, dentists and veterinarians, on the other. For the government- and mission-operated health services, the main sources of data are government and receipt records, and the survey of religious organizations. Government health operations basically related to expenditure associated with the Department of Health (excluding their medical training facilities). The operations of private doctors, dentists and veterinarians have been estimated using taxation statistics in regard to claimed expenditure on medical services. In using this source, allowance has been made for medicaments included in the estimate and some attempt has also been made to allow for a slight exaggeration in the estimates provided by private persons when completing their taxation returns. Indigenous persons who do not complete tax returns are regarded as not using the services provided by private medical practitioners but relying instead upon government-provided medical services. As a check against this method of estimation, an attempt was made to derive a gross output for medical practitioners from unpublished taxation statistics on income. From these two methods a mutually consistent estimate of total output has been derived.

33. Data on the amusement, hotels and cafes sector have been obtained mainly from taxation statistics, the Department of Labour Employment Census, the Bureau of Statistics Survey of Retail Trade, government expenditure and receipts records, and privately obtained company records. The operations of hotels, clubs, restaurants and motels have been estimated as a single group because of the basic interrelation that exists among them. In the calculation of commercial mark-ups on aerated waters and alcoholic beverages, estimates have been derived of the mark-ups on these commodities which form part of the output of hotels, clubs and restaurants. This calculation has been based upon company records of sales to these types of outlets as distinct from supermarkets and trade stores. Unpublished details obtained from the survey of retail trade have been used to estimate the value of other takings. These results have also been used as an estimate of meals sold and accommodation services provided by industry groups in this survey which correspond to the amusement, hotel, and cafe sectors. This estimate of total output has been compared to some company reports and appears to be reasonably consistent. For the remaining part of this sector covering cinemas, squash courts and other amusement activities, it has been necessary to rely upon privately collected company records and unpublished Department of Labour Employment Census results.

34. The largest part of the personal services sector relates to the activities of household domestic servants. The estimated number of household domestic servants is derived from the 1971 Population Census, adjusted to 1972/73 in accordance with the movement in non-indigenous population since 1971. The services of household domestic servants are valued at the estimated average rate applying in 1972/73. The remaining part of this sector relates to the activities of laundries, dry cleaners, hairdressers and similar types of services. Estimates of output and operating costs are obtained from completed Secondary Industries Census returns for dry cleaning and laundry services. Unpublished details from the survey of retail trade relating to other retail takings of hairdressers and other miscellaneous personal services provide an estimate of the output of the

remaining part of this sector. Operating costs for this component of the sector have had to be estimated from the Employment Census.

35. Data on the other community and business services sector were obtained from taxation statistics and unpublished details obtained from the Department of Labour Employment Census. The sector includes the activities of the legal profession, consultant engineers and surveyors, architects, accountants and auditors, advertising agencies and typing and copying agencies.

Final demand and imports

36. Private consumption expenditure has been estimated on the basis of a detailed product analysis conducted on each of the 100 commodity groups used in the compilation of the input-output table. As a cross-check on the estimates derived from this commodity approach, an estimate of consumption expenditure has been constructed using the Bureau of Statistics Survey of Retail Trade. In addition, use was made of the results of household expenditure surveys and a number of minor data sources. The results were adjusted to account for inflation and observed changes in consumption patterns between periods.

37. Data on government consumption have been obtained from national accounts estimates slightly modified in cases where noted discrepancies with other data sources existed. The non-market component has been derived from the national accounts.

38. Estimates of change in stock have been derived in two ways: directly, from calculation of the supply and usage of domestically produced goods where sources of data permit an exact calculation of the quantity variation in stocks (for example, the difference between copper concentrate production and export sales); and indirectly, as a residual after the allocation of total commodity supplies to all using sectors. The official national accounts estimate was also used as a guide to the overall value of the change in stocks.

39. The main sources of data covering the gross fixed capital formation of general Government are government records of receipts and expenditure, special surveys and investigations conducted into the expenditure of Australian government departments operating in Papua New Guinea, and statistics on the activities of local government councils collected by the Commissioner for Local Government. Data on private capital formation were obtained mainly from the Survey of Capital Expenditure, the Rural Industries Bulletin (to cover own account capital formation on rural holdings) and unpublished details from the Agriculture and Pastoral Census (to obtain the value of new areas of crops and plantations laboured by non-indigenous producers). The non-market estimate was obtained directly from the national accounts.

40. Data on exports and imports are mainly derived from the International Trade Statistics Bulletin.

Papua New Guinea (aggregated)

Reference year: 1972

Entries in table: Total flows

Source: Institute of Applied Social and Economic Research of Papua New Guinea, *An input-output matrix for Papua New Guinea 1972-1973, Monograph 5*

Computerized: Wirtschaftsuniversität, Vienna

Currency units: Kina of Y 1972/73

Scale factor: 1,000

Pricing system: Purchasers' current prices

Intermediate sectors: 20 × 20

Treatment of trade margins: Sector 15

Treatment of imports: Absorption matrix for 64 commodities

Availability of import matrix: Available

Total number of rows: 31 (aggregated)

Statistical unit of quadrant 1: Industry

Total number of columns: 28 (aggregated)

Statistical unit of quadrant 1: Industry

Fourth quadrant: Occupied

Aggregated scheme for Papua New Guinea (1972)

Aggregated sector	Original sector	Aggregated sector	Original sector
1. Agriculture	1. Plantation copra 2. Smallholder copra 3. Plantation cocoa 4. Smallholder cocoa 5. Plantation coffee 6. Smallholder coffee 7. Plantation oil palm 8. Smallholder oil palm 9. Plantation rubber 10. Smallholder rubber 11. Plantation tea 12. Smallholder tea 13. Plantation cattle 14. Smallholder cattle 15. Pig, poultry, milk 16. Rice 17. Other crops 18. Fishing 19. Forest products 20. Non-market agriculture	8. Non-metallic mineral products	38. Cement products
		9. Basic metal industries	23. Joineries
		10. Metal products, machinery	24. General engineering 25. Sheet metal and wire working 26. Electrical machinery repair and manufacturing 27. Motor vehicle repair and building 28. Aircraft repairs 29. Ship and boat building
		11. Village industries	45. Village industries
		12. Other manufacturing	46. Other manufacturing
		13. Electricity, gas and steam	47. Electricity and sanitary services
2. Mining and quarrying	21. Mining and quarrying	14. Construction	48. Building and construction
3. Manufacture of food	30. Bakeries 31. Beverages (breweries/soft drinks) 32. Tobacco and cigarettes 33. Tea processing 34. Cocoa processing 36. Coffee processing 37. Other food processing	15. Trade (distribution)	53. Commerce
		16. Restaurants and hotels	63. Amusements, hotels, cafes
		17. Transport and storage	49. Road transport and storage 50. Water transport and storage 51. Air transport and storage
4. Textiles, clothing	40. Canvas goods, rope and cordage 41. Clothing	18. Communications	52. Communication
5. Wood and wood products	22. Sawmills 42. Furniture	19. Finance, insurance	54. Financial institutions 55. Property and investment services 56. Owner occupied dwellings—market 57. Owner occupied dwellings—nonmarket 64. Personal services 65. Business expenses 66. Unallocated rent
6. Paper, printing	43. Printing, paper products		
7. Chemicals	35. Chemicals and oils 39. Paints, varnishes 44. Fibreglass and plastic products		

Aggregated sector	Original sector
20. Public services	58. Education
	59. Health
	60. Government and defence
	61. Welfare and religion
	62. Other community and business service

Primary inputs

Aggregated sector	Original sector
22. Imports c.i.f.	142. Imports f.o.b.
	143. Freight/insurance
	144. Other transport, communications, insurance, services import
	145. Other commodities imported
	146. Imports of other goods and services
23. Import duties	75. Duty on imports
24. Imports including duties	75. Duty on imports
	142. Imports f.o.b.
	143. Freight insurance
	144. Other transport, communications, insurance, services import
	145. Other commodities imported
	146. Imports of other goods and services
25. Gross fixed capital consumption	72. Consumption of fixed capital
26. Compensation of employees	68. Compensation of employees—indigenous
	69. Compensation of employees—non-indigenous
27. Indirect taxes less subsidies	72. Consumption of fixed capital
	73. Other indirect taxes less subsidies
28. Operating surplus	70. Operating surplus—market compensation
	71. Operating surplus—non-market compensation

Aggregated sector	Original sector
29. Sales by final buyers	74. Sales by final buyers
30. Gross value added	68. Compensation of employees—indigenous
	69. Compensation of employees—non-indigenous
	70. Operating surplus—market compensation
	71. Operating surplus—non-market compensation
	72. Consumption of fixed capital
	73. Other indirect taxes less subsidies
	74. Sales by final buyers

Final demand

Aggregated sector	Original sector
22. Private consumption	68. Private final consumption—market
	69. Private final consumption—nonmarket
23. Government consumption	70. General government final consumption
24. Gross fixed capital formation	72. Private capital formation—market
	73. Private capital formation—non-market
	74. General government capital formation
25. Changes in stock	71. Stock change
26. Exports	75. Exports f.o.b.
	76. Transport, communications, insurance, services export
	77. Other commodities exported
	78. Direct purchase by non-resident

Aggregated Input-Output Table of Papua New Guinea for the Year 1972

PAPUA NEW GUINEA 1972   FLOWS in thousands of kina of y 1972-73   PURCHASERS CURRENT MARKET PRICES

INDUSTRY:	1 Agriculture	2 Mining and Quarrying	3 Manufacture of Food	4 Textiles, Clothing	5 Wood and Wood Products	8 Paper, Printing
* DOMESTIC TRANSACTIONS *						
INDUSTRY						
1 Agriculture	1344	0	617	0	4204	0
2 Mining and Quarrying	6681	0	0	0	0	0
3 Manufacture of Food	534	0	0	0	0	0
4 Textiles, Clothing	712	100	2	1	81	0
5 Wood and Wood Products	110	13	34	0	278	12
6 Paper, Printing	1219	134	0	0	0	0
7 Chemicals			324	14	138	68
8 Non-Metallic Mineral Prod.		0	1017	0	0	0
9 Basic Metal Industries	7	1195	1613	8	97	64
10 Metal Products, Machinery	72	4	515	0	17	19
11 Village Industries	506	45	194	323	1421	291
12 Other Manufacturing		71	9093	0	1037	8
13 Electricity, Gas and Steam	6967	5076	5740	6	1057	88
14 Construction	18	438	1912		42	63
15 Trade (Distribution)	7844	2320	193	27	174	136
16 Restaurants and Hotels	196	679	872			
17 Transport and Storage	2063	5129	853	27	174	58
18 Communications					205	
19 Finance, Insurance	1068	1548		12		
20 Public Services						
21 Domestic Intermed. Inputs	29342	16751	24090	402	7736	805
22 Imports c.i.f	10025	30618	8711	261	1449	1191
23 Import Duties	710	1790	950	22	93	117
24 Imports incl. Duties	10935	32408	9681	283	1542	1308
25 Gross Fixed Capital Conspt	3581	2946	1897	15	984	181
26 Compensation of Employees	21630	20468	4784	211	4014	1538
27 Indirect Taxes less Subsid.	3722	89120	13238	19	976	191
28 Operating Surplus	215440		7010	111	1338	577
29 Sales by Final Buyers	0	0	0	0	0	0
30 Gross Value added	240801	131731	25033	341	6326	2306
31 Total Supply	281076	180869	58803	1026	15603	4419

Aggregated Input-Output Table of Papua New Guinea for the Year 1972

PAPUA NEW GUINEA 1972 FLOWS in thousands of kina of Y 1972-73 PURCHASERS CURRENT MARKET PRICES

INDUSTRY:	Chemicals 7	Non-Metallic Mineral Prod. 8	Basic Metal Industries 9	Metal Products Machinery 10	Village Industries 11	Other Manufacturing 12
* DOMESTIC TRANSACTIONS *						
1 Agriculture	5842	0	0	0	0	0
2 Mining and Quarrying	0	275	0	0	0	82
3 Manufacture of Food	0	0	0	0	0	0
4 Textiles, Clothing	0	0	0	55	0	0
5 Wood and Wood Products	0	0	1538	108	0	3
6 Paper, Printing	13	3	160	0	0	2
7 Chemicals	111	0	0	0	2	38
8 Non-Metallic Mineral Prod.	0	3	0	837	0	0
9 Basic Metal Industries	0	46	500	5	0	0
10 Metal Products, Machinery	238	0	0	284	0	73
11 Village Industries	0	0	0	145	0	70
12 Other Manufacturing	0	0	39	4077	515	0
13 Electricity, Gas and Steam	84	26	217	9	0	97
14 Construction	15	10	15	1034	81	10
15 Trade (Distribution)	1329	70	126	233	0	155
16 Restaurants and Hotels	0	0	14	837	0	4
17 Transport and Storage	259	173	25	363	0	126
18 Communications	151	12	71		0	9
19 Finance, Insurance	184	31			0	80
20 Public Services	69	27			0	13
21 Domestic Intermed. Inputs	8197	677	2258	7805	578	673
22 Imports c.i.f.	1609	508	308	9356	33	348
23 Imports Duties	105	15	40	470	2	48
24 Imports incl. Duties	1714	523	349	9826	35	394
25 Gross Fixed Capital Conspt.	408	95	136	851	0	280
26 Compensation of Employees	1227	504	1098	8699	15	438
27 Indirect Taxes less Subsid.	419	100	140	870	0	283
28 Operating Surplus	1448	489	127	5637	814	167
29 Sales by Final Buyers	0	0	0	0	0	0
30 Gross Value added	3092	1093	1365	15206	829	866
31 Total Supply	13002	2283	3969	32837	1242	1953

200

Aggregated Input-Output Table of Papua New Guinea for the Year 1972

PAPUA NEW GUINEA 1972 FLOWS in thousands of kina of Y 1972-73 PURCHASERS CURRENT MARKET PRICES

INDUSTRY:

DOMESTIC TRANSACTIONS / INDUSTRY	13 Electricity, Gas and Steam	14 Construction	15 Trade (Distribution)	16 Restaurants and Hotels	17 Transport and Storage	18 Communications
1 Agriculture	2	0	0	336	74	0
2 Mining and Quarrying	195	866	0	0	1634	0
3 Manufacture of Food	0	0	284	212	75	0
4 Textiles, Clothing	0	0	30	0	155	0
5 Wood and Wood Products	6	7120	455	93	243	76
6 Paper, Printing	9	129	39	0	104	0
7 Chemicals	0	1439	0	0	0	0
8 Non-Metallic Mineral Prod.	0	2293	0	332	34	24
9 Basic Metal Industries	202	8388	0	0	8387	0
10 Metal Products, Machinery	0	0	1259	0	0	0
11 Village Industries	0	0	0	0	10	0
12 Other Manufacturing	0	608	0	0	260	189
13 Electricity, Gas and Steam	252	631	817	785	1239	214
14 Construction	455	0	1445	1185	4493	316
15 Trade (Distribution)	450	7433	2330	446	891	712
16 Restaurants and Hotels	491	305	287	32	2441	713
17 Transport and Storage	65	4104	4458	1140	1125	110
18 Communications	147	1041	1356	742	6763	159
19 Finance, Insurance	61	2653	18303	2495	6763	101
20 Public Services		1863	3483	1367	3343	
21 Domestic Intermed. Inputs	1938	41206	34547	9167	31291	1905
22 Imports c.i.f.	1266	3018	4914	2027	24415	1200
23 Import Duties	66	194	432	79	742	34
24 Imports incl. Duties	1332	3211	5346	2106	25157	1234
25 Gross Fixed Capital Conspt	1578	1994	4833	657	6957	1134
26 Compensation of Employees	2823	68407	22385	5537	19997	5517
27 Indirect Taxes less Subsid	1478	2408	5380	547	7323	1134
28 Operating Surplus	2241	6050	17207	2782	1497	4109
29 Sales by Final Buyers	0	0	0	0	0	0
30 Gross Value added	6540	74915	44972	8665	28817	10760
31 Total Supply	9808	148292	84865	20138	85265	13399

Aggregated Input-Output Table of Papua New Guinea for the Year 1972

PAPUA NEW GUINEA 1972   FLOWS in thousands of kina of Y 1972-73   PURCHASERS CURRENT MARKET PRICES

INDUSTRY:	19 Finance, Insurance	20 Public Services	21 Total Intermd Consumption	22 Private Consumption	23 Government Consumption	24 Gross Fixed Capital Form
* DOMESTIC TRANSACTIONS * INDUSTRY						
1 Agriculture	396	557	13373	194135	1422	9593
2 Mining and Quarrying	405	123	3580		74	
3 Manufacture of Food	1166	135	8554	49213	0	0
4 Textiles, Clothing	20	10	110	802	0	0
5 Wood and Wood Products	168	239	9210	372	0	230
6 Paper, Printing	247	1865	9841	315	0	
7 Chemicals	60	547	4289	183	0	2
8 Non-Metallic Mineral Prod.			3287		0	0
9 Basic Metal Industries	77		3597		0	
10 Metal Products, Machinery	477	1211	24974	7	14	3573
11 Village Industries	0		1662	3702	0	
12 Other Manufacturing		15	7552	124		
13 Electricity, Gas and Steam	235	3309	7765	291		0
14 Construction	1143	51003	67787	2245		75365
15 Trade (Distribution)	765	2511	48287	28768	5124	6186
16 Restaurants and Hotels	289	231	10350	4393	2168	
17 Transport and Storage	1930	14174	44456	15581	1989	536
18 Communications	685	4139	10651	2756	301	
19 Finance, Insurance	3172	1216	44448	24581	1030	0
20 Public Services	3391	3889	20785	24536	217544	0
21 Domestic Intermed. Inputs	23892	87005	330391	354458	229647	95485
22 Imports c.i.f.	12383	25559	166569	104941	0	35157
23 Import Duties	431	878	8769	11510	0	1554
24 Imports incl. Duties	12814	26237	175338	116451	0	36711
25 Gross Fixed Capital Conspt	7601	3580	58656	0	0	0
26 Compensation of Employees	12713	143788	345838	0	0	0
27 Indirect Taxes less Subsid	7441	3741	69544	0	0	0
28 Operating Surplus	20249	2249	378475	0	0	0
29 Sales by Final Buyers	0	0	0	-12844	0	-5741
30 Gross Value added	40403	149776	793857	-12844	0	-5741
31 Total Supply	77109	263098	1299986	458065	229647	126455

202

Aggregated Input-Output Table of Papua New Guinea for the Year 1972

PAPUA NEW GUINEA 1972   FLOWS in thousands of kina of Y 1972-73   PURCHASERS CURRENT MARKET PRICES

* DOMESTIC TRANSACTIONS *

INDUSTRY	25 Changes in Stock	26 Exports	27 Total Final Demand	28 Total Supply
1 Agriculture	2186	60388	267704	281076
2 Mining and Quarrying	9029	168280	177309	180889
3 Manufacture of Food	375	587	50249	58020
4 Textiles, Clothing	110	514	5782	15026
5 Wood and Wood Products	-372	5343	5130	15603
6 Paper, Printing	-928	187	9214	4419
7 Chemicals		8100		13002
8 Non-Metallic Mineral Prod.	412		422	2293
9 Basic Metal Industries	122	453	7862	3969
10 Metal Products, Machinery		1118	1242	32837
11 Village Industries	0		291	1242
12 Other Manufacturing	0			1953
13 Electricity, Gas and Steam	0	7	2252	9608
14 Construction	927		80529	148292
15 Trade (Distribution)	223	697	36578	84865
16 Restaurants and Hotels	262	3002	9788	20138
17 Transport and Storage		22521	40809	85265
18 Communications	0	386	3248	13899
19 Finance Insurance	0	4037	32663	77109
20 Public Services	0	236	242315	263098
21 Domestic Intermed. Inputs	14211	275378	989177	1299586
22 Imports C.i.f.	4481	822	144752	31952
23 Import Duties	379	274	13717	22488
24 Imports incl Duties	4840	1096	158469	33438
25 Gross Fixed Capital Conspt	0	0	0	56056
26 Compensation of Employees	0	0	0	345838
27 Indirect Taxes less Subsid	0	0	0	89544
28 Operating Surplus	0	18585	0	378475
29 Sales by Final Buyers	0	18585	0	0
30 Gross Value added	0		0	793857
31 Total Supply	19052	295058	1128281	0

203

PHILIPPINES

Reference year: 1974

Entries in table: Total flows

Source: National Economic and Development Authority, National Census and Statistics Office, *Interindustry (Input-Output) Accounts of the Philippines* (Manila, 1974)

Computerized: Economics University of Vienna

Currency units: Pesos of Y 1974
Scale factor: 100,000

Pricing system: Producers' current prices
Intermediate sectors: 61 × 61
Treatment of trade margins: Inputs, row 52

Treatment of imports: Imports column 68
Availability of import matrix: Not available

Total number of rows: 68
Statistical unit of quadrant 1: Industry

Total number of columns: 70
Statistical unit of quadrant 1: Industry

Fourth quadrant: Not occupied

Input-Output Table of Philippines for the Year 1974

PHILIPPINES 1974   FLOWS in hundred thousand pesos of Y 1974   PRODUCERS CURRENT PRICES

INDUSTRY:	1 Palay	2 Corn	3 Fruits & Nuts	4 Vegetables	5 Tubers & Root Crops	6 Coffee & Cacao
* TOTAL TRANSACTIONS *						
1 Palay	1586.30	0.00	0.00	0.00	0.00	0.00
2 Corn	0.00	669.30	0.00	0.00	0.00	0.00
3 Fruits & Nuts	0.00	0.00	935.09	240.19	0.00	0.00
4 Vegetables	0.00	0.00	0.00	0.00	0.00	0.00
5 Tubers & Root Crops	0.00	0.00	0.00	0.00	263.77	30.75
6 Coffee & Cacao	0.00	0.00	0.00	0.00	0.00	0.00
7 Sugar Cane	0.00	0.00	0.00	0.00	0.00	0.00
8 Coconut incl Copra (in Farm)	0.00	0.00	0.00	0.00	0.00	0.00
9 Tobacco (Native & Virginia)	0.00	0.00	0.00	0.00	0.00	0.00
10 Abaca & Other Fiber Crops	0.00	0.00	0.00	0.00	0.00	0.00
11 Other Crops	0.00	0.00	0.00	0.00	0.00	0.00
12 Livestock	0.00	0.00	0.00	0.00	0.00	0.00
13 Poultry	0.00	0.00	0.00	0.00	0.00	21.13
14 Oth. Agricultural Activities	731.78	170.42	193.48	29.54	32.30	21.00
15 Fisheries	0.00	0.00	0.00	0.00	0.00	0.00
16 Forestry & Logging	0.00	0.00	0.00	0.00	0.00	0.00
17 Gold & Silver Mining	0.00	0.00	0.00	0.00	0.00	0.00
18 Oth. Metallic Mining	0.00	0.00	0.00	0.00	0.00	0.00
19 Non-Metall. Min. & Quarr.	0.00	0.00	0.00	0.00	0.00	0.00
20 Meat Products	0.00	0.00	0.00	0.00	0.00	0.00
21 Dairy Products	0.00	0.00	0.00	0.00	0.00	0.00
22 Rice Milling	0.00	0.00	0.00	0.00	0.00	0.00
23 Sugar Milling & Refining	0.00	0.00	0.00	0.00	0.00	0.00
24 Oth. Manufactured Foods	0.00	0.00	0.00	0.00	0.00	0.00
25 Beverages	0.00	0.00	0.00	4.03	0.00	0.00
26 Tobacco Products	9.06	1.15	10.90	0.03	1.54	0.00
27 Textile Manufactures	20.06	0.00	0.00	0.23	20.60	0.00
28 Wearing Apparel, Made-up Text	1.49	0.00	4.65	7.10	0.00	0.00
29 Lumber	0.00	0.00	1.55	6.70	0.13	0.00
30 Plywood & Veneer Plants	0.00	0.00	258.97	6.12	0.00	0.00
31 Furniture & Fixtures	0.45	0.00	0.10	0.00	0.00	0.00
32 Paper & Paper Products	0.00	0.00	0.74	0.00	0.00	0.23
33 Printing, Publishing, etc.	0.00	0.00	0.00	0.00	0.00	0.00
34 Leather & Leather Products	0.00	0.00	0.00	0.00	0.00	0.00
35 Rubber Products	0.00	0.00	0.00	0.00	0.00	0.00
36 Basic Industrial Chemicals	0.00	0.00	0.00	0.00	0.00	0.00
37 Coconut & oth. Oils & Fats	2722.09	969.88	1309.87	654.57	61.42	206.91
38 Oth. Chemical Products	100.79	41.67	69.16	28.93	4.76	14.63
39 Petroleum Refineries & Prods	0.00	0.00	0.00	0.00	0.00	0.00
40 Hydraulic Cement	0.00	0.00	0.00	0.00	0.00	0.00
41 Oth. Non-Metall. Mineral Prods	0.00	0.00	0.00	0.00	0.93	0.00
42 Basic Metals	3.42	0.00	0.61	5.86	0.00	0.00
43 Metal Prods, exc. Machinery	112.61	22.10	0.00	60.64	0.00	0.00
44 Machinery, exc. Electr. Mach.	0.00	0.00	0.00	0.00	0.00	0.00
45 Electr. Machinery & Apparatus	0.92	0.00	0.93	0.00	0.00	0.00
46 Motor Vehicles	0.72	0.00	0.00	0.00	0.00	0.00
47 Oth. Transport Equipment	0.00	0.00	0.00	0.55	0.00	0.00
48 Misc. Manufactures	87.88	0.00	0.00	0.00	0.00	0.00
49 Scrap	0.00	0.00	0.00	0.00	0.00	0.00
50 Electricty, Gas & Water Svc.	0.00	0.00	1.58	0.45	0.00	0.00

Input-Output Table of Philippines for the Year 1974

PHILIPPINES 1974   FLOWS in hundred thousand pesos of Y 1974   PRODUCERS CURRENT PRICES

INDUSTRY:

	1 Palay	2 Corn	3 Fruits & Nuts	4 Vegetables	5 Tubers & Root Crops	6 Coffee & Cacao
51 Construction	0.00	20.00	30.00	0.00	0.00	0.00
52 Wholesale & Retail Trade	665.54	223.90	33.96	143.31	45.19	36.75
53 Banking & Oth. Financing	71.65	28.81	37.58	23.50	7.68	6.62
54 Insurance	0.00	0.00	3.49	0.00	0.00	0.00
55 Real Estate	0.00	0.00	5.70	0.00	0.00	0.00
56 Transport Services	3.48	20.21	2.86	5.98	2.55	2.50
57 Storage & Warehousing	3.69	-1.42	3.01	5.08	0.00	1.73
58 Communications	0.00	0.00	0.26	0.00	0.00	-1.92
59 Private Services	181.30	105.24	76.13	0.98	0.21	1.30
60 Government Services	0.00	0.00	0.00	0.00	0.00	0.00
61 National Industry	0.00	0.00	0.00	0.00	0.00	
62 Total Intermed. Inputs	6360.29	2254.20	3283.52	1158.86	441.08	323.47
63 Compensation of Employees	21157.04	8603.81	6980.87	5920.67	2943.01	993.27
64 Capital Consumpt. Allowance	1188.18	497.20	744.16	454.90	90.91	80.78
65 Indirect Taxes less Subsid.	667.74	188.06	645.62	187.57	113.27	187.65
66 Other Value Added	19754.35	7455.10	11767.19	7691.38	3697.08	2516.71
87 Gross Value Added	42767.31	16743.97	20141.64	14254.52	6844.27	3642.41
68 Gross Output	49127.60	18998.17	23425.16	15413.38	7285.35	3965.88

206

Input-Output Table of Philippines for the Year 1974

PHILIPPINES 1974 FLOWS in hundred thousand pesos of Y 1974 PRODUCERS CURRENT PRICES

#	INDUSTRY:	7 Sugar Cane	8 Coconut & Copra (in Farm)	9 Tobacco	10 Abaca & Other Fiber Crops	11 Other Crops	12 Livestock
	TOTAL INDUSTRY						
1	Palay	0.000	0.000	0.000	0.000	0.000	583.29
2	Corn	0.000	0.000	0.000	0.000	0.000	77.09
3	Fruits & Nuts	0.000	0.000	0.000	0.000	0.000	77.56
4	Vegetables	0.000	0.000	0.000	0.000	0.000	0.000
5	Tubers & Root Crops	0.000	0.000	0.000	0.000	0.000	0.000
6	Coffee & Cacao	0.000	0.000	0.000	0.000	0.000	0.000
7	Sugar Cane	807.48	0.000	0.000	0.000	0.000	0.000
8	Coconut incl.Copra (in Farm)	0.000	5918.87	26.08	0.000	0.000	0.000
9	Tobacco (Native & Virginia)	0.000	0.000	0.000	20.00	2.11	0.000
10	Abaca & Other Fiber Crops	0.000	0.000	0.000	2.00	0.000	0.000
11	Other Crops	0.000	0.000	0.000	0.000	0.000	1427.14
12	Livestock	0.000	0.000	0.000	0.000	0.000	246.24
13	Poultry	0.000	0.000	0.000	0.000	3.87	0.000
14	Oth.Agricultural Activities	252.63	130.33	50.33	32.00	2.45	0.000
15	Fisheries	0.000	0.000	0.000	0.000	0.000	0.000
16	Forestry & Logging	11.47	11.47	9.87	0.000	0.77	21.72
17	Gold & Silver Mining	0.000	0.000	13.07	0.000	5.33	0.000
18	Non-Metallic Min. & Quarr.	0.000	0.000	0.18	0.000	0.000	0.000
19	Oth.Metallic Min. & Quarr.	0.000	0.000	0.000	0.000	0.000	0.000
20	Meat Products	0.000	0.000	0.000	0.000	0.000	88.93
21	Dairy Products	0.000	0.000	0.000	0.000	0.000	4.95
22	Rice Milling	0.000	0.000	0.000	0.000	0.000	2610.97
23	Sugar Milling & Refining	0.000	0.000	0.000	0.000	0.000	0.000
24	Oth.Manufactured Foods	0.000	0.000	0.000	0.000	0.000	0.000
25	Beverage	0.000	0.000	0.000	0.000	0.000	0.000
26	Tobacco Products	0.000	0.000	0.000	0.000	0.000	0.000
27	Textile Manufactures	0.000	0.000	0.000	0.000	0.000	0.000
28	Wearing Apparel,Made-up Text	0.000	0.000	0.000	0.000	0.000	0.000
29	Lumber	0.000	1.75	0.000	0.000	0.77	0.000
30	Plywood & Veneer Plants	14.23	4.87	0.000	0.000	0.000	0.000
31	Furniture & Fixtures	1.85	0.50	0.000	0.000	0.30	0.000
32	Paper & Paper Products	0.000	0.000	0.000	0.000	0.000	0.000
33	Printing,Publishing,etc.	0.000	0.000	0.000	0.000	0.000	0.000
34	Leather & Leather Products	0.000	0.000	0.000	0.000	0.000	0.000
35	Rubber Products	0.000	0.000	0.000	0.000	0.000	0.000
36	Basic Industrial Chemicals	0.000	42.92	249.68	261.93	66.95	0.000
37	Coconut & Oth. Oils & Fats	2846.28	475.31	9.17	18.20	10.16	569.05
38	Oth.Chemical Products	274.50	34.70	0.000	18.20	0.000	58.87
39	Petroleum Refineries & Prods	0.000	0.000	0.000	0.000	0.000	0.000
40	Hydraulic Cement	0.000	0.000	0.000	0.000	0.000	0.000
41	Oth.Non-Metall.Mineral Prods	0.000	0.000	0.000	0.000	0.000	0.000
42	Basic Metals	0.42	0.000	2.05	0.48	0.23	0.23
43	Metal Prods. exc. Machinery	7.54	11.95	0.000	0.000	0.000	2.89
44	Machinery,exc.Electr.Mach.	0.75	0.10	0.000	0.000	0.000	2.40
45	Electr.Machinery & Apparatus	0.00	0.00	0.000	0.000	0.000	0.000
46	Motor Vehicles	0.000	0.000	0.000	0.000	0.000	0.000
47	Oth.Transport Equipment	2.89	0.000	0.000	0.000	1.09	0.39
48	Misc. Manufactures	0.000	0.000	0.000	0.000	0.000	0.000
49	Scrap	0.000	0.000	0.000	0.000	0.000	0.000
50	Electricty, Gas & Water Svc.	24.37	0.00	0.000	6.55	0.00	36.93

Input-Output Table of Philippines for the Year 1974

PHILIPPINES 1974   FLOWS in hundred thousand pesos of Y 1974   PRODUCERS CURRENT PRICES

INDUSTRY:	7 Sugar Cane	8 Coconut & Copra (in Farm)	9 Tobacco	10 Abaca & Other Fiber Crops	11 Other Crops	12 Livestock
51 Construction	0.00	0.00	0.00	2.86	10.62	210.92
52 Wholesale & Retail Trade	499.68	175.97	52.97	43.89	18.62	690.87
53 Banking & oth. Financing	39.00	33.00	5.49	0.00	0.39	4.80
54 Insurance	0.00	0.00	0.00	0.00	0.16	0.00
55 Real Estate	45.88	2.90	0.00	0.00	0.00	0.00
56 Transport Services	4.47	8.42	2.23	0.85	8.00	200.15
57 Storage & Warehousing	0.00	0.00	0.00	0.00	0.00	0.00
58 Communications	103.15	1.26	1.54	0.01	0.00	10.47
59 Private Services	0.00	0.00	1.00	7.10	5.04	103.77
60 Government Services	0.00	0.00	0.00	0.00	0.00	0.00
61 National Industry						
62 Total Intermedt. Inputs	4722.45	6863.33	432.78	401.18	139.89	7018.40
63 Compensation of Employees	10483.50	8654.34	1024.61	1113.78	400.01	11237.63
64 Capital Consumpt. Allowance	1470.23	766.66	81.57	150.77	40.36	138.28
65 Indirect Taxes less Subsid.	774.55	742.10	23.66	84.65	21.55	775.90
66 Other Value Added	8422.06	13353.61	2007.52	1889.19	569.83	10476.76
67 Gross Value Added	21150.34	23516.71	3137.36	3238.39	1031.75	2387.57
68 Gross Output	25872.79	30380.04	3570.12	3639.57	1171.84	30889.97

208

Input-Output Table of Philippines for the Year 1974

PHILIPPINES 1974   FLOWS in hundred thousand pesos of Y 1974   PRODUCERS CURRENT PRICES

INDUSTRY:

#	INDUSTRY	13 Poultry	14 Oth. Agricult. Activities	15 Fisheries	16 Forestry & Logging	17 Gold & Silver Mining	18 Oth. Metallic Mining
	* TOTAL TRANSACTIONS *	.00	.000	.00	.000	.00	.000
1	Palay	317.02	.000	.00	.000	.00	.000
2	Corn	65.51	.000	.00	.000	.00	.000
3	Fruits & Nuts	.00	.000	.00	.000	.00	.000
4	Vegetables	.00	.000	37.47	.000	.00	.000
5	Tubers & Root Crops	.00	.000	.00	.000	.00	.000
6	Coffee & Cacao	.00	.000	.00	.000	.00	.000
7	Sugar Cane	.00	.000	.00	.000	.00	.000
8	Coconut incl.Copra (in Farm)	75.79	.000	18.93	.000	.00	.000
9	Tobacco (Native & Virginia)	.00	.000	.00	.000	.00	.000
10	Abaca & Other Fiber Crops	.00	.000	84.59	.000	.00	.000
11	Other Crops	.00	85.49	.00	.000	.00	.000
12	Livestock	165.73	.000	.00	.000	.00	.000
13	Poultry	18.11	.000	.00	.000	.00	.000
14	Oth. Agricultural Activities	.00	.000	346.52	1887.35	95.92	154.18
15	Fisheries	.00	.000	.00	.000	62.87	101.27
16	Forestry & Logging	.00	.000	.00	.000	.00	.000
17	Gold & Silver Mining	.00	.000	.00	.000	.00	.000
18	Oth.Metallic Min. & Quarr.	.00	.000	.00	.000	.00	.000
19	Non-Metal.Min. & Quarr.	.00	.000	30.34	.000	2.68	1.08
20	Meat Products	.00	.000	9.50	.000	.00	.000
21	Dairy Products	.00	.000	.00	.000	.00	.000
22	Rice Milling	.00	.000	258.29	.000	.00	.000
23	Sugar Milling & Refining	.00	.000	736.25	.000	.00	.000
24	Oth.Manufactured Foods	3385.78	.000	8.48	.000	.00	.000
25	Beverages	.00	.000	30.94	.78	.00	.000
26	Tobacco Products	.00	.000	.00	.000	.00	.000
27	Textile Manufactures	.00	2.45	.00	.45	.00	.000
28	Wearing Apparel,Made-up Text	.00	2.43	254.02	.000	80.51	34.35
29	Lumber	.00	2.63	.00	19.80	.00	.000
30	Plywood & Veneer Plants	.00	.000	.00	.000	.00	.000
31	Furniture & Fixtures	40.50	.000	1.56	1.40	.14	33.07
32	Paper & Paper Products	.36	.000	.00	2.90	6.08	37.09
33	Printing,Publishing,etc.	.00	.000	4.43	.000	.00	.000
34	Leather & Leather Products	.00	.000	32.19	77.37	.22	1.25
35	Rubber Products	.00	.000	.00	2.40	3.66	82.63
36	Basic Industrial Chemicals	725.89	18.73	400.47	2.00	300.71	546.50
37	Coconut&oth.Oils & Fats	160.00	24.36	2431.96	677.95	510.57	579.56
38	Oth.Chemical Products	.00	28.07	.00	1101.06	205.80	1554.63
39	Petroleum Refineries & Prods	.00	.000	5.32	15.88	.00	.000
40	Hydraulic Cement	.00	.000	.00	.000	.00	.000
41	Oth.Non-Metall.Mineral Prods	.00	.000	.00	.000	.00	.000
42	Basic Metals	.00	1.27	45.27	2.14	9.88	12.37
43	Metal Prods.exc.Machinery	3.36	.000	30.74	624.98	8.40	74.30
44	Machinery,exc.Electr.Mach.	3.00	.19	16.34	16.34	195.31	1590.44
45	Electr.Mach.& Apparatus	.00	.000	.00	158.89	16.39	82.22
46	Motor Vehicles	.00	.000	65.07	73.93	5.68	242.27
47	Oth.Transport Equipment	.00	.21	.00	.000	2.17	52.09
48	Misc.Manufactures	1.56	.000	28.80	.48	.83	11.00
49	Scrap	.00	.000	28.84	.000	.00	4.95
50	Electricty, Gas & Water Svc.	53.77	2.55	28.86	25.82	87.40	145.41

Input-Output Table of Philippines for the Year 1974

PHILIPPINES 1974   FLOWS in hundred thousand pesos of Y 1974   PRODUCERS CURRENT PRICES

INDUSTRY:	13 Poultry	14 Oth. Agricult. Activities	15 Fisheries	16 Forestry & Logging	17 Gold & Silver Mining	18 Oth. Metallic Mining
51 Construction	50.26	0.00	0.00	747.00	0.86	85.13
52 Wholesale & Retail Trade	979.36	19.56	714.86	37.14	233.89	86.16
53 Banking & Oth. Financing	39.79	2.59	45.33	37.00	4.53	33.83
54 Insurance	0.00	1.74	0.00	312.02	20.41	49.80
55 Real Estate	0.00	5.22	34.53	73.97	0.10	4.04
56 Transport Services	142.91	2.80	11.90	3.45	45.92	220.37
57 Storage & Warehousing	0.00	0.00	54.70	3.45	0.00	0.00
58 Communications	7.68	7.45	56.37	86.23	5.79	18.92
59 Private Services	38.29	96.14	156.13	384.81	72.38	554.84
60 Government Services	0.00	0.00	0.00	0.00	0.00	0.00
61 National Industry	0.00	0.00	0.00	0.00		
62 Total Intermed. Inputs	7763.27	303.28	6097.75	6499.86	1987.09	7084.92
63 Compensation of Employees	5035.87	866.32	19265.56	7713.29	1142.19	6280.77
64 Capital Consumpt. Allowance	1261.96	98.48	2467.75	5811.28	589.30	2978.49
65 Indirect Taxes less Subsid.	1385.65	85.64	2417.06	2544.66	243.74	2210.73
66 Other Value Added	8033.25	1181.64	26156.91	15032.32	2537.68	13595.09
67 Gross Value Added	14716.73	2212.08	52510.28	31101.55	4512.91	25065.08
68 Gross Output	22480.00	2515.36	58608.03	37601.41	8500.00	32150.00

Input-Output Table of Philippines for the Year 1974

PHILIPPINES 1974   FLOWS in hundred thousand pesos of Y 1974   PRODUCERS CURRENT PRICES

INDUSTRY:

	19 Non-Metallic Mining &Quarryg	20 Meat Products	21 Dairy Products	22 Rice Milling	23 Sugar Milling & Refining	24 Oth. Manufact. Foods
* TOTAL TRANSACTIONS *						
1 Palay	0.00	0.00	0.00	47254.62	0.00	0.00
2 Corn	0.00	0.36	1.04	0.00	0.00	15114.56
3 Fruits & Nuts	0.00	39.89	24.12	0.00	0.00	2034.56
4 Vegetables	0.00	0.45	0.02	0.00	0.00	439.25
5 Tubers & Root Crops	0.00	0.00	0.00	0.00	0.00	422.02
6 Coffee & Cacao	0.00	0.00	3.88	0.00	24877.06	3644.02
7 Sugar Cane	0.00	0.00	0.00	0.00	0.00	0.00
8 Coconut incl Copra (in Farm)	0.00	0.00	101.95	0.00	0.00	1717.12
9 Coconut (Native & Virginia)	0.00	0.00	0.00	0.00	0.00	0.00
10 Abaca & Other Fiber Crops	0.00	0.00	0.00	0.00	0.00	1.63
11 Other Crops	0.00	0.00	1.18	0.00	0.00	6462.74
12 Livestock	0.00	2207.70	533.51	0.00	0.00	507.00
13 Poultry	0.00	3355.68	51.50	0.00	0.00	0.00
14 Oth Agricultural Activities	0.00	0.00	0.00	0.00	0.00	5141.08
15 Fisheries	0.00	0.00	0.00	0.00	0.00	103.80
16 Forestry & Logging	10.75	0.00	0.00	0.00	0.00	0.00
17 Gold & Silver Mining	0.00	0.00	0.00	0.00	0.00	0.00
18 Oth Non-Metallic Mining	0.00	5.45	0.00	0.00	0.00	304.04
19 Non-Metall. Min. & Quarr.	0.00	0.00	0.00	0.00	0.00	144.29
20 Meat Products	0.00	2007.03	1629.54	0.00	0.00	489.17
21 Dairy Products	0.00	0.00	481.27	0.00	0.00	215.94
22 Rice Milling	0.00	4.14	399.08	0.00	0.00	1067.18
23 Sugar Milling & Refining	0.00	94.48	0.00	0.00	611.51	12032.27
24 Oth. Manufactured Foods	0.00	0.00	0.00	0.00	0.00	0.00
25 Beverages	0.00	0.00	0.00	0.00	0.00	103.37
26 Tobacco Products	0.00	0.06	0.06	0.00	0.00	279.40
27 Textile Manufactures	0.00	0.04	0.00	0.00	0.19	0.00
28 Wearing Apparel,Made-up Text	0.06	0.00	-0.50	7.00	0.00	29.40
29 Lumber	0.17	3.00	89.14	0.76	18.20	20.07
30 Plywood & Veneer Plants	3.97	4.97	33.88	2.07	1.50	857.07
31 Furniture & Fixtures	1.43	1.43	0.00	4.48	68.12	154.64
32 Paper & Paper Products	13.57	10.93	9.26	17.65	46.20	66.29
33 Printing, Publishing, etc.	13.78	8.42	8.68	0.00	3.81	66.45
34 Leather & Leather Products	0.00	2.67	62.71	0.00	3.00	2724.45
35 Rubber Products	237.02	0.88	21.00	0.00	84.07	5727.70
36 Basic Industrial Chemicals	0.44	90.21	157.00	565.52	1118.01	5129.46
37 Coconut & Oth. Oils & Fats	0.06	0.00	0.00	25.21	0.07	1587.05
38 Oth. Chemical Products	0.00	0.11	106.35	10.37	7.45	431.59
39 Petroleum Refineries & Prods	5.37	0.84	592.65	1.34	7.77	726.06
40 Oth.Non-Metall.Mineral Prods	9.66	106.96	1.37	1.54	9.77	12.05
41 Hydraulic Cement	3.94	4.03	0.54	3.79	13.23	12.29
42 Basic Metals	1.59	0.94	4.21	1.07	1.79	0.00
43 Metal Prods. exc. Machinery	0.04	0.00	3.79	0.00	0.00	0.00
44 Machinery, exc. Electr. Mach.	0.00	0.00	1.07	0.74	1.07	303.04
45 Electr. Machinery & Apparatus	0.00	50.00	2.00	0.00	189.33	0.00
46 Motor Vehicles			36.00			
47 Oth. Transport Equipment						
48 Misc. Manufactures	0.00	50.00				303.04
49 Scrap			36.00			
50 Electricty, Gas & Water Svc.	25.56	35.50	51.17	35.43	157.16	462.94

Input-Output Table of Philippines for the Year 1974

PHILIPPINES 1974   FLOWS in hundred thousand pesos of Y 1974   PRODUCERS CURRENT PRICES

INDUSTRY:	Non-Metallic Mining &Quarryg 19	Meat Products 20	Dairy Products 21	Rice Milling 22	Sugar Milling & Refining 23	Oth. Manufact. Foods 24
51 Construction	1.38	0.28	0.07	9.06	5.24	1.86
52 Wholesale & Retail Trade	48.40	5325.27	637.09	6349.84	4507.00	8193.23
53 Banking & Oth. Financing	15.38	2.60	10.13	15.79	102.07	51.15
54 Insurance	10.00	20.86	20.75	75.58	134.20	232.27
55 Real Estate	6.90	30.24	21.98	219.14	154.74	365.84
56 Transport Services	31.58	112.84	68.33	201.34	335.74	392.96
57 Storage & Warehousing	0.00	1.82	1.18	31.62	1.00	2.98
58 Communications	4.96	22.27	7.21	26.23	7.80	108.20
59 Private Services	34.35	46.89	98.75	0.00	302.00	615.51
60 Government Services	0.00	0.00	0.00	0.00	0.00	0.00
61 National Industry						
62 Total Intermedt. Inputs	473.54	33439.33	5290.45	54965.94	32797.20	71039.15
63 Compensation of Employees	783.33	3021.28	791.92	2438.12	4503.44	7513.86
64 Capital Consumpt. Allowance	306.43	866.54	379.50	1439.43	3025.66	3517.48
65 Indirect Taxes less Subsid.	209.16	928.95	569.66	807.65	2493.51	2309.03
66 Other Value Added	1927.42	5849.66	1792.16	4437.81	13747.12	14749.82
67 Gross Value Added	3226.54	10666.43	3533.24	9123.01	23769.73	28090.19
68 Gross Output	3700.08	44105.76	8823.69	64088.95	56566.93	99129.34

212

Input-Output Table of Philippines for the Year 1974

PHILIPPINES 1974   FLOWS in hundred thousand pesos of Y 1974   PRODUCERS CURRENT PRICES

INDUSTRY:	25 Beverages	26 Tobacco Products	27 Textile Manufact. Made-up Textile	28 Wearing Apparl. Made-up Textile	29 Lumber	30 Plywood & Veneer Plants
* TOTAL TRANSACTIONS *						
1 Palay	0.000	0.000	0.000	0.000	0.000	0.000
2 Corn	2.53	0.000	0.000	0.000	0.000	0.000
3 Fruits & Nuts	0.000	0.000	0.000	0.000	0.000	0.000
4 Vegetables	0.000	0.000	0.000	0.000	0.000	0.000
5 Tubers & Root Crops	0.74	0.000	0.000	0.000	0.000	0.000
6 Coffee & Cacao	0.000	0.000	63.85	0.000	0.000	0.000
7 Sugar Cane	0.000	0.000	0.000	0.000	0.000	0.000
8 Coconut incl.Copra (in Farm)	0.000	0.000	3009.76	0.000	0.000	0.000
9 Tobacco (Native & Virginia)	0.000	3001.80	0.10	0.000	0.000	0.000
10 Abaca & Other Fiber Crops	0.000	1.05	0.00	78.42	0.000	0.000
11 Other Crops	0.000	0.000	0.01	0.00	0.000	0.000
12 Livestock	0.000	0.000	0.000	0.000	0.000	0.000
13 Poultry	0.000	0.000	0.000	0.000	0.000	0.000
14 Oth.Agricultural Activities	0.000	0.000	0.000	0.000	0.000	0.000
15 Fisheries	0.000	0.000	0.000	0.000	0.000	0.000
16 Forestry & Logging	0.000	35.48	0.000	6.95	4685.35	3048.91
17 Gold & Silver Mining	0.000	0.000	0.000	2.36	0.000	0.00
18 Non-Metall.Min. & Quarr.	0.000	0.000	0.000	0.000	0.000	0.000
19 Non-Metal Min. & Quarr.	0.000	0.000	0.14	0.000	0.000	0.000
20 Meat Products	3.92	0.000	0.000	0.35	0.000	0.000
21 Dairy Products	0.000	0.000	0.000	0.000	0.000	0.000
22 Rice Milling	0.000	0.000	0.000	0.000	0.000	0.000
23 Sugar Milling & Refining	627.49	52.59	0.000	0.000	0.000	57.74
24 Oth.Manufactured Foods	128.53	52.00	210.32	0.000	0.000	0.00
25 Beverages	1499.09	4132.35	0.00	0.000	0.000	0.000
26 Tobacco Products	0.000	18.00	0.000	4830.44	0.000	0.00
27 Textile Manufactures	0.000	0.000	9115.11	454.15	0.000	9.97
28 Wearing Apparel,Made-up Text	0.000	0.000	0.94	5.44	90.92	0.00
29 Lumber	17.56	13.37	23.26	0.22	0.00	0.000
30 Plywood & Veneer Plants	2.22	5.65	7.78	1.86	0.00	0.00
31 Furniture & Fixtures	215.97	41.24	182.52	201.86	18.21	9.97
32 Paper & Paper Products	270.74	931.20	31.17	28.93	5.88	28.99
33 Printing, Publishing, etc.	84.41	47.00	0.00	758.54	0.00	14.82
34 Leather & Leather Products	0.000	0.000	58.52	27.46	18.79	13.29
35 Rubber Products	43.81	18.50	2082.70	35.93	478.91	5.23
36 Basic Industrial Chemicals	343.96	298.17	0.00	52.50	0.00	18.26
37 Coconut & Oth.Oils & Fats	48.39	0.000	1986.07	58.26	9.89	82.01
38 Oth.Chemical Products	621.51	406.11	1138.93	275.26	481.12	83.83
39 Petroleum Refineries & Prods	610.82	28.71	3.87	0.00	0.00	252.75
40 Hydraulic Cement	886.72	0.000	0.00	0.99	0.02	387.58
41 Oth.Non-Metal.Mineral Prods	0.000	0.000	3.12	30.05	0.00	2.00
42 Basic Metals	382.10	0.000	0.00	6.67	2.68	4.37
43 Metal Prods. exc. Machinery	126.73	6.83	6.89	3.29	2.36	2.37
44 Machinery,exc.Electr.Mach.	6.60	3.50	6.45	3.75	2.44	1.82
45 Electr.Machinery & Apparatus	5.00	5.97	3.95	0.00	2.00	0.00
46 Motor Vehicles	0.000	3.54	0.00	156.00	0.71	0.80
47 Oth.Transport Equipment	0.000	0.000	0.00	0.00	0.00	0.00
48 Misc. Manufactures	10.34	118.15	131.04	556.80	0.71	0.71
49 Scrap	0.000	0.000	239.30	119.03	66.85	55.92
50 Electricty, Gas & Water Svc.	139.78	63.38	366.96			

Input-Output Table of Philippines for the Year 1974

PHILIPPINES 1974   FLOWS in hundred thousand pesos of Y 1974   PRODUCERS CURRENT PRICES

INDUSTRY:	25 Beverages	26 Tobacco Products	27 Textile Manufact.	28 Wearing Apparl, Made-up Textile	29 Lumber	30 Plywood & Veneer Plants
51 Construction	10.06	4.96	1.85	0.13	0.00	0.00
52 Wholesale & Retail Trade	714.90	1179.93	3013.27	1443.67	652.42	386.92
53 Banking & Oth. Financing	39.42	35.59	83.17	29.68	10.20	9.98
54 Insurance	56.76	73.84	173.54	71.67	22.06	31.01
55 Real Estate	78.75	58.66	149.68	185.03	20.08	14.62
56 Transport Services	119.42	86.96	279.89	107.39	142.59	97.88
57 Storage & Warehousing	4.58	0.46	2.73	0.00	0.00	0.24
58 Communications	19.81	14.23	25.08	31.95	5.21	13.10
59 Private Services	675.17	514.94	757.29	160.03	11.83	93.03
60 Government Services	0.00	0.00	0.00	0.00	0.00	0.00
61 National Industry	0	0	0	0	0	0
62 Total Intermed. Inputs	7079.01	11459.03	23160.28	9676.95	6836.56	4638.75
63 Compensation of Employees	2096.12	1719.70	2150.01	2831.08	701.07	658.08
64 Capital Consumpt. Allowance	1084.59	7875.63	1546.68	558.01	332.26	246.40
65 Indirect Taxes less Subsid.	3290.14	7859.33	901.31	395.80	306.14	253.78
66 Other Value Added	4270.62	2862.20	4393.96	2817.77	828.67	1099.08
67 Gross Value Added	10741.47	13116.86	8991.96	6602.66	2163.14	2257.34
68 Gross Output	17820.48	24575.89	32152.24	16279.61	8999.70	6896.09

214

Input-Output Table of Philippines for the Year 1974

PHILIPPINES 1974 FLOWS in hundred thousand pesos of Y 1974 PRODUCERS CURRENT PRICES

INDUSTRY:

* TOTAL TRANSACTIONS * INDUSTRY	31 Furniture & Fixtures	32 Paper & Paper Products	33 Printing, Publishing, etc	34 Leather & Leather Prods	35 Rubber Products	36 Basic Indust. Chemicals
1 Palay	0.000	0.000	0.000	0.000	0.000	0.000
2 Corn	0.000	0.000	0.000	0.000	0.000	0.000
3 Fruits & Nuts	0.000	0.000	0.000	0.000	0.000	0.000
4 Vegetables	0.000	0.000	0.000	0.000	0.000	0.000
5 Tubers & Root Crops	0.000	0.000	0.000	0.000	0.000	0.000
6 Coffee & Cacao	0.000	0.000	0.000	0.000	0.06	0.000
7 Sugar Cane	0.000	0.000	0.000	0.000	0.000	0.000
8 Coconut incl.Copra (in Farm)	22.08	0.000	0.000	0.000	0.000	0.000
9 Tobacco (Native & Virginia)	0.000	0.000	0.000	0.000	0.000	0.000
10 Abaca & Other Fiber Crops	5.29	0.000	0.000	0.000	0.000	0.000
11 Other Crops	0.000	0.000	0.000	0.000	0.000	460.08
12 Livestock	0.000	0.000	0.000	0.000	0.000	0.000
13 Poultry	0.000	0.000	0.000	0.000	0.000	0.000
14 Oth.Agricultural Activities	0.000	0.000	0.000	0.000	0.000	0.000
15 Fisheries	0.000	0.000	0.000	0.000	0.000	0.000
16 Forestry & Logging	300.40	80.57	0.000	0.000	0.000	8.38
17 Gold & Silver Mining	300.51	0.000	0.000	0.000	0.000	0.78
18 Oth.Metallic Mining	0.000	0.00	0.000	0.000	0.000	0.000
19 Non-Metall.Min. & Quarr.	0.000	0.75	0.14	5.17	7.58	24.77
20 Meat Products	0.000	0.000	0.00	235.17	0.000	20.00
21 Dairy Products	0.000	0.000	0.000	0.000	0.000	0.000
22 Rice Milling & Refining	0.000	0.000	0.000	0.000	0.000	5.09
23 Sugar Milling & Refining	0.000	0.000	0.000	0.000	0.000	5.06
24 Oth.Manufactured Foods	0.000	38.47	0.000	0.000	0.21	0.000
25 Beverages	0.000	0.000	0.000	0.000	0.000	0.000
26 Tobacco Products	0.000	53.35	1.43	26.35	529.00	0.000
27 Textile Manufactures	127.82	41.31	0.00	12.50	3.25	0.000
28 Wearing Apparel,Made-up Text	1190.89	4.31	0.29	0.52	0.15	0.000
29 Lumber	404.85	2.57	0.27	0.52	1.00	14.42
30 Plywood & Veneer Plants	39.97	0.28	6.44	4.82	79.61	10.47
31 Furniture & Fixtures	3.95	0.28	0.21	4.49	0.84	10.43
32 Paper & Paper Products	4.31	532.30	1502.41	56.42	10.91	1.00
33 Printing, Publishing, etc.	21.71	36.53	3.21	42.55	367.69	11.31
34 Leather & Leather Products	15.53	18.02	8.59	56.42	868.69	783.37
35 Rubber Products	151.36	484.91	44.73	42.55	5.36	134.76
36 Basic Industrial Chemicals	74.56	4.54	4.73	42.15	1139.58	131.11
37 Coconut & Oth.Oils & Fats	7.68	105.17	291.19	44.22	193.09	355.48
38 Oth.Chemical Products	16.70	1036.08	79.06	10.38	2.62	72.66
39 Petroleum Refineries & Prods	174.78	2.82	0.88	0.00	2.25	40.48
40 Hydraulic Cement	4.74	4.85	18.86	6.85	0.58	34.78
41 Oth.Non-Metall.Mineral Prods	1.23	17.05	32.87	0.29	30.40	5.94
42 Basic Metals	0.000	15.25	2.45	0.35	6.63	2.96
43 Metal Prods.exc.Machinery	0.000	21.44	1.34	0.48	2.82	1.62
44 Machinery,exc.Electr.Mach.	0.000	5.23	0.00	0.000	2.76	0.00
45 Electr.Machinery & Apparatus	0.000	2.32	15.89	28.99	0.57	3.24
46 Motor Vehicles	1.04	0.00	0.00	0.000	0.000	0.00
47 Oth.Transport Equipment	0.000	0.00	0.00	0.000	0.000	0.00
48 Misc.Manufactures	10.23	56.90	15.89	28.99	80.57	3.24
49 Scrap	12.10	56.90	0.00	0.000	0.00	0.00
50 Electricity, Gas & Water Svc.	57.74	227.23	97.94	12.93	86.82	115.82

Input-Output Table of Philippines for the Year 1974

PHILIPPINES 1974   FLOWS in hundred thousand pesos of Y 1974   PRODUCERS CURRENT PRICES

INDUSTRY:	31 Furniture & Fixtures	32 Paper & Paper Products	33 Printing, Publishing, etc	34 Leather & Leather Prods	35 Rubber Products	36 Basic Indust. Chemicals
51 Construction	353.67	73.92	25.94	0.14	10.00	210.58
52 Wholesale & Retail Trade	47.07	799.52	20.57	72.13	606.51	5.40
53 Banking & oth. Financing	46.68	147.27	10.30	5.07	70.52	24.28
54 Insurance	24.40	36.00	36.84	2.03	20.58	19.04
55 Real Estate	3.00	208.05	61.48	6.49	87.17	76.02
56 Transport Services			1.00	0.00	0.06	70.04
57 Storage & Warehousing	10.63	100.87	17.98	2.31	20.14	0.59
58 Communications	44.82	100.88	314.45	7.69	114.11	98.80
59 Government Services		140.00	314.00	0.00	0.00	0.00
61 National Industry	0.00	0.00	0.00	0.00	0.00	0.00
62 Total Intermedt. Inputs	3278.58	8965.82	2879.14	616.82	4822.33	2117.62
63 Compensation of Employees	1103.21	3131.51	1429.00	153.96	817.36	398.86
64 Capital Consumpt. Allowance	340.45	1191.43	347.86	44.21	383.95	231.70
65 Indirect Taxes less subsid	179.25	750.99	399.28	38.52	303.57	232.01
66 Other Value Added	1234.21	4653.16	1726.00	267.14	1406.03	1214.79
67 Gross Value Added	2857.12	9727.09	3902.14	503.83	2810.91	2077.36
68 Gross Output	6135.70	18692.91	6781.28	1120.65	7733.24	4194.98

Input-Output Table of Philippines for the Year 1974

PHILIPPINES 1974 FLOWS in hundred thousand pesos of Y 1974 PRODUCERS CURRENT PRICES

* TOTAL TRANSACTIONS * INDUSTRY	37 Coconut & Oth. Oils & Fats	38 Other Chemical Products	39 Petroleum Refineries	40 Hydraul. Cement	41 Non-Metallic Mineral Prods	42 Basic Metals
1 Palay	0.00	0.00	0.00	0.00	0.00	0.00
2 Corn	106.00	0.00	0.00	0.00	0.00	0.00
3 Fruits & Nuts	28.41	0.78	0.00	0.00	0.00	0.00
4 Vegetables	0.00	0.00	0.00	0.00	0.00	0.00
5 Tubers & Root Crops	0.00	0.78	0.00	0.00	0.00	0.00
6 Coffee & Cacao	0.00	0.00	0.00	0.00	0.00	0.00
7 Sugar Cane	0.00	0.00	0.00	0.00	0.00	0.00
8 Coconut incl.Copra(in Farm)	12113.000	-0.03	0.000	0.000	0.000	0.000
9 Tobacco (Native & Virginia)	0.000	3.54	0.000	0.000	0.000	0.000
10 Abaca & Other Fiber Crops	0.000	6.04	0.000	0.000	0.000	0.000
11 Other Crops	0.000	4.11	0.000	0.000	0.000	0.000
12 Livestock	0.000	2.05	0.000	0.000	0.000	0.000
13 Poultry	0.00	0.00	0.00	0.00	0.00	0.00
14 Oth.Agricultural Activities	0.04	0.04	0.00	0.00	0.00	0.00
15 Fisheries	0.00	60.01	0.00	0.00	0.00	0.00
16 Forestry & Logging	0.00	0.00	0.00	0.00	0.00	0.00
17 Gold & Silver Mining	0.00	0.00	0.00	104.37	0.00	0.00
18 Non-Metallic Min. & Quarr.	0.00	4.25	0.00	537.52	386.24	82.41
19 Meat Products	0.00	1100.71	41990.10	0.00	0.00	0.34
20 Dairy Products	0.00	20.32	0.00	0.00	0.00	0.00
21 Rice Milling	0.00	28.23	0.00	0.00	0.00	0.00
22 Sugar Milling & Refining	25.31	98.91	0.00	0.00	0.99	0.00
23 Oth.Manufactured Foods	0.00	0.00	0.00	0.00	0.00	0.00
24 Beverages	0.00	-0.21	0.61	6.80	0.00	0.31
25 Tobacco Products	0.00	0.00	0.99	8.50	13.21	2.09
26 Textile Manufactures	0.00	11.50	0.00	0.00	0.00	0.00
27 Wearing Apparel,Made-up Text	0.00	4.12	0.00	0.00	2.32	0.00
28 Lumber	2.54	0.00	55.36	0.00	46.03	19.83
29 Plywood & Veneer Plants	-0.30	0.00	58.09	296.13	57.66	5.75
30 Furniture & Fixtures	6.60	0.00	0.00	17.62	0.00	3.18
31 Paper & Paper Products	5.96	988.41	29.38	0.00	4.83	145.53
32 Printing,Publishing etc.	0.00	235.96	802.36	67.75	390.17	100.19
33 Leather & Leather Products	21.39	0.00	34.13	12.54	0.00	1135.97
34 Rubber Products	598.01	578.68	0.00	0.00	71.63	23.86
35 Basic Industrial Chemicals	530.97	4321.47	672.97	2930.18	629.18	10290.57
36 Coconut & Oth.Oils & Fats	22.70	3209.10	3.71	45.92	451.05	24.74
37 Oth.Chemical Products	595.15	1098.35	0.60	13.54	362.46	1.82
38 Petroleum Refineries & Prods	1.58	426.52	10.57	3.81	42.92	1.15
39 Hydraulic Cement	3.46	235.52	40.84	2.85	30.16	1.54
40 Basic Metals	284.92	16.63	9.32	1.34	5.88	0.00
41 Oth.Non-Metall.Mineral Prods	4.09	16.32	4.71	0.81	1.54	3.47
42 Metal Prods. exc. Machinery	3.18	6.34	7.33	0.00	0.50	0.00
43 Machinery,exc.Electr.Mach.	-0.18	0.00	0.00	0.00	0.00	0.00
44 Electr.Machinery & Apparatus	0.00	0.00	32.26	0.81	0.00	166.50
45 Motor Vehicles	0.10	27.93	0.00	0.00	35.18	0.00
46 Oth.Transport Equipment	0.00	0.00	0.00	0.00	157.70	0.00
47 Misc. Manufactures	0.00	0.00	91.87	270.30	174.86	166.50
48 Scrap	0.00	0.00	0.00	0.00	0.00	0.00
49 Electricty, Gas & Water Svc.	56.14	395.20	91.87	270.30	174.86	166.50

Input-Output Table of Philippines for the Year 1974

PHILIPPINES 1974 FLOWS in hundred thousand pesos of Y 1974 PRODUCERS CURRENT PRICES

INDUSTRY:	37 Coconut & Oth. Oils & Fats	38 Other Chemical Products	39 Petroleum Refineries	40 Hydraul. Cement	41 Non-Metallic Mineral Prods	42 Basic Metals
51 Construction	4.26	9.41	164.56	5.24	27.53	48.66
52 Wholesale & Retail Trade	2102.70	2647.12	6793.15	690.77	360.98	1388.76
53 Banking & Oth. Financing	32.67	47.71	33.31	12.54	11.92	32.09
54 Insurance	202.78	191.67	181.51	52.03	48.16	124.60
55 Real Estate	8.57	209.27	616.66	29.03	34.55	28.83
56 Transport Services	362.09	506.04	931.12	133.68	70.65	48.75
57 Storage & Warehousing	7.66	1.78	27.22	0.35	0.26	0.95
58 Communications	9.08	72.07	49.27	6.72	15.10	20.81
59 Private Services	371.16	2262.69	1287.87	373.83	174.30	207.53
60 Government Services	0.00	0.00	0.00	0.00	0.00	0.00
61 National Industry						
62 Total Intermedt. Inputs	17016.15	23957.50	53880.05	5644.79	3612.07	14351.30
63 Compensation of Employees	5918.94	3961.53	4085.70	826.73	890.52	983.48
64 Capital Consumpt. Allowance	1965.85	1537.64	3057.31	624.74	448.25	1112.33
65 Indirect Taxes less Subsid.	1398.14	1209.41	1843.70	232.02	260.08	541.26
66 Other Value Added	10497.93	7414.15	4947.80	1076.57	2044.86	374.22
67 Gross Value Added	18780.86	14122.73	30524.51	2760.06	3643.71	6422.29
68 Gross Output	36797.01	38080.23	84404.56	8404.85	7255.78	20773.59

Input-Output Table of Philippines for the Year 1974

PHILIPPINES 1974   FLOWS in hundred thousand pesos of Y 1974   PRODUCERS CURRENT PRICES

INDUSTRY:	43 Metallic Prods exc. Machinery	44 Machinery exc. Electr.M.	45 Electr. Mach. & Apparatus	46 Motor Vehicles	47 Oth. Transport Equipment	48 Misc. Manufactures
* TOTAL TRANSACTIONS * INDUSTRY						
1 Palay	0.000	0.000	0.000	0.000	0.000	0.000
2 Corn	0.000	0.000	0.000	0.000	0.000	0.000
3 Fruits & Nuts	0.000	0.000	0.000	0.000	0.000	0.000
4 Vegetables & Root Crops	0.000	0.000	0.000	0.000	0.000	0.000
5 Tubers & Root Crops	0.000	0.000	0.000	0.000	0.000	0.000
6 Coffee & Cacao	0.000	0.000	0.000	0.000	0.000	0.000
7 Sugar Cane	0.000	0.000	0.000	0.000	0.000	0.000
8 Coconut incl.Copra(in Farm)	0.000	0.000	0.000	0.000	0.000	0.005
9 Tobacco (Native & Virginia)	0.000	0.000	0.000	0.000	0.000	2.05
10 Abaca & Other Fiber Crops	0.000	0.000	0.000	0.000	0.000	2.75
11 Other Crops	0.000	0.000	0.000	0.000	0.000	0.000
12 Livestock	0.000	0.000	0.000	0.000	0.000	0.000
13 Poultry	0.000	0.000	0.000	0.000	0.000	0.000
14 Oth.Agricultural Activities	0.000	0.000	0.000	0.000	0.000	0.59
15 Fisheries	0.000	0.000	0.000	0.000	0.000	0.000
16 Forestry & Logging	0.000	0.000	0.000	0.000	0.000	23.63
17 Gold & silver Mining	-.45	0.51	43.55	0.00	2.73	3.35
18 Non-Metallic Min. & Quarr.	5.55	-1.00	0.3	0.00	0.00	0.48
19 Meat Products	0.000	0.000	0.000	0.000	0.000	0.000
20 Dairy Products	0.000	0.000	0.000	0.000	0.000	0.000
21 Sugar Milling & Refining	0.000	0.000	0.000	0.000	0.000	0.000
22 Oth.Manufactured Foods	0.000	0.000	0.000	0.000	0.000	6.05
23 Beverages	0.000	0.000	0.000	0.000	0.000	0.000
24 Tobacco Products	41.000	0.000	4.24	13.67	0.02	19.62
25 Textile Manufactures	9.46	43.99	7.39	4.60	0.08	2.77
26 Wearing Apparel,Made-up Text	9.00	23.89	6.41	2.60	12.07	15.75
27 Lumber	79.60	13.07	5.50	2.60	-1.55	10.62
28 Plywood & Veneer Plants	58.40	28.78	153.91	12.28	2.85	78.34
29 Furniture & Fixtures	20.64	16.29	18.50	14.58	2.41	5.18
30 Paper & Paper Products	20.41	0.00	0.3	21.25	0.00	5.60
31 Printing,Publishing,etc.	17.99	66.80	159.97	200.32	16.64	176.17
32 Leather & Leather Products	13.0	7.32	237.96	99.54	3.59	3.00
33 Rubber Products	239.50	0.00	212.84	202.40	0.00	2086.91
34 Basic Industrial Chemicals	473.88	97.49	247.78	226.79	37.59	102.60
35 Coconut & Oth.Oils & Fats	5.26	132.44	0.00	0.00	62.55	1.09
36 Oth.Chemical Products	4.57	17.52	168.72	14.92	0.54	24.91
37 Petroleum Refineries & Prods	6103.62	806.04	823.61	1185.34	22.99	116.54
38 Hydraulic Cement	894.55	195.81	149.58	46.42	39.22	50.21
39 Oth.Non-Metall.Mineral Prods	9.12	364.57	936.24	62.65	5.21	3.75
40 Basic Metals	123.92	54.74	1.86	1283.66	104.18	3.02
41 Metal Prods.exc.Machinery	2.00	1.50	0.00	0.00	0.77	127.00
42 Machinery.exc.Electr.Mach.	0.000	10.00	48.00	64.96	0.70	60.30
43 Electr.Machinery & Apparatus	21.68	10.52	0.00	0.00	14.86	75.39
44 Motor Vehicles	89.60	0.00	0.00	0.00		
45 Oth.Transport Equipment						
46 Misc.Manufactures						
47 Scrap						
48 Electricty, Gas & Water Svc.	151.95	50.36	115.55	77.76		

Input-Output Table of Philippines for the Year 1974

PHILIPPINES 1974

FLOWS in hundred thousand pesos of Y 1974

PRODUCERS CURRENT PRICES

INDUSTRY:	43 Metallic Prods exc. Machinery	44 Machinery. exc. Electr.M.	45 Electr. Mach. & Apparatus	46 Motor Vehicles	47 Oth. Transport Equipment	48 Misc. Manufactures
51 Construction	22.15	4.85	12.57	21.54	1.35	4.84
52 Wholesale & Retail Trade	1205.44	358.52	788.93	750.99	105.59	417.96
53 Banking & Oth. Financing	23.34	33.17	86.45	41.49	4.94	32.35
54 Insurance	142.50	50.60	89.30	38.09	13.12	68.06
55 Real Estate	39.00	21.20	41.97	43.35	7.99	40.83
56 Transport Services	167.01	100.65	11.78	288.08	26.99	88.64
57 Storage & Warehousing	4.44	0.74	2.11	10.05	0.21	0.20
58 Communications	41.42	10.68	30.48	17.14	7.62	17.85
59 Private Services	213.70	120.10	367.71	421.99	48.96	178.24
60 Government Services	0.00	0.00	0.00	0.00	0.00	0.00
61 National Industry						
62 Total Intermed. Inputs	10345.16	2637.80	4895.78	5173.09	789.71	3867.30
63 Compensation of Employees	1530.55	711.75	1306.81	3037.85	324.56	872.35
64 Capital Consumpt. Allowance	790.49	311.39	603.78	1186.72	105.28	368.79
65 Indirect Taxes less Subsid	461.57	206.18	393.90	872.01	74.18	219.31
66 Other Value Added	3356.88	1788.14	3119.34	4150.40	655.14	1702.98
67 Gross Value Added	6139.49	2997.46	5423.83	9246.98	1159.14	3164.43
68 Gross Output	16484.65	5635.26	10319.61	14420.07	1948.85	7031.73

Input-Output Table of Philippines for the Year 1974

PHILIPPINES 1974   FLOWS in hundred thousand pesos of Y 1974   PRODUCERS CURRENT PRICES

INDUSTRY:	49 Scrap	50 Electr., Gas & Water Svcs	51 Construction	52 Wholesale & Retail Trade	53 Banking & oth. Financing	54 Insurance
* TOTAL INDUSTRY TRANSACTIONS *						
1 Palay	0.00	0.00	0.00	0.00	0.00	0.00
2 Corn	0.00	0.00	0.00	0.00	0.00	0.00
3 Fruits & Nuts	0.00	0.00	0.00	0.00	0.00	0.00
4 Vegetables	0.00	0.00	0.00	0.00	0.00	0.00
5 Tubers & Root Crops	0.00	0.00	0.00	0.00	0.00	0.00
6 Coffee & Cacao	0.00	0.00	0.00	0.00	0.00	0.00
7 Sugar Cane	0.00	0.00	0.00	0.00	0.00	0.00
8 Coconut incl. Copra (in Farm)	0.82	0.00	0.00	0.00	0.00	0.00
9 Tobacco (Native & Virginia)	17.59	0.00	0.00	0.00	0.00	0.00
10 Abaca & Other Fiber Crops	17.09	0.00	0.00	0.00	0.00	0.00
11 Other Crops	0.00	0.00	0.00	0.00	0.00	0.00
12 Livestock	0.00	0.00	0.00	0.00	0.00	0.00
13 Poultry	0.00	0.00	0.00	0.00	0.00	0.00
14 Oth. Agricultural Activities	0.00	0.00	0.00	0.00	0.00	0.00
15 Fisheries	0.16	76.35	403.09	0.00	0.00	0.00
16 Forestry & Logging	0.00	0.00	0.00	0.00	0.00	0.00
17 Gold & Silver Mining	0.00	0.00	0.00	0.00	0.00	0.00
18 Non-Metallic Mining	0.01	0.01	1536.82	0.00	0.00	0.00
19 Oth. Metallic Min. & Quarr.	0.00	0.00	0.00	0.00	0.00	0.00
20 Meat Products	0.00	0.00	0.00	0.00	0.00	0.00
21 Dairy Products	0.00	0.00	0.00	0.00	0.00	0.00
22 Rice Milling & Refining	0.00	0.00	0.00	0.00	0.00	0.00
23 Sugar Milling & Refining	0.00	0.00	0.00	0.00	0.00	0.00
24 Oth. Manufactured Foods	0.00	0.00	0.00	0.00	0.00	0.00
25 Beverage Products	0.00	0.00	0.00	0.00	0.00	0.00
26 Tobacco Products	0.00	0.00	0.00	1.93	0.00	0.00
27 Textile Manufactures	231.64	0.42	3.12	18.23	17.30	5.72
28 Wearing Apparel.Made-up Text	1.56	0.00	0.00	6.79	13.13	0.00
29 Lumber	1.64	3.92	324.66	10.31	0.00	0.00
30 Plywood & Veneer Plants	1.13	0.31	998.93	56.17	0.00	0.00
31 Furniture & Fixtures	27.17	63.34	404.03	2277.15	244.89	100.58
32 Paper & Paper Products	1.22	105.06	251.79	839.27	448.65	96.96
33 Printing, Publishing, etc.	1.03	0.21	118.89	0.00	0.00	0.00
34 Leather & Leather Products	2.55	86.40	223.45	453.55	25.42	4.70
35 Rubber Products	0.00	136.68	95.01	35.50	0.00	0.00
36 Basic Industrial Chemicals	0.00	106.09	0.00	0.00	125.09	12.60
37 Coconut & Oth. Oils & Fats	21.67	4850.30	267.92	520.22	218.24	63.11
38 Oth. Chemical Products	0.00	0.99	1729.51	2926.52	2.80	0.00
39 Petroleum Refineries & Prods	0.01	62.52	4591.94	0.00	0.00	0.00
40 Hydraulic Cement	0.00	237.34	3321.94	35.85	39.45	7.55
41 Oth. Non-Metall.Mineral Prods	0.48	67.92	3561.90	64.35	23.24	1.55
42 Basic Metals	34.41	4.85	3472.88	90.45	3.24	3.07
43 Metal Prods. exc. Machinery	0.35	233.91	1137.25	47.68	3.67	0.67
44 Machinery. exc. Electr.Mach.	1.98	8.19	1133.04	29.68	0.00	0.00
45 Electr.Machinery & Apparatus	0.00	0.00	59.20	0.00	88.94	7.88
46 Motor Vehicles	0.00	24.61	0.00	65.73	0.00	0.00
47 Oth. Transport Equipment	1.89	0.00	24.65	0.00	0.00	0.00
48 Misc. Manufactures	0.00	0.00	73.64	0.00	0.00	0.00
49 Scrap	0.93	926.06	198.29	4471.29	254.13	48.74
50 Electricty, Gas & Water Svc.						

Input-Output Table of Philippines for the Year 1974

PHILIPPINES 1974 | FLOWS in hundred thousand pesos of Y 1974 | PRODUCERS CURRENT PRICES

INDUSTRY:	49 Scrap	50 Electr. Gas & Water Svcs	51 Construction	52 Wholesale & Retail Trade	53 Banking & Oth. Financing	54 Insurance
51 Construction	0.44	23.30	617.70	953.57	21.80	18.76
52 Wholesale & Retail Trade	107.49	1053.34	3574.40	837.49	221.63	48.29
53 Banking & Oth. Financing	0.42	14.88	54.18	1244.80	155.49	28.47
54 Insurance	0.00	229.31	443.64	2672.87	258.61	73.99
55 Real Estate	4.34	121.00	58.00	4805.54	1020.48	210.25
56 Transport Services	9.98	106.71	988.14	1510.61	93.82	33.70
57 Storage & Warehousing	0.18	6.55		119.76	0.00	0.00
58 Communications	-1.14	40.46	248.94	1070.67	238.11	122.32
59 Private Services	1.48	515.04	3530.36	4864.75	2284.30	859.80
60 Government Services	0.00	0.00	0.00	0.00	0.00	0.00
61 National Industry	0.00	0.00	0.00	0.00	0.00	0.00
62 Total Intermedt. Inputs	628.07	9118.06	37728.48	3010.50	5798.67	1748.34
64 Compensation of Employees	131.61	2337.10	16862.27	4407.14	7740.14	4026.49
65 Capital Consumpt. Allowance	35.87	1990.65	3694.86	8124.00	1608.25	441.25
66 Indirect Taxes less Subsid.	23.89	1854.15	3826.71	1505.81	3318.17	828.01
Other Values Added	44.68	4357.74	18211.80	9589.16	17017.09	6711.22
67 Gross Value Added	638.85	10539.64	42595.64	16016.11	29683.65	12006.97
68 Gross Output	1266.92	19657.70	80324.12	19020.61	35482.32	13755.31

Input-Output Table of Philippines for the Year 1974

FLOWS in hundred thousand pesos of Y 1974

PRODUCERS CURRENT PRICES

INDUSTRY:

* TOTAL TRANSACTIONS * INDUSTRY	55 Real Estate	56 Transport Services	57 Storage & Warehousing	58 Communications	59 Private Services	80 Government Services
1 Palay	0.00	0.00	0.000	0.000	0.00	0.000
2 Corn	0.00	22.47	0.000	0.000	27.88	0.000
3 Fruits & Nuts	0.00	24.88	0.000	0.000	456.70	0.000
4 Vegetables	0.00	3.11	0.000	0.000	653.08	0.000
5 Tubers & Root Crops	0.00	0.00	0.000	0.000	652.11	0.000
6 Coffee & Cacao	0.00	0.00	0.000	0.000	0.00	0.000
7 Sugar Cane	0.00	0.00	0.000	0.000	0.00	0.000
8 Coconut (incl.Copra (in Farm)	0.00	0.00	0.000	0.000	77.74	0.000
9 Tobacco (Native & Virginia)	0.00	0.00	0.000	0.000	0.00	0.000
10 Abaca & Other Fiber Crops	0.00	0.00	0.000	0.000	0.00	0.000
11 Other Crops	0.00	0.00	0.000	0.000	0.00	0.000
12 Livestock	0.00	0.00	0.000	0.000	0.00	0.000
13 Poultry	0.00	9.20	0.000	0.000	1082.42	0.000
14 Agricultural Activities	0.00	0.00	0.000	0.000	119.53	0.000
15 Fisheries	0.00	536.34	0.000	0.000	1012.05	0.000
16 Forestry & Logging	0.00	0.00	0.000	0.000	11.67	0.000
17 Gold & Silver Mining	0.00	0.00	0.000	0.000	0.00	0.000
18 Oth.Metallic Mining	0.00	0.00	0.000	0.000	0.00	0.000
19 Non-Metal.Min.& Quarr.	59.91	638.12	0.000	0.000	9.02	0.000
20 Meat Products	0.00	45.29	0.000	0.000	2230.06	0.000
21 Dairy Products	0.00	106.62	0.000	0.000	1092.58	0.000
22 Rice Milling	0.00	259.53	0.000	0.000	874.80	0.000
23 Sugar Milling & Refining	0.00	43.18	0.000	0.000	186.71	0.000
24 Oth.Manufactured Foods	0.00	0.00	0.000	0.000	1801.18	0.000
25 Beverages	0.00	95.96	0.000	0.000	722.82	0.000
26 Tobacco Products	0.00	35.25	0.000	0.74	0.00	0.000
27 Textile Manufactures	-0.47	39.23	0.000	0.000	1.38	0.000
28 Wearing Apparel,Made-up Text	0.00	21.47	0.000	0.000	0.00	0.000
29 Lumber	53.79	247.27	3.16	141.34	205.17	0.000
30 Plywood & Veneer Plants	596.83	325.07	0.000	119.90	0.00	0.000
31 Furniture & Fixtures	10.31	0.00	0.000	0.000	1.59	0.000
32 Paper & Paper Products	45.02	1044.84	1.71	12.35	11.59	0.000
33 Printing,Publishing,etc.	84.97	22.16	0.000	0.000	1059.66	0.000
34 Leather & Leather Products	0.00	0.00	0.000	0.000	637.07	0.000
35 Rubber Products	14.91	330.94	0.52	0.000	0.00	0.000
36 Basic Industrial Chemicals	0.00	7017.78	0.000	61.12	81.90	0.000
37 Coconut & oth.Oils & Fats	81.90	2.68	0.85	0.000	230.24	0.000
38 Oth.Chemical Products	305.08	42.78	0.000	112.31	513.36	0.000
39 Petroleum Refineries & Prods	575.28	118.60	4.59	0.000	0.00	0.000
40 Hydraulic Cement	0.00	163.20	3.45	38.45	1853.63	0.000
41 Oth.Non-Metall.Mineral Prods	0.00	175.59	0.000	3.40	1503.35	0.000
42 Basic Metals	29.66	575.90	0.45	0.000	0.00	0.000
43 Metal Prods,exc.Machinery	33.53	258.59	0.46	199.00	40.00	0.000
44 Machinery,exc.Electr.Mach.	16.22	0.00	0.000	0.000	101.95	0.000
45 Electr.Machinery & Apparatus	40.36	0.00	0.47	0.25	50.49	0.000
46 Motor Vehicles	2.72	0.00	0.000	0.000	114.09	0.000
47 Oth.Transport Equipment	3.04	0.00	0.000	0.000	0.00	0.000
48 Misc.Manufactures	0.00	0.00	0.04	4.93	509.24	0.000
49 Scrap	20.00	0.00	0.03	0.000	7.30	0.000
50 Electricty,Gas & Water Svc.	312.10	201.70	4.43	85.82	2354.87	0.000

Input-Output Table of Philippines for the Year 1974

PHILIPPINES 1974   FLOWS in hundred thousand pesos of Y 1974   PRODUCERS CURRENT PRICES

INDUSTRY:	55 Real Estate	56 Transport Services	57 Storage & Warehousing	58 Communications	59 Private Services	60 Government Services
51 Construction	1295.28	48.18	-.31	12.73	668.97	0.00
52 Wholesale & Retail Trade	313.78	203.23	2.44	164.07	2403.74	0.000
53 Banking & Oth. Financing	103.06	76.92	0.96	109.72	85.49	0.00
54 Insurance	851.49	54.00	2.81	109.00	486.13	0.000000
55 Real Estate	998.04	462.1	4.10	36.97	1895.00	0.00000
56 Transport Services	189.32	1963.88	0.00	37.54	531.67	0.00000
57 Storage & Warehousing		28.02	0.43	0.00	0.01	0.000
58 Communications	78.90	388.96	-1.28	40.72	107.42	0.00
59 Private Services	792.00	1771.51	8.04	268.00	5807.65	0.00
60 Government Services	0.00	0.00	0.00	0.00	0.00	0.00
61 National Industry	0	0	0		0	0
62 Total Intermedt. Inputs	7468.85	2006.20	41.15	1477.02	32724.18	0.00
63 Compensation of Employees	5609.73	9615.05	82.44	2692.92	25594.45	47030.00
64 Capital Consumpt. Allowance	4158.74	533.40	33.06	945.30	4429.19	0.00
65 Indirect Taxes less Subsid.	5522.27	4768.96	20.83	699.81	5317.93	0.00
66 Other Value Added	26177.28	1167.67	200.04	2340.25	31175.12	0.00
67 Gross Value Added	41468.00	3139.08	336.37	6678.28	66380.69	47030.00
68 Gross Output	48936.85	51402.28	377.52	8155.30	99104.87	47030.00

224

Input-Output Table of Philippines for the Year 1974

PHILIPPINES 1974

PRODUCERS CURRENT PRICES

FLOWS in hundred thousand pesos of Y 1974

*	TOTAL TRANSACTIONS *	61 National Industry	62 Total Intrmdt. Consumption	63 Private Consumption	64 Government Consumption	65 Gross Fixed Capital Formt.	66 Change in Inventories
1	Palay	0.000	4840.92	265.90	0.00	0.000	20.78
2	Corn	0.000	16819.57	2972.31	0.00	0.000	513.18
3	Fruits & Nuts	0.000	1350.02	15861.33	133.73	0.000	444.08
4	Vegetables	0.000	1587.38	13277.34	305.96	0.000	66.04
5	Tubers & Root Crops	0.000	3678.80	6505.13	0.00	0.000	207.42
6	Coffee & Cacao	0.000	25685.28	114.83	0.00	0.000	272.68
7	Sugar Cane	0.000	20010.42	1447.92	0.54	0.000	281.04
8	Coconut incl.Copra (in Farm)	0.000	3028.80	43.61	0.00	0.000	46.78
9	Tobacco (Native&Virginia)	0.000	3376.53	122.37	0.00	0.000	617.33
10	Abaca & Other Fiber Crops	0.000	6995.01			0.000	577.36
11	Other Crops	0.000	23982.49	4665.46	221.98	0.000	2302.99
12	Livestock	0.000	8874.49	14501.38		0.000	2984.88
13	Poultry	0.000	2123.18	5085.54	393.50	0.000	13.10
14	Oth.Agricultural Activities	0.000	7047.97	5017.39	24.46	0.000	5908.37
15	Fisheries	0.000	10977.08		0.00	0.000	3090.34
16	Forestry & Logging	0.000	341.76	0.00		0.000	3753.91
17	Gold & Silver Mining	0.000		0.00	241.49	0.000	224.78
18	Oth.Metallic Mining	0.000		0.00	741.76	0.000	1008.22
19	Non-Metal.Min.& Quarr.	0.000	4605.26	374.25	299.34	0.000	35.22
20	Meat Products	0.000	5265.00	7329.60	137.62	0.000	48.34
21	Dairy Products	0.000	3288.82	6058.08	432.60	0.000	2413.88
22	Rice Milling	0.000	1598.56	71690.70	0.00	0.000	386.96
23	Sugar Milling & Refining	0.000	2936.81	1988.85	398.02	679.32	387.48
24	Oth.Manufactured Foods	0.000	4272.97	20654.94	405.55	5.05	2756.75
25	Beverages	0.000	15372.43	12029.14	101.14	0.000	1300.75
26	Tobacco Products	0.000	5095.19	1068.50	164.78	0.000	298.58
27	Textile Manufactures	0.000	5789.32	2383.10	33.96	558.46	880.43
28	Wearing Apparel.Made-up Text	0.000	2213.72	1152.31	707.40	13.58	106.55
29	Lumber	0.000	1127.04	2964.31	18.70	0.000	2853.72
30	Plywood & Veneer Plants	0.000	16241.94	4427.10	312.76	0.000	173.87
31	Furniture & Fixtures	0.000	21.00	552.73	476.45	0.000	14.93
32	Paper & Paper Products	0.000	3656.05	752.72	0.08	0.000	653.47
33	Printing, Publishing,etc.	0.000	15570.88	16788.40	4129.94	0.000	4339.39
34	Leather & Leather Products	0.000	10308.34	31363.98	7491.47	0.000	1407.65
35	Rubber Products	0.000	29353.46	1266.41	96.52	0.000	9556.80
36	Basic Industrial Chemicals	0.000	42437.06	1266.40	52.64	0.000	8259.60
37	Coconut&Veget.Oils&Fats	0.000	5885.55	2104.70	146.73	146.53	1308.11
38	Petroleum Refineries & Prods	0.000	6147.64	2400.81	0.00	6769.57	8083.53
39	Oth.Chem.Prod.& Prods	0.000	25879.52	916.48	186.40	30924.31	1886.06
40	Hydraulic Cement	0.000	3423.69	5502.01	425.38	7294.71	1456.47
41	Oth.Non-Metall.Mineral Prods	0.000	1644.87	9959.33	1100.50	13719.60	1433.40
42	Basic Metals	0.000	3409.77	773.86	230.37	9850.26	2252.30
43	Metal Prods.exc.Machinery	0.000	2192.97	4345.65	578.00	204.80	2330.94
44	Machinery exc.Electr.Mach.	0.000	391.52			0.00	666.87
45	Electr.Machinery & Apparatus	0.000	2619.08				87.11
46	Motor Vehicles	0.000	1253.04				0.00
47	Oth.Transport Equipment	0.000					
48	Misc.Manufactures	0.000					
49	Scrap	0.000					
50	Electricty,Gas & Water Svc.	0.000	13090.93	5825.97	662.90	0.00	0.00

Input-Output Table of Philippines for the Year 1974

PHILIPPINES 1974   FLOWS in hundred thousand pesos of Y 1974   PRODUCERS CURRENT PRICES

INDUSTRY:	61 National Industry	62 Total Intrmdt. Consumption	63 Private Consumption	64 Government Consumption	65 Gross Fixed Capital Formt.	66 Change in Inventories
51 Construction	0.00	4371.85	254.13	1678.32	73864.72	0.000
52 Wholesale & Retail Trade	30320.19	69516.90	67166.95	4360.95	2065.78	0.000
53 Banking & Oth. Financing		33454.27	1647.95	138.26	0.00	0.000
54 Insurance		8205.53	6015.74			0.000
55 Real Estate		1258.97	23797.93	3028.40	5405.72	0.000
56 Transport Services		12178.45	28636.59	1724.91	2957.22	0.000
57 Storage & Warehousing		362.58		9.00	0.000	0.000
58 Communications		4154.18	3364.49	393.59		0.000
59 Private Services		3290.61	61896.72	4391.90	0.000	0.000
60 Government Services		0	0.00	47030.00	0.000	0.000
61 National Industry		0			0	
62 Total Intermedt. Inputs	30320.19	670006.51	667143.36	87270.98	18462O.64	70720.85
63 Compensation of Employees	0.00	346839.36	0.000	0.000	0.000	0.000
64 Capital Consumpt. Allowance	0.00	81836.39	0.000	0.000	0.000	0.000
65 Indirect Taxes less Subsid.	-30320.19	96199.90	0.000	0.000	0.000	0.000
66 Other Value Added		453779.82				
67 Gross Value Added	-30320.19	978655.47	0.00	0.00	0.00	0.00
68 Gross Output	0.00	1648661.98	667143.36	87270.98	18462O.64	70720.85

Input-Output Table of Philippines for the Year 1974

PHILIPPINES 1974

FLOWS in hundred thousand pesos of Y 1974

PRODUCERS CURRENT PRICES

* TOTAL TRANSACTIONS * / Industry	67 Exports	68 Imports (less)	Total 69 Final Demand	Gross 70 Output
1 Palay	0.00	0.00	286.68	49127.60
2 Corn	0.07	-1306.76	2178.60	18998.17
3 Fruits & Nuts	3579.63	-98.63	19922.14	23425.38
4 Vegetables	341.02	-164.36	6534.55	7285.89
5 Tubers & Root Crops	28.00	0.00	287.23	3965.89
6 Coffee & Cacao	0.00	-625.02	187.51	20850.04
7 Sugar Cane	0.00	0.00	10269.62	30380.12
8 Coconut incl.Copra (in Farm)	8540.12	-1243.74	541.32	3639.57
9 Tobacco (Native & Virginia)	1692.67	-2478.32	263.07	31.64
10 Abaca & Other Fiber Crops	2128.58	-6483.47	-5763.57	32089.00
11 Other Crops	0.00	0.00	6907.51	2515.97
12 Livestock	0.37	-63.92	15732.51	56500.03
13 Poultry	0.00	0.00	-392.06	3600.41
14 Oth.Agricultural Activities	31.08	-55.14	51564.06	3650.00
15 Fisheries	0.43	-40.77	2641.33	3150.08
16 Forestry & Logging	154.62	0.00	-43354.39	3770.08
17 Gold & Silver Mining	16010.73	0.00	-35542.87	44105.76
18 Oth.Metallic Mining	6413.90	0.00	-48804.24	8823.69
19 Non-Metall.Min.& Quarr.	28774.23	-4363.37	62490.39	64088.95
20 Meat Products	568.09	-5972.39	53438.25	56566.93
21 Dairy Products	587.75	-3452.49	77192.43	99129.34
22 Rice Milling	0.03	0.00	15540.51	17820.48
23 Sugar Milling & Refining	42518.60	-5809.81	20443.11	24575.89
24 Oth.Manufactured Foods	8465.06	-209.81	16776.42	23125.24
25 Beverages	250.89	-9677.40	15176.42	16679.61
26 Tobacco Products	1065.67	0.00	3212.80	8999.70
27 Textile Manufactures	1794.41	-967.43	4682.37	696.09
28 Wearing Apparel.Made-up Text	2569.13	-10.89	5008.07	6130.70
29 Lumber	2085.09	0.00	2450.97	6781.28
30 Plywood & Veneer Plants	527.46	-20.47	3060.18	1120.65
31 Furniture & Fixtures	124.47	-158.56	288.69	7773.24
32 Paper & Paper Products	176.78	-6472.38	4076.09	4194.98
33 Printing, Publishing etc.	256.20	-830.22	26448.07	36797.01
34 Leather & Leather Products	2631.40	-13.63	8726.77	84404.56
35 Rubber Products	613.49	-1393.42	41957.30	8404.85
36 Basic Industrial Chemicals	1003.23	-17003.67	2519.30	7255.78
37 Coconut & oth.Oils & Fats	1784.50	-1983.20	-1108.14	20777.59
38 Oth.Chemical Products	539.43	-2238.49	-5105.93	16484.65
39 Petroleum Refineries & Prods	1384.84	-6142.86	-7760.96	563.26
40 Hydraulic Cement	292.14	-61.31	3990.39	10319.61
41 Oth.Non-Metall.Mineral Prods	227.40	-2201.31	6909.84	14420.07
42 Basic Metals	173.89	-21820.30	12227.10	1948.85
43 Metal Prods.exc.Machinery	26.05	-29071.66	1557.10	703.73
44 Machinery.exc.Electr.Mach.	30.89	-29979.49	4412.65	1266.92
45 Electr.Machinery & Apparatus	1557.83	-8593.95	6413.88	19657.70
46 Motor Vehicles	535.61	-13960.69	6566.77	
47 Oth.Transport Equipment		-9586.97		
48 Misc.Manufactures	77.90	-3755.38		
49 Scrap	0.00			
50 Electricty, Gas & Water Svc.		0.00		

227

Input-Output Table of Philippines for the Year 1974

PHILIPPINES 1974　　　　FLOWS in hundred thousand pesos of Y 1974

PRODUCERS CURRENT PRICES

	67 Exports	68 Imports (less)	69 Total Final Demand	70 Gross Output
51 Construction	442.40	-287.30	75952.27	80024.12
52 Wholesale & Retail Trade	28520.33	0.00	12070.71	19220.61
53 Banking & oth. Financing	0.00	0.00	2028.05	35482.32
54 Insurance	434.10	-1038.32	5549.78	13755.31
55 Real Estate	4642.93	-501.10	36354.88	48936.85
56 Transport Services	8112.97	-2242.80	39223.83	51402.28
57 Storage & Warehousing	492.65	-249.11	-14.94	377.52
58 Communications	15987.08	-209.44	400.12	8155.30
59 Private Services	0.00	-1502.44	66203.26	99104.87
60 Government Services	0.00	0.00	47030.00	47030.00
61 National Industry				0
62 Total Intermedt. Inputs	222895.62	-253995.98	978655.47	1646661.98
63 Compensation of Employees	0.00	0.00	0.000	34638.36
64 Capital Consumpt. Allowance	0.00	0.00	0.000	88836.39
65 Indirect Taxes less Subsid.	0.00	0.00	0.000	88199.90
66 Other Value Added				453779.82
67 Gross Value Added	0.00	0.00	0.00	978655.47
68 Gross Output	222895.62	-253995.98	978655.47	0.00

228

REPUBLIC OF KOREA

Reference year: 1975

Entries in table: Domestic flows, import matrix

Source: Bank of Korea, *1975 Input-Output Tables* (Seoul, 1978)

Computerized: Deutsches Institut für Wirtschaftsforschung, Berlin

Currency units: Won of Y 1975
Scale factor: 100,000,000

Pricing system: Producers' current prices
Intermediate sectors: 60 × 60
Treatment of trade margins: Inputs, row 49 (wholesale and retail trade)

Treatment of imports: Import matrix and rows 123, 124
Availability of import matrix: Available

Total number of rows: 131
Statistical unit of quadrant 1: Industry

Total number of columns: 70
Statistical unit of quadrant 1: Industry

Fourth quadrant: Not occupied

#	INDUSTRY (DOMESTIC TRANSACTIONS)	1 Rice,Barley,Wheat (polished)	2 Vegetab.Fruits & Other Grains	3 Industrial Crops	4 Livestock Breed & Sericulture	5 Forestry Products	6 Fishery Products
1	Rice, Barley, Wheat (pol)	322148	80193	15385	436537	2239	72
2	Vegetab.Fruits &Othgrains		225248	33804	16398		
3	Industrial Crops	335170	99389	58305	231818	4093	
4	Livestck Breedng &Sericul S.	253897	159289	48547	125726	10497	81
5	Forestry Products				131967		17297
6	Fishery Products			2448			69942
7	Coal				0	0	0
8	Metallic Ores						
9	Non-Metallic Minerals						
10	Slaughter,Dairy Fruit Proc.	380	487	706	2037	1604	6598
11	Seafood Processing				0	0	0
12	Grain Polishing	706472					8
13	Cereal Flours		42	6502	8185		109
14	Other Food Preparations				69282	303	35182
15	Beverages				0	0	
16	Tobacco				0	0	
17	Fibre Yarn		1178	1591	2049	1534	303
18	Textile Fabrics	25994		1304	1773	11503	775
19	Fabricated Textile Products						1209
20	Leather & Leather Products						74074
21	Lumber and Plywood	1031	340	2943	1598	804	
22	Wood Products & Furniture		9728	3366	5476	1436	3450
23	Pulp & Paper		20918	291	2366		23078
24	Printing & Publishing		455	205	86	50	1246
25	Basic Organic Chemicals	2208		5131	22		1271
26	Basic Inorganic Chemicals			22		1258	
27	Chemical Fertilizers	475456	232315	1214	15510	14396	489
28	Drugs & Cosmetics		80		719		614
29	Synth Resins,Rubber,Fibres	-2007	26087		1204	374	13838
30	Other Chemical Products	153484	149888	24004		2851	3839
31	Petroleum Products	2372	24402	23308	4834		269607
32	Coal Products	129	4168	561		100	100
33	Rubber Products	1070	408	1193		1056	11210
34	Non-Metallic Mineral Prods.				160084	1968	12588
35	Pig Iron & Raw Steel				1111		317
36	Non-F. Met.Ingots&Prim.P.						407
37	Primry Iron & Steel Prods.				200		21034
38	Fabricated Metal Products	11145	6156	4218	5837	2528	31990
39	General Machinery	7788	2227	1174	1728	9907	7450
40	Electrical Machinery		1088	1305	547	416	7240
41	Electronic & Commnc. Mach.	1053	610	685	565		73648
42	Transportation Equipment			797	1360		146
43	Measrg.Medical,Optical Inst.		64	147	2243	178	2382
44	Misc.Manufacturing	1746		28	108	69	1892
45	Building Constcn & Maint.		3880	2883	7607		
46	Public Works & Oth. Constcn.				1882	76	76
47	Electric Power & Gas Svcs.			274	7954	102	1414
48	Water Services			73	330	181	914
49	Wholesale & Retail Trade	-63209	10988	17284		18295	134765
50	Restaurant & Hotel Services						
51	Transportation & Warehousing	50084		1899	107857	7255	49130
52	Communications		31375	844	1700	254	13037

Input-Output Table of Republic of Korea for the Year 1975

FLOWS in hundred thousand won of Y 1975   PRODUCERS CURRENT PRICES

INDUSTRY:	1 Rice,Barley & Wheat(Polished)	2 Vegetab.Fruits & Other Grains	3 Industrial Crops	4 Livestock Breed & Sericulture	5 Forestry Products	6 Fishery Products
53 Financing & Insurance	70038	2625	7456	19297	2582	76397
54 Real Estate	0	0	0	1413	277	4117
55 Government Services	0	0	0	0	0	0
56 Social Services	0	0	240	17492	268	5143
57 Other Services	0	0	2035	4169	209	8341
58 Office Supplies	0	177	143	1138	14456	1380
59 Business Consumption	0	0	5564	19284	4912	46518
60 Unclassifiable	1423	21029	1180	1365	0	18168
61 Domestic Intermediate Input	2373606	1150525	357028	1929708	233431	1037170

* IMPORT TRANSACTIONS *

	1	2	3	4	5	6
62 Rice Barley Wheat (pol)	0	0	6	7417	0	0
63 Vegetab.Fruits &OthGrains	0	283	0	0	0	0
64 Industrial Crops	0	0	0	0	1882	11329
65 Livestock Breedng &Sericult.	0	0	0	0	0	1072
66 Forestry Products	0	0	0	0	0	0
67 Fishery Products	0	0	0	0	0	0
68 Coal	0	0	0	0	0	0
69 Metallic Ores Minerals	0	0	0	0	0	0
70 Non-Metallic Ores Minerals	0	0	0	0	0	0
71 Slaughter,Dairy,Fruit Proc.	0	0	0	0	0	0
72 Seafood Processing	0	0	0	0	0	0
73 Grain Polishing	0	0	0	5810	0	0
74 Cereal Flours	0	0	0	0	0	0
75 Other Food Preparations	0	0	0	0	0	0
76 Beverages	0	0	0	0	0	0
77 Tobacco	0	0	0	0	0	0
78 Fibre Yarn	0	0	1825	0	0	0
79 Textile Fabrics	0	0	0	0	0	1673
80 Fabricated Textile Prods	0	0	0	0	0	0
81 Leather & Leather Products	0	0	0	0	0	0
82 Lumber and Plywood	0	0	0	0	0	0
83 Wood Products & Furniture	0	0	0	0	0	0
84 Pulp & Paper Publishing	0	0	0	0	5512	0
85 Printing & Publishing	0	0	0	0	0	0
86 Basic Organic Chemicals	4605	0	0	0	0	0
87 Basic Inorganic Chemicals	190884	97433	18342	3	0	0
88 Chemical Fertilizers	0	0	0	0	0	0
89 Drugs & Cosmetics	0	0	0	0	0	1456
90 Synth.Resins,Rubber,Fibres	11329	13318	2033	0	1438	286623
91 Other Chemical Products	0	0	0	0	0	0
92 Petroleum Products	0	0	0	0	0	485
93 Coal Products	0	0	0	0	0	0
94 Rubber Pdoucts	0	0	0	0	0	0
95 Non-Metallic Mineral Prods.	32	0	0	0	0	0
96 Pig Iron & Raw Steel	0	0	0	0	0	0
97 Primary Iron & Steel Prods.	0	0	0	0	0	0
98 Non-Fer Met Ingots&Prim.P.	0	0	0	0	0	0
99 Fabricated Metal Products	0	0	0	0	0	3814
100 General Machinery	0	0	0	19	1007	18508
101 Electrical Machinery	0	0	0	0	0	629
102 Electronic & Commnc. Mach.	0	0	0	0	0	632
103 Transportation Equipment	0	0	0	0	0	4987

Input-Output Table of Republic of Korea for the Year 1975

KOREA RP. 1975   FLOWS in hundred thousand won of Y 1975   PRODUCERS CURRENT PRICES

INDUSTRY:	1 Rice,Barley & Wheat(polished)	2 Vegetab.Fruits & Other Grains	3 Industrial Crops	4 Livestock Breed & Sericulture	5 Forestry Products	6 Fishery Products
104 Measrg,Medical,Optical Inst.	0	0	0	123	0	0
105 Misc.Manufacturing	0	0	0	0	0	211
106 Building Constcn & Maint.	0	0	0	0	0	0
107 Public Works & Oth.Constcn.	0	0	0	0	0	0
108 Electric Power & Gas Svcs.	0	0	0	0	0	0
109 Water Services	0	0	0	0	0	0
110 Wholesale & Retail Trade	0	0	0	0	0	0
111 Restaurant & Hotel Services	0	0	0	0	0	0
112 Transportation & Warehousing	0	0	0	0	0	0
113 Communications	0	0	0	0	0	1283
114 Financing & Insurance	0	0	0	0	0	283
115 Real Estate	0	0	0	0	0	0
116 Government Services	0	0	0	0	0	0
117 Social Services	0	0	0	0	0	0
118 Other Services	0	0	0	0	0	0
119 Office Supplies	0	0	0	0	0	0
120 Business Consumption	0	0	101	203	907	739
121 Unclassifiable	714	10628	589	728		907
122 Imported Intermediate Input	207364	121662	22890	14411	10544	322077
123 Compet. Imports (cif & Dut)	204984	121662	22890	14411	10544	322077
124 Non-Comp. Imports (cif &Dut)	2380	0	0	0	0	0
125 Total Intermediate Input	2580970	1272187	379916	1944117	243975	1359247
126 Compensation of Employees	81951	348411	239565	287448	344739	830066
127 Other Value Added	11935063	3349613	830241	872144	1004364	564008
128 Consumption of Fixed Capital	167088	59008	30387	102683	13096	388275
129 Indir. Taxes Less Subsidies	20384		37933	572	7809	7802
130 Total Value Added	12742088	3774611	1144126	1262845	1370008	1800452
131 Negative Flows from Quad.	-85218	0	0	0	0	0
132 Total Input	15323058	5046798	1524042	3206962	1613983	3159899

232

Input-Output Table of Republic of Korea for the Year 1975

KOREA RP. 1975

FLOWS in hundred thousand won of Y 1975

INDUSTRY:

#	Industry	7 Coal	8 Metallic Ores	9 Non-Metallic Minerals	10 Slaughtrg.Dairy & Fruit Proc.	11 Canning & Proc. of Sea Foods	12 Grain Polishing
	* DOMESTIC TRANSACTIONS * INDUSTRY						
1	Rice,Barley,Wheat(pol)	0	0	0	8038	0	0
2	Vegetab,Fruits &OthGrains	0	0	0	95784	5108	0
3	Industrial Crops	19	0	4009	1724	244	30
4	Livestck Breedng &Sericul S.	8	4042	203	1671088	868	0
5	Forestry Products	4448	440	3789	5321	420144	80
6	Fishery Products	1820	0	0	372	246	0
7	Coal	0	0	0	428	8806	0
8	Metallic Ores	10	0	0	483	89	0
9	Non-Metallic Minerals	0	0	0	27383	357	0
10	Slaughter,Dairy,Fruit Proc.	0	0	0	211	1511	0
11	Seafood Processing	0	0	0	560	0	18333
12	Grain Polishing	0	0	0	52174	70	1292
13	Cereal Flours	0	0	0	546	662	222
14	Other Food Preparations	0	0	0	0	130	176
15	Beverages	0	0	0	17	857	680
16	Tobacco	0	0	0	768	2567	44
17	Fibre Yarn	155	422	8198	130	1753	395
18	Textile Fabrics	513	568	217	437	190	969
19	Fabricated Textile Products		799	590	16223	154	89
20	Leather & Leather Products	494	19	387	4963	234	7535
21	Lumber and plywood	59	435	684	356	187	528
22	Wood Pducts & Furniture	832	252	10	2056	16855	1263
23	Pulp & Paper	765	928	1286	1930	273	1368
24	Print & Publishing		7255		12066	910	
25	Basic Organic Chemicals	43	3	530	4088	140	1389
26	Basic Inorganic Chemicals	31	192	380	33788	675	2127
27	Chemical Fertilizers	28847	9008	29433	400	9740	5248
28	Drugs & Cosmetics	9766	6178	41141	6366	931	1387
29	Synth Resins,Rubber,Fibres		153	1563	2988	654	1234
30	Other Chemical Products		809	1242	272	253	327
31	Petroleum Products	829	1163		122	1378	74
32	Coal Products	1370			82819	170	66
33	Rubber Products	9		3441	2679	1438	216
34	Non-Metallic Mineral Prods.	104	10459	6924	1795		
35	Pig Iron & Raw Steel	18213	28	4112	13		
36	Primary Iron & Steel Prods.	20	2305	1920	6093		
37	Non-F Met.Ingots &Prim.P.	3515	1744	13	225		
38	Fabricated Metal Products	5216	46	3025	645		
39	General Machinery	1944	551	206	1387		
40	Electrical Machinery	7264	57				
41	Electronic & Commnc Mach.	437	12				
42	Transportation Equipment	4887	578	2223			
43	Measrg.Medical.Optical Inst.	78					
44	Misc.Manufacturing	8					
45	Building Constcn & Maint.	999					
46	Public Works & Oth.Constcn.						
47	Electric Power & Gas Svcs.	53395	21948	12810	11549	8919	116082
48	Water Services	125	9180	2229	2568	1084	1318
49	Wholesale & Retail Trade	25813	9129	23847	238728	91630	9545
50	Restaurant & Hotel Services	0	0	0	0	0	0

233

Input-Output Table of Republic of Korea for the Year 1975

KOREA RP. 1975   FLOWS in hundred thousand won of Y 1975   PRODUCERS CURRENT PRICES

INDUSTRY:	7 Coal	8 Metallic Ores	9 Non-Metallic Minerals	10 Slaughtrg,Dairy & Fruit Proc	11 Canning & Proc of Sea Foods	12 Grain Polishing
51 Transportation & Warehousing	4509	2732	1361	21871	13097	1682
52 Communications	1189	348	2699	3843	5112	1177
53 Financing & Insurance	28429	8323	9009	24048	7918	5782
54 Real Estate	0	172	3248	1073	2714	585
55 Government Services						
56 Social Services	1175	210	470	583	3011	5250
57 Other Services	1738	728	1623	18231	1915	1743
58 Office Supplies	1369	583		873	615	390
59 Business Consumption	6480	5857	17224	10180	12812	12530
60 Unclassifiable	7380	1375	8768	8090	1345	5246
61 Domestic Intermediate Input	258977	102903	206379	236092	656923	204195

* IMPORT TRANSACTIONS *

	7 Coal	8 Metallic Ores	9 Non-Metallic Minerals	10 Slaughtrg,Dairy & Fruit Proc	11 Canning & Proc of Sea Foods	12 Grain Polishing
62 Rice Barley, Wheat (pol)	0	0	0	0	0	0
63 Vegetab.Fruits &OthGrains	0	0	0	0	0	0
64 Industrial Crops	50205	0	0	0	0	0
65 Livestck Breedg &Sericult.	0	85	0	599	0	0
66 Forestry Products	0	0	0	0	0	0
67 Fishery Products	0	0	2912	1934	3219	0
68 Metallic Ores	0	0	0	0	0	0
69 Non-Metallic Minerals	0	0	0	0	0	0
70 Sla-Metallic Minerals	0	0	0	0	0	0
71 Slaughter,Dairy/Fruit Proc.	0	0	0	0	0	0
72 Seafood Processing	0	0	0	11915	599	0
73 Grain Polishing	0	0	0	0	0	0
74 Cereal Flours	0	0	1120	933	0	0
75 Other Food Preparations	0	0	0	4653	349	0
76 Beverages	0	0	0	226	0	0
77 Tobacco	0	0	0	0	0	0
78 Fibre Yarn	0	0	0	0	0	12
79 Textile Fabrics	0	0	0	0	0	0
80 Fabricated Textile Prods	0	0	0	0	0	0
81 Leather & Leather Products	0	0	0	0	0	0
82 Lumber and Plywood Products	0	0	0	0	0	0
83 Wood Products & Furniture	0	0	0	0	0	0
84 Pulp & Paper	0	0	0	0	0	0
85 Printing & Publishing	0	0	0	0	0	0
86 Basic Organic Chemicals	0	447	62	0	0	0
87 Basic Inorganic Chemicals	0	1423	1	0	0	0
88 Chemical Fertilizers	0	0	0	0	0	0
89 Drugs & Cosmetics	512	0	0	248	114	0
90 Synth.Resins,Rubber,Fibres	950	0	0	196	9	0
91 Other Chemical Products	487	0	821	234	8	0
92 Petroleum Products	0	0	0	172	4	0
93 Coal Products	0	0	0	786	0	0
94 Rubber Products	0	0	0	0	0	0
95 Non-Metallic Mineral Prods.	0	114	0	0	0	1205
96 Pig Iron & Raw Steel	1500	308	0	0	0	82
97 Primary Iron & Steel Prods.	0	0	0	0	0	0
98 Non-F. Met. Ingots &Prim.P.	0	0	0	0	0	0
99 Fabricated Metal Products	1098	380	300	0	0	0
100 General Machinery	7511	0	1354	8991	2408	0
101 Electrical Machinery	7321	0	4421	1051	1097	1594

234

Input-Output Table of Republic of Korea for the Year 1975

KOREA RP. 1975   FLOWS in hundred thousand won of Y 1975   PRODUCERS CURRENT PRICES

INDUSTRY:	7 Coal	8 Metallic Ores	9 Non-Metallic Minerals	10 Slaughtrg.Dairy & Fruit Proc.	11 Canning & Proc. of Sea Foods	12 Grain Polishing
102 Electronic & Commnc. Mach.	0	0	0	0	0	0
103 Transportation Equipment	0	0	0	0	0	0
104 Measrg.Medical,Optical Inst.	118	0	0	0	0	0
105 Misc. Manufacturing	0	0	0	0	0	0
106 Building Constcn.& Maint.	0	0	0	0	0	0
107 Public Works & Oth. Constcn.	0	0	0	0	0	0
108 Electric Power & Gas Svcs.	0	0	0	0	0	0
109 Water Service	0	0	0	0	0	0
110 Wholesale & Retail Trade	0	0	0	0	0	0
111 Restaurant & Hotel Services	0	0	0	0	0	0
112 Transportation & Warehousing	0	0	0	0	103	0
113 Communications	0	0	0	0		0
114 Financing & Insurance	0	0	0	0	0	0
115 Real Estate	0	0	0	0	0	0
116 Government Services	0	0	0	0	0	0
117 Social Services	0	0	0	0	0	0
118 Other Services	0	0	0	0	0	0
119 Office Supplies	0	0	0	0	0	0
120 Business Consumption	39	125	18	49	459	0
121 Unclassifiable	3690	441	1653	3466	577	2249
122 Imported Intermediate Input	66414	6525	12474	32811	37827	5122
123 Compet. Imports (cif & Dut.)	66413	5628	12411	30913	37812	5122
124 Non-Comp. Imports (cif &Dut)	1	899	63	1898	15	0
125 Total Intermediate Input	325391	109428	218853	2400703	894850	209317
126 Compensation of Employees	598025	114640	285136	165683	98329	178182
127 Other Value Added	49431	55718	270802	136587	61288	294688
128 Consumption of Fixed Capital	62753	44514	41985	20615	16468	16024
129 Indir.Taxes Less Subsidies	-62753	516	2210	49912	10938	8261
130 Total Value Added	688114	215388	600133	372997	187021	497155
131 Negative Flows from Quad.	0	0	0	0	0	0
132 Total Input	993505	324816	818986	2773700	881871	708472

235

Input-Output Table of Republic of Korea for the Year 1975

KOREA RP. 1975   FLOWS in hundred thousand won of Y 1975   PRODUCERS CURRENT PRICES

INDUSTRY:	13 Cereal Flours	14 Other Food Preparations	15 Beverages	16 Tobacco	17 Fibre Spinning	18 Textile Fabrics
* DOMESTIC TRANSACTIONS *						
1 Rice, Barley, Wheat (pol)	5213	312638	42448	0	13	7
2 Vegetab,Fruits &OthGrains	0	150039	82631	82	0	0
3 Industrial Crops	0	132228	48507	372150	5685	0
4 Livestock Breedng &Sericul s	0	10874	140	384	492198	116
5 Forestry Products	0	10005	21	0	0	0
6 Fishery Products	0	16766	1874	0	204	5182
7 Coal	8	3708	-4327	0	0	139
8 Metallic Ores	0	8	-4410	0	9	
9 Non-Metallic Minerals	0	16648	0	0	0	
10 Slaughter,Dairy Fruit Proc.	0	4921	0	0	0	
11 Seafood Processing	0	1173	0	0	0	
12 Grain Polishing	14	0	273521	0	16	2518
13 Cereal Flours		458721	143862	3387	57	2492
14 Other Food Preparations		429908	501685	5875	0	0
15 Beverages		12487		2405	0	2053763
16 Tobacco			37		425379	504018
17 Fibre Yarn	370	533	1793	223	97882	5750
18 Textile Fabrics	922	7635	2977	1895	4226	2030
19 Fabricated Textile Products	942	265	75	2094	1929	3312
20 Leather &Leather Products	265	1694	485	921	1250	1154
21 Lumber and plywood Products	335	5518	25140	98103	17474	18272
22 Wood Products & Furniture	13188	7274	8162	16050	1396	2321
23 Pulp & Paper	145	3115	1533	16625	6279	55064
24 Printing & Publishing	62	26701	2690	0	4917	24500
25 Basic Organic Chemicals	378	51357	0	446	0	0
26 Basic Inorganic Chemicals	20	20	627	692	185	185
27 Chemical Fertilizers	389	40563	4531	8831	26	83
28 Drugs & Cosmetics	7210	18097	8286	20375	2106369	55969
29 Synth Resins Rubber,Fibres	555	13442	43133	2195	4492	18387
30 Other Chemical Products	13	1946	1363	2517	69337	186852
31 Petroleum Products	555	1398	1633	1190	203	1714
32 Coal Products	295	335	18334	789	2496	6698
33 Rubber Products	671	3524	2384	224	570	1052
34 Non-Metallic Mineral Prods.	178	15735	24002	7178	2229	2540
35 Pig Iron & Raw Steel	422	3894	3091	1251	357	122
36 Primary Iron & Steel Prods.	425	8413	3289	1888	3065	8835
37 Non-F. Met Ingots&Prim P.	94	565	505	1809	9914	17848
38 Fabricated Metal Products	175	1194	2206	1	2300	4618
39 General Machinery		7439		12941	2646	145
40 Electrical Machinery				255	453	4189
41 Electronic & Commnc Mach.					985	826
42 Transportation Equipment						1878
43 Measrg,Medical,Optical Inst.						1423
44 Misc.Manufacturing						0
45 Building Constcn & Maint.			1460	10553	121351	0
46 Public Works & Oth. Constcn.	13804	7127	7419	446	2357	106231
47 Electric Power & Gas Svcs.	231	6938	208248	34044	108045	5689
48 Water Services	44154	321852				269303
49 Wholesale & Retail Trade						
50 Restaurant & Hotel Services						
51 Transportation & Warehousing	19044	68512	42628	25349	26878	30518
52 Communications	779	9318	4668	792	8777	8839

Input-Output Table of Republic of Korea for the Year 1975

KOREA RP. 1975

FLOWS in hundred thousand won of Y 1975

PRODUCERS CURRENT PRICES

INDUSTRY:	13 Cereal Flours	14 Other Food Preparations	15 Beverages	16 Tobacco	17 Fibre Spinning	18 Textile Fabrics
53 Financing & Insurance	33923	35102	34747	1281	6735	153350
54 Real Estate Services	196	5632	2495		3749	3287
55 Government Services		0		0		
56 Social Services	1578	426	4242	118	7464	8768
57 Other Services	2031	33605	50185	2790	12370	3445
58 Business Supplies	427	3776	2928	1738	3558	4578
59 Office Consumption	6770	48138	47532	5803	4408	41658
60 Unclassifiable	3	14874	24724	3044	2456	14451
61 Domestic Intermediate Input	154377	2685286	1873523	789611	3674221	3629731

* IMPORT TRANSACTIONS *

	13 Cereal Flours	14 Other Food Preparations	15 Beverages	16 Tobacco	17 Fibre Spinning	18 Textile Fabrics
62 Rice Barley,Wheat (pol)	1175845	534551	41737	0	0	0
63 Vegetab.Fruits &OthGrains	0	18559	40349	60827	1020918	0
64 Industrial Crops	0	16616	35328	0	148975	0
65 Livestck Breedng &Sericult.	0	1210	0	0	0	0
66 Forestry Products	0	0	0	0	0	0
67 Fishery Products	0	0	0	0	0	0
68 Coal	0	0	0	0	0	0
69 Metallic Ores Minerals	0	0	0	0	0	0
70 Non-Metallic Minerals	0	0	0	0	0	0
71 Slaughter,Dairy,Fruit Proc.	0	3815	154	0	0	58
72 Seafood Processing	0	2477	1467	0	0	0
73 Grain Polishing	1840	0	0	1177	0	0
74 Cereal Flours	0	5842	1325	0	0	0
75 Other Food Preparations	0	1203001	25286	0	0	0
76 Beverages	0	213	18011	0	0	0
77 Tobacco	0	0	0	0	0	0
78 Fibre Yarn	0	1837	0	18194	87910	3764
79 Textile Fabrics	0	0	0	0	210	34881
80 Fabricated Textile Prods	0	0	0	0	3095	1939
81 Leather & Leather Products	0	0	183	0	294	134
82 Lumber and Plywood	0	0	0	0	0	0
83 Wood Products & Furniture	0	0	0	0	0	0
84 Pulp & Paper	0	0	0	0	0	0
85 Printing & Publishing	0	95	224	14684	28	179097
86 Basic Organic Chemicals	0	7227	2245	2158	31528	27257
87 Basic Inorganic Chemicals	0	14135	246	0	2279	5
88 Chemical Fertilizers	0	127	0	0	5	0
89 Drugs & Cosmetics	0	0	17471	14225	0	7484
90 Synth.Resins,Rubber,Fibres	0	0	0	185	284152	25471
91 Other Chemical Products	0	2833	0	0	2204	2350
92 Petroleum Products	132	143	103	1267	1416	75
93 Coal Products	908	0	0	0	0	70
94 Rubber Products	0	492	654	0	0	0
95 Non-Metallic Mineral Prods.	0	0	0	0	0	0
96 Pig Iron & Raw Steel Prods.	0	1452	0	308	0	0
97 Primary Iron & Steel Prods.	0	0	6781	1953	20057	24468
98 Non-Fer.Met Ingots &Prim.P.	0	4851	1642	872	880	310
99 Fabricated Metal Products	455	0	0	0	0	0
100 General Machinery	0	0	0	0	0	0
101 Electrical Machinery	0	0	0	0	0	0
102 Electronic & Commc. Mach.	0	0	0	0	0	0
103 Transportation Equipment	0	0	0	0	0	0

Input-Output Table of Republic of Korea for the Year 1975

KOREA RP. 1975   FLOWS in hundred thousand won of Y 1975   PRODUCERS CURRENT PRICES

INDUSTRY:	13 Cereal Flours	14 Other Food Preparations	15 Beverages	16 Tobacco	17 Fibre Spinning	18 Textile Fabrics
104 Measrg.Medical.Optical Inst	0	182	0	210	0	0
105 Misc.Manufacturing	0	0	0	2401	0	0
106 Building Constr.& Maint	0	0	0	0	0	0
107 Public Works & Oth.Constcn	0	0	0	0	0	0
108 Electric Power & Gas Svcs.	0	0	0	0	0	0
109 Water Services	0	0	0	0	0	0
110 Wholesale & Retail Trade	0	0	0	0	0	0
111 Restaurant & Hotel Services	0	0	0	0	0	0
112 Transportation & Warehousing	0	0	0	0	0	245
113 Communications	0	0	0	0	0	0
114 Financing & Insurance	0	0	0	0	0	0
115 Real Estate	0	0	0	0	0	0
116 Government Services	0	0	0	0	0	0
117 Social Services	0	0	0	0	0	0
118 Other Services	0	0	0	0	0	0
119 Office Supplies	0	0	0	0	0	0
120 Business Consumption	8397	6397	10597	1305	1371	1279
121 Unclassifiable			82		1049	6194
122 Imported Intermediate Input	1178980	1849530	201063	117764	1594962	348695
123 Compet. Imports (cif & Dut.)	1178980	736702	187606	107836	379209	316015
124 Non-Comp. Imports (cif &Dut)	0	112828	34351	9928	1215663	33880
125 Total Intermediate Input	1333357	4514618	2075486	887375	5269183	3978426
126 Compensation of Employees	64040	413343	195438	163990	339701	480551
127 Other Value Added	435058	526345	409184	457673	213693	497191
128 Consumption of Fixed Capital	12162	113572	102584	45263	198796	152877
129 Indir.Taxes Less Subsidies	-530525	272263	998218	1362889	349024	62098
130 Total Value Added	-19265	1326143	1705412	2028375	1102214	1192715
131 Negative Flows from Quad.	0	0	-4327	0	0	0
132 Total Input	1314092	5840959	3780898	2915750	6371397	5171141

238

Input-Output Table of Republic of Korea for the Year 1975

KOREA RP. 1975   FLOWS in hundred thousand won of Y 1975   PRODUCERS CURRENT PRICES

INDUSTRY:

#	DOMESTIC TRANSACTIONS INDUSTRY	19 Apparel &Fabrc. Textile Prods.	20 Leather and Leather Prods.	21 Lumber & Plywood	22 Wood Products & Furniture	Paper	23 Paper & Products	24 Printing & Publishing
1	Rice,Barley,Wheat (pol)	66516	44	0	0		1938	0
2	Vegetab.,Fruits &OthGrains	12137	0	0	0		0	17
3	Industrial Crops	3103	6163	2723	2928		671	0
4	Livestck Breedng &Sericul s.	3238	1113	0	5250		30298	2
5	Forestry Products		6	734	330		1074	529
6	Fishery Products		0	15225	27		2814	0
7	Coal		871	1501	13		0	0
8	Metallic Ores	29	19507	92	15			
9	Non-Metallic Minerals		133	238	8		1478	134
10	Slaughter,Dairy,Fruit Proc.		1728	1988	1387		10399	106
11	Seafood Processing		438		538			
12	Grain Polishing				85			
13	Cereal Flours							
14	Other Food Preparations	375						
15	Beverages	348						385
16	Tobacco							
17	Fibre Yarn	2536628	7362				38874	962
18	Textile Fabrics	1733558	18592				4855	1994
19	Fabricated Textile Products	171247	9221				3833	126
20	Leather & Leather Products	1407	373080				683	243
21	Lumber and Plywood	5927	1634	45251	11284		164	548
22	Wood Products & Furniture	4699	4362	93	4405			
23	Pulp & Paper	60554	2061	2652	942		399185	403407
24	Printing & Publishing	80731	1769	1239	812		1224	22995
25	Basic Organic Chemicals	11936	5670	25098	2320		8496	2048
26	Basic Inorganic Chemicals	5288	15	1007	106		15142	1458
27	Chemical Fertilizers	99	20	6282	8		7425	841
28	Drugs & Cosmetics	146111	19200	136	670		24589	29075
29	Synth.Resins,Rubber,Fibres	17780	13660	46503	14876		54815	11474
30	Other Chemical Products	115421	29171	14395	4096		428	1933
31	Petroleum Products	8668	520	35243	419		1354	1599
32	Coal Products	20080	29260	119	1415		4105	706
33	Rubber Products	2172	5890	1669	3887		1158	942
34	Non-Metallic Mineral Prods.	3881	1785	3521	86		3558	4931
35	Pig Iron & Raw Steel	718	302	531	12		3880	873
36	Primary Iron & Steel Prim.Prods.	30855	9118	12	4968		3191	898
37	Non-F. Met.Ingots &Prim.P.	29163	3750	7521	1003		582	782
38	Fabricated Metal Products	10381	1581	3682	172		123	104
39	General Machinery	175	57	1134	130		2280	2717
40	Electrical Machinery	4160	1183	407	238		149	624
41	Electronic & Commnc. Mach.	296	296	1378	61		1222	752
42	Transportation Equipment	5795	1351	47	203		3374	955
43	Measrng.Medical.Optical Inst.	1986	5770	1458	170			
44	Misc.Manufacturing		10179	2773				
45	Building Constcn & Maint.		861					
46	Public Works & Oth.Constcn.							
47	Electric Power & Gas Svcs.	96158		2646	2345		73348	13781
48	Water Services	5715		828	368		1216	1527
49	Wholesale & Retail Trade	674639	134062	17336	36387		14315	56961
50	Restaurant & Hotel Services	0		0				0

Input-Output Table of Republic of Korea for the Year 1975

KOREA RP. 1975   FLOWS in hundred thousand won of Y 1975   PRODUCERS CURRENT PRICES

INDUSTRY:	19 Apparel &Fabrc Textile Prods	20 Leather and Leather Prods	21 Lumber & Plywood	22 Wood Products & Furniture	23 Paper & Products	24 Printing & Publishing
51 Transportation & Warehousing	85339	1194	16491	8635	22980	27855
52 Communications	23925	2829	3864	1869	3506	16517
53 Financing & Insurance	73008	20172	53621	12007	46404	13048
54 Real Estate	16671	2907	1180	242	14395	13029
55 Government Services						
56 Social Services	9053	894	1539	423	1835	1258
57 Other Services	35756	4518	3703	2668	3303	17722
58 Office Supplies	6459	11903	1753	444	2007	4408
59 Business Consumption	79222	832	25838	4633	20954	23214
60 Unclassifiable	38150		7463	4976	4581	2627
61 Domestic Intermediate Input	6063798	777982	585485	238781	963784	676002

* IMPORT TRANSACTIONS *

	19	20	21	22	23	24
62 Rice,Barley,Wheat(pol)	0	0	0	0	0	0
63 Vegetab[Fruits&OthGrains	0	0	0	0	0	0
64 Industr'l Crops	18465					
65 Livestock Breeing &Sericult.						
66 Forestry Products	886	4850	1215814	9979	40991	
67 Fishery Products		18		4388		
68 Coal	0	0	0	0	0	0
69 Metallic Ores		240634				
70 Non-Metallic Minerals	0	0	0	0	0	0
71 Slaughter,Dairy,Fruit Proc.	0	0	0	0	0	0
72 Seafood Processing	0	0	0	0	0	0
73 Grain Polishing	0	0	0	0	0	0
74 Cereal Flours	0	0	0	0	0	0
75 Other Food Preparations	0	11543	0	0	0	0
76 Beverages	0	0	0	0	865	0
77 Tobacco	0	0	0	0	0	0
78 Fibre Yarn	87894					
79 Textile Fabrics	583847	338			513	150
80 Fabricated Textile Prods	512	2963	398		1773	197
81 Leather & Leather Products		23184				
82 Lumber and Plywood				7082		
83 Wood Products & Furniture	0	0	0	210	0	0
84 Pulp & Paper	8513		8516		52224	11537
85 Printing & Publishing	30359					1471
86 Basic Organic Chemicals	3357	2785	9151		6990	2285
87 Basic Inorganic Chemicals		1074	228		8937	2364
88 Chemical Fertilizers	142					
89 Drugs & Cosmetics	79484	870			2127	294
90 Synth.Resins,Rubber,Fibres	6238	404	12865	2358	5454	16307
91 Other Chemical Products	4628	7111	4996		140	225
92 Petroleum Products	0	0	0	0	0	0
93 Coal Products	0	0	0	0	0	0
94 Rubber Products	8628	3075	105	888	187	105
95 Non-Metallic Mineral Prods.		117	500	4697	5155	13
96 Pig Iron & Raw Steel	0	0	0	0	0	0
97 Primary Iron & Steel Prods						
98 Non-F. Met.Ingots &Prim.P.	0	0	0	0	0	0
99 Fabricated Metal Products	24424	2216	8634	254	10714	1239
100 General Machinery	13753	1327	2632	292	473	2518
101 Electrical Machinery	2935				2930	

240

Input-Output Table of Republic of Korea for the Year 1975

INDUSTRY:	19 Apparel &Fabrc Textile Prods.	20 Leather and Leather Prods.	21 Lumber & Plywood	22 Wood Products & Furniture	23 Paper & Paper Products	24 Printing & Publishing
102 Electronic & Commnc. Mach.	0	0	0	0	0	0
103 Transportation Equipment	198	0	0	0	0	0
104 Measrg.Medical.Optical Inst.			112		81	61
105 Misc.Manufacturing	58295	4429		0	71	87
106 Building Constcn & Maint.	0	0	0	0	0	0
107 Public Works & Oth. Constcn.	0	0	0	0	0	0
108 Electric Power & Gas Svcs.	0	0	0	0	0	0
109 Water Services	0	0	0	0	0	0
110 Wholesale & Retail Trade	0	0	0	0	0	0
111 Restaurant & Hotel Services	2575	0	254	0	0	371
112 Transportation & Warehousing	5	0	0	0	0	341
113 Communications	0	0	0	0	0	0
114 Financing & Insurance	0	0	0	0	0	0
115 Real Estate	0	0	0	0	0	0
116 Government Services	778	0	205	0	0	0
117 Social Services	0	0	0	0	0	0
118 Other Services	0	0	0	0	0	0
119 Office Supplies	4862	233	1188	2130	119	1042
120 Business Consumption	15493	357	3197	2132	1966	35
121 Unclassifiable						1127
122 Imported Intermediate Input	948196	537334	1260852	32208	811539	39769
123 Compet.Imports (cif & Dut)	93301	462145	164960	30887	360723	28795
124 Non-Comp. Imports (cif &Dut)	34595	55189	195892	1341	350816	9974
125 Total Intermediate Input	701994	1315296	1826317	270988	1575303	715771
126 Compensation of Employees	1290064	240453	197777	68501	226118	234848
127 Other Value Added	1730008	240853	107475	39005	213878	126635
128 Consumption of Fixed Capital	271591	33870	54167	8897	71824	26808
129 Indir.Taxes Less Subsidies	115618	21839	52025		62951	61894
130 Total Value Added	2819559	516868	401444	120214	574565	401823
131 Negative Flows from Quad.	0	0	0	0	0	0
132 Total Input	9831553	1832164	2227761	391203	2149868	1117894

241

Input-Output Table of Republic of Korea for the Year 1975

KOREA RP. 1975 FLOWS in hundred thousand won of Y 1975 PRODUCERS CURRENT PRICES

INDUSTRY:	25 Basic Organic Chemicals	26 Basic Inorganic Chemicals	27 Chemical Fertilizer	28 Drugs & Cosmetics	29 Synthetic Resin Rubber &Fibres	30 Other Chemical Products
* DOMESTIC TRANSACTIONS * INDUSTRY						
1 Rice, Barley, Wheat (pol)	0	0	0	0	0	801
2 Vegetab Fruits &OthGrains	0	0	0	6075	0	18
3 Industrial Crops	0	0	0	3528	2620	0
4 Livestck Breedng &Sericul S.	24	548	0	21	0	2844
5 Forestry Products	0	1108	0	334	397	340
6 Fishery Products	19	12192	0	385	19	902
7 Coal						1335
8 Metallic Ores Minerals	492	10921	416	8465		0
9 Non-Metallic Minerals	0	0	0	381	19	150
10 Slaughter,Dairy,Fruit Proc.	0	0	0	568		15560
11 Seafood Processing	0	0	0			645
12 Grain Polishing	0	0	0	35979		0
13 Cereal Flours	0	0	0	568	35	
14 Other Food Preparations	2642	367	0		21233	2091
15 Beverages		0	0	414	16364	441
16 Tobacco	3	0	0	1493	5068	1786
17 Fibre Yarn	431	38	324	430	18151	1530
18 Textile Fabrics	457	526	46	175	2042	969
19 Fabricated Textile Products	43	269	573	3288	1358	6096
20 Leather & Leather Products	188	383	92	5683	35914	29490
21 Lumber and Plywood	1998	358	429	40560	25074	1852
22 Wood Products & Furniture	1372	2838		8617	551135	101736
23 Pulp & Paper	215895	2476	849937		51695	33394
24 Printing & Publishing	57392	1370	11934	18152	23563	242
25 Basic Organic Chemicals		8369	13840	11585		-171
26 Basic Inorganic Chemicals	698	0	13823	33318	805364	30984
27 Chemical Fertilizers	717	1969	139173	27704	36229	44367
28 Drugs & Cosmetics	2518	1884	753	48	175571	42010
29 Synth.Resins,Rubber,Fibres	376171	1673	830	4950	794	8682
30 Other Chemical Products		326357	1103	1941	2481	951
31 Petroleum Products	173	173			1046	5375
32 Coal Products	2602	1268	1121	437	9498	1575
33 Rubber Products	101	3073	828	212	358	32315
34 Non-Metallic Mineral Prods.	1182		1962	10700	8405	26638
35 Pig Iron & Raw Steel		4785	146	689	7299	1447
36 Primary Iron & Steel Prods.	2639	356	487	892	178	15906
37 Non-F. Met.Ingots &Prim.P.	1314	5006	129	1866	2303	1216
38 Fabricated Metal Products	1539	9870	192	1851	753	1533
39 General Machinery	630	630		595	403	260
40 Electrical Machinery	715	1068	84122	1728	1139	33
41 Electronic & Commnc. Mach.	414	329	55237	192		420
42 Transportation Equipment	88	88	55109			0
43 Measrg Medical,Optical Inst.	98	98		12568	14979	19788
44 Misc.Manufacturing	219	219		124555	37879	5021
45 Building Constrn & Maint					378793	181821
46 Public Works & Oth.Constn.	28306	94896				
47 Elec.Power & Gas Svcs.	88629	51054				
48 Water Services	54686	54686				
49 Wholesale & Retail Trade						
50 Restaurant & Hotel Services						
51 Transportation & Warehousing	14399	19800	30319	29804	54002	25136
52 Communications	1719	1376	778	7402	9664	4595

242

Input-Output Table of Republic of Korea for the Year 1975

KOREA RP. 1975   FLOWS in hundred thousand won of Y 1975   PRODUCERS CURRENT PRICES

INDUSTRY:	25 Basic Organic Chemicals	26 Basic Inorganic Chemicals	27 Chemical Fertilizer	28 Drugs & Cosmetics	29 Synthetic Resin Rubber & Fibres	30 Other Chemical Products
53 Financing & Insurance	1808	13713	33940	32488	34091	21932
54 Real Estate	1044	651	517	7035	6035	2365
55 Government Services	0	0	0	0	0	0
56 Other Services	771	490	324	5857	6138	1555
57 Office Supplies	3113	1578	1187	129170	14986	9787
58 Business Consumption	1086	972	705	48610	8489	2454
59 Unclassifiable	13372	11282	5362	40474	48708	17873
60 Unclassifiable	6703	2817	706	2690	20730	2643
61 Domestic Intermediate Input	847402	689719	1128948	857510	2321572	705550

* IMPORT TRANSACTIONS *

	25	26	27	28	29	30
62 Rice, Barley, Wheat (pol)	0	0	0	0	0	0
63 Vegetab,Fruits &OthGrains	0	0	0	0	0	0
64 Industrial Crops	0	0	0	2166	0	2298
65 Livestock Breedng &Sericult.	0	0	0	0	0	0
66 Forestry Products	0	0	0	212	1444	0
67 Fishery Products	0	0	0	0	0	677
68 Coal	0	0	0	0	0	216
69 Metallic Ores	258	167311	79923	365	336	0
70 Non-Metallic Minerals	0	0	0	1187	0	103438
71 Slaughter,Dairy,Fruit Proc.	0	0	0	0	0	0
72 Seafood Processing	0	0	0	0	0	0
73 Grain Polishing	0	0	0	918	1469	0
74 Cereal Flours	21079	0	0	128	5200	327
75 Other Food Preparations	0	0	0	325	6388	545
76 Beverages	125	0	0	0	4576	0
78 Tobacco	0	0	0	123	30529	10406
79 Fibre Yarn	0	0	0	1193	1091864	140411
80 Textile Fabrics	0	0	313	1326	25246	40662
81 Fabricated Textile Prods	0	14809	17849	85067	432	11340
82 Leather & Leather Products	18579	49368	82770	9694	341843	22828
83 Lumber and Plywood	16970	150	5312	127458	57485	211832
84 Wood Products & Furniture	93	4384	77	7025	8722	8533
85 Pulp & Paper	8650	441	0	74893	0	4837
86 Printing & Publishing	655	280	450	48222	145	2689
87 Basic Organic Chemicals	0	339	309	230	812	1842
88 Basic Inorganic Chemicals	85	1803	3151	1432	6136	1848
89 Chemical Fertilizers	242	2303	93	3846	1213	1038
90 Drugs & Cosmetics	697	1144	0	880	0	0
91 Synth.Resins,Rubber,Fibres	0	0	0	0	0	0
92 Other Chemical Products						
93 Petroleum Products						
94 Coal Products						
95 Rubber Products						
96 Non-Metallic Mineral Prods.						
97 Primary Iron & Raw Steel						
98 Primary Met.Products &Prim.						
99 Fabricated Metal Products						
100 General Machinery						
101 Electrical Machinery						
102 Electronic & Commnc. Mach.						
103 Transportation Equipment						

Input-Output Table of Republic of Korea for the Year 1975

KOREA RP. 1975   FLOWS in hundred thousand won of Y 1975   PRODUCERS CURRENT PRICES

INDUSTRY:	25 Basic Organic Chemicals	26 Basic Inorganic Chemicals	27 Chemical Fertilizer	28 Drugs & Cosmetics	29 Synthetic Resin Rubber & Fibres	30 Other Chemical Products
104 Measrg,Medical,Optical Inst	10	216	473	1214	49	107
105 Misc. Manufacturing	12	0	0	0	1032	0
106 Building,Constcn & Maint.	0	0	0	0	0	0
107 Public Works & Oth. Constcn	0	0	0	0	0	0
108 Electric Power & Gas Svcs.	0	0	0	0	0	0
109 Water Services	0	0	0	0	0	0
110 Wholesale & Retail Trade	0	0	0	0	0	0
111 Restaurant & Hotel Services	0	0	0	133	604	0
112 Transportation & Warehousing	0	0	0	7	0	0
113 Communication	0	0	0	0	0	0
114 Financing & Insurance	0	0	0	0	8	0
115 Real Estate	0	0	0	0	0	0
116 Government Services	0	0	0	0	0	0
117 Social Services	0	0	0	0	0	0
118 Office Supplies	0	0	0	808	484	0
119 Business Consumption	88	35	44	498	1322	0
120 Unclassifiable	2873	1205	302	1153	8884	1131
122 Imported Intermediate Input	215008	243501	191086	335639	1594222	588195
123 Compet. Imports (cif & Dut)	71742	84178	99791	241778	678380	281437
124 Non-Comp. Imports (cif & Dut)	143284	158615	91295	93861	814862	304758
125 Total Intermediate Input	1062408	913310	1320014	1193149	3915784	1271745
126 Compensation of Employees	63525	86312	89052	232223	350293	140029
127 Other Value Added	127189	158009	90812	290665	350394	172180
128 Consumption of Fixed Capital	84881	74875	-131580	60139	350803	46009
129 Indir. Taxes Less Subsidies	18172	17999	-394778	64173	96492	28008
130 Total Value Added	293767	335255	-83334	647420	1302874	386316
131 Negative Flows from Quad. I	0	0	0	0	0	0
132 Total Input	1356175	1248565	1236680	1840569	5218668	1658081

Input-Output Table of Republic of Korea for the Year 1975

KOREA RP. 1975   FLOWS in hundred thousand won of Y 1975   PRODUCERS CURRENT PRICES

INDUSTRY:

INDUSTRY	31 Petroleum Ref. & Related Prods	32 Coal Products	33 Rubber Products	34 Non-Metallic Mineral Prod.	35 Pig Iron & Raw Steel	36 Primary Iron & Steel Products
DOMESTIC TRANSACTIONS						
1 Rice Barley Wheat(pol)	0	0	0	369	0	17
2 Vegetab.Fruits &OthGrains	0	0	0	0	0	0
3 Industrial Crops	0	0	0	0	0	0
4 Livestck Breedng &Sericul S.	38	0	26	2085	520	211
5 Forestry Products	0	0	403	0	0	0
6 Fishery Products	0	0	1031	0	0	0
7 Coal	0	651842	0	32867	13758	12408
8 Metallic Ores Minerals	938	174	0	11991	31887	2909
9 Non-Metallic Minerals	0	0	0	293510	15361	82
10 Slaughter,Dairy,Fruit Proc.	0	0	18	22	45	245
11 Seafood Processing	0	0	0	0	366	650
12 Grain Polishing	0	0	0	0	230	226
13 Cereal Flours	0	0	0	135	746	2058
14 Other Food Preparations	87	0	0	725	340	1258
15 Beverages	0	0	0	690	762	1508
16 Tobacco	0	492	41148	4029	113	1249
17 Fibre Yarn	44	431	115399	1959	11455	1855
18 Textile Fabrics	740	11	5569	13148	159	13856
19 Fabricated Textile Products	128	161	3336	2244	377	15
20 Leather & Leather Products	1878	107	28110	5440	4360	2253
21 Lumber and Plywood	1240	822	1735	5210	22192	8543
22 Wood Products & Furniture	13161	103	14928	120	331	68287
23 Pulp & Paper	1569	728	5583	3309	46447	2581
24 Printing & Publishing	1887	2	88570	8587	690497	805
25 Basic Organic Chemicals	308	527	90809	489768	11753	10763
26 Basic Inorganic Chemicals	4481	15315	49059	4259	1017	1714208
27 Chemical Fertilizers	372123	22214	1067	3647	2636	485102
28 Drugs & Cosmetics	2128	692	33792	181801	207	45587
29 Synth.Resins,Rubber,Fibres	519	255	839	1968	1786	14484
30 Other Chemical Products	1025	859	2443	22041	3	7199
31 Petroleum Products	124	126	905	7642	868	2056
32 Coal Products	12240	2443	12184	29151	428	52
33 Rubber Products	1652	1985	5195	12424	8	1727
34 Non-Metallic Mineral Prods.	3461	174	1078	361	3639	402
35 Pig Iron & Raw Steel	29	29	87	3504	12419	33
36 Primary Iron & Steel Prods.	87	2837	1417	276	952	862
37 Non-Fer Met.Ingots &Prim.P.	2483	968	211	235	10784	88010
38 Fabricated Metal Products	968	1145	811	1580	0	992
39 General Machinery	276	489	782			17835
40 Electrical Machinery	1145					0
41 Electronic & Commnc.Mach.	157					
42 Transportation Equipment						
43 Measrg.Medical,Optical Inst.						
44 Misc.Manufacturing						
45 Building Constrn. & Maintn.						
46 Public Works & Oth.Constrn						
47 Electric Power & Gas Svcs.	25131	13251	36940	193607		
48 Water Services	1543	345	1642	2281		
49 Wholesale & Retail Trade	48547	24943	140808	212864		
50 Restaurant & Hotel Services	0			0		

Input-Output Table of Republic of Korea for the Year 1975

KOREA RP. 1975   FLOWS in hundred thousand won of Y 1975   PRODUCERS CURRENT PRICES

INDUSTRY:	31 Petroleum Ref. & Related Prods.	32 Coal Products	33 Rubber Products	34 Non-Metallic Mineral Prods.	35 Pig Iron & Raw Steel	38 Primary Iron & Steel Products
51 Transportation & Warehousing	29312	140195	24527	101267	57736	39008
52 Communications	3679	1470	35517	7359	52160	33733
53 Financing & Insurance	54154	7658	35759	66684	2995	52091
54 Real Estate	3785	1971	32548	6331	471	1385
55 Government Services	1078	1788	2494	8743	827	1748
56 Social Services	10934	2808	11718	8100	1212	4577
57 Other Services	5398	1127	2104	4830	910	1929
58 Office Supplies	48380	11730	18433	45272	7521	21378
59 Business Consumption	3		2900	3480	1953	1405
80 Unclassifiable						
61 Domestic Intermediate Input	663145	891047	896289	1955224	1243679	2792019

* IMPORT TRANSACTIONS *

	31 Petroleum Ref. & Related Prods.	32 Coal Products	33 Rubber Products	34 Non-Metallic Mineral Prods.	35 Pig Iron & Raw Steel	38 Primary Iron & Steel Products
62 Rice,Barley,Wheat (pol)	0	0	0	0	0	0
63 Vegetbl,Fruits&Othgrains	0	0	0	0	0	0
85 Industrial Crops	0	0	0	0	0	0
85 Livestock Breedng &Sericult.	0	0	0	0	0	0
66 Forestry Products	0	0	0	0	0	0
67 Fishery Products	0	0	259797	0	0	0
68 Coal	6058386	8481	0	0	0	0
69 Metallic Ores	0	0	0	281	177180	0
70 Non-Metallic Minerals	0	0	0	127	134064	0
71 Slaughter Dairy Fruit Proc.	0	0	0	114612	11707	0
72 Seafood Processing	0	0	0	0	0	0
73 Grain Polishing	0	0	0	0	0	0
74 Cereal Flours	0	0	0	0	0	0
75 Other Food Preparations	0	0	0	0	0	0
76 Beverages	0	0	0	0	0	0
77 Tobacco	0	0	0	0	0	0
78 Fibre Yarn	0	0	1355	0	0	0
79 Textile Fabrics	0	0	35212	0	0	214
80 Fabricated Textile Prods	0	0	27527	374	91	0
81 Leather & Leather Products	0	0	3527	0	0	0
82 Lumber and Plywood	0	0	0	0	0	0
83 Wood Products & Furniture	0	0	0	0	0	0
84 Pulp & Paper	0	0	483	0	0	0
85 Printing & Publishing	3593	0	0	0	0	0
86 Basic Organic Chemicals	175	0	2709	5838	153	817
87 Basic Inorganic Chemicals	0	0	2930	21848	1323	314
88 Chemical Fertilizers	0	0	0	0	0	0
89 Drugs & Cosmetics	0	0	0	0	0	0
90 Synth Resins,Rubber,Fibres	0	0	59807	2087	2119	367
91 Other Chemical Products	0	0	877	287	4525	1071
92 Petroleum Products	32171	2523	0	0	0	3862
93 Coal Products	20558	3932	0	0	0	4146
94 Rubber Products	0	3236	6708	405	0	1199
95 Non-Metallic Mineral Prods.	0	0	128	17688	38719	0
96 Pig Iron & Raw Steel	218	18	0	0	581640	295038
97 Primary Iron & Steel Prod.	188	0	0	0	162	690551
98 Non-F. Met.Ingots&Prim.P.	1175	0	0	0	236	166644
99 Fabricated Metal Products	4341	0	2770	3710	0	644
100 General Machinery	3322	513	9473	14188	3837	10784
101 Electrical Machinery	1791	0	1309	423	41306	2104

246

Input-Output Table of Republic of Korea for the Year 1975

KOREA RP. 1975   FLOWS in hundred thousand won of Y 1975   PRODUCERS CURRENT PRICES

INDUSTRY:	Petroleum Ref. 31 & Related Prods	Coal 32 Products	Rubber 33 Products	Non-Metallic 34 Mineral Prods	Pig Iron & 35 Raw Steel	Primary Iron & 38 Steel Products
02 Electronic & Commnc. Mach.	0	0	0	0	0	0
04 Transportation Equipment	0	0	0	0	0	0
05 Measrg.Medical,Optical Inst	778	214	1949	121	478	331
06 Misc.Manufacturing	0	0	0	0	0	0
07 Public Works& Oth.Constn	0	0	0	0	0	0
08 Electr.Power & Gas Svcs	0	0	0	0	0	0
09 Water Services	0	0	0	0	0	0
10 Wholesale & Retail Trade	0	0	0	0	0	0
11 Restaurant & Hotel Services	0	0	236	0	184	0
12 Transportation & Warehousing	2	0	5	2	0	0
13 Communications	0	0	0	0	0	0
14 Financing & Insurance	0	0	0	0	0	0
15 Real Estate	0	0	0	0	0	0
16 Government Services	0	0	0	0	0	0
17 Social Services	0	0	0	0	0	0
18 Other Services	0	0	719	0	0	0
19 Office Supplies	1031	0	590	337	15	184
20 Business Consumption	0	0	1243	1493	836	602
21 Unclassifiable						
122 Imported Intermediate Input	6127742	15915	541855	188202	1008773	1028852
123 Compet. Imports (cif & Dut)	64552	4911	205897	170000	829463	942084
124 Non-Comp. Imports (cif &Dut)	6063190	11004	335758	18202	179310	86768
125 Total Intermediate Input	6790887	908962	1437944	2141426	2252652	3820871
126 Compensation of Employees	190053	82238	217408	408890	95126	155408
127 Other Value Added	511772	71355	107129	480267	80389	217532
128 Consumption of Fixed Capital	311175	24397	54424	262125	51836	118172
129 Indir.Taxes Less Subsidies	1251256	16221	27446	111477	30139	56939
130 Total Value Added	2264856	174211	406205	1242759	257300	548051
131 Negative Flows from Quad.	0	0	0	0	0	0
132 Total Input	9055743	1081173	1844149	3384185	2509952	4368922

Input-Output Table of Republic of Korea for the Year 1975

KOREA RP. 1975   FLOWS in hundred thousand won of Y 1975   PRODUCERS CURRENT PRICES

INDUSTRY:	Non-Ferr. Metal Ingot &Prl.Prod 37	Fabricated Metal Products 38	General Machinery 39	Electrical Machinery 40	Electronic & Communic. Mach. 41	Transport Equipment 42
* DOMESTIC TRANSACTIONS						
INDUSTRY						
1 Rice, Barley, Wheat (pol)	0	3	1	9	0	0
2 Vegetab.Fruits &OthGrains	0	0	0	0	0	0
3 Industrial Crops	0	0	0	25	6	2
4 Livestck Breedng &Sericul s.	298	219	609	771	24	510
5 Forestry Products						
6 Fishery Products	0	0	4234	587	530	772
7 Coal	1961	3208	23	348	883	4
8 Metallic Ores	80037	1841	1356	4435		2264
9 Non-Metallic Minerals	391					0
10 Slaughter.Dairy.Fruit Proc.	0	0	0	0	4	
11 Seafood Processing	0	21	25	369	124	0
12 Grain Polishing	0	514	26	138		1
13 Cereal Flours	0	0	0	0	0	
14 Other Food Preparations	30				0	0
15 Beverages	0	0	0	0	0	0
16 Tobacco	0	0	0	0	0	0
17 Fibre Yarn	87	6385	84	2197	17	435
18 Textile Fabrics	16	6511	195	1180	242	1873
19 Fabricated Textile Products	586	485	1686	1680	3593	6177
20 Leather & Leather Products	724	8702	113	5715	2550	1351
21 Lumber and Plywood	231	4366	6318	202	9954	29265
22 Wood Products & Furniture	779	12015	1465	1499	22926	1691
23 Pulp & Paper	305	6150	5431	1666	24592	4090
24 Printing & Publishing	698	13319	1057	361	2287	3587
25 Basic Organic Chemicals	1567		568	4442	2754	1525
26 Basic Inorganic Chemicals			5322		5379	17825
27 Chemical Fertilizers	5					
28 Drugs & Cosmetics	214	8758	65	78183	21	118
29 Synth.Resins,Rubber,Fibres	547	13329	7601	8706	90074	12326
30 Other Chemical Products	1849	42574	6324	4637	16774	48680
31 Petroleum Products	1664	2285	29215	675	26820	39241
32 Coal Products	935	6486	4064	8665	234	193
33 Rubber Products	2067	15820	13766	4329	8390	63215
34 Non-Metallic Mineral Prods.	844		5797		18908	16099
35 Pig Iron & Raw Steel	2738	528307	309094	138650		40912
36 Pri.Iron.Met.Ingots&Prim.P.	129861	76449	51394	302467	57170	348763
37 Non-Ferr.Met.Metal Products	1318	43026	21545	37113	76478	20203
38 General Machinery	1470	1318	159936	20336	21995	66025
39 Electrical Machinery Mach.		7027	5225	170241	2766	165576
40 Electronic Machinery	1870	2504	22223	43796	404300	47129
41 Transportation&Commnc. Equipment	236	2893	2060		644299	7062
42 Transportation&Commnc.	250	607	2089	1910	3688	375845
43 Measrng.Medical.Optical Inst.		610	2984	2020	2351	4502
44 Misc.Manufacturing			572	2314	1065	852
45 Building Constn & Maint.			716		3210	1921
46 Public Works,Oth Constn.						
47 Electric Power & Gas Svcs.	49788	53774	26892	21549	42287	4978
48 Water Services	43996		844	1004	1066	5234
49 Wholesale & Retail Trade		127688	101676	14550	217700	254297
50 Restaurant & Hotel Services	127688	29040				41803
51 Transportation & Warehousing	8538	8445	23888	24971	35257	41803
52 Communication	1319		6148	5321	15257	12946

Input-Output Table of Republic of Korea for the Year 1975

KOREA RP. 1975   FLOWS in hundred thousand won of Y 1975   PRODUCERS CURRENT PRICES

INDUSTRY:	37 Non-Ferr. Metal Ingot &Pri.Prod	38 Fabricated Metal Products	39 General Machinery	40 Electrical Machinery	41 Electronic & Communic. Mach.	42 Transport Equipment
53 Financing & Insurance	11581	36103	44709	24443	3087	6611
54 Real Estate	282	1513	3353	2009	4158	3792
55 Government Services	954	1985	1639	1966	2373	3510
56 Social Services	788	8712	6800	15341	1080	13847
57 Other Services	720	2760	3397	3228	3235	8195
58 Office Supplies	8942	16385	25131	28582	58130	50391
59 Business Consumption	1598	1948	8157	8692		21632
60 Unclassifiable						
61 Domestic Intermediate Input	390353	1121181	945157	1210388	1535983	1890476

* IMPORT TRANSACTIONS *

	37	38	39	40	41	42
62 Rice, Barley, Wheat (pol)	0	0	0	0	0	0
63 Vegetab.Fruits.&OthGrains	0	0	0	0	0	0
64 Industrial Crops	0	0	42	24	0	0
65 Livestock Breeding &Sericult.	0	0	0	0	0	0
66 Forestry Products	0	0	0	0	0	1645
67 Fishery Products	0	0	0	0	0	0
68 Coal	0	0	0	0	0	0
69 Metallic Ores	50253	0	0	1412	4752	1474
70 Non-Metallic Minerals		3572	0	4828	0	0
71 Slaughter,Dairy,Fruit Proc.	0		0	0	0	0
72 Seafood Processing	0		0	0	0	0
73 Grain Polishing	0		0	0	0	0
74 Cereal Flours	0		0	0	0	0
75 Other Food Preparations	0		0	0	0	0
76 Beverages	0		0	0	0	0
77 Tobacco	0		0	0	0	0
78 Fibre Yarn		112	0	0	0	0
79 Textile Fabrics			469	1067	470	1501
80 Fabricated Textile Prods	0	217	0	0	848	213
81 Leather & Leather Products	0		0	0	580	20
82 Lumber and Plywood			0	0	0	0
83 Wood Products & Furniture	0		0	0	0	0
84 Pulp & Paper	0		0	1440	10906	0
85 Printing& Publishing	371	2372	347	765	843	42
86 Basic Organic Chemicals	21198	2813	1344	2417	2306	1617
87 Basic Inorganic Chemicals	0		0	0	2955	4252
88 Chemical Fertilizers			0	0	0	0
89 Drugs & Cosmetics	72	115	1870	26223	4843	7544
90 Synth.Resins,Rubber,Fibres	811	4844	1853	3189	7276	37353
91 Other Chemical Products		1632	442	19	43	2283
92 Petroleum Products	3482		3132	205		2297
93 Coal Products	9	28	2223		540	5542
94 Rubber Products	75	249	2671	12851		
95 Non-Metallic Mineral Prods.		2871	3430	9022	35476	28560
96 Pig Iron & Raw Steel Prods.		5503	45584	15280	6015	57508
97 Primary.Iron & Steel Prods.	223982	235240	19151	15101	60872	55601
98 Non-F.Met.Ingots &Prim.P.	286	72643	115608	87101	9328	18427
99 Fabricated Metal Products	3521	6621	9038	10348	49101	28509
100 General Machinery	3658					
101 Electrical Machinery					144542	
102 Electronic & Commnc. Mach.						
103 Transportation Equipment	0	0	159		0	280476

249

Input-Output Table of Republic of Korea for the Year 1975

KOREA RP. 1975

FLOWS in hundred thousand won of Y 1975

PRODUCERS CURRENT PRICES

INDUSTRY:	37 Non-Ferr.Metal Ingot &Pri.Prod	38 Fabricated Metal Products	39 General Machinery	40 Electrical Machinery	41 Electronic & Communic. Mach.	42 Transport Equipment
104 Measrg.Medical.Optical Inst	0	353	1407	5331	2928	11371
105 Misc.Manufacturing	0	0	0	0	0	0
106 Building Constrcn & Maint.	0	0	0	0	0	0
107 Public Works & Oth Constcn.	0	0	0	0	0	0
108 Electric Power & Gas Svcs.	0	0	0	0	0	0
109 Water Services	0	0	0	0	0	0
110 Wholesale & Retail Trade	0	174	0	0	0	0
111 Restaurant & Hotel Services	0	0	0	240	2215	498
112 Transportation & Warehousing	0	0	0	0	15	0
113 Communications	0	0	0	0	0	0
114 Financing & Insurance	0	0	0	0	0	0
115 Real Estate	0	0	0	0	0	0
116 Government Services	0	0	0	0	0	0
117 Social Services	0	0	0	0	0	0
118 Other Services	0	0	0	0	0	0
119 Office Supplies	0	210	102	322	525	0
120 Business Consumption	81	834	3538	2988	780	1183
121 Unclassifiable	685				2204	9272
122 Imported Intermediate Input	305480	352753	234771	301577	1695372	1048412
123 Compet. Imports (cif & Dut.)	283242	348658	207284	300297	1689359	985322
124 Non-Comp. Imports (cif &Dut)	22238	4095	27487	1280	26013	83090
125 Total Intermediate Input	695533	1473834	1179928	1511983	3231335	2938888
126 Compensation of Employees	89094	205435	252437	205214	433155	607188
127 Other Value Added	89651	162674	243527	180795	476838	400105
128 Consumption of Fixed Capital	32198	54852	64714	57339	171155	106238
129 Indir.Taxes Less Subsidies	20843	39014	33363	228213	307907	169228
130 Total Value Added	211786	461975	594041	675581	1389055	1282755
131 Negative Flows from Quad.	0	0	0	0	0	0
132 Total Input	907819	1935909	1773969	2187524	4820390	4221643

250

Input-Output Table of Republic of Korea for the Year 1975

INDUSTRY:

#	DOMESTIC TRANSACTIONS INDUSTRY	43 Measuring,Medic & Optical Inst.	44 Miscellaneous Manufacturing	45 Building Constr & Maintenance	46 Public Works &Oth.Construc.	47 Electric Power Gas Services	48 Water Services
1	Rice, Barley, Wheat(pol)	0	388	11760	1	0	0
2	Vegetab,Fruits &OthGrains	0	0	0	4405	0	0
3	Industrial Crops	2	1318	0	0	0	49
4	Livestck Breedng &Sericul s.	86	2632	28539	23506	9	64
5	Forestry Products	0	5215	514	0	0	0
6	Fishery Products	34	326	0	0	7329	0
7	Coal	0	0	0	0	0	0
8	Metallic Ores Minerals	0	0	0	0	0	0
9	Non-Metallic Minerals	1164	1969	109924	125655	205	333
10	Slaughter,Dairy,Fruit Proc.	0	0	0	0	0	0
11	Seafood Processing	0	0	0	0	0	0
12	Grain Polishing	0	163	0	0	0	0
13	Cereal Flours	0	30	0	0	0	20
14	Other Food Preparations	0	0	0	0	0	0
15	Beverages	0	0	0	0	0	0
16	Tobacco	0	0	0	0	0	0
17	Fibre Yarn	284	2290	897	211	9	0
18	Textile Fabrics	213	71436	3927	294	1350	229
19	Fabricated Textile Products	954	6372	4254	4254	29	5
20	Leather & Leather Products	3728	8772	701062	152499	342	8
21	Lumber and Plywood	3092	28914	11456	-1507	70	198
22	Wood Products & Furniture	3186	51067	107057	2848	2017	2266
23	Pulp & Paper	3641	3170	2730	2884	3879	5019
24	Printing & Publishing	2	18893	16897	1210	3908	0
25	Basic Organic Chemicals	11791	14218	9387	4	0	8
26	Basic Inorganic Chemicals	9258	178	0	39	48	866
27	Chemical Fertilizers	5410	184920	51176	8553	98	945
28	Drugs & Cosmetics	0	23305	87201	34465	474	3598
29	Synth.Resin,Rubber,Fibres	0	15775	47679	312324	134551	3524
30	Oth.Chemical Products	0	0	0	198	77	177
31	Petroleum Products	736	969	465	4168	123	1043
32	Coal Products	10584	11034	79752	41313	2013	0
33	Rubber Products	-1530	9832	1652783	-1228	1869	1737
34	Non-Metallic Mineral Prods.	24599	3932	-2957	449588	160	0
35	Pig Iron & Raw Steel	16702	33011	748260	25541	621	870
36	Primary Iron & Steel Prods.	959	74826	25021	133848	3785	2794
37	Non-F. Met Ingots &Prim P.	4745	49933	17461	205227	2116	2688
38	Fabricated Metal Products	7611	4253	130770	393897	374	44
39	General Machinery	12178	2651	-1336	23749	2436	413
40	Electrical Machinery	118	1957	2808	3809	165	1564
41	Electronic & Commnc. Mach.	218	1456	3921	1586	71	46
42	Transportation Equipment	0	0	433	307	6634	1247
43	Measr.Medical,Optical Inst.	0	2458	2092	845	0	0
44	Misc.Manufacturing	0	2382	0	0	0	0
45	Building Constcn & Maint.	5048	18839	10563	5373	17460	875516
46	Public Works&Oth. Constcn.	422	2353	1719	793	2558	6411
47	Electric Power & Gas Svcs.	31105	141666	499237	324924	274700	0
48	Water Services	0	0	0	0	0	0

Input-Output Table of Republic of Korea for the Year 1975

KOREA RP. 1975   FLOWS in hundred thousand won of Y 1975   PRODUCERS CURRENT PRICES

INDUSTRY:	43 Measuring,Medic & Optical Inst.	44 Miscellaneous Manufacturing	45 Building Constr & Maintenance	46 Public Works &oth Construc	47 Electric Power Gas Services	48 Water Services
51 Transportation & Warehousing	6837	23377	316835	280719	77247	2818
52 Communications	2338	4807	8827	7043	1293	1014
53 Financing & Insurance	12602	47611	137799	44081	71626	4697
54 Real Estate	907	9651	6645	3624	719	0
55 Government Services	0	0	0	0	0	0
56 Social Services	880	1724	5601	4466	400	3789
57 Other Services	7624	14094	15187	48229	3653	315
58 Office Supplies	1059	12425	13815	3195	1080	3908
59 Business Consumption	7764	20359	139344	107021	5903	227
60 Unclassifiable	179	7640	38224	23651	4598	0
61 Domestic Intermediate Input	204631	933824	521857	292448	1929867	116390

	43	44	45	46	47	48
62 Rice,Barley,Wheat (pol)	0	0	0	0	0	0
63 Vegetab,Fruits &Othgrains	0	0	0	0	0	0
64 Industrial Crops &Othgrains	0	0	0	0	0	0
65 Livestck Breedng &Sericult.	0	7466	25087	19774	0	0
66 Forestry Products	0	8089	0	0	0	0
67 Fishery Products	0	0	0	0	0	0
68 Metallic Ores	918	0	0	0	0	0
69 Non-Metallic Minerals	0	3533	314	0	0	0
70 Slaughter,Dairy,Fruit Proc.	0	0	0	0	0	0
71 Grain Processing	0	0	0	0	0	0
72 Seafood Processing	0	0	0	0	0	0
73 Cereal Flours	0	0	0	0	0	0
74 Other Food Preparations	0	0	0	0	0	0
75 Beverages	0	0	0	0	0	0
76 Tobacco	0	0	0	0	0	0
77 Fibre Yarn	441	1313	509	439	0	0
78 Textile Fabrics	0	7230	532	430	0	0
79 Fabricated Textile Prods	0	6109	215	0	0	0
80 Leather & Leather Products	0	57328	14	0	0	0
81 Lumber and Plywood	0	2023	0	0	0	0
82 Wood Products & Furniture	0	0	0	0	0	0
83 Pulp & Paper	1543	2752	0	0	1242	0
84 Printing & Publishing	470	1116	0	0	0	0
85 Basic Organic Chemicals	0	6364	0	0	0	4937
86 Basic Inorganic Chemicals	0	3805	0	0	0	0
87 Chemical Fertilizers	0	0	54197	2853	190142	0
88 Drugs & Cosmetics	7080	4531	0	9946	0	0
89 Other Chemical Products	69	8093	0	52	0	0
90 Synth.Resins,Rubber,Fibres	400	810	21859	42562	0	287
91 Petroleum Products	1117	5772	119810	103767	0	0
92 Coal Products	0	0	0	0	0	0
93 Rubber Products	1641	3330	47098	38643	101	0
94 Non-Metallic Mineral Prods.	7817	28130	24595	18841	2032	0
95 Pig Iron & Raw Steel	313	12136	53656	237938	2650	0
96 Primary Iron & Steel Prods.	75	240	0	0	0	0
97 Non-F.Met.Ingots&Prim.P.	23					

252

Input-Output Table of Republic of Korea for the Year 1975

KOREA RP. 1975

FLOWS in hundred thousand won of Y 1975

PRODUCERS CURRENT PRICES

INDUSTRY:	43 Measuring.Medic & Optical Inst.	44 Miscellaneous Manufacturing	45 Building Constr & Maintenance	46 Public Works &Oth.Construc.	47 Electric Power Gas Services	48 Water Services
102 Electronic & Commnc. Mach.	5448	280	108	24803	0	0
103 Transportation Equipment	0	0	0	0	0	0
104 Measrg,Medical,Optical Inst.	195137	0	0	0	0	1802
105 Misc.Manufacturing	265	8301	2394	574	0	0
106 Building Constn & Maint.	0	0	0	0	0	0
107 Public Works & Oth.Constcn.	0	0	0	0	0	0
108 Electric Power & Gas Svcs.	0	0	0	0	0	0
109 Water Services	0	0	0	0	0	0
110 Wholesale & Retail Trade	0	0	0	0	0	0
111 Restaurant & Hotel Services	348	518	0	0	104	0
112 Transportation & Warehousing	0	0	0	0	0	0
113 Communications	0	0	0	0	0	0
114 Financing & Insurance	0	0	0	0	0	0
115 Real Estate	0	0	0	0	0	0
116 Government Services	236	0	0	0	0	0
117 Social Services	0	0	0	0	0	0
118 Other Services	18	0	0	0	0	0
119 Office Supplies	77					
120 Business Consumption		215				
121 Unclassifiable	77	3276	14686	10139	1969	99
122 Imported Intermediate Input	235271	223815	366452	508752	198247	7125
123 Compet. Imports (cif & Dut;)	115587	136378	366443	506303	198059	7084
124 Non-Comp. Imports (cif &Dut)	119684	87737	9	2449	188	41
125 Total Intermediate Input	439902	1157439	5579309	3501200	2127514	123515
126 Compensation of Employees	66289	172992	1934767	1324958	273839	29219
127 Other Value Added	43300	346664	885310	588663	382424	36971
128 Consumption of Fixed Capital	6907	23062	53503	74851	253573	41314
129 Indir.Taxes Less Subsidies	21108	48527	136773	39717	154998	4
130 Total Value Added	137604	591245	3010353	2008187	1064834	107508
131 Negative Flows from Quad.	0	0	-2957	-2735	0	0
132 Total Input	577506	1748684	8589662	5509387	3192148	231023

253

Input-Output Table of Republic of Korea for the Year 1975

KOREA RP. 1975   FLOWS in hundred thousand won of Y 1975   PRODUCERS CURRENT PRICES

INDUSTRY:	49 Wholesale & Retail Trade	50 Restaurant & Hotel Services	51 Transportation & Warehousing	52 Communications	53 Financing Insurance	54 Real Estate
* DOMESTIC TRANSACTIONS *						
1 Rice, Barley Wheat (pol)	0	0	0	0	0	0
2 Vegetab.Fruits &Othgrains	5517	222	261	28	1020	0
3 Industrial Crops	0	330		10	2	0
4 Livestck Breedng &Sericul 9.	0		38	4	0	0
5 Forestry Products	0	499	753	0	0	0
6 Fishery Products	0		1614	0	0	0
7 Coal	0			0	0	0
8 Metallic Ores	1867			0	0	0
9 Non-Metallic Minerals	0			0	0	0
10 Slaughter.Dairy.Fruit Proc.	0			0	0	0
11 Seafood Processing	0			0	0	0
12 Grain Polishing	0			0	0	0
13 Cereal Flours	0			0	0	0
14 Other Food Preparations	9363	778		0	0	0
15 Beverages	0			0	0	0
16 Tobacco	0			0	0	0
17 Fibre Yarn	0		9	131	498	439
18 Textile Fabrics	31101	5290	1468	136	4031	
19 Fabricated Textile Products	81594	4087	31759	2863	46	
20 Leather & Leather Products	907	907	13033	279	656	918
21 Lumber and Plywood	15613	799	13081	313	4939	
22 Wood Products & Furniture	124485	1855	29995	293	7524	
23 Pulp & Paper	25952	8834	98	1378	524	1238
24 Printing & Publishing	83	5520	6665	13331	34	
25 Basic Organic Chemicals	1355	499	772			
26 Basic Inorganic Chemicals	0		3429			
27 Chemical Fertilizers	0		0			
28 Drugs & Cosmetics	858	1669		142	78	
29 Synth.Resins.Rubber.Fibres	9227	1382			709	
30 Other Chemical Products	14609	9788	202658	17	603	
31 Petroleum Products	113975	83638	2102659	295	30580	19578
32 Coal Products	68264	49628	13055	516	830	543
33 Rubber Products	40785	11326	224551	22657	484	
34 Non-Metallic Mineral Prods.	5916	11226	18366	763	344	
35 Pig Iron & Raw Steel	0		0	346		
36 Primary Iron & Steel Prods.	1361	68	12297	4821	65	428
37 Non-F.Met.Ingots &Prim.P.	0		1704	0		
38 Fabricated Metal Products	2538	491	28592	1792	16334	1774
39 General Machinery	15298	6914	150160	1579	85	
40 Electrical Machinery	33482	1837	11091	1018	1285	363
41 Electronic & Commnc. Mach.	33202	1120	380097	34232	3534	102
42 Transportation Equipment	2418		1232	9582	6513	2013
43 Misc.Manufacturing	32762	2555	5072	227	122	
44 Measg.Medical.Optical Inst.		28670	7962	169	288	474
45 Building Constrn & Maint.	0			8246	2390	
46 Public Works & Oth.Constcn.	0		0			460821
47 Electr.Power & Gas Svcs.	43185	72463	8894	10307	12755	24221
48 Water Services	16168	15318		840	2687	1508
49 Wholesale & Retail Trade	295344	49532	481106	23852	35037	9875
50 Restaurant & Hotel Services	0					
51 Transportation & Warehousing	367986	2023?	315358	19859	39781	2744
52 Communications	264410	54090	83832	393	61156	8584

254

Input-Output Table of Republic of Korea for the Year 1975

KOREA RP. 1975   FLOWS in hundred thousand won of Y 1975   PRODUCERS CURRENT PRICES

INDUSTRY:	49 Wholesale & Retail Trade	50 Restaurant & Hotel Services	51 Transportation & Warehousing	52 Communications	53 Financing Insurance	54 Real Estate
53 Financing & Insurance	250830	2424	11877	4645	55712	10458
54 Real Estate	216909	8331	31302	900	7207	8802
55 Government Services	0	0	0	0	0	0
56 Social Services	33302	6933	32865	281	16507	1273
57 Other Services	180424	1924	90375	6253	124818	4148
58 Office Supplies	11524	1231	6986	3179	5934	3170
59 Business Consumption	842917	59856	317532	29883	100249	18574
60 Unclassifiable	71384	20060	44424	7189	9692	2977
61 Domestic Intermediate Input	3308010	631595	4564911	216170	843885	581020
* IMPORT TRANSACTIONS *						
62 Rice Barley Wheat (pol)	0	0	0	0	0	0
63 Vegetabl.Fruits &OthGrains	0	0	0	0	0	0
64 Industrial Crops	0	0	0	0	0	0
65 Livestock Breedng &sericult.	0	0	0	0	0	0
66 Forestry Products	0	0	0	0	0	0
67 Fishery Products	0	0	0	0	0	0
68 Coal	0	0	0	0	0	0
69 Metallic Ores	0	0	0	0	0	0
70 Non-Metallic Minerals	0	0	0	0	0	0
71 Slaughter.Dairy Fruit Proc.	0	0	0	0	0	0
72 Seafood Processing	0	0	0	0	0	0
73 Grain Polishing	0	0	0	0	0	0
74 Cereal Flours	0	0	0	0	0	0
75 Other Food Preparations	0	0	0	0	0	0
76 Beverages	0	0	0	0	0	0
77 Tobacco	0	0	0	0	0	0
78 Fibre Yarn	5942	1871	2365	0	0	0
79 Textile Fabrics	23488	625	2520	773	829	0
80 Fabricated Textile Prods	0	0	0	0	0	0
81 Leather & Leather Products	0	0	0	0	0	0
82 Lumber and Plywood	0	152	0	0	0	0
83 Wood Products & Furniture	0	0	0	0	0	0
84 Pulp & Paper	9322	251	2134	1621	0	0
85 Printing & Publishing	3360	68	0	0	2787	0
86 Basic Organic Chemicals	0	0	0	0	0	0
87 Basic Inorganic Chemicals	0	0	0	0	0	0
88 Chemical Fertilizers	0	0	0	0	0	0
89 Drugs & Cosmetics	0	0	0	0	0	0
90 Synth.Resins,Rubber,Fibres	2899	2011	0	0	0	0
91 Other Chemical Products	6638	1500	5767	0	0	0
92 Petroleum Products	3312	0	374817	0	0	0
93 Coal Products	0	0	0	0	0	0
94 Rubber Products	359	247	4745	0	0	0
95 Non-Metallic Mineral Prods.	231	0	0	0	0	0
96 Pig Iron & Raw Steel	0	0	0	0	0	0
97 Primary Iron & Steel Prods.	0	0	0	0	0	0
98 Non-F. Met Ingots&Prim.P.	0	0	188	0	0	0
99 Fabricated Metal Products	324	384	26108	0	475	0
100 General Machinery	3649	518	2590	3838	145	0
101 Electrical Machinery	0	0	36494	18888	0	0
102 Electronic & Commnc. Mach.	0	0	0	0	0	0
103 Transportation Equipment	0	0	0	0	0	0

Input-Output Table of Republic of Korea for the Year 1975

KOREA RP. 1975

FLOWS in hundred thousand won of Y 1975

PRODUCERS CURRENT PRICES

INDUSTRY:	49 Wholesale & Retail Trade	50 Restaurant & Hotel Services	51 Transportation & Warehousing	52 Communications	53 Financing Insurance	54 Real Estate
104 Mesrg.Medical,Optical Inst	6280	0	314	307	0	0
105 Misc.Manufacturing	117	0	0	0	0	0
106 Building Constr.& Maint.	0	0	0	0	0	0
107 Public Works&Oth Consicn	0	0	0	0	0	0
108 Electric Power & Gas Svcs.	0	0	0	0	0	0
109 Water Services	0	0	0	0	0	0
110 Wholesale & Retail Trade	71390	0	0	0	0	0
111 Restaurant & Hotel Services	0	0	326024	0	1363	0
112 Transportation & Warehousing	23498	0	1054	0	328	0
113 Communications	1056	0	0	0	136128	0
114 Financing & Insurance	0	0	0	0		0
115 Real Estate	0	0	0	0	0	0
116 Government Services	0	0	0	0	0	0
117 Social Services	2781	0	0	0	0	0
118 Other Services	0	0	0	0	0	0
119 Office Supplies	0	0	0	0	0	0
120 Business Consumption	0	0	1055	0	0	0
121 Unclassifiable	30585	8597	19040	3081	4154	1278
122 Imported Intermediate Input	195411	16075	807464	28525	145990	1276
123 Compet. Imports (cif & Dut.)	195341	16075	786800	28234	145847	1278
124 Non-Comp. Imports(cif &Dut)	70	0	20864	281	143	0
125 Total Intermediate Input	3503421	647870	5372375	244695	789675	582298
126 Compensation of Employees	2364777	840191	1995093	416837	1183487	140853
127 Other Value Added	12652843	1367392	1781932	434922	885616	2070324
128 Consumption of Fixed Capital	505399	36980	1109675	93206	69347	373704
129 Indir.Taxes Less Subsidies	-147492	118411	216330	100894	160820	763101
130 Total Value Added	15375577	2168954	5087030	1045859	2299270	3347990
131 Negative Flows from Quad. 1	0	0	0	0	0	0
132 Total Input	18878998	2816824	10439405	1290554	3088945	3930288

Input-Output Table of Republic of Korea for the Year 1975

KOREA RP. 1975   FLOWS in hundred thousand won of Y 1975   PRODUCERS CURRENT PRICES

INDUSTRY:

	55 Government Services	58 Social Services	57 Other Services	58 Office Supplies	59 Business Consumption	60 Unclassifiable
DOMESTIC TRANSACTIONS * INDUSTRY						
1 Rice, Barley, Wheat (pol)	0	931	1117	0	50257	194408
2 Vegetab.Fruits.&OthGrains	0	406	1021	0	3070	3110
3 Industrial Crops	0	54034	103	0	4530	2345
4 Livestck Breedng &Sericul S.	0	6471	231	0	19186	3045
5 Forestry Products	0	2744	103	0	1229	4914
6 Fishery Products	0	48	0	0	8963	4096
7 Coal	0	2962	1727	0		3949
8 Metallic Ores	0	509		0	3009	
9 Non-Metallic Minerals	0	1070	157	0	86241	
10 Slaughter,Dairy Fruit Proc.	0	737		0	4934	
11 Seafood Processing	0	0	0	0	0	3117
12 Grain Polishing	0	-3	83	0	18129	21349
13 Cereal Flours	0	3590	2912	0	213325	52552
14 Other Food Preparations	0	279	530	0	900350	
15 Beverages	0	704	768	0	142829	17545
16 Tobacco	0	8152	14302	304		42699
17 Fibre Yarn	0	15138	3753		3347	10497
18 Textile Fabrics	0	37	888		170	17972
19 Fabricated Textile Products	0	6320	10818	183		
20 Leather & Leather Products	0	8065	1358	87008	468	10705
21 Lumber and Plywood	0	38051	3064	11893		981
22 Wood Products & Furniture	0	103950	21300		1190	11798
23 Pulp & Paper	0	5864	6838			6212
24 Printing & Publishing	0	3189	6		11494	13805
25 Basic Organic Chemicals	0	235205	61474		2053	12081
26 Basic Inorganic Chemicals	0	3706	13030	2189	9283	16719
27 Chemical Fertilizers	0	8342	5749			18410
28 Drugs & Cosmetics	0	125540	14221			37210
29 Synth.Resins,Rubber,Fibres	0	25689	3451	673	14720	3863
30 Other Chemical Products	0	14708	4425	89		22575
31 Petroleum Products	0		6498			17288
32 Coal Products	0	2189	3002			1552
33 Rubber Products	0	3982	85907	3003	718	3434
34 Non-Metallic Mineral Prods.	0	8943	1386	449		3583
35 Pig Iron & Raw Steel	0	3679	11908			13074
36 Primary Iron & Steel Prods.	0	10758	15312			12841
37 Non-F. Met.Ingots&Prim.P.	0	20541	21341			3747
38 Fabricated Metal Products	0	25538	3821	407	512	595
39 General Machinery	0	55618	6587	88892	12499	1581
40 Electrical Machinery	0	18418	24805			0
41 Electronic & Commnc. Mach.	0	155452				
42 Transportation Equipment	0					169
43 Measg.Medical,Optical Inst.	0	66848	64584			0
44 Misc.Manufacturing	0	14431	2488	32244	308202	88683
45 Building Constn.& Maint.	0	155288	94722	0	935033	25659
46 Public Works & Oth Constn.	0					
47 Electric Power & Gas Svcs.	0					
48 Water Service	0					
49 Wholesale & Retail Trade	0					
50 Restaurant & Hotel Services	0					

257

Input-Output Table of Republic of Korea for the Year 1975

KOREA RP. 1975   FLOWS in hundred thousand won of Y 1975   PRODUCERS CURRENT PRICES

INDUSTRY:	55 Government Services	56 Social Services	57 Other Services	58 Office Supplies	59 Business Consumption	80 Unclassifiable
51 Transportation & Warehousing	0	64234	47872	5530	174700	28822
52 Communication	0	56375	47908	0	0	9508
53 Financing & Insurance	0	20552	27088	0	0	984
54 Real Estate	0	43227	128747	0	0	0
55 Government Services	0	0	8048	0	0	0
56 Social Services	0	22262	340452	0	62991	1051
57 Other Services	0	57392	5307	0	4049	14334
58 Office Supplies	0	15946	78777	0	0	80597
59 Business Consumption	0	185047	27525	534	186114	0
60 Unclassifiable	0	48811				0
61 Domestic Intermediate Input	0	1888193	1497788	211358	3245087	858060

*   IMPORT   TRANSACTIONS   *

	55 Government Services	56 Social Services	57 Other Services	58 Office Supplies	59 Business Consumption	80 Unclassifiable
62 Rice, Barley, Wheat (pol)	0	8255	0	0	0	7445
63 Vegetab, Fruits & OthGrains	0	2619	0	0	0	9500
64 Industrial Crops	0	1451	0	0	0	9588
65 Livestock Breeding	0	6	0	0	0	1498
66 Forestry Products & sericult.	0	0	0	0	0	433
67 Fishery Products	0	0	0	0	0	0
68 Coal	0	0	0	0	0	0
69 Metallic Ores	0	65	0	0	0	1429
70 Non-Metallic Minerals	0	96	0	0	13209	6558
71 Slaughter, Dairy, Fruit Proc.	0	0	0	0	0	2102
72 Seafood Processing	0	0	0	0	0	0
73 Grain Polishing	0	0	317	0	217	0
74 Cereal Flours	0	0	0	0	0	0
75 Other Food Preparations	0	0	0	0	9785	753
76 Beverages	0	0	0	0	0	0
77 Tobacco	0	0	0	0	0	0
78 Fibre Yarn	0	2011	2488	288	870	155
79 Textile Fabrics	0	4775	200	0	2537	849
80 Fabricated Textile Prods	0	0	0	0	0	217
81 Leather & Leather Products	0	0	0	0	0	95
82 Lumber and Plywood	0	0	0	0	0	0
83 Wood Products & Furniture	0	0	0	0	0	370
84 Pulp & Paper	0	11575	845	881	0	156
85 Printing & Publishing	0	8331	2010	1415	0	6263
86 Basic Organic Chemicals	0	995	42	0	0	8613
87 Basic Inorganic Chemicals	0	236	31	0	0	7141
88 Chemical Fertilizers	0	0	774	0	0	4539
89 Drugs & Cosmetics	0	38156	2982	0	0	7478
90 Synth. Resins, Rubber, Fibres	0	18503	54555	290	1590	8603
91 Other Chemical Products	0	1140	0	0	0	0
92 Petroleum Products	0	0	68	0	0	531
93 Coal Products	0	573	1325	0	0	1441
94 Rubber Products	0	5349	0	0	0	0
95 Non-Metallic Mineral Prods.	0	0	0	0	0	9844
96 Pig Iron & Raw Steel	0	167	242	773	0	845
97 Primary Iron & Steel Prods.	0	807	1590	425	0	382
98 Non-F. Met. Ingots & Prim. P.	0	822	3314	0	0	2305
99 Fabricated Metal Products	0	2521	0	0	0	2305
100 General Machinery	0	0	0	0	0	2305
101 Electrical Machinery	0	0	0	0	0	8432

258

Input-Output Table of Republic of Korea for the Year 1975

KOREA RP. 1975   FLOWS in hundred thousand won of Y 1975   PRODUCERS CURRENT PRICES

INDUSTRY:	55 Government Services	56 Social Services	57 Other Services	58 Office Supplies	59 Business Consumption	60 Unclassifiable
102 Electronic & Commnc. Mach.	0	1554	24978		0	10976
103 Transportation Equipment	0		1655		0	2186
104 Measrg.Medical.Optical Inst.	0	24095	2827	415	1848	885
105 Misc. Manufacturing	0	4179	384	572	0	0
106 Building Constcn & Maint.	0	0	0	0	0	0
107 Public Works & Oth. Constcn	0	0	0	0	0	0
108 Electric Power & Gas Svcs.	0	0	0	0	0	0
109 Water Services	0	0	0	0	0	0
110 Wholesale & Retail Trade	0	0	0	0	0	0
111 Restaurant & Hotel Services	0	2018	8970	0	7350	0
112 Transportation & Warehousing	0		705	0	0	0
113 Communications	0	0	0	0	0	0
114 Financing & Insurance	0	0	0	0	0	0
115 Real Estate	0	0	1462	0	0	0
116 Government Services	0	0	0	0	0	0
117 Social Services	0	0	0	0	0	0
118 Other Services	0	0	0	0	0	0
119 Office Supplies	0	0	0	0	0	0
120 Business Consumption	0	20922	11798	229	73829	
121 Unclassifiable	0					
122 Imported Intermediate Input	0	171719	135318	5288	111327	120075
123 Compet. Imports (cif & Dut.)	0	149038	111057	5288		101310
124 Non-Comp. Imports (cif &Dut)	0	22680	24259		111327	18765
125 Total Intermediate Input	0	1857912	1633102	218648	3356414	978141
126 Compensation of Employees	3927625	3638384	1055272	0	0	184759
127 Other Value Added	64480	782459	1460487	0	0	88028
128 Consumption of Fixed Capital		314855	61059	0	0	0
129 Indir. Taxes Less Subsidies	7201	12272	203431	0	0	0
130 Total Value Added	3999306	4747870	2780229	0	0	272787
131 Negative Flows from Quad.	0	0	0	0	0	0
132 Total Input	3999306	6605882	4413331	218648	3356414	1250928

259

Input-Output Table of Republic of Korea for the Year 1975

KOREA RP. 1975

FLOWS in hundred thousand won of Y 1975

PRODUCERS CURRENT PRICES

*

DOMESTIC TRANSACTIONS *

INDUSTRY	Interm. Demand	61 Total Demand	62 Private Consump Expenditures	63 Govt. Consumptn Expenditures	84 Private Fixed Capital Formn	65 Govt. Fixed Capital Formn	66 Increase in Stocks
1 Rice,Barley,Wheat (po1)	1551485		12538841	24230	0	0	1207727
2 Vegetab(Fruits &OthGrains	607443		4316555	6394	0	0	90217
3 Industrial Crops	925739		2213914	3256	15396	2097	-55130
4 Livestck Breedng &Sericul S.	2836632		725109	70898	37382	4	-482439
5 Forestry Products	822883		326136	927	313186	1272	-29706
6 Fishery Products	524138		1442675	42872	0	0	
7 Coal	867028				0	0	836605
8 Metallic Ores	140443				0	0	21654
9 Non-Metallic Minerals	626294		7826	22706	0	0	-9923
10 Slaughter,Dairy;Fruit Proc.	197909		270626	6653	0	0	-7273
11 Seafood Processing	706472		220395	2065	0	0	4324
12 Grain Polishing	6415		356619		0	0	
13 Cereal Flours	7082865		505577	28777	0	0	-8639
14 Other Food Preparations	1700262		3437755	41039	0	0	17648
15 Beverages	1475431		2161590	188	0	0	22111
16 Tobacco	145803		2759152	127	0	0	8080
17 Fibre Yarn	5180345		10221	3839	6648	656	144172
18 Textile Fabrics	2641314		700389	6892	3143	0	143989
19 Fabricated Textile Products	6402360		3957044	2087	0	0	89383
20 Leather & Leather Products	426336		573314	26051	0	0	22479
21 Lumber and Plywood	1212067		3889	9061	5384	1435	24140
22 Wood Products & Furniture	1870060		86072	22070	0	0	4339
23 Pulp & paper	1942187		37625	153767	0	0	27103
24 Printing&Publishing	592187		305497	-1633	0	0	-4401
25 Basic Organic Chemicals	1203352		53	6356	0	0	24463
26 Basic Inorganic Chemicals	1995095			2338	0	0	2629
27 Chemical Fertilizers	938831		1179029	10009	0	0	209849
28 Drugs & Cosmetics	3758092		599397	34894	0	0	337193
29 Synth. Resins&Rubber,Fibres	1726670		368881	31125	0	0	92437
30 Other. Chemical Pproducts	7276076		209142	63299	0	0	22447
31 Petroleum Products	5770045		775457		0	0	75199
32 Coal Products	2515538		240447		0	0	2102
33 Rubber Products	3587641		318651		0	0	13156
34 Non-Metallic Mineral Prods.	1004867		-5176		0	0	53120
35 Pig Iron & Raw Steel	1069937				-3544	-10347	13080
36 Primary Iron & Steel Prods.	1024260		149323	5685	-11900	-231	30460
37 Non-Ferr. Met Ingots &Prim.P.	53569			1338	-52347	30283	-23189
38 Fabricated Metal Products	276802		490039	19556	879083	6148	6673
39 General Machinery	844502		906299	88097	2395105	752	49934
40 Electrical Machinery			155268		1723624	180087	32524
41 Electronic & Commnc. Mach			41731	100098	33464	109567	275078
42 Transportation Equipment			0	14357	9742	9875	9132
43 Measrg Medical.Optical Inst.						2627	1470
44 Misc.Manufacturing					6803907	97840	
45 Building Constcn & Maint.					2203532	291478	
46 Public Works & Oth. Constcn.							0
47 Electric Power & Gas Svcs	2368809		884104	3287	0	0	0
48 Water Services			64483	15114	0	0	
49 Wholesale & Retail Trade	8169744		7724098	233430	886270	87270	-9431
50 Restaurant & Hotel Services			1845249				0
51 Transportation & Warehousing	3145302		4239922	435054			
52 Communications	801346		327578	114850	32206	5805	90905

260

Input-Output Table of Republic of Korea for the Year 1975

KOREA RP. 1975   FLOWS in hundred thousand won of Y 1975   PRODUCERS CURRENT PRICES

	81 Interm. Total Demand	62 Private Consump Expenditures	63 Govt. Consumptn Expenditures	84 Private Fixed Capital Formn	65 Govt. Fixed Capital Formn	66 Increase in Stocks
53 Financing & Insurance	2273815	590410	143012	0	0	0
54 Real Estate	621313	2911128	12305	380972	0	0
55 Government Services	314210	3581534	399306	0	0	0
56 Social Services	1423035	2740530	2729401	0	0	0
57 Other Services	163344		201856	0	0	0
58 Office Supplies	3087196		51988	0	0	0
59 Business Consumption	777214		250142	0	0	0
60 Unclassifiable		-25079	35471	0	0	0
61 Domestic Intermediate Input	83830572	87063570	10217810	1379203	4412484	2341228

* IMPORT TRANSACTIONS *

	81 Interm. Total Demand	62 Private Consump Expenditures	63 Govt. Consumptn Expenditures	84 Private Fixed Capital Formn	65 Govt. Fixed Capital Formn	66 Increase in Stocks
62 Rice, Barley, Wheat (pol)	1767594	1424973	0	0	0	247081
63 Vegetab,Fruits &OthGrains	59191	15131	0	0	0	168634
64 Industrial Crops	1170159	406	0	0	0	168630
65 Livestck Breedng &Sericult.	165440	142	0	0	0	-32558
66 Forestry Products	1656432	5814	1405	5831	0	0
67 Fishery Products	137663	10416	0	0	0	-2892
68 Coal	185661		0	0	0	
69 Metallic Ores Minerals	187061		0	0	0	13592
70 Non-Metallic Minerals	6453093	119692	0	0	0	668
71 Slaughter,Dairy,Fruit Proc.	273327	13490	0	0	0	-8
72 Seafood Processing			0	0	0	
73 Grain Polishing	10	10614	403	0	0	-388
74 Cereal Flours	7534	14368	0	0	0	4786
75 Other Food Preparations	138635	24551	0	0	0	-94
76 Beverages	2644	1417	0	0	0	
77 Tobacco		1680	0	0	0	455
78 Fibre Yarn	179138		0	0	0	29283
79 Textile Fabrics	875802	84395	0	817	0	5538
80 Fabricated Textile Prods	138500	11750	289	1137	0	5305
81 Leather & Leather Products	299860	117508	148	0	0	5175
82 Lumber and Plywood	12450	1960	152	0	0	-40
83 Wood Products & Furniture		1778	586	1263	83	-244
84 Pulp & Paper	849370	18608	2739	0	0	-212
85 Printing Publishing	235773		733	0	0	-142
86 Basic Organic Chemicals	1842290		818	0	0	4294
87 Basic InOrganic Chemicals	342290		233	0	0	267774
88 Chemical Fertilizers	415530	414	3192	0	0	3538
89 Drugs & Cosmetics	161541	2688	936	0	0	9482
90 Synth. Resins Rubber,Fibres	980563	1526	16132	0	0	8120
91 Other Chemical Products	845263		13053	0	0	3518
92 Petroleum Products	924482			0	0	1822
93 Coal Products	627744			0	0	446
94 Rubber Products	366693	88	2868	0	0	4302
95 Non-Metallic Mineral Prods.	2212887	447	344	0	0	8057
96 Primary Iron & Raw Steel	5109033			0	0	-1292
97 Prim. Iron & Steel Prods.	15190033			0	0	-5960
98 Non-F. Met Ingots &Prim.P	2607608		1083	0	0	6078
99 Fabricated Metal Products	260099	19621	87058	25022	10115	24518
100 General Machinery	672991	157176	18070	3290530	80881	13157
101 Electrical Machinery	585761	17176	11437	3335873	7030	32473
102 Electronic & Commnc Mach.	1585761	48789	25554	3965579	88053	-2480
103 Transportation Equipment	3259935	11287		2345460	175858	

Input-Output Table of Republic of Korea for the Year 1975

KOREA RP. 1975   FLOWS in hundred thousand won of Y 1975   PRODUCERS CURRENT PRICES

	61 Total Demand Interm. Demand	82 Private Consump Expenditures	83 Govt. Consump'n Expenditures	84 Private Fixed Capital Formn	85 Govt. Fixed Capital Formn	86 Increase in Stocks
104 Measrg.Medical.Optical Inst.	262331	19490	5436	184457	25946	11601
105 Misc.Manufacturing	85361	48413	2298	2043	50	4157
106 Building Constrcn & Maint.	0	0	301	0	5075	0
107 Public Works & Oth.Constcn.	0	0	0	0	0	0
108 Electric Power & Gas Svcs.	0	0	2182	0	0	0
109 Water Services	0	0	755	0	0	0
110 Wholesale & Retail Trade	71390	0	0	0	0	0
111 Restaurant & Hotel Services	36935	17620	1337	0	0	0
112 Transportation & Warehousing	138610	10762	3565	0	0	0
113 Communications	0	0	3565	0	0	0
114 Financing & Insurance	0	0	6660	0	0	0
115 Real Estate	0	0	0	0	0	0
116 Government Services	22198	8713	913	0	0	0
117 Social Services	0	1346	449	0	0	0
118 Other Services	0	0	0	0	0	0
119 Office Supplies	0	0	0	0	0	0
120 Business Consumption	1943	0	71980	0	0	0
121 Unclassifiable	327504	23144	36758	0	0	0
122 Imported Intermediate Input	28852984	2146283	355583	8588806	391091	988661
123 Compet. Imports (cif & Dut.)	16034695	2128441	29091	5276283	228208	658185
124 Non-Comp. Imports (cif &Dut)	12818289	17842	60092	1312523	164883	310496
125 Total Intermediate Input	112683538	69209853	10573393	20382009	4803575	3309889
126 Compensation of Employees	31077571	0	0	0	0	
127 Other Value Added	52142888	0	0	0	0	
128 Consumption of Fixed Capital	7093700	0	0	0	0	
129 Indir.Taxes Less Subsidies	6906320	0	0	0	0	
130 Total Value Added	97220459	0	0	0	0	
131 Negative Flows from Quad. I	0.	0.	0.	0.	0.	
132 Total Input	209903995	69209853	10573393	20382009	4803575	3309889

Input-Output Table of Republic of Korea for the Year 1975

PRODUCERS CURRENT PRICES

KOREA RP. 1975   FLOWS in hundred thousand won of Y 1975

DOMESTIC TRANSACTIONS INDUSTRY	87 Exports	88 Final Total Demand	89 Negative Flows From Quad. 1	70 Total Output
1 Rice, Barley, Wheat (pol)	773	13711571	0	15323058
2 Vegetab Fruits &OthGrains	28189	4439355	0	5048798
3 Industrial Crops	418770	588303	0	1524042
4 Livestck Breedng &Sericul S.	17376	368330	0	3206962
5 Forestry Products	41896	691100	0	1613983
6 Fishery Products	1191959	2635581	0	3159699
7 Coal		184477	0	993505
8 Metallic Ores	162719	184373	-437	324816
9 Non-Metallic Minerals	101283	192692	0	2739906
10 Slaughter,Dairy Fruit Proc.	291470	2577579	0	881871
11 Seafood Processing	512448	875456	0	3104092
12 Grain Polishing		51227	0	1340892
13 Cereal Flours	512	4140697	0	5840898
14 Other Food Preparations	647455	2369047	0	2015750
15 Beverages	10578	2709527	0	6371397
16 Tobacco	1033507	2590922	0	9831553
17 Fibre Yarn	1594092	9101933	0	2232184
18 Textile Fabrics	5194163	1452828	0	2227781
19 Fabricated Textile Products	807164	1015554	0	391203
20 Leather & Leather Products	861474	207143	0	2149668
21 Lumber and & Plywood	849911	201784	-1507	1117694
22 Wood Pdoucrs & Furniture	120388	525507	0	1356175
23 Pulp&paper,Publishing	70644	152923	0	1240505
24 PrlPrtng and Publishing	125903	45470	0	1239680
25 Basic Organic Chemicals	149145	298349	0	1840569
26 Basic Inorganic Chemicals	1142	1320088	0	5216668
27 Chemical Fertilizers	35485	1460576	0	1658061
28 Drugs & Cosmetics	769408	431087	-2007	9055743
29 Synth Resins Rubber,Fibres	488	1278865	0	1061173
30 Other Chemical Products	567580	811128	0	1844149
31 Petroleum Products	1644	1274108	0	3364185
32 Coal Products	985234	606661	0	2509952
33 Rubber Products	451581	5286	0	4360922
34 Non-Metallic Mineral Prods.	32597	108128	-4185	807619
35 Pig Iron & Raw Steel	1038956	1563	0	1935909
36 Primary Iron & Steel Prods.	5286	831042	0	1773969
37 Non-F. Met. Ingots &Prim. P.	565578	1147046	0	2167524
38 Fabricated Metal Products	562607	1117527	0	4620590
39 General Machinery	1747640	3809433	0	4221643
40 Electrical Machinery	258668	3197434	0	577506
41 Electronic & Commnc. Mach.	2335382	523365	0	1748684
42 Transportation Equipment	831610	1471668	0	8589662
43 Measrg.Medical Optical Inst.	300131	7745160	0	5509387
44 Misc. Manufacturing	1017995	5509387	0	3191128
45 Building Constrn & Maint.			0	
46 Public Works & Oth. Constcn	62803	82652	0	
47 Electric Power & Gas Svcs.	10004		0	
48 Water Services	485		0	
49 Wholesale & Retail Trade	1780490	1071725	-63209	18873998
50 Restaurant & Hotel Services	210889	1855933	0	2816624

KOREA RP. 1975   FLOWS in hundred thousand won of Y 1975   PRODUCERS CURRENT PRICES

		67 Exports	88 Final Total Demand	69 Negative Flows From Quad	70 Total Output
51	Transportation & Warehousing	2506131	7284103	0	1043845
52	Communications	46778	489206	0	1290554
53	Financing & Insurance	81708	815130	0	3088895
54	Real Estate	24570	3308973	0	3930286
55	Government Services		3999306	0	3999306
56	Office Services	737	6291672	0	6605682
57	Office Supplies	47107	2990296	0	4413331
58	Business Consumption	19074	253002	0	4216646
59	Unclassifiable	46372	269218	0	3356414
60			473714	0	1250928
61	Domestic Intermediate Input	28245128	126073423	-75235	209903895

*   IMPORT   TRANSACTIONS   *

		67 Exports	88 Final Total Demand	69 Negative Flows From Quad	70 Total Output
62	Rice, Barley, Wheat (pol)	0	1672054	0	3439648
63	Vegetab,Fruits &OthGrains	0	16765	0	175556
64	Industrial Crops	0	189236	0	1339395
65	Livestck Breedng &Sericult.	0	-227309	0	163042
66	Forestry Products	0	25339	0	1631095
67	Fishery Products	0	10416	0	480709
68	Coal	0	-2708	0	182709
69	Metallic Ores Minerals	0	-2892	0	185253
70	Non-Metallic Minerals	0	133592	0	6586685
71	Slaughter,Dairy Fruit Proc.	0	13308	0	399995
72	Seafood Processing	0	13482	0	13493
73	Cereal Polishing	0		0	
74	Cereal Flours	0	14631	0	22165
75	Other Food Preparations	0	19074	0	1405379
76	Beverages	0	23610	0	50053
77	Tobacco	0	2144	0	1417
78	Fibre Yarn	0	14269	0	181263
79	Textile Fabrics	0	126618	0	790069
80	Fabricated Textile Prods	0	22025	0	251127
81	Leather & Leather Products	0	3321	0	321693
82	Lumber and Plywood	0	3500	0	12571
83	Wood Products & Furniture	0	-1502	0	3978
84	Pulp & Paper	0	18173	0	648848
85	Printing & Publishing	0	8117	0	46806
86	Basic Organic Chemicals	0	267977	0	1855352
87	Basic Inorganic Chemicals	0	210877	0	340020
88	Chemical Fertilizers	0	37239	0	663327
89	Drugs & Cosmetics	0	39519	0	172283
90	Synth. Resins,Rubber,Fibres	0	10622	0	1017283
91	Other Chemical Products	0	3160	0	841076
92	Petroleum Products	0	5093	0	9169
93	Coal Products	0	8057	0	308873
94	Rubber Products	0	-2292	0	228352
95	Non-Metallic Mineral Prods.	0	-4877	0	809944
96	Pig Iron & Raw Steel	0		0	152125
97	Primary Iron & Steel Prods.	0		0	567731
98	Non-F. Met.Ingots &Prim.P	0	63106	0	323285
99	Fabricated Metal Products	0	3498702	0	4171693
100	General Machinery	0	391900	0	912660
101	Electrical Machinery	0		0	

Input-Output Table of Republic of Korea for the Year 1975

KOREA RP. 1975

FLOWS in hundred thousand won of Y 1975

#	Sector	67 Exports	68 Final Total Demand	69 Negative Flows From Quad.	70 Total Output
102	Electronic & Commnc. Mach.	0	575333	0	2181094
103	Transportation Equipment	0	2555678	0	2881614
104	Measrg.Medical.Optical Inst.	0	248930	0	509261
105	Misc.Manufacturing	0	56961	0	142328
106	Building Constcn & Maint.	0	5378	0	5378
107	Public Works & Oth.Constcn.	0		0	0
108	Electric Power & Gas Svcs.	0	2182	0	2182
109	Water Services	0	755	0	755
110	Wholesale & Retail Trade	0	17623	0	71390
111	Restaurant & Hotel Services	0	24135	0	24973
112	Transportation & Warehousing	0	3565	0	394071
113	Communications	0	341	0	137375
114	Financing & Insurance	0	8660	0	136470
115	Real Estate	0		0	8660
116	Government Services	0	6713	0	6713
117	Social Services	0	2259	0	2449
118	Other Services	0	449	0	449
119	Office Supplies	0	71880	0	91449
120	Business Consumption	0	59902	0	387406
121	Unclassifiable	0		0	
		0	10450424	0	38303388
122	Imported Intermediate Input	0	8584188	0	24618883
123	Compet. Imports (cif & Dut.)	0	1886636	0	14884505
124	Non-Comp. Imports (cif &Dut)			-75235	
125	Total Intermediate Input	2845128	136523847	-75235	249207383
126	Compensation of Employees	0	0	0	0
127	Other Value Added	0	0	0	0
128	Consumption of Fixed Capital	0	0	0	0
129	Indir.Taxes Less Subsidies	0	0	0	0
130	Total Value Added	0	0	0	0
131	Negative Flows from Quad.	0	0	75235	0
132	Total Input	2845128	136523847	0	249207383

SENEGAL (1959)

Reference year: 1959

Entries in table: Domestic flows, import matrix

Source: Sénégal, Ministère de l'économie et des finances, Direction de la statistique, Tableau d'échanges interindustriels—année 1959, Tableau No. 27

Computerized: Not available

Currency units: CFA francs of Y 1959
Scale factor: 1,000,000,000

Pricing system: Producers' current prices
Intermediate sectors: 18 × 18
Treatment of trade margins: Not available (inputs row 18 = commercial services)

Treatment of imports: Import matrix
Availability of import matrix: Available

Total number of rows: 44
Statistical unit of quadrant 1: Industry

Total number of columns: 44
Statistical unit of quadrant 1: Industry

Fourth quadrant: Not occupied

Input-Output Table of Senegal for the Year 1959

SENEGAL 1959   FLOWS in billions of CFA francs of Y 1959   PRODUCERS CURRENT MARKET PRICES

INDUSTRY:	1 Agriculture and Fisheries	2 Fats	3 Grain and Flour	4 Sugar Refining and Beverages	5 Livestock(Meat) & Canning	6 Energy
* DOMESTIC TRANSACTIONS * INDUSTRY						
1 Agriculture and Fisheries	3.74	13.23	1.43	0.00	2.96	0.00
2 Fats	0.00	0.19	0.00	0.00	0.00	0.00
3 Grain and Flour	0.00	0.00	0.20	0.00	0.00	0.00
4 Sugar Refining and Beverages	0.00	0.00	0.00	0.00	0.00	0.00
5 Livestock (Meat) & Canning	0.00	0.00	0.00	0.00	0.00	0.00
6 Energy	0.36	0.31	0.05	0.06	0.02	0.23
7 Mining	0.00	0.00	0.00	0.00	0.00	0.00
8 Chemical Industry	0.00	0.00	0.00	0.00	0.00	0.00
9 Construction Materials	0.08	0.03	0.02	0.02	0.05	0.03
10 Metal Products	0.04	0.00	0.00	0.00	0.00	0.03
11 Wood and Furniture	0.00	0.00	0.00	0.00	0.00	0.00
12 Textiles and Leather	0.07	0.01	0.04	0.00	0.01	0.00
13 Tabacco and Matches	0.00	0.01	0.03	0.01	0.00	0.00
14 Polygraph Industries & Other	0.08	0.00	0.00	0.00	0.02	0.01
15 Construction & Public Works	0.01	0.00	0.03	0.01	0.06	0.04
16 Transport	0.01	0.41	0.14	0.01	0.10	0.04
17 Services	0.22	2.54	0.51	0.05	0.89	0.45
18 Commercial Services				0.11		
19 Total Domestic Inputs	4.80	17.94	3.57	0.28	4.22	0.82
* IMPORT TRANSACTIONS *						
20 Agriculture and Fisheries	0.01	0.00	2.39	0.14	1.84	0.00
21 Fats	0.00	0.00	0.00	0.00	0.00	0.00
22 Grain and Flour	0.00	0.00	0.00	0.00	0.00	0.00
23 Sugar Refining and Beverages	0.00	0.56	0.16	0.05	0.00	0.00
24 Livestock (Meat) & Canning	0.00	0.00	0.07	0.74	0.00	0.00
25 Energy	0.00	0.04	0.05	0.01	0.01	0.22
26 Mining	0.08	0.05	0.05	0.01	0.00	0.00
27 Chemical Products	0.07	0.05	0.02	0.05	0.00	0.00
28 Construction Materials	0.00	0.00	0.00	0.00	0.00	0.00
29 Metal Products	0.03	0.00	0.00	0.00	0.00	0.00
30 Wood and Furniture	0.00	0.10	0.04	0.00	0.00	0.00
31 Textiles and Leather	0.04	0.00	0.04	0.00	0.00	0.00
32 Tabacco and Matches	0.00	0.00	0.00	0.00	0.00	0.00
33 Polygraph Industries & Other	0.00	0.00	0.02	0.02	0.00	0.00
34 Construction						
35 Transport	0.00	0.00	0.00		0.00	
36 Services						
37 Total Imported Inputs	0.23	0.75	2.75	1.01	1.85	0.22
38 Wages of Migrants	0.00	0.00	0.00	0.00	0.00	0.24
39 Wages of Africans	0.00	0.45	0.16	0.00	0.07	0.20
40 Import-Export Taxes	0.00	0.97	0.30	0.20	0.15	0.06
41 Other Indiris Taxes - Subsid.	0.00	0.00	0.05	0.04	0.04	1.71
42 Gross Profits	34.57	1.50	0.93	0.47	0.32	
43 Gross Value Added	34.57	3.67	1.57	0.81	0.58	2.21
44 Total Inputs	39.40	22.36	7.89	2.10	6.45	3.25

267

Input-Output Table of Senegal for the Year 1959

SENEGAL 1959 — FLOWS in billions of CFA francs of Y 1959 — PRODUCERS CURRENT MARKET PRICES

INDUSTRY:	7 Mining	8 Chemical Industry	9 Construction Materials	10 Metal Products	11 Wood and Furniture	12 Textiles and Leather
* DOMESTIC TRANSACTIONS *						
1 Agriculture and Fisheries	0.00	0.04	0.00	0.00	0.10	0.03
2 Fats	0.000	0.000	0.000	0.000	0.000	0.000
3 Grain and Flour	0.000	0.000	0.000	0.000	0.000	0.000
4 Sugar Refining and Beverages	0.00-	0.00-	0.00	0.000	0.00	0.00
5 Livestock (Meat) & Canning	0.000	0.000	0.002	0.002	0.002	0.000
6 Energy	0.01	0.01	0.02	0.00	0.02	0.09
7 Mining	0.000	0.04	0.000	0.000	0.000	0.000
8 Chemical Industry	0.000	0.05	0.02	0.06	0.04	0.04
9 Construction Materials	0.00-	0.000	0.03	0.00	0.00-	0.00
10 Metal Products	0.000	0.000	0.02	0.18	0.09	0.08
11 Wood and Furniture	0.00	0.000	0.000	0.000	0.00	0.00-
12 Textiles and Leather	0.000	0.000	0.04	0.01	0.01	0.06
13 Tabacco and Matches	0.00	0.00	0.00	0.02	0.000	0.000
14 Polygraph Industries & Other	0.00	0.01	0.04	0.02	0.01	0.02
15 Construction & Public Works	0.00	0.01	0.01	0.00	0.01-	0.06
16 Transport	0.12	0.02	0.07	0.02	0.08	0.11
17 Services	0.18	0.06	0.24	0.37	0.28	0.21
18 Commercial Services	0.10					
19 Total Domestic Inputs	0.54	0.24	0.57	0.71	0.74	0.66
* IMPORT TRANSACTIONS *						
20 Agriculture and Fisheries	0.000	0.000	0.000	0.05	0.14	0.49
21 Fats	0.000	0.000	0.000	0.000	0.000	0.000
22 Grain and Flour	0.000	0.000	0.000	0.000	0.000	0.000
23 Sugar Refining and Beverages	0.000	0.00	0.00	0.02	0.00	0.00
24 Livestock (Meat) & Canning	0.03	0.01	0.11	0.00	0.06	0.01-
25 Energy	0.01	0.15	0.03	0.00	0.03	0.00
26 Mining	0.000	0.000	0.000	0.00	0.00-	0.13
27 Chemical Products	0.08	0.000	0.000	0.59	0.00	0.000
28 Construction Materials	0.01-	0.000	0.000	0.00	0.08	0.82
29 Metal Products	0.00	0.000	0.02	0.00	0.00	0.02
30 Wood and Furniture						
31 Textiles and Leather						
32 Tabacco and Matches						
33 Polygraph Industries & Other						
34 Construction	0	0	0	0	0	0
35 Transport						
36 Services						
37 Total Imported Inputs	0.11	0.16	0.16	0.66	0.32	1.47
38 Wages of Migrants	0.16	0.05	0.25	0.30	0.16	0.23
39 Wages of Africans	0.22	0.05	0.25	0.25	-.13	0.36
40 Import-Export Taxes	-.05	0.01	0.06	0.07	-.00	0.05
41 Other Indir. Taxes - subsid.	-.31	0.02	0.11	0.51	0.16	3.15
42 Gross Profits						
43 Gross Value Added	0.02	0.13	0.87	1.13	0.50	3.95
44 Total Inputs	0.67	0.53	1.40	2.50	1.56	6.08

268

Input-Output Table of Senegal for the Year 1959

SENEGAL 1959

FLOWS in billions of CFA francs of Y 1959

PRODUCERS CURRENT MARKET PRICES

INDUSTRY:	13 Tabacco Polygraph Matches	14 Polygraph Indus & Other	15 Construction & Public Works	16 Transport	17 Services	18 Commercial Services
DOMESTIC TRANSACTIONS						
1 Agriculture and Fisheries	0.00	0.00	0.00	0.00	0.02	0.00
2 Fats	.00	.00	.00	.00	.01	.00
3 Grain and Flour	.00	.00	.00	.00	.00	.00
4 Sugar Refining and Beverages	.00	.00	.00	.00	.04	.00
5 Livestock (Meat) & Canning	.00	.01	.06	.09	.07	.07
6 Energy	.00	.00	.00	.00	.00	.00
7 Mining	.00	.00	.00	.00	.00	.00
8 Chemical Industry	.00	.01	.18	.00	.02	.20
9 Construction Materials	.00	.00	.28	-.15	.02	.01
10 Metal Products	.00	.00	.43	.00	.00	.06
11 Wood and Furniture	.00	.00	.12	.00	.00	.02
12 Textiles and Leather	.01	.00	.00	.05	.05	.05
13 Tabacco and Matches	.00	.00	.02	.00	.23	.82
14 Polygraph Industries & Other	.02	.00	2.01	.17	.00	.01
15 Construction & Public Works	.04	.01	.55	.27	.75	3.76
16 Transport	.00	.07	.64	.32	.33	.31
17 Services	.02	.09	.14			
18 Commercial Services						
19 Total Domestic Inputs	0.09	0.19	6.43	3.16	2.88	9.26
IMPORT TRANSACTIONS						
20 Agriculture and Fisheries	0.18	.00	.00	.00	.03	.00
21 Fats	.00	.00	.00	.00	.00	.00
22 Grain and Flour	.00	.00	.00	.00	.00	.00
23 Sugar Refining and Beverages	.00	.00	.00	.00	.01	.00
24 Livestock (Meat) & Canning	.00	.00	.00	.00	.00	.15
25 Energy	.03	.00	.10	.57	.05	.00
26 Mining	.00	.00	.00	.00	.00	.09
27 Chemical Products	.00	.01	.47	.08	.05	.01
28 Construction Materials	.08	.00	.25	.00	.02	.01
29 Metal Products	.00	.00	.42	.24	.00	.00
30 Wood and Furniture	.00	.00	2.00	.00	.00	.00
31 Textiles and Leather	.01	.00	.00	.00	.00	.04
32 Tabacco and Matches	.00	.00	.02	.04	.03	
33 Polygraph Industries & Other		.34				
34 Construction			.00			
35 Transport			.00	.00	.00	
36 Services						
37 Total Imported Inputs	0.30	0.35	2.46	0.93	0.31	0.39
38 Wages of Migrants	.06	.18	2.15	1.58	2.22	3.02
39 Wages of Africans	.05	.13	2.42	.71	.89	3.46
40 Import-Export Taxes	.04	.00	.00	-.01	.00	15.11
41 Other Indir. Taxes - Subsid	.34	.03	.44	-.2	.55	2.63
42 Gross Profits		.17	3.13	2.47	10.58	13.08
43 Gross Value Added	1.49	0.49	8.14	5.83	14.24	38.30
44 Total Inputs	1.88	1.03	17.03	9.72	17.43	47.95

269

Input-Output Table of Senegal for the Year 1959

SENEGAL 1959   FLOWS in billions of CFA francs of Y 1959   PRODUCERS CURRENT MARKET PRICES

	19 Total Intmdt. Consumption	20 African Househ Consumption Dom	21 European Househ Consumption Dom	22 Government Consumption Dom	23 Stocks Domestic Dom	24 Gross Fixed Cap Formation Dom
DOMESTIC TRANSACTIONS — INDUSTRY						
1 Agriculture and Fisheries	21.55	16.20	0.05	0.52	0.00	0.00
2 Fats	0.21	2.32	0.03	0.05	0.00	0.00
3 Grain and Flour	0.22	4.32	-0.03	-0.03	0.00	0.00
4 Sugar Refining and Beverages	0.04	4.50	0.24	-0.09	-0.02	0.00
5 Livestock (Meat) & Canning	0.07	0.80	0.42	0.49	-0.01	0.00
6 Energy	0.54	0.06	0.00	0.00	0.00	0.00
7 Mining	0.05				0.00	0.00
8 Chemical Industry	0.23	0.13	0.00	0.00	0.00	0.00
9 Construction Materials	0.40	0.00	0.00	0.00	0.00	0.00
10 Metal Products	1.43	0.00	0.21	0.00	0.00	0.42
11 Wood and Furniture	0.35	0.74	0.20	0.25	0.12	0.27
12 Textiles and Leather	0.25	5.26	0.39	0.33	0.00	0.00
13 Tabacco and Matches	0.00	1.08	0.00	0.58	0.00	0.40
14 Polygraph Industries & Other	0.31	0.55	0.39	0.83	0.00	0.00
15 Construction & Public Works	3.50	0.00	0.00	0.51	0.00	10.40
16 Transport	5.69	1.32	0.80	0.90	0.00	0.00
17 Services	9.87	3.22	2.93			1.88
18 Commercial Services	9.19	15.33	7.35			
19 Total Domestic Inputs	56.90	59.00	14.79	7.69	0.15	12.97
IMPORT TRANSACTIONS						
20 Agriculture and Fisheries	5.07	3.49	1.00	0.15	0.00	0.00
21 Fats	0.58	0.09	0.15	0.02	0.00	0.00
22 Grain and Flour	0.93	3.65	0.91	0.05	0.00	0.00
23 Sugar Refining and Beverages	0.01	0.00	0.45	0.01	0.00	0.00
24 Livestock (Meat) & Canning	0.12	0.31	0.19	0.02	0.07	0.00
25 Energy	0.52	0.00	0.02	0.29	0.09	0.00
26 Mining	0.00	0.00	0.00	0.00	0.00	0.00
27 Chemical Products	0.27	0.44	0.88	0.00	0.04	4.39
28 Construction Materials	0.25	0.00	0.40	0.00	0.00	0.00
29 Metal Products	2.39	0.00	2.07	0.00	0.05	4.00
30 Wood and Furniture	0.10	2.43	0.42	0.22	0.00	0.00
31 Textiles and Leather	0.00	0.00				
32 Tabacco and Matches	0.58	0.00				
33 Polygraph Industries & Other						
34 Construction						
35 Transport						
36 Services						
37 Total Imported Inputs	14.23	12.81	6.78	1.36	0.25	4.39
38 Wages of Migrants	1.34	0.00	0.00	0.00	0.00	0.00
39 Wages of Africans	2.77	0.00	0.00	0.00	0.00	0.00
40 Import-Export Taxes	15.11	0.00	0.00	0.00	0.00	0.00
41 Other Indir Taxes - Subsid.	5.86	0.00	0.00	0.00	0.00	0.00
42 Gross Profits	73.22					
43 Gross Value Added	118.10	0.00	0.00	0.00	0.00	0.00
44 Total Inputs	189.23	0.00	0.00	0.00	0.00	0.00

270

Input-Output Table of Senegal for the Year 1959

SENEGAL 1959   FLOWS in billions of CFA francs of Y 1959   PRODUCERS CURRENT MARKET PRICES

* DOMESTIC TRANSACTIONS *

INDUSTRY	25 Exports	26 Adjustment	27 Total Fin.Dmnd. Domestic	28 African Househ. Consumption Imp	29 European Househ. Consumption Imp	30 Government Consumption Imp
1 Agriculture and Fisheries	0.93	0.00	17.85	3.49	1.00	0.15
2 Fats	19.62	0.000	22.15	3.09	0.15	0.02
3 Grain and Flour	2.22	0.000	6.67	3.00	0.91	0.10
4 Sugar Refining and Beverages	2.56	0.000	2.06	0.31	0.45	0.05
5 Livestock (Meat) & Canning	0.84	0.000	6.38	0.00	0.02	0.01
6 Energy	0.00	0.000	0.62	0.10	0.10	0.12
7 Mining	0.55	0.000	0.30	0.44	0.00	0.29
8 Chemical Industry	0.17	0.000	0.07	0.00	0.88	0.40
9 Construction Materials	0.00	0.000	1.21	1.00	0.04	0.00
10 Metal Products	0.44	0.000	5.83	2.43	2.40	0.00
11 Wood and Furniture	0.00	0.000	1.88	0.00	0.07	0.22
12 Textiles and Leather	0.32	0.000	0.72	0.00	0.42	0.00
13 Tabacco and Matches	0.68	0.000	13.53	0.00	0.00	0.00
14 Polygraph Industries & Other	0.00	0.000	7.56	0.00	0.00	0.00
15 Construction & Public Works	0.00	0.000	38.76	0.00	0.00	
16 Transport	0.00	0.000				
17 Services	0.00	-0.100				
18 Commercial Services	11.70	0.00				
19 Total Domestic Inputs	37.83	-0.10	132.33	12.61	6.78	1.36

* IMPORT TRANSACTIONS *

	25 Exports	26 Adjustment	27 Total Fin.Dmnd. Domestic	28	29	30
20 Agriculture and Fisheries	0.67	0.000	5.31	0.000	0.000	0.000
21 Fats	1.59	0.000	1.85	0.000	0.000	0.000
22 Grain and Flour	0.09	0.000	3.99	0.000	0.000	0.000
23 Sugar Refining and Beverages	2.42	0.000	4.36	0.000	0.000	0.000
24 Livestock (Meat) & Canning	0.21	0.000	0.98	0.000	0.000	0.000
25 Energy	4.93	0.000	5.41	0.000	0.000	0.000
26 Mining	0.00	0.000	0.02	0.000	0.000	0.000
27 Chemical Products	0.90	0.000	0.34	0.000	0.000	0.000
28 Construction Materials	0.34	0.000	0.32	0.000	0.000	0.000
29 Metal Products	2.51	0.000	0.13	0.000	0.000	0.000
30 Wood and Furniture	0.09	0.000	8.24	0.000	0.000	0.000
31 Textiles and Leather	3.36	0.000	0.12	0.000	0.000	0.000
32 Tabacco and Matches	0.05	0.000	0.88	0.000	0.000	0.000
33 Polygraph Industries & Other	0.26	-0.02		0.000	0.000	0.000
34 Construction	0	0	0	0	0	0
35 Transport						
36 Services						
37 Total Imported Inputs	17.42	-.02	42.79	0.00	0.00	0.00
38 Wages of Migrants	0.00	0.000	0.000	0.00	0.000	0.000
39 Wages of Africans	0.00	0.000	0.000	0.00	0.000	0.000
40 Import Export Taxes	0.00	0.000	0.000	0.00	0.000	0.000
41 Other Export Taxes - Subsid	0.00	0.000	0.000	0.00	0.000	0.000
42 Gross Profits	0.00	0.000	0.000	0.00	0.000	0.000
43 Gross Value Added	0.00	0.00	0.00	0.00	0.00	0.00
44 Total Inputs	0.00	0.00	0.00	0.00	0.00	0.00

Input-Output Table of Senegal for the Year 1959

SENEGAL 1959   FLOWS in billions of CFA francs of Y 1959   PRODUCERS CURRENT MARKET PRICES

		31 Stocks Imported Goods	32 Gross Fixed Cap Form. Imported Goods	33 Re-Exports of Imported Goods	34 Adjustment	35 Total Fin. Dmnd. Imported Goods	36 African Househ. Consumption All
*	DOMESTIC TRANSACTIONS *						
	INDUSTRY						
1	Agriculture and Fisheries	0.000	0.000	0.67	0.000	5.31	19.69
2	Fats	0.000	0.000	0.59	0.000	1.85	2.52
3	Grain and Flour	0.000	0.000	2.42	0.000	3.99	7.38
4	Sugar Refining and Beverages	0.000	0.000	0.00	0.000	4.98	4.81
5	Livestock (Meat) & Canning	0.007	0.000	4.03	0.000	0.41	0.90
6	Energy	0.009	0.000	0.00	0.000	5.02	0.06
7	Mining	0.000	0.000	0.34	0.000	0.82	0.57
8	Chemical Industry	0.009	0.000	2.09	0.000	0.34	0.02
9	Construction Materials	0.004	4.39	0.34	0.000	9.32	0.10
10	Metal Products	0.005	0.000	0.09	0.000	0.13	0.74
11	Wood and Furniture	0.000	0.000	3.08	0.000	0.24	7.69
12	Textiles and Leather	0.000	0.000	3.05	0.000	0.08	1.08
13	Tabacco and Matches	0.000	0.000	0.28	-0.02	0.12	0.55
14	Polygraph Industries & Other	0.000	0.000	0.00	0.000	0.86	1.40
15	Construction & Public Works	0.000	0.000	0.00	0.000	0.00	0.00
16	Transport	0.000	0.000	0.00	0.000	0.00	3.22
17	Services	0.000	0.000	0.00	0.000	0.00	15.93
18	Commercial Services	0.00	0.00	0.00	0.00	0.00	
19	Total Domestic Inputs	0.25	4.39	17.42	-0.02	42.79	71.61
*	IMPORT TRANSACTIONS *						
20	Agriculture and Fisheries	0.000	0.000	0.000	0.000	0.000	0.000
21	Fats	0.000	0.000	0.000	0.000	0.000	0.000
22	Grain and Flour	0.000	0.000	0.000	0.000	0.000	0.000
23	Sugar Refining and Beverages	0.000	0.000	0.000	0.000	0.000	0.000
24	Livestock (Meat) & Canning	0.000	0.000	0.000	0.000	0.000	0.000
25	Energy	0.000	0.000	0.000	0.000	0.000	0.000
26	Mining	0.000	0.000	0.000	0.000	0.000	0.000
27	Chemical Products	0.000	0.000	0.000	0.000	0.000	0.000
28	Construction Materials	0.000	0.000	0.000	0.000	0.000	0.000
29	Metal Products	0.000	0.000	0.000	0.000	0.000	0.000
30	Wood and Furniture	0.000	0.000	0.000	0.000	0.000	0.000
31	Textiles and Leather	0.000	0.000	0.000	0.000	0.000	0.000
32	Tabacco and Matches	0.000	0.000	0.000	0.000	0.000	0.000
33	Polygraph Industries & Other	0.000	0.000	0.000	0.000	0.000	0.000
34	Construction	0.000	0.000	0.000	0.000	0.000	0.000
35	Transport	0.000	0.000	0.000	0.000	0.000	0.000
36	Services	0.000	0.000	0.000	0.000	0.000	0.000
37	Total Imported Inputs	0.00	0.00	0.00	0.00	0.00	0.00
38	Wages of Migrants	0.000	0.000	0.000	0.000	0.000	0.000
39	Wages of Africans	0.000	0.000	0.000	0.000	0.000	0.000
40	Import-Export Taxes	0.000	0.000	0.000	0.000	0.000	0.000
41	Other Indir. Taxes - Subsid.	0.000	0.000	0.000	0.000	0.000	0.000
42	Gross Profits	0.000	0.000	0.000	0.000	0.000	0.000
43	Gross Value Added	0.00	0.00	0.00	0.00	0.00	0.00
44	Total Inputs	0.00	0.00	0.00	0.00	0.00	0.00

Input-Output Table of Senegal for the Year 1959

SENEGAL 1959   FLOWS in billions of CFA francs of Y 1959   PRODUCERS CURRENT MARKET PRICES

	37 European Househ Consumption All	38 Government Consumption All	39 Stocks Origines All	40 Gross Fixed Cap Form. -All Gds	41 Exports All Origines	42 Adjustment
* DOMESTIC TRANSACTIONS *						
INDUSTRY						
1 Agriculture and Fisheries	1.20	0.67	0.00	0.00	21.60	0.00
2 Fats	0.07	0.07	0.00	0.00	21.21	0.00
3 Grain and Flour	0.18	0.20	0.00	0.00	2.31	0.00
4 Sugar Refining and Beverages	1.00	0.08	0.02	0.00	2.98	0.00
5 Livestock (Meat) & Canning	1.57	0.11	0.07	0.00	0.85	0.00
6 Energy	0.61	0.61	0.01	0.00	4.93	0.00
7 Mining	0.02	0.00	0.09	0.00	0.55	0.00
8 Chemical Industry	0.10	0.29	0.00	0.00	1.07	0.00
9 Construction Materials	0.00	0.00	0.04	4.81	0.34	0.00
10 Metal Products	0.09	0.40	0.00	4.27	2.95	0.00
11 Wood and Furniture	0.24	0.00	0.05	0.00	0.09	0.00
12 Textiles and Leather	2.40	0.25	0.12	0.00	3.88	0.00
13 Tabacco and Matches	0.07	0.00	0.00	0.00	0.73	0.00
14 Polygraph Industries & Other	0.81	0.55	0.00	0.00	0.26	-0.02
15 Construction & Public Works	0.00	1.58	0.00	10.40	0.00	0.00
16 Transport	0.80	0.83	0.00	0.00	0.00	-0.00
17 Services	2.93	1.51	0.00	0.00	11.70	0.00
18 Commercial Services	7.35	1.90	0.00	1.88		-0.10
19 Total Domestic Inputs	21.57	9.05	0.40	17.36	55.45	-0.12
* IMPORT TRANSACTIONS *						
20 Agriculture and Fisheries	0.000	0.000	0.000	0.000	0.000	0.000
21 Fats	0.000	0.000	0.000	0.000	0.000	0.000
22 Grain and Flour	0.000	0.000	0.000	0.000	0.000	0.000
23 Sugar Refining and Beverages	0.000	0.000	0.000	0.000	0.000	0.000
24 Livestock (Meat) & Canning	0.000	0.000	0.000	0.000	0.000	0.000
25 Energy	0.000	0.000	0.000	0.000	0.000	0.000
26 Mining	0.000	0.000	0.000	0.000	0.000	0.000
27 Chemical Products	0.000	0.000	0.000	0.000	0.000	0.000
28 Construction Materials	0.000	0.000	0.000	0.000	0.000	0.000
29 Metal Products	0.000	0.000	0.000	0.000	0.000	0.000
30 Wood and Furniture	0.000	0.000	0.000	0.000	0.000	0.000
31 Textiles and Leather	0.000	0.000	0.000	0.000	0.000	0.000
32 Tabacco and Matches	0.000	0.000	0.000	0.000	0.000	0.000
33 Polygraph Industries & Other	0.000	0.000	0.000	0.000	0.000	0.000
34 Construction	0.000	0.000	0.000	0.000	0.000	0.000
35 Transport	0.000	0.000	0.000	0.000	0.000	0.000
36 Services	0.000	0.000	0.000	0.000	0.000	0.000
37 Total Imported Inputs	0.00	0.00	0.00	0.00	0.00	0.00
38 Wages of Migrants	0.000	0.000	0.000	0.000	0.000	0.000
39 Wages of Africans	0.000	0.000	0.000	0.000	0.000	0.000
40 Import-Export Taxes	0.000	0.000	0.000	0.000	0.000	0.000
41 Other Indir Taxes - Subsid.	0.000	0.000	0.000	0.000	0.000	0.000
42 Gross Profits	0.000	0.000	0.000	0.000	0.000	0.000
43 Gross Value Added	0.00	0.00	0.00	0.00	0.00	0.00
44 Total Inputs	0.00	0.00	0.00	0.00	0.00	0.00

Input-Output Table of Senegal for the Year 1959

SENEGAL 1959   FLOWS in billions of CFA francs of Y 1959

PRODUCERS CURRENT MARKET PRICES

	43 Total Fin.Dmnd. All Origines	44 Total Domestic Outputs
* DOMESTIC TRANSACTIONS *		
INDUSTRY		
1 Agriculture and Fisheries	23.16	39.40
2 Fats	24.00	22.36
3 Grain and Flour	10.66	7.89
4 Sugar Refining and Beverages	6.44	2.10
5 Livestock (Meat) & Canning	7.36	6.45
6 Energy	7.12	3.25
7 Mining	0.64	0.67
8 Chemical Industry	2.12	0.53
9 Construction Materials	0.34	1.40
10 Metal Products	20.39	2.50
11 Wood and Furniture	1.34	1.56
12 Textiles and Leather	14.27	6.08
13 Tabacco and Matches	2.00	.88
14 Polygraph Industries & Other	1.60	1.03
15 Construction & Public Works	13.53	17.03
16 Transport	4.03	9.72
17 Services	7.56	17.43
18 Commercial Services	38.76	47.95
19 Total Domestic Inputs	175.32	189.23
* IMPORT TRANSACTIONS *		
20 Agriculture and Fisheries	0.00	0.00
21 Fats	0.00	0.00
22 Grain and Flour	0.00	0.00
23 Sugar Refining and Beverages	0.00	0.00
24 Livestock (Meat) & Canning	0.00	0.00
25 Energy	0.00	0.00
26 Mining	0.00	0.00
27 Chemical Products	0.00	0.00
28 Construction Materials	0.00	0.00
29 Metal Products	0.00	0.00
30 Wood and Furniture	0.00	0.00
31 Textiles and Leather	0.00	0.00
32 Tabacco and Matches	0.00	0.00
33 Polygraph Industries & Other	0.00	0.00
34 Construction	0.00	0.00
35 Transport	0.00	0.00
36 Services	0.00	0.00
37 Total Imported Inputs	0.00	0.00
38 Wages of Migrants	0.00	0.00
39 Wages of Africans	0.00	0.00
40 Import-Export Taxes	0.00	0.00
41 Other Indir. Taxes - Subsid.	0.00	0.00
42 Gross Profits	0.00	0.00
43 Gross Value Added	0.00	0.00
44 Total Inputs	0.00	0.00

SENEGAL (1974)

Reference year: 1974

Entries in table: Domestic flows,

Source: Sénégal, Ministère de l'économie et des finances, Direction de la statistique

Computerized: Deutsches Institut für Wirtschaftsforschung, Berlin

Currency units: CFA francs of Y 1974
Scale factor: 1,000,000

Pricing system: Producers' current prices
Intermediate sectors: 26 × 26
Treatment of trade margins: Inputs row 26 = Trade

Treatment of imports: Imports row 28
Availability of import matrix: Not available

Total number of rows: 34
Statistical unit of quadrant 1: Industry

Total number of columns: 29
Statistical unit of quadrant 1: Industry

Fourth quadrant: Not occupied

Input-Output Table of Senegal for the Year 1974

SENEGAL 1974   FLOWS in millions of CFA francs of Y 1974   PRODUCERS CURRENT PRICES

INDUSTRY: DOMESTIC TRANSACTIONS INDUSTRY	Agriculture 1	Livestock 2	Fishing Forestry 3	Mining Industry 4	Freezing, Pres. of Fish 5	Misc. Food Industries 6
1 Agriculture	3731	800	0	0	0	74
2 Livestock	274	5160	0	0	0	290
3 Fishing Forestry	11	230	0	2	5513	0
4 Mining Industries	0	0	2	0	0	0
5 Freezing, Preserv. of Fish	0	0	228	78	0	0
6 Misc. Food Industries	0	280	0	0	27	23
7 Fats and Vegetable Oils	0	0	0	0	122	0
8 Grain and Flour Processing	0	240	0	0	0	0
9 Sugar, Confectionary Prods.	0	0	0	0	0	0
10 Beverages	0	0	0	0	20	215
11 Tobacco and Matches	0	0	0	0	6	0
12 Textiles	45	0	293	0	40	0
13 Wrg. Apparel - Leather Tan.	13	0	85	0	0	0
14 Wood	68	0	5	50	0	0
15 Paper, Paperboard	0	0	0	0	0	0
16 Polygraphics	0	0	0	0	0	0
17 Chemicals	644	0	1536	592	82	134
18 Construction Materials	45	0	267	200	210	1
19 Machinery	114	0	100	990	168	5
20 Energy	137	300	25	1	0	298
21 Miscellaneous Manufacturing	30	0	38	8	34	5
22 Construction, Public Works	45	0	45	0	0	18
23 Hotels	0	0	0	0	8	14
24 Transport & Communications	210	100	1098	1955	458	474
25 Other Services	206	42	1652	1860	248	235
26 Trade	252	90	346	130	290	74
27 Total Domest. Intmdt. Inputs	5825	7012	5721	4699	7041	1858
28 Total Import. Intmdt. Inputs	794	360	1380	1572	493	1493
29 Compensation of Employees	480	1180	4868	1497	1080	710
30 Indirect Taxes less Subsid.	-240	20	382	1106	268	171
31 Interest	-1290	0	556	-12	198	130
32 Operating Surplus	38648	18728	17394	18899	354	-78
33 Gross Value Added	37598	19928	23200	21490	1900	933
34 Gross Output	44215	27300	30301	27781	9434	4284

Input-Output Table of Senegal for the Year 1974

SENEGAL 1974 FLOWS in millions of CFA francs of Y 1974 PRODUCERS CURRENT PRICES

INDUSTRY:

DOMESTIC TRANSACTIONS	7 Fats and Vegetable Oils	8 Grain and Flour Processing	9 Sugar, Cnfctry Industry	10 Beverages	11 Tobacco and Matches	12 Textiles
1 Agriculture	13180	0	86	0	112	1117
2 Livestock	0	4	0	0	0	0
3 Fishing Forestry	0	44	0	0	0	0
4 Mining Industries	0	7	0	0	0	0
5 Freezing, Preserv. of Fish	0	0	0	0	0	0
6 Misc. Food Industries	20	0	0	0	0	0
7 Fats and Vegetable Oils	0	1344	0	0	0	0
8 Grain and Flour Processing	0	116	70	0	0	0
9 Sugar, Confectionary Prods.	0	0	0	130	0	0
10 Beverages	0	0	0	0	0	0
11 Tobacco and Matches	0	0	0	0	0	0
12 Textiles	0	0	0	0	0	2168
13 Wrg. Apparel - Leather Tan.	0	0	0	0	0	0
14 Wood	0	22	0	0	0	0
15 Paper, Paperboard	37	103	11	5	5	5
16 Polygraphics	33	96	0	2	4	10
17 Chemicals	2	36	300	10	1	579
18 Construction Materials	51	0	0	0	0	10
19 Machinery	90	119	19	30	25	0
20 Energy	89	39	15	0	9	467
21 Miscellaneous Manufacturing	3	14	0	4	8	0
22 Construction, Public Works	0	5	0	0	0	19
23 Hotels	42	3	0	0	0	11
24 Transport & Communications	2089	303	206	82	145	719
25 Other Services	813	173	80	54	118	183
26 Trade	4399	100	31	15	0	868
27 Total Domest. Intmdt. Inputs	20848	2528	818	332	427	8151
28 Total Import. Intmdt. Inputs	684	4510	5728	348	673	3590
29 Compensation of Employees	2042	703	1310	444	375	1878
30 Indirect Taxes less Subsid.	12327	400	-1422	784	1520	1781
31 Interest	377	61	352	21	32	214
32 Operating Surplus	8955	800	169	279	459	3737
33 Gross Value Added	23701	1964	409	1528	2386	7590
34 Gross Output	45231	9000	6955	2208	3488	17331

Input-Output Table of Senegal for the Year 1974

SENEGAL 1974   FLOWS in millions of CFA francs of Y 1974   PRODUCERS CURRENT PRICES

INDUSTRY:

* DOMESTIC TRANSACTIONS

INDUSTRY	13 Wrg. Apparel - Leather Tanning	14 Wood	15 Paper Paperboard	16 Polygraphics	17 Chemicals	18 Construction Materials
1 Agriculture	0	0	0	0	0	0
2 Livestock	0	0	0	0	0	0
3 Fishing Forestry	0	0	0	0	0	0
4 Mining Industries	0	0	0	0	616	26
5 Freezing Preserv. of Fish	0	0	0	0	0	0
6 Misc. Food Industries	0	0	0	0	0	0
7 Fats and Vegetable Oils	0	0	0	0	0	0
8 Grain and Flour Processing	0	0	0	0	0	0
9 Sugar, Confectionary Prods.	0	0	0	0	0	0
10 Beverages	0	0	0	0	0	0
11 Tobacco and Matches	0	0	0	0	0	0
12 Textiles	79	0	0	0	105	0
13 Wrg. Apparel - Leather Tan.	60	0	0	0	0	0
14 Wood	0	170	0	0	0	0
15 Paper, Paperboard	1	0	3	75	31	0
16 Polygraphics	5	0	10	4	13	0
17 Chemicals	16	23	4	8	221	0
18 Construction Materials	6	40	8	24	302	708
19 Machinery	91	18	2	6	132	175
20 Energy	39	16	5	4	10	473
21 Miscellaneous Manufacturing	7	2	0	0	51	19
22 Construction. Public Works	5	0	0	0	12	5
23 Hotels	0	0	0	0	0	0
24 Transport & Communications	145	218	286	99	625	265
25 Other Services	182	122	60	112	450	242
26 Trade	9	72	3	33	65	85
27 Total Domest. Intmdt. Inputs	645	681	422	365	2633	1998
28 Total Import. Intmdt. Inputs	1095	1103	606	821	18177	811
29 Compensation of Employees	880	577	158	360	1054	551
30 Indirect Taxes less Subsid.	492	326	229	213	938	520
31 Interest	122	42	17	5	234	70
32 Operating Surplus	231	859	268	341	2946	947
33 Gross Value Added	1725	1804	672	919	5172	2088
34 Gross Output	3465	3588	1700	2105	25982	4895

Input-Output Table of Senegal for the Year 1974

SENEGAL 1974   FLOWS in millions of CFA francs of Y 1974   PRODUCERS CURRENT PRICES

INDUSTRY:

* DOMESTIC TRANSACTIONS *

INDUSTRY	19 Machinery	20 Energy	21 Miscellaneous Manufacturing	22 Construction; Public Works	23 Hotels	24 Transport and Communications
1 Agriculture	0	0	0	0	70	0
2 Livestock	0	0	0	0	115	0
3 Fishing Forestry	0	0	0	0	0	0
4 Mining Industries	0	0	0	0	0	117
5 Freezing, Preserv. of Fish	0	0	0	0	40	0
6 Misc. Food Industries	0	0	0	0	120	0
7 Fats and Vegetable Oils	0	0	0	0	0	0
8 Grain and Flour Processing	0	0	0	0	0	0
9 Sugar, Confectionary Prods.	0	0	0	0	0	0
10 Beverages	0	0	0	0	90	0
11 Tobacco and Matches	11	0	0	0	0	0
12 Textiles	0	0	0	0	0	0
13 Wrg. Apparel - Leather Tan.	18	0	0	0	32	12
14 Wood	69	100	0	17	0	0
15 Paper, Paperboard	5	0	0	0	0	0
16 Polygraphics	341	4	0	20	27	4305
17 Chemicals	7	1440	18	967	48	10
18 Construction Materials	72	350	0	3195	9	0
19 Machinery	18	40	37	1108	0	9
20 Energy	45	326	2	527	370	332
21 Miscellaneous Manufacturing	0	13	0	0	65	159
22 Construction, Public Works	0	24	0	90	0	0
23 Hotels	0	0	0	14	0	23
24 Transport & Communications	440	307	107	1510	238	1276
25 Other Services	347	573	0	2323	346	2703
26 Trade	91	150	4	1184	310	668
27 Total Domest. Intmdt. Inputs	1425	3327	172	10955	1880	9814
28 Total Import. Intmdt. Inputs	4501	666	627	7544	416	1685
29 Compensation of Employees	1406	2210	176	4113	1324	9507
30 Indirect Taxes less Subsid.	205	1284	176	1871	546	2698
31 Operating Surplus	1857	1853	170	7720	782	12066
32 Gross Value Added	3466	5647	489	13704	2687	24271
34 Gross Output	9382	9640	1288	32203	4983	35550

Input-Output Table of Senegal for the Year 1974

SENEGAL 1974   FLOWS in millions of CFA francs of Y 1974   PRODUCERS CURRENT PRICES

INDUSTRY:

* DOMESTIC TRANSACTIONS *

INDUSTRY	Other Services 25	Trade 26	Total Intmdt Consumption 27	Total Final Demand 28	Gross Output 29
1 Agriculture	0	0	19170	25045	44215
2 Livestock	0	0	5843	21457	27300
3 Fishing Forestry	0	0	5598	24703	30301
4 Mining Industries	0	0	1088	26673	27761
5 Freezing, Preserv. of Fish	0	0	40	9394	9434
6 Misc. Food Industries	0	0	678	3606	4284
7 Fats and Vegetable Oils	0	0	143	45088	45231
8 Grain and Flour Processing	0	0	1584	7416	9000
9 Sugar, Confectionary Prods.	0	0	534	6421	6955
10 Beverages	0	0	90	2118	2208
11 Tobacco and Matches	0	0		3486	3486
12 Textiles	0	0	2795	14536	17331
13 Wrg. Apparel - Leather Tan.	0	0	137	3348	3485
14 Wood	0	162	406	3102	3508
15 Paper, Paperboard	0	55	655	1045	1700
16 Polygraphics	0	438	201	1904	2105
17 Chemicals	588	22	13140	12842	25982
18 Construction Materials	15	495	3898	997	4895
19 Machinery	271	55	2507	6885	9392
20 Energy	518	465	5851	3789	9640
21 Miscellaneous Manufacturing		114	221	1047	1268
22 Construction. Public Works	492		1615	30588	32203
23 Hotels	131		482	4501	4983
24 Transport & Communications	1352	4801	19401	16149	35550
25 Other Services	3609	4535	20375	16060	36435
26 Trade	214	168	9425	70196	79621
27 Total Domest. Intmdt. Inputs	7186	11310	115877	362476	478353
28 Total Import. Intmdt. Inputs	2509	925	63091	0	63091
29 Compensation of Employees	5728	10212	53528	0	53528
30 Indirect Taxes less Subsid.	2525	14807	43187	0	43187
31 Interest	-5422	3150	2101	0	2101
32 Operating Surplus	23909	39217	200569	0	200569
33 Gross Value Added	26740	67386	299385	0	299385
34 Gross Output	36435	79621	478353	362476	840829

SRI LANKA (aggregated)

Reference year: 1970

Entries in table: Domestic flows

Source: ILO-UNDP Special Fund Project, ILO Research Team, 1973

Computerized: UNIDO

Currency units: Rupees of Y 1970
Scale factor: 1,000,000

Pricing system: Producers' current prices
Intermediate sectors: 20 × 20
Treatment of trade margins: Inputs row 15 = Trade

Treatment of imports: Imports c.i.f. row 22
 Import duties row 23
Availability of import matrix: Not available

Total number of rows: 28
Statistical unit of quadrant 1: Industry

Total number of columns: 28
Statistical unit of quadrant 1: Industry

Fourth quadrant: Occupied

Aggregated scheme for Sri Lanka (1970)

Aggregated sector	*Original sector*	*Aggregated sector*	*Original sector*
1. Agriculture	1. Tea 2. Rubber 3. Coconut 4. Paddy 5. Livestock 6. Fish 7. Logging and firewood 8. Other agriculture	8. Petroleum refineries	28. Petroleum and coal products
		9. Non-metallic mineral products	29. Structural clay products 30. Ceramics, glass and pottery 31. Cement and cement products
2. Mining and quarrying	9. Mining and quarrying	10. Basic metal industries	32. Basic metals
3. Manufacture of food	10. Rice and grinding mills 11. Flour mill 12. Dairy products 13. Bread 14. Other bakery and confect products 15. Carbonated beverages 16. Desiccated coconut and copra 17. Other processed food 18. Distilling of spirits etc. 19. Tobacco products	11. Metal products, machinery	33. Light engineering 34. Transport equipment 35. Machinery and other equipment
		12. Other manufacturing	36. Other manufactures n.e.s.
		13. Electricity, gas and steam	38. Electricity
		14. Construction	37. Construction
		15. Trade (distribution)	41. Wholesale trade 42. Retail trade
4. Textiles, clothing	20. Textiles 23. Leather and leather products 27. Coconut fibre and yarn	16. Restaurants and hotels	45. Hotels and restaurants
		17. Transport and storage	39. Road passenger transport 40. Rail transport 43. Other transport
5. Wood and wood products	21. Wood products	18. Communications	44. Communications
6. Paper, printing	22. Paper, printing and publishing	19. Finance, insurance	46. Professional services 47. Dwellings
7. Chemicals	24. Rubber products 25. Chemicals and chemical products 26. Oils and fats	20. Public services	48. Other services n.e.s.

Aggregated Input-Output Table of Sri Lanka for the Year 1970

SRI LANKA 1970   FLOWS in millions of rupees of Y 1970   PRODUCERS CURRENT PRICES

INDUSTRY:	Agriculture 1	Mining and Quarrying 2	Manufacture of Food 3	Textiles, Clothing 4	Wood and Wood Products 5	Paper, Printing 8
* DOMESTIC TRANSACTIONS *						
INDUSTRY						
1 Agriculture	177	2	1316	17	19	4
2 Mining and Quarrying	1	0	0	0	0	1
3 Manufacture of Food	0	0	33	0	0	0
4 Textiles,Clothing	15	0	0	26	0	0
5 Wood and Wood Products	26	0	5	3	80	0
6 Paper,Printing	12	0	5	5	0	0
7 Chemicals	10	0	19	30	0	8
8 Petroleum Refineries	0	0	4	0	0	3
9 Non-metallic Mineral prod.	0	0	0	0	0	0
10 Basic Metal Industries	0	5	0	6	0	0
11 Metal Products,Machinery	55	0	13	0	0	4
12 Other Manufacturing	0	0	0	5	0	0
13 Electricity, Gas and Steam	7	3	6	2	0	2
14 Construction	0	0	0	0	0	0
15 Trade (distribution)	55	3	81	21	26	7
16 Restaurants and Hotels	0	0	0	0	0	0
17 Transport and Storage	42	3	52	1	14	4
18 Communications	9	0	0	0	0	0
19 Finance, Insurance	0	0	0	0	0	0
20 Public Services	23	0	4	0	0	0
21 Total Intmdt Domestic Inputs	552	18	1535	101	122	34
22 Imports cif (inputs)	179	3	207	129	2	23
23 Import Duties	-4	-8	33	9	0	15
24 Imports incl. Duties	175	-5	240	138	2	38
25 Indirect Taxes less Subsid.	33	0	258	2	0	3
26 Other Value Added	4034	95	354	217	113	82
27 Gross Value added	4067	95	810	219	113	85
28 Gross Output	4794	108	2385	458	237	157

Aggregated Input-Output Table of Sri Lanka for the Year 1970

SRI LANKA 1970　　　　FLOWS in millions of rupees of Y 1970　　　　PRODUCERS CURRENT PRICES

INDUSTRY:	7 Chemicals	8 Petroleum Refineries	9 Non-metallic Mineral Prod.	10 Basic Metal Industries	11 Metal Products, Machinery	12 Other Manufacturing
* DOMESTIC TRANSACTIONS * INDUSTRY						
1 Agriculture	8	0	2	0	0	0
2 Mining and Quarrying	188	0	20	0	0	0
3 Manufacture of Food	1	0	0	0	0	0
4 Textiles, Clothing	3	0	0	0	0	0
5 Wood and Wood Products	16	0	1	0	1	1
6 Paper, Printing	36	0	0	0	2	2
7 Chemicals	3	0	0	0	5	0
8 Petroleum Refineries	0	168	3	0	2	0
9 Non-metallic Minerals prod.	0	0	18	1	5	0
10 Basic Metal Industries	0	0	0	0	35	3
11 Metal Products,Machinery	0	0	9	0	34	0
12 Other Manufacturing	5	3	9	0	0	0
13 Electricity,Gas and Steam	5	0	6	5	3	0
14 Construction	0	0	9	0	0	3
15 Trade (Distribution)	32	5	9	0	48	0
16 Restaurants and Hotels	0	0	0	0	0	3
17 Transport and Storage	16	0	5	0	24	2
18 Communications	0	0	0	0	0	0
19 Finance,Insurance	0	0	0	0	0	0
20 Public Services	0	0	0	0	0	0
21 Total Intmdt.Domestic Inputs	313	188	74	9	161	13
22 Imports cif (Inputs)	52	0	12	20	121	5
23 Import Duties	29	-23	7	13	77	1
24 Imports incl. Duties	81	-23	19	33	198	6
25 Indirect Taxes less Subsid.	9	0	8	0	1	0
26 Other Value Added	158	105	88	17	238	20
27 Gross Value added	167	105	96	17	239	20
28 Gross Output	581	270	189	59	598	39

Aggregated Input-Output Table of Sri Lanka for the Year 1970

SRI LANKA 1970   FLOWS in millions of rupees of Y 1970   PRODUCERS CURRENT PRICES

INDUSTRY:	13 Electricity, Gas and Steam	14 Construction	15 Trade (Distribution)	16 Restaurants & Hotels	17 Transport and Storage	18 Communications
* DOMESTIC TRANSACTIONS * INDUSTRY						
1 Agriculture	0	3	0	47	0	0
2 Mining and Quarrying	0					0
3 Manufacture of Food	0	56	0	44	0	0
4 Textiles. Clothing	0	50	5	3		0
5 Wood and Wood Products	0	82	5	0	0	0
6 Paper, Printing	0	1	4			2
7 Chemicals	1	1	0		42	0
8 Petroleum Refineries Prod.	0	180	8		20	0
9 Non-metallic Mineral Prod.	7	24		0		0
10 Basic Metal Industries	0	83			69	0
11 Metal Products, Machinery	0		13	0	2	0
12 Other Manufacturing	0				2	2
13 Electricity, Gas and Steam	5			0		3
14 Construction	2	13	100	0	54	5
15 Trade (Distribution)	0		0	9	0	0
16 Restaurants and Hotels	0	75	4	0	28	8
17 Transport and Storage	2	3	20	4	4	0
18 Communications	0	2	1	0		3
19 Finance, Insurance						
20 Public Services		4	7		6	
21 Total Inimdt Domestic Inputs	15	635	79	113	234	28
22 Imports cif (inputs)	3	65	6	0	64	5
23 Import Duties	2	43	3	-8	29	0
24 Imports incl Duties	5	108	9	-8	93	5
25 Indirect Taxes less Subsid	0	23	95	0	-9	0
26 Other Value Added	94	979	1423	107	921	97
27 Gross Value added	94	1002	1518	107	912	97
28 Gross Output	114	1745	1606	212	1239	130

285

Aggregated Input-Output Table of Sri Lanka for the Year 1970

SRI LANKA 1970   FLOWS in millions of rupees of Y 1970   PRODUCERS CURRENT PRICES

INDUSTRY:	19 Finance, Insurance	20 Public Services	21 Total Intermd. Consumption	22 Private Consumption	23 Government Consumption	24 Gross Fixed Capital Form
* DOMESTIC TRANSACTIONS INDUSTRY						
1 Agriculture	0	0	1595	1841	22	82
2 Mining and Quarrying	0	0	80	9	0	0
3 Manufactured Food	0	0	276	1896	26	0
4 Textiles Clothing	0	0	36	292	5	0
5 Wood and Wood Products	0	0	173	54	0	8
6 Paper Printing	0	0	75	75	7	0
7 Chemicals	10	2	254	220	0	0
8 Petroleum Refineries	-1	0	226	55	-0	0
9 Non-metallic Mineral Prod.	0	-1	182	7	0	0
10 Basic Metal Industries	0	0	159	0	0	0
11 Metal Products Machinery	0	0	311	179	0	26
12 Other Manufacturing	5	1	8	30	23	0
13 Electricity, Gas and Steam	2	2	58	27	0	0
14 Construction	7	5	58	0	0	1595
15 Trade (Distribution)	0	4	518	769	28	108
16 Restaurants and Hotels	0	0	0	198	92	0
17 Transport and Storage	3	3	305	837	39	46
18 Communications	0	0	16	16	0	0
19 Finance Insurance	10	25	77	898	20	0
20 Public Services	0	10	49	198	30	0
21 Total Intmdt.Domestic Inputs	81	53	4358	7601	302	1885
22 Imports cif (Inputs)	7	121	1024			
23 Import Duties	5	-39	184	1298	43	328
24 Imports incl. Duties	12	82	1208	1320	48	249
25 Indirect Taxes less Subsid	15	39	475	-110	28	577
26 Other Value Added	818	335	10295	-100	1275	0
27 Gross Value added	833	374	10770	-10	1301	0
28 Gross Output	926	509	16336	8911	1849	2442

286

Aggregated Input-Output Table of Sri Lanka for the Year 1970

SRI LANKA 1970   FLOWS in millions of rupees of Y 1970   PRODUCERS CURRENT PRICES

DOMESTIC TRANSACTIONS INDUSTRY	25 Changes in Stock	26 Exports	27 Total Final Demand	28 Gross Output
1 Agriculture	-34	1288	3199	4794
2 Mining and Quarrying	83	19	128	108
3 Manufacture of Food	50	94	2109	2385
4 Textiles, Clothing	0	75	422	458
5 Wood and Wood Products	0	0	64	237
6 Paper, Printing	0	0	82	151
7 Chemicals	-69	87	307	561
8 Petroleum Refineries	0	57	44	290
9 Non-metallic Mineral Prod.	0	0	7	189
10 Basic Metal Industries	57	0	0	59
11 Metal Products, Machinery	0	2	287	598
12 Other Manufacturing	0	0	35	539
13 Electricity, Gas and Steam	0	0	114	114
14 Construction	0	0	1655	1745
15 Trade (Distribution)	172	172	1688	1606
16 Restaurants and Hotels	0	14	212	212
17 Transport and Storage	0	31	334	1239
18 Communications	0	7	53	130
19 Finance, Insurance	0	0	909	928
20 Public Services	0	258	460	509
21 Total Intmdt.Domestic Inputs	97	2113	11978	16338
22 Imports cif. (Inputs)	35	0	1497	2521
23 Import Duties	21	-197	305	489
24 Imports incl. Duties	56	-197	1802	3010
25 Indirect Taxes less Subsid.	0	0	243	718
26 Other Value Added	0	327	1375	11670
27 Gross Value added	0	327	1618	12388
28 Gross Output	153	2243	15398	31734

ZAMBIA

The present report is based on *National Accounts and Input-Output Tables, 1973,* published by the Central Statistical Office of Zambia.

A.   General information

1.   Input-output tables have been compiled approximately every two years since 1965. The present report describes the latest table available which refers to 1973 and was compiled by the Central Statistical Office with technical assistance provided by the United Nations Office of Technical Co-operation. In 1971, two major methodological changes were introduced: make tables were compiled; and the compilation of import matrices was discontinued since the data available were considered to be insufficient.

2.   Input-output tables are compiled jointly with the national accounts. Both sets of accounts are based on the same conventions and definitions and use the same data base.

3.   Main deviation from SNA recommendations include: the inclusion of the dummy sector of unspecified activities (para. 10); disaggregation of value added (para. 12); treatment of imports (para. 13); evaluation standards (para. 7); treatment of secondary production (para. 14); and distribution of output of the financial sector (para. 19).

B.   Analytical framework

Tables and derived matrices available

4.   Two basic tables are compiled, an absorption matrix and a make matrix, both of which are valued at producers' prices. Neither input-output tables nor derived matrices are available. The row and column totals of each intermediate sector generally record different figures. This is due to two main reasons:

   (a)   Row totals refer to commodity outputs while column totals refer to industry outputs;

   (b)   Column totals refer to domestic outputs while row totals refer to total supply, i.e., domestic supply plus imports.

Valuation standards

5.   Transactions are valued at producers' prices which exclude distribution margins. Imports are valued c.i.f. (import duties are recorded in a separate row) and exports are valued f.o.b. Contrary to SNA recommendations, commodity taxes are not recorded separately and therefore no valuation at approximate basic values can be derived.

Statistical units and classification standards

6.   Commodities are the statistical units adopted for row data while establishments are taken as the unit for column data. Commodities and establishments (industries) are defined as in SNA.

7.   Commodities and industries are classified according to a national system which generally follows the ISIC classification.

8.   The classification of the intermediate consumption quadrant differs from SNA recommendations in that:

   (a)   A dummy sector of unspecified activities is included to account for statistical errors and omissions;

   (b)   The distribution of output of private non-profit institutions and of producers of government services are recorded together in a row describing the consumption of goods and services other than commodities. However, in agreement with SNA recommendations, inputs into these two sectors (i.e., private non-profit institutions and producers of government services) are recorded in two separate columns.

9.   Final demand is disaggregated as recommended in SNA. Categories of final demand are also defined as in SNA. Private consumption is defined on a national basis.

10.   The breakdown of value added recommended in SNA is adopted, except for subsidies which are recorded together with indirect taxes. Categories of value added are defined as in SNA.

11.   Imports are distributed together with domestic output in the absorption matrix. No imports classification is presented in the absorption matrix. However, a commodity classification of imports is provided in the make matrix. Imports in this table are disaggregated into c.i.f. values and import duties. Contrary to SNA recommendations, no distinction is made between competitive and complementary imports.

Treatment and presentation of selected transactions

12.   Neither outputs of secondary products nor their corresponding inputs are transferred to their characteristic sectors. This is contrary to SNA recommendations. The extent and pattern of secondary production are described in the make matrix.

13.   Intermediate inputs which are used and produced by the same sector and are characteristic products of a different sector (such as electricity used and produced by mining industries, trade and transportation activities carried out by manufacturers etc.) are not recorded as commodity inputs. Instead, the inputs needed for their production are recorded.

14.   Scrap generated as part of the production process is treated as any other secondary product. Sales of second-hand goods are treated as recommended in SNA.

15. Domestic output of industries is recorded gross, that is, it includes intra-sector consumption of characteristic and secondary products.

16. Non-monetary output (such as own-consumption of traditional farmers, imputed rents of owner-occupied homes etc.) and its corresponding inputs have been recorded together with the monetary output and inputs in the corresponding input-output sector.

17. Output of the financial sector is defined as in SNA but it is distributed to input-output sectors in proportion to their domestic ouput, which is contrary to SNA recommendations.

18. The input structure of the government sector mostly refers to its production of goods and services other than commodities and includes such activities as public administration, defence, health, education, social services and promotion of economic growth. Output of this sector is measured as recommended in SNA and is allocated to private and to government final consumption. The output share allocated to private consumption is equal to the value of government commodity and non-commodity sales. As recommended in SNA, government services are recorded in the intermediate consumption quadrant.

C. Statistical sources and compilation methodology

19. Data were obtained from existing regular sources and the results of the 1971 Agriculture Census and the Annual Census of Industrial Production. No special surveys were carried out for the purpose of compiling the input-output table.

Gross output and intermediate consumption

Agriculture, forestry and fishing

20. Data for marketed production of main crops were obtained from the Quarterly Agricultural Statistical Bulletin (Ministry of Lands and Agriculture), the Annual Agricultural and Pastoral Production Surveys (APPS) of Commercial Farms and the 1970/71 Census of Agriculture. Data on prices and values were also obtained from household budget surveys, monthly surveys of prices etc. Data on inputs became available for the first time through the 1972 APPS of Commercial Farms.

21. For the subsistence sector covering own-consumed production of traditional farms, use was made of the APPS (non-commercial farms) supplemented by the household budget surveys of rural areas. Estimates for this sector are considered to be less than satisfactory, since the APPS (non-commercial farms) only covers main crops, and since annual changes are still based on the assumption of volume changes associated to population growth and mark-ups for price increases.

Mining, manufacturing, electricity, water and construction

22. Data were mainly obtained from the Annual Census of Industrial Production. Response rates for this survey vary from full response in the metal mining sector to low rate of response in the construction sector.

Services

23. Data were obtained from the Annual National Income Inquiry covering all large and medium-size enterprises. Small units are covered on a sample basis. The coverage of the informal sector is considered to be less than satisfactory, except for bars and domestic services. Unorganized trading activity, small repair shops etc. are still practically left out.

24. Regarding the government sector, data contained in the financial statistics of the government sector, issued by the Central Statistical Office (CSO) and supplemented by special CSO tabulations, were used. Data in respect of the central Government are processed through the computer, while for local Government estimates are made on the basis of replies received from them.

Value added

25. Employment data are collected from the establishments through employment inquiries conducted by the CSO. Grossing-up factors for non-responding units are worked out on the basis of employment data reported by the responding units. In the estimation for services sectors grossing-up is done after carefully comparing employment data of companies responding to both the employment inquiry and the national income inquiry.

26. Estimates for consumption of fixed capital are usually obtained from the financial provisions for depreciation computed by enterprises on the basis of historical costs and expected economic lifetime of their fixed assets. However, efforts are made to obtain estimates on the basis of replacement costs (as recommended in SNA) for as many sectors as possible.

Final demand and imports

27. Data on private consumption expenditure are derived from the Urban Household Budget Survey in Low-cost Housing Areas, 1966-1968, supplemented by preliminary estimates from household budget surveys conducted in urban and rural areas during 1974-1975. Estimates of the total number of households were based on population projections prepared by the CSO. Data in this column also include statistical discrepancies found in the process of compilation of the table.

28. Transactions with the rest of the world are taken from the balance of payments statistics for 1973 issued by the CSO. Details on imports and exports of commodities are obtained from the Annual Statement of External Trade published by the CSO.

Zambia

Reference year: 1973

Entries in table: Total flows, absorption matrix

Source: Central Statistical Office, *National Accounts and Input-Output Tables, 1973* (Lusaka, 1980)

Computerized: UNIDO

Currency units: Kwacha of Y 1973
Scale factor: 100,000

Pricing system: Producers' current prices
Intermediate sectors: 30 × 30

Treatment of trade margins: Intermediate demand row 17 and column 17

Treatment of imports: Rows 38, 39 and 40 in primary inputs
Availability of import matrix: Not available

Total number of rows: 41
Statistical unit of quadrant 1: Commodity

Total number of columns: 39
Statistical unit of quadrant 1: Industry

Fourth quadrant: Not occupied

292

Absorption Table of Zambia for the Year 1973 (Revised)

ZAMBIA 1973   FLOWS in hundred thousand kwacha of Y 1973   PRODUCERS CURRENT PRICES

INDUSTRY:	1 Agriculture Forest & Fishg.	2 Metal Mining	3 Other Mining	4 Food Manufacturing	5 Beverages and Tobacco	6 Textiles and Wearing Apparel
* TOTAL COMMODITY TRANSACTIONS *						
1 Agricult.Forestry & Fishing	99	1	0	471	33	38
2 Metal Mining	0	0	0	0	1	0
3 Other Mining	7	37	3	2	0	0
4 Food Manufacturing	57	29	4	100	48	4
5 Beverages and Tobacco	3	131	2	8	4	134
6 Textiles and Wearing Apparel	3	19	0	1	0	3
7 Wood and Wood Products	0	20	0	17	14	45
8 Paper-Prod.,Printg.& Publ.	0	84	2	17	12	0
9 Rubber Products	10	573	5	30	0	9
10 Non-Metals & Chem. Prods	136	21	0	0	6	2
11 Basic Metal Products	10	462	5	2	0	0
12 Fabricated Metal Products	0	10	2	0	0	2
13 Other Manufacturing Industr.	1	207	0	9	6	0
14 Electricity,Gas and Water	2	16	3	2	0	0
15 Construction	0	298	2	0	0	0
16 Wholesale and Retail Trade	9	9	3	39	12	7
17 Hotels and Restaurants	0	45	-1	1	6	7
18 Rail Transport	2	63	0	35	17	15
19 Road Transport	20	20	0	30	24	3
20 Other Transport	0	14	0	0	0	0
21 Posts and Telecommunications	0	64	0	0	0	0
22 Financial Inst. & Insurance	0	8	0	0	0	0
23 Real Estate	0	90	0	0	0	0
24 Business Services	0	0	0	0	0	0
25 Education	0	0	0	0	0	0
26 Health	0	0	0	0	0	0
27 Recreational & Cultural Svc.	0	10	0	0	0	0
28 Personal & Household Servc.	5	0	0	0	0	0
29 Statistical Adjustments	40	54	2	-50	2	2
31 Total Intermediate Inputs	420	2313	55	756	215	309
32 Gross Fxd.Capital Consumpt.	222	1417	34	124	73	98
33 Compensation of Employees	1333	2763	2	86	82	54
34 Indirect Taxes less Subsidie	-17	-80	0	-89	562	4
35 Operating Surplus	55	852	33	29	18	13
36 Gross Value Added	1593	5032	69	170	735	167
37 Gross Output	2013	7345	124	926	950	476
38 Imports CIF.	88	0	241	283	27	428
39 Import duties	0	0	0	28	24	100
40 Imports incl. Duties	88	0	241	311	51	528
41 Total Resources	2101	7345	365	1237	1001	1004

Absorption Table of Zambia for the Year 1973 (Revised)

ZAMBIA 1973   FLOWS in hundred thousand kwacha of Y 1973   PRODUCERS CURRENT PRICES

INDUSTRY: COMMODITY	7 Wood and Wood Products	8 Paper-Prod. Prtng.& Publ.	9 Rubber Products	10 Chemicals & Chem. Prods	11 Non-Metallic Mineral Prods	12 Basic Metal Products
* TOTAL TRANSACTIONS *						
1 Agricult. Forestry & Fishing	4	0	8	0	0	0
2 Metal Mining	0	0	0	0	0	0
3 Other Mining	0	0	0	253	27	0
4 Food Manufacturing	0	0	0	30	3	0
5 Beverages and Tobacco	0	2	2	5	4	0
6 Textiles and Wearing Apparel	5	0	9	0	0	0
7 Wood and Wood Products	16	0	0	2	5	2
8 Paper-Prod.Prtng.& Publ.	2	66	26	1	3	9
9 Rubber Products	13	4	0	2	18	0
10 Chemicals & Chem. Prods	0	0	0	12	14	0
11 Non-Metallic Mineral Prods.	7	3	0	3	18	3
12 Basic Metal Products	0	0	3	0	0	0
13 Fabricated Metal Products	0	0	2	7	5	2
14 Other Manufacturing Industr.	2	0	0	0	0	0
15 Electricity, Gas and Water	0	9	2	24	9	3
16 Construction	0	0	0	2	2	0
17 Wholesale and Retail Trade	5	1	1	53	30	3
18 Hotels and Restaurants	0	2	2	6	7	0
19 Rail Transport	0	8	8	2	3	0
20 Road Transport	4	0	4	50	11	0
21 Other Transport	3	5	0	5	7	7
22 Posts and Telecommunications	0	0	0	3	1	0
23 Financial Inst. & Insurance	0	0	0	0	0	0
24 Real Estate	0	2	0	0	0	0
25 Business Services	1	1	4	3	2	0
26 Education						
27 Health						
28 Recreational & Cultural Svc.						
29 Personal & Household Servc.						
30 Statistical Adjustments						
31 Total Intermediate Inputs	102	107	88	829	136	29
32 Gross Fxd Capital Consumpt.	38	46	24	83	66	14
33 Compensation of Employees	15	19	35	50	4	1
34 Indirect Taxes less Subsidie	10	0	4		-4	0
35 Operating Surplus	7	6	7	43	25	2
36 Gross Value Added	81	71	70	177	88	27
37 Gross Output	163	178	138	806	224	56
38 Imports CIF	36	115	89	682	89	238
39 Import duties				691	8	2
40 Imports incl. Duties	37	122	94	753	97	240
41 Total Resources	200	300	232	1559	321	296

Absorption Table of Zambia for the Year 1973 (Revised)

ZAMBIA 1973   FLOWS in hundred thousand kwacha of Y 1973   PRODUCERS CURRENT PRICES

INDUSTRY: COMMODITY	13 Fabricated Metal Products	14 Other Manufact. Industries	15 Electricity Gas and Water	16 Construction	17 Wholesale and Retail Trade	18 Hotels and Restaurants
* TOTAL TRANSACTIONS *						
1 Agricult. Forestry & Fishing	0	0	0	1	6	12
2 Metal Mining	39	0	0	0	0	0
3 Other Mining	2	0	0	45	7	4
4 Food Manufacturing	7	0	0	13	16	5
5 Beverages and Tobacco	56	0	1	110	0	0
6 Textiles and Wearing Apparel	0	0	2	54	2	2
7 Wood and Wood Products	5	0	0	8	16	0
8 Paper-Prod.,Printg & Publ.	13	0	0	2	40	1
9 Rubber Products	4	0	2	6		0
10 Chemicals & Chem. Prods	160	1	6	178	5	2
11 Non-Metallic Mineral Prods.	124	0	4	56	36	0
12 Basic Metal Products	16	1	0	244	1	2
13 Fabricated Metal Products	2	0	9	16	3	0
14 Other Manufacturing Industr.	59	1	0	7	24	0
15 Electricity, Gas and Water	2	0	100	154	0	0
16 Construction	0	0	0	127	12	0
17 Wholesale and Retail Trade	15	0	4	5	10	7
18 Hotels and Restaurants	2	0	0	3	28	0
19 Rail Transport	3	0	2	47	43	7
20 Road Transport	27	1	7	13	81	1
21 Other Transport	5	0	2	46	147	7
22 Posts and Telecommunications	24	0	0	17	5	1
23 Financial Inst. & Insurance	0	0	9	81	0	0
24 Real Estate	0	0	0	147	0	0
25 Business Services	1	0	0	5	3	1
26 Education	0	0	0	0	0	0
27 Health	0	0	0	0	0	0
28 Recreational & Cultural Svc.	0	0	0	7	0	0
29 Personal & Household Serv.	0	0	0	0	3	0
30 Statistical Adjustments	1	0	0	93	3	1
31 Total Intermediate Inputs	584	5	59	1397	535	87
32 Gross Fxd Capital Consumpt.	181	3	118	655	722	92
33 Compensation of Employees	107	3	120	223	827	81
34 Indirect Taxes less Subsidie	23	0	0	74	-203	5
35 Operating Surplus		0	81		-88	3
36 Gross Value Added	292	8	302	957	1432	181
37 Gross Output	876	8	361	2354	1967	268
38 Imports CIF.	1800	42	73	0	0	0
39 Import duties	90	46	0	0	0	0
40 Imports incl. Duties	1966	50	73	0	0	0
41 Total Resources	2842	81	434	2354	1967	268

Absorption Table of Zambia for the Year 1973 (Revised)

ZAMBIA 1973 FLOWS in hundred thousand kwacha of Y 1973 PRODUCERS CURRENT PRICES

INDUSTRY:

	COMMODITY	19 Rail Transport	20 Road Transport	21 Other Transport	22 Posts and Telecommunic.	23 Financial Inst. & Insurance	24 Real Estate
	TOTAL TRANSACTIONS *						
1	Agricult. Forestry & Fishing						
2	Metal Mining						
3	Other Mining						
4	Food Manufacturing						
5	Beverages and Tobacco						
6	Textiles and Wearing Apparel						
7	Wood and Wood Products						
8	Paper-Prod.,Printg.& Publ.						
9	Rubber Products						
10	Chemicals & Chem. Prods						
11	Non-Metallic Mineral Prods.						
12	Basic Metal Products						
13	Fabricated Metal Products						
14	Other Manufacturing Industr.						
15	Electricity, Gas and Water						
16	Construction						
17	Wholesale and Retail Trade						
18	Hotels and Restaurants						
19	Rail Transport						
20	Road Transport						
21	Other Transport						
22	Posts and Telecommunications						
23	Financial Inst. & Insurance						
24	Real Estate						
25	Business Services						
26	Education						
27	Health						
28	Recreational & Cultural Svc.						
29	Personal & Household Servc.						
30	Statistical Adjustment						
31	Total Intermediate Inputs	95	314	135	57	124	253
32	Gross Fxd Capital Consumpt.	129	147	78	81	194	50
33	Compensation of Employees	-21	75	-5	-0	297	172
34	Indirect Taxes less Subsidie	-75	-0	-0	1	-4	-4
35	Operating Surplus	-28	88	20	13	48	144
36	Gross Value Added	101	296	93	85	535	362
37	Gross Output	196	610	228	142	659	615
38	Imports CIF	0	215	199	0	0	0
39	Import duties	0	0	0	0	0	0
40	Imports Incl. Duties	0.	215.	199.	0.	0.	0.
41	Total Resources	198	825	427	142	659	815

Absorption Table of Zambia for the Year 1973 (Revised)

ZAMBIA 1973　　FLOWS in hundred thousand kwacha of Y 1973　　PRODUCERS CURRENT PRICES

* TOTAL TRANSACTIONS *

INDUSTRY: COMMODITY	Business Services 25	Education 26	Health 27	Recreational & Cultural Svc 28	Personal & Household Svc 29	Statistical Adjustment 30
1 Agricult.Forestry & Fishing	0	0	0	0	0	0
2 Metal Mining	0	0	0	0	0	0
3 Other Mining	0	0	0	0	0	0
4 Food Manufacturing	0	0	0	0	2	0
5 Beverages and Tobacco	5	1	1	0	0	0
6 Textiles and Wearing Apparel	0	0	0	0	0	0
7 Wood and Wood Products	8	0	0	0	0	0
8 Paper.-Prod.,Printg.& Publ.	5	0	0	0	1	0
9 Rubber-Products	0	0	0	0	0	0
10 Chemicals & Chem. Prods	6	0	0	0	3	0
11 Non-Metallic Mineral Prods.	0	0	0	0	1	0
12 Basic Metal Products	0	0	0	0	0	0
13 Fabricated Metal Products	0	0	0	4	2	0
14 Other Manufacturing Industr.	0	0	0	0	0	0
15 Electricity, Gas and Water	18	0	0	0	1	-58
16 Construction	0	0	0	0	0	0
17 Wholesale and Retail Trade	0	0	0	0	0	0
18 Hotels and Restaurants	0	0	0	0	0	0
19 Road Transport	2	0	0	0	4	0
20 Other Transport	2	0	0	0	4	0
21 Posts and Telecommunications	6	0	0	0	4	0
22 Financial Inst. & Insurance	3	0	0	0	3	0
23 Real Estate	-1	0	0	2	0	0
24 Business Services	30	0	0	0	0	0
25 Education	0	0	0	0	0	0
26 Health		0	0	0	0	0
27 Recreational & Cultural Svc.		0	0	0	1	0
28 Personal & Household Serv.		0	0	0	5	56
29						
30 Statistical Adjustments		2	0	2		
31 Total Intermediate Inputs	102	2	2	11	92	0
32 Gross Fxd.Capital Consumpt.	193			12	61	0
33 Compensation of Employees	85	0	2	4	4	0
34 Indirect Taxes less Subsidie	0	0	0	2	0	0
35 Operating Surplus	25	0	0	0	18	0
36 Gross Value Added	303	1	4	18	83	0
37 Gross Output	405	3	8	29	175	343
38 Imports CIF.	237	17	0	0	0	8
39 Import duties	0	0	0	0	0	
40 Imports Incl. Duties	237	17	0	0	0	352
41 Total Resources	642	20	8	29	175	352

297

Absorption Table of Zambia for the Year 1973 (Revised)

ZAMBIA 1973   FLOWS in hundred thousand kwacha of Y 1973   PRODUCERS CURRENT PRICES

* TOTAL TRANSACTIONS * COMMODITY	31 Total Intermed. Consumption	32 Private Consumption	33 Government Consumption	34 Gr.Fxed.Capital Formation	35 Changes in Stocks	36 Export (f.o.b.)
1 Agricult.Forestry & Fishing	710	1317	70	12	-97	90
2 Metal Mining	39				161	7092
3 Other Mining	408				24	12
4 Food Manufacturing	240	809	128		1	4
5 Beverages and Tobacco	184	788	34		-4	
6 Textiles and Wearing Apparel	530	398	59		-12	3
7 Wood and Wood Products	92	36		74	-2	
8 Paper.-Prod.Printg.& Publ.	199	92	87	72	-5	8
9 Rubber Products	35					
10 Chemicals & Chem. Prods.	204	106	87		119	
11 Non-Metallic Mineral Prods.	1272	92		1504		43
12 Basic Metal Products	265		107		-25	2
13 Fabricated Metal Products	278	62			-1	5
14 Other Manufacturing Industr.	112				-7	4
15 Electricity,Gas and Water	47	48	55	1900		
16 Construction	319		233	591	-6	
17 Wholesale and Retail Trade	228	497	48		37	70
18 Hotels and Restaurants	620	196	45			
19 Rail Transport	21	89	69		1	214
20 Road Transport	71		152	24	3	82
21 Other Transport	339		40	6		
22 Posts and Telecommunications	161	20	159			
23 Financial Inst. & Insurance	82	449	10			
24 Real Estate	413	468		74		
25 Business Services	200		3			10
26 Education	610		2			
27 Health	19	8				
28 Recreational & Cultural Svc.		3				
29 Personal & Household Serv.	66	35				
30 Statistical Adjustments	264	-9	141	41	24	48
31 Total Intermediate Inputs	8993	5000	1529	4229	420	7804
32 Gross Fxd.Capital Consumpt.	4917		1506	0	0	0
33 Compensation of Employees	6475	297		0	0	0
34 Indirect Taxes less Subsidie	218			0	0	0
35 Operating Surplus	1701	4	412	0	0	0
36 Gross Value Added	13311	302	1919	0	0	0
37 Gross Output	22304	5302	3448	4229	420	7804
38 Imports CIF.	5290	0	0	0	0	0
39 Import duties	381	0	0	0	0	0
40 Imports incl. Duties	5671	0	0	0	0	0
41 Total Resources	27975	5302	3448	4229	420	7804

Absorption Table of Zambia for the Year 1973 (Revised)

ZAMBIA 1973   FLOWS in hundred thousand kwacha of Y 1973

		37 Total Final Demand	38 Stat.Adjust.for Indust./Commod.	39 Total Resources
	* TOTAL TRANSACTIONS * COMMODITY			
1	Agricult.Forestry & Fishing	1392	-1	2101
2	Metal Mining	7253	53	7345
3	Other Mining	368	-79	365
4	Food Manufacturing	968	-29	1237
5	Beverages and Tobacco	819	22	1001
6	Textiles and Wearing Apparel	452	22	1004
7	Wood and Wood Products	96	12	300
8	Paper,Prod.,Printg & Publ.	101	0	232
9	Rubber Products	24	-4	232
10	Chemicals & Chem. Prods	305	-18	1559
11	Non-Metallic Mineral Prods.	48	8	321
12	Basic Metal Products	-4	0	296
13	Fabricated Metal Products	1787	-57	2842
14	Other Manufacturing Industr.	-3	1	61
15	Electricity Gas and Water	108	-5	434
16	Construction	2131	173	2354
17	Wholesale and Retail Trade	1174	-6	1967
18	Hotels and Restaurants	241	7	268
19	Rail Transport	108	17	196
20	Road Transport	404	82	825
21	Other Transport	250	16	427
22	Posts and Telecommunications	60	-8	142
23	Financial Inst. & Insurance	208	38	659
24	Real Estate	476	-61	615
25	Business Services	189	-157	642
26	Education	5	-4	20
27	Health		-2	29
28	Recreational & Cultural Svc.	38	-7	175
29	Personal & Household Serv.	170	-81	352
30	Statistical Adjustments	106	-18	
31	Total Intermediate Inputs	18982	0	27975
32	Gross Fxd Capital Consumpt.	1803	0	6720
33	Compensation of Employees	0	0	6475
34	Indirect Taxes less Subsidie	2	0	220
35	Operating Surplus	416	0	2117
36	Gross Value Added	2221	0	15532
37	Gross Output	21203	0	43507
38	Imports CIF	0	0	5280
39	Imports duties	0	0	381
40	Imports Incl.Duties	0	0	567
41	Total Resources	21203	0	49178

B